ROMAN BRITAIN
A NEW HISTORY

ROMAN BRITAIN
A NEW HISTORY

Guy de la Bédoyère

with 285 illustrations, 75 in color

Thames & Hudson

Half-title: Uley (Gloucestershire).
Bronze figurine of Mercury holding a caduceus, a staff entwined with two serpents.
Such figures were probably sold in and around cult sites for pilgrims to use as
offerings, or to take away as souvenirs. Height 10 cm.

Title page: Hadrian's Wall (Northumberland).
Milecastle 39 ('Castle Nick'). Milecastles, built roughly every Roman mile along
the Wall, accommodated small garrisons that supervised transit across the frontier
through these fortified gateways. This milecastle was built *c*. AD 124, probably by
the legion, *VI Victrix*.

First published in 2006 in hardcover in the United States of America by
Thames & Hudson Inc., 500 Fifth Avenue, New York, New York 10110

thamesandhudsonusa.com

Library of Congress Catalog Card Number 2005907162

ISBN-13: 978-0-500-05140-5
ISBN-10: 0-500-05140-2

Printed and bound in Singapore by Tien Wah Press Pte Ltd

CONTENTS

PREFACE

Roman Britain was Britain's first truly historical period, and as such it has deservedly been the subject of many books, especially in the last thirty years. Today, thanks to excavations, scientific techniques and new research, we know far more about this unique mixture of classical and Celtic civilization. However, the basic history has not altered much. Instead it is the archaeology that has changed, and with it there has been a reappraisal of the architectural, material and social structure of Roman Britain. In the process, the history has become a little lost, or at any rate taken for granted.

Some of the greatest excavations of Romano-British archaeological sites were conducted in the late nineteenth and early twentieth centuries. These included the work at Silchester and numerous digs along Hadrian's Wall, and at other military sites nearby. The techniques of the time meant many features in the ground went unnoticed, whilst contemporary attitudes had their own effect. A preoccupation with the Roman army in Britain was common, and lay to a large extent in personal experience of Britain's own imperial armed forces. Military documents found at Vindolanda in the 1970s show that the Roman army was far from being the rigid and predictable organization archaeologists once assumed, and probably also reflect other aspects of the way Roman Britain and other provinces were managed.

Perhaps this mirrors how our world has also changed. Equally, each generation of historians and archaeologists wants to make its mark. Part of this process is a ritual re-examination of some of the assumptions and attitudes of previous generations. An old dogma is supplanted by a new one. But just as the certainties of older scholarly attitudes now seem easy to question, we also need to bear in mind that the certainties of our own time are just as likely to be flawed. Today, dendrochronology and other modern archaeological techniques are often treated as infallible sources of objective information. Archaeologists also sometimes infer more from their excavations than the evidence can really support. The reality is that flawed historical and literary material cannot be made good by archaeology,

1. Gresham Street (London). This bronze cauldron was found in a well at Gresham Street, constructed *c.* AD 100. After the well was destroyed by fire, it was back-filled with rubbish, including this cauldron, perhaps used initially for collecting water.

not least because the evidence is of an entirely different kind. The two complement one another, but they are not mutual substitutes.

Even so, the archaeological record has been transformed. New techniques have made it possible to recognize environmental evidence in unprecedented detail, or to identify occupation levels that would entirely have escaped the notice of a Victorian archaeologist. Despite its usefulness, the metal-detector is regretted by many archaeologists because of the reckless way some detectorists have used it. However, some extraordinary finds have changed our view of Roman Britain forever. The fact that some finds have turned up in places that archaeologists either would not, or could not, have looked only goes to show how selective the 'official' record can be. The Mildenhall Treasure (see pp. 258–59), found in the 1940s, was even thought by some at the time to have been a modern import from North Africa. Since then, the discovery of exceptional treasure hoards such as Thetford and Hoxne, along with a very large number of minor finds, have radically altered our knowledge of the sheer quantity of Romano-British sites. The remarkable coinage of the rebel emperor Carausius (286–93), with its dramatic series of unprecedented mythical and literary types, was once rare. Now far more is known about this emperor from his numismatic record.

Archaeology and history belong to their own time. Today, old certainties have been replaced by doubt, and a palpable fear for the future. A parallel often drawn today is how the increase in American power mirrors Rome's rise, and how America has come to define today's world order. Now that international terrorism and environmental concerns have challenged our sense of security, it becomes easier to see what the dramatic decline of Roman power in the West in the fourth century meant for the Empire's population. Likewise, an increasing focus on native identities in Roman Britain reflects an increased respect for ethnic identities in our own time. Imperialism has increasingly become condemned as a purely oppressive force, given weight by its appalling excesses in the twentieth century, and reinforced by a contemporary sense of the 'victim'. Yet life is rarely quite so simple. The complex relationships between native society and Roman culture in Britain were just that, and evidently reached some sort of equilibrium which was surprisingly stable, and which seems to have been eventually acceptable to most of the participants. A new approach to the late Iron Age has made a very good case for the idea that some tribal aristocracies welcomed, and even coveted, Roman influence.

Archaeology has also been transformed in modern times. What was once the preserve of an exclusive few has become the everyday fare of popular television, magazines and weekend relaxation. Far more people now have access to the subject, with many seeking to further their

2. Birdoswald (Cumbria).
A gilt-copper figure of Hercules, said to have been found near Hadrian's Wall, at Birdoswald. It is possible that this statuette was intended as a portrait of the emperor Commodus (AD 180–92), who from 191 identified himself with the deified mythical hero. Height 50 cm. (British Museum).

knowledge as students. Others take part in excavations, often paying for the privilege of instruction 'in the field'. Roman Britain is an especially popular component in this new world of archaeology. The Roman world is one that we can recognize, with its towns, roads, political structure, economy and multicultural society. Like all the most absorbing historical periods, it is at once a mirror for our own lives, and a portal into an age of mystery and intrigue.

Roman Britain is also a source of perpetual frustration, thanks to the sporadic and limited nature of the historical record. Traditionally this contributed to a sense that Britain was palpably different from other provinces, by being fundamentally less integrated into the Roman world and all its systems. It was also true that archaeological thought inclined to the idea that the Roman world was so systematized, that fragmentary evidence could be joined together by filling in the gaps. In recent years, more time has been given to an increasingly sophisticated analysis of the evidence. Not surprisingly, a broader range of interpretations has been the result. These help to invigorate academic debate, but often leave the general reader floundering in a jungle of limitless and inconclusive possibilities. Yet the basic chronological framework is much as it has always been.

Peter Salway has recently made the important observation that the writing tablets at Vindolanda near Hadrian's Wall, and an increasing number of other documents from similar waterlogged deposits, show that Britain functioned as a Roman province much as any other. Its administrative systems and military units used the same methods of recording, communication and government as other provinces of the Empire. So we should be more confident about being able to use parallels from other, better-recorded parts of the Empire to understand how Roman Britain worked. However, the record we have is so biased to the military that it leaves us still unsure of the extent to which the Roman world impacted on the indigenous British population. Another problem that arises from recent discoveries, especially the Vindolanda letters, is the natural tendency to treat these extraordinary pieces of evidence, each of which is highly individual, uncritically as templates for everything else that went on.

The study of Roman Britain, like most academic disciplines, has increasingly been divided up amongst a proliferating array of specialists. This inclination to disperse what is in fact a fairly cohesive subject means that it is commonplace for a specialist in one field to know little about other fields beyond his or her immediate interest. Since Roman Britain is a fairly small subject, this means that often only one or two people end up monopolizing their own particular topics, or even sites. Two recent books attempting to sum up current work on Roman Britain were written by an array of different specialists, each responsible for different chapters. Many of the contributions are in fact interesting and worthwhile, but overall create an impression of a fragmented and incomplete subject.

Ironically, despite the expansion in specialisms, a major facet of the Roman world has taken a back seat. Today it is commonplace for lecturers and archaeologists teaching Roman history to have no Latin, and therefore no direct access to the history, literature and graffiti of the period they profess to be experts in. The result is a literal acceptance of published translations, and a distancing between our time and the one we are studying. To a Victorian antiquarian, despite his shortcomings, this would have been regarded as an impossible handicap.

This book has been written to try and balance old and new attitudes, and to draw as much of what went to make up Roman Britain into a single whole, by taking into account new discoveries and perceptions for a contemporary audience. With a subject as wide-ranging as this, and with limited space, it is impossible to cover everything. Rather than include a litany of examples, each only briefly alluded to, I have preferred to discuss fewer examples of artifacts, sites and other subjects in greater detail. The basic chronology of events is tackled in the first three chapters, before turning to a variety of themes that allow us to explore the complex strata of developments that characterized Britain in the Roman Empire. With its unique combination of history and archaeology, Roman Britain bridges the world between prehistory and the Middle Ages, providing not just a vital link, but also a special opportunity to examine how history and archaeology complement and contradict one another.

I would like to record my thanks to Colin Ridler, Elain McAlpine, Sarah Vernon-Hunt, Neil Palfreyman, Rowena Alsey and Celia Falconer at Thames & Hudson. I am also immensely grateful to Catherine Johns, formerly of the British Museum, for her detailed comments on the text. Thanks are also due to Stewart Ainsworth, Mick Aston, Mark Corney, Neil Faulkner, Richard Reece and Tony Wilmott who contributed wittingly and unwittingly in a variety of discussions about general issues and specific sites.

Guy de la Bédoyère
Welby, Lincolnshire

CHAPTER 1

CAESAR & IRON AGE BRITAIN

3. Stonehenge (Wiltshire).
Britain's most famous prehistoric
monument remains a powerful
testimony to the sophistication of
Neolithic and Bronze Age society,
erected between 3000 and 1600 BC.

Britain is a cluster of islands off northwest Europe. It is easy to forget
how fundamentally this fact has characterized everything about Britain's
geography and history. Despite covering only a small area, Britain features a phenomenal array of landscape and environmental conditions,
but escapes the worst extremes the Earth is capable of imposing. There is
no desert or frozen tundra. Instead, much of the south and east is fertile
agricultural land, and the abundant rivers and streams make viable
human habitation possible almost everywhere. Bathed in the Gulf
Stream, Britain benefits from the warmth of tropical seas, thereby cheat-
ing the consequences of a latitude that places it as far north as Calgary
and Moscow. It is, of course, the sea that defines Britain, just as much as

its landscape does. It provides Britain with a natural security, as important thousands of years before as it was in 1940. The crossing might be short, but it is also dangerous, the sea being *impetu atque aperto*, 'boisterous and open'.[1] Conversely, the sea is neither wide enough nor cold enough to prevent it being a thoroughfare for those sailing past Britain or to her. The sea protects Britain, but it does not isolate her.

Caesar's arrival was not the first time that the Britons had encountered the inhabitants of Continental Europe. There had been movement and contact as long as people could move about at will over land and sea. This much we can infer from prehistoric artifacts and structures that resemble those found on both sides of the English Channel. They tell us nothing substantive about the personalities or events that characterize a historical period, but they do tell us that the Britons were organized into complex societies capable of sophisticated production and management of resources. We might know little about how they did this, but the results are there for all to see to this day, in sites ranging from countless small settlements and henge monuments to Stonehenge [3].

The ability of Neolithic peoples in Britain to coordinate the movement of stone into monumental tombs and circles by the fourth millennium BC, quite apart from the cultural and religious motivations to do so, shows that societies in Britain had already evolved into communities capable of sustained cooperative activity. The production and migration of pottery and stone axes is evidence for active trade and gift exchange, as well as for the expression of status through possessions. By the late Iron Age, it becomes possible to look at the archaeological evidence of settlements, graves and prestige goods in the context of written observations by travellers and geographers from the classical world. Clearly Iron Age Britain was made up of many different communities whose settlements, artifacts and practices differed widely from one another and from communities on the Continent, while at the same time showing common influences [4]. By the first century BC, of all the influences and factors that affected Britain, the Roman Empire was the most pervasive and decisive.

REFERENCES TO BRITAIN

The Greeks, at least by the fourth century BC, knew Britain as *Albion*. Originally applied to a Spanish tribe called the 'Albiones', the term was later adopted for Britain, perhaps because of its similarity to the Greek word for white, *alphos*, thanks to the white chalk cliffs of the southeast coast. Pliny the Elder, writing in the first century AD, says that Britain had 'previously' been called *Albion*, so by then the name must have fallen out of common use.[2] By the time Britain began to be referred to more frequently, the Greeks called it *Prettannia*, or *Brettannia*.[3] What does seem

4. Battersea (London).
Late Iron Age bronze ceremonial shield from the Thames. This distinctively Celtic object is an example of the high standard of production that British craftsmen were capable of in the centuries prior to the Roman invasion. It belongs to a large group of military equipment deliberately deposited in rivers, including the Thames and the Witham in Lincolnshire. (British Museum).

certain is that in the fourth century BC, Pytheas of Massilia (Marseilles) sailed to Britain. Pytheas wrote down his experiences, but these only survive as incidental third-hand references by later writers. Most of our authorities belong to the late first century BC or to the first two centuries AD, by which time Britain had ceased to seem quite so remote. Historians such as Pliny the Elder, conscious that Britain was now a place of importance, scavenged older records for information. They knew that the British Isles consisted of two main islands, Britain and Ireland, with a host of lesser islands scattered about. Since some of their information had come from older, now lost sources, Britain's location and general geographical arrangement was known from at least the time of Pytheas, and perhaps for a while before that. Nevertheless, there was a certain amount of scepticism. Strabo, writing in the late first century BC, accused Pytheas of being a liar and doubted many of his claims.[4]

Until the time of Caesar, it seems that few people knew much about the Britons themselves. Pytheas, according to Strabo, had reported rather vaguely on conditions in Thule (Shetland Islands), probably compiled from information generally applicable to Britain. He talked of a reliance on millet, vegetables, roots and fruits in 'the frozen area', along with a lack of cultivated crops and domesticated animals. Elsewhere those who had grain made a drink from it, and threshed their grain in barns to protect it from the weather. Strabo's doubts about the general veracity of Pytheas' claims was founded on his own ignorance, and recalls the kind of scepticism that faced early explorers of the Northwest Passage, Africa and Australia in modern times. Pytheas might have failed to understand what he had seen, but Strabo was in no better position to make a judgment.

The Greeks had established that Earth was a globe, and even measured its size surprisingly accurately, but most people still treated the world as flat. All civilizations have a tendency to centricity, and for Mediterranean peoples the physical geography encouraged that perception. Their world was centred on the sea, and more especially on whichever city was in the ascendancy – at least by those who lived there. When news of Britain's existence filtered through, it was generally information that promoted the place as barbarous and almost exotically sensational. Britain provoked the same kind of fascination that discoveries in the North American West promoted in cities like Chicago and New York in the 1800s. At the time of Caesar's invasions and the Claudian conquest of AD 43, crossing the sea into Britain involved not just a colossal logistical problem, but also a psychological leap of faith. This cut both ways. The more dreadful, forbidding and terrifying Britain was made out to be, the more effective the propaganda coup in going there at all.

MARITIME LINKS

The prospect of sailing to Britain might have been daunting to the Romans, but it was of far less consequence to the traders of northwestern Europe and the Greeks and Phoenicians. By the late fourth century BC, trade routes existed that brought tin out of Britain's southwest into Gaul, and then overland to the Mediterranean.[5] Ships left the key Continental rivers (the Rhine, Seine, Garonne and Loire), and waited for the outgoing evening tide to carry them out to sea. The following morning the incoming tide carried them onshore to Britain.[6] The Veneti were the most accomplished of the maritime Gaulish tribes. By Caesar's time, their many ships, proficiency in navigation, and control of the few ports allowed them to dictate movement across the sea by exacting tribute from their neighbours.[7] But cross-Channel movement was not yet a normal part of everyday life. Caesar claimed that while traders knew their way across to Britain, most Gauls knew little or nothing of the place.[8]

Caesar describes the Veneti ships as relatively flat-bottomed, allowing them to exploit shallow water and tides, and to be safely beached when storms erupted. Made of heavy oak beams, with high prows and sterns and iron anchors on chains, they were built deliberately to withstand the unpredictable weather of the English Channel and North Sea. Even cloth sails were spurned in favour of hide and leather. Caesar thought Roman ships faster and their crews better disciplined, but otherwise believed that the Gaulish ships were stronger and more easily defended.[9] Not only had maritime technology of this level existed in the mid-first century BC, but it had been evolving for some time, as shown by occasional finds of far more ancient ships, such as the Ferriby boat of *c.* 2000–1800 BC. Coastal tribal communities had established local control of offshore waters, for passenger traffic, ferrying, trade and fishing. Their knowledge of creeks, marshes, submerged rocks, tides and other dangers will have been handed down for centuries.

The ancient tradition of prehistoric monuments, particularly graves, suggests that the concepts of tribal hierarchies and status were already well established. In East Yorkshire, as in Gaul, in the middle of the first millennium BC, distinctive burials containing chariots appeared, providing evidence for the existence of a component of society that expressed its wealthy status in death in an ostentatious form, as well as the technical skills that provided the equipage. Those chariots incidentally illustrate the literal mobility of British élite society, which would reach its zenith in the resistance to the Roman conquest. At the same time, burials across late Iron Age Britain increasingly incorporated prestige goods associated with a mounted, or chariot-riding, warrior élite. This general practice of utilizing death as part of social display, usually known as 'conspicuous consumption', was mirrored on the Continent at the same time. Parallel

5. Maiden Castle (Dorset).
Reconstruction painting of the Iron Age hillfort. Although such installations were effective defences against local warfare, they were vulnerable to assault by Roman artillery.

6. *Opposite above. Stater* of the Corieltauvi.
This gold *stater* was struck in the Corieltauvi region of the East Midlands and Lincolnshire. Derived from coins of Philip of Macedon, the images represent abstractions of Philip's hair and a horse. After Caesar's invasion, some southern tribes adopted realistic Roman imagery and lettering. Mid-first century BC.

development is a well-established phenomenon in which human societies follow similar patterns, without necessarily learning all their practices from one another.

By the mid-second century BC, trade with the Continent began to include goods that have left far more physical evidence. Wealthy members of tribal communities were showing their status in an increasingly sophisticated and conspicuous way. Whether their standing had actually increased, as a result of successfully maintaining their positions in the face of growing pressure on land and resources, or they were simply finding new ways to express their prestige, is difficult to say. The development of major hillforts in the south, such as Danebury (Hampshire) and Maiden Castle (Dorset), right up to *c.* 100 BC, each apparently controlling, or at least reflecting control of, a block of territory, must reflect a hierarchical society in which leadership was clearly defined [5].

Around the same time, coinage started to circulate in parts of Britain. Made in Gaul, the gold and silver *staters* were progressively abstract versions of coins issued by the Macedonian Greeks in the fourth century BC. The Macedonian coins had simply established an accepted standard, and the Gaulish copies emulated them for that reason. These coins reflected trading links with Gaul and tribal links as gifts, and probably also represented payment for goods that had been exported to the Continent. As high-value bullion pieces, the coins were not used for everyday trivial transactions, but were instead a means of storing and displaying wealth. Over the next century production of British copies followed, before some of the southern and eastern tribes started to produce dynastic issues that named their kings and rulers [6].

Coinage marks a significant change in late Iron Age society in southern Britain, with a clear regional difference. Coinage was not habitually used or struck north and west of a line between the Humber and Devon. Occasionally coins turn up here, but, unlike further south, hoards and deposits at shrines in this region are unknown. The same discrepancy affects all sorts of other artifacts in late Iron Age settlements and graves. Brooches, for example, become commonplace in the south and east, but remain rare in the north and west. It is easy to assume that this was a straightforward consequence of relative differences in wealth, but it could also have been due to cultural differences. Wealth stored and displayed, for example, in cattle is far less archaeologically visible than wealth stored in coins and manufactured goods.

By around 100 BC, the major hillforts seem to have declined or been abandoned, while smaller enclosure settlements seem to have proliferated. Marginal areas, previously scarcely occupied (if at all), became settled. The appearance of rectangular houses in the south marks a radical change from the ancient tradition of living in round structures. These changes are difficult to explain unless the developments of industry and coinage were all somehow linked to changes in how wealth, power and status were expressed. This complex interdependence of social and economic phenomena would reach its climax in Roman Britain, but at this stage late Iron Age society in Britain was laying the foundations for integration into the Roman world. The exploitation of metal resources, for example, to fuel the demand for coinage and manufactured goods may have materially altered the balance of power, while also altering expectations. If money and goods had become the arbitrating icons of power and status in Iron Age Britain, then Rome, whose capacity to endow its favoured servants with comparatively limitless quantities of either, was inevitably going to become the biggest player in Britain's tribal politics [7].

7. Snettisham (Norfolk).
A small part of one of at least eleven hoards deposited at Snettisham, *c.* 70 BC. The hoard may have belonged to an Iceni tribal leader, buried for safekeeping, or a ritual burial. The pits incorporated false bottoms to conceal their contents. (British Museum).

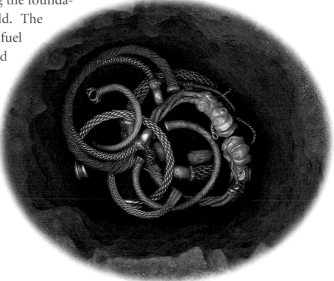

Caesar's arrival played a pivotal role in accelerating that process. As Roman influence stretched across Gaul and Spain, so the Romans absorbed the contacts and coastal routes that had enabled that trade. The political stability that followed in their wake, reinforced by standardized coinage and improved communications, promoted long-distance trade. Britain was drawn closer into the net. In return for its natural resources, Britain was paid with the fruits of the Roman Empire: manufactured goods, and the money with which to buy more manufactured goods. Characteristically, this benefited only a very small segment of late Iron Age Britain's population, not only in terms of social strata, but also in geographical terms. Britain's tribal societies were not egalitarian paradises.

The classic marker of this trade is the Mediterranean universal container, the amphora [8]. In every sense the cardboard box, oil drum and packing case of its age, the amphora was ubiquitous. Amphorae mark the movement of goods from the Roman world into a very small part of central southern Britain during at least the 50 years that preceded Caesar's arrival. The trade included a route that headed north from St Servan (Brittany) to Hengistbury Head (Dorset). The latter was ideally placed. Easy to locate from the sea, it also provided sheltered beaching sites for ships. Close to natural resources and agriculturally productive areas, it was also easily reached from inland southern Britain.

Hengistbury itself was a fully-fledged trading settlement with service industries, including metalworking and the slaughter and preparation of cattle. Large quantities of Armorican pottery from Brittany show where some of the Continental trade came from. Hengistbury was not the only place where cross-Channel trade had started to reach quasi-industrial levels. Evidence has been found in Poole Harbour (Dorset), about 25 miles to the west, of the manufacture of jewelry from Kimmeridge shale. Finds of imported Roman pottery here suggest that some of the finished goods were being shipped across to Gaul, though the pottery could either have been imported in exchange for resale or been used by traders in the manufacturing settlements. Strabo famously recorded a list of Britain's exports: grain, cattle, gold, silver and iron, as well as hunting dogs and slaves.[10] It is tempting to see Hengistbury and Poole as Iron Age versions of an outlet mall, a place to which all kinds of products were channelled so that they could reach their Continental customers. Strabo goes on to tell us that the Britons bought in jewelry and fine wares, and were prepared to pay exorbitant customs duties levelled on trade with Gaul.

Strabo's words and the finds from Hengistbury emphasize the importance of combining the evidence. Most of the perishable materials Strabo refers to could not possibly survive in the archaeological record.

8. Italian Dressel amphora. Amphorae of this type (1B) were produced in large numbers in central Italy, and shipped widely around the Mediterranean and to Spain, Gaul, and as far away as Britain.

Even if they did, they would be unidentifiable as British exports or imports. Beyond a place like Hengistbury, the amphorae serve as the only significant manifestation of this trade that we can recognize. At that time anything that could be reused generally was, with the result that much of what might have entered the archaeological record did not. What mattered to the importers at Hengistbury Head was not the amphorae themselves, but what they contained.

The route the amphorae seem to have travelled is around 130 miles as the crow flies, rather than the shortest cross-Channel route. The distance between Dover and Calais is around one-sixth of the distance. What dictated the existence of such trade and its maintenance was who was importing it, and who controlled the trade routes. The distribution of the amphorae of the first century BC is restricted to an area roughly equivalent to part of Hampshire and the Isle of Wight. The logical deduction from this is that the tribal élite in control of that area was sufficiently aware of the Roman world to favour some of its products, and that it was able to monopolize at least part of the trans-Channel trade. The evidence from Hengistbury shows that either the economic base of the trade was powerful enough to attract people there to work, or that the tribal leadership was organizing the settlement in a centralized way.

Much has been made of Hengistbury Head, but equally important is the fact that this sort of trade link and settlement was generally absent elsewhere in Britain, apart from north Kent, Essex and Hertfordshire. This had profound implications for the process of the Roman conquest more than a century later, and the nature of the province of Britain throughout its history. In the mid-first century BC, parts of southern Britain had far more in common with northern Gaul than with other parts of Britain, and were also more aware of the Roman world. This drew them more closely into the Roman net, especially in the aftermath of Caesar's invasions.

9. Distribution of amphorae in Britain.
Italian Dressel 1A/B amphorae are found in southern Britain, mainly along the south coast between Hengistbury Head and Portsmouth, north Kent, Essex and Hertfordshire, reflecting maritime trade links with the Continent. (After Tyers).

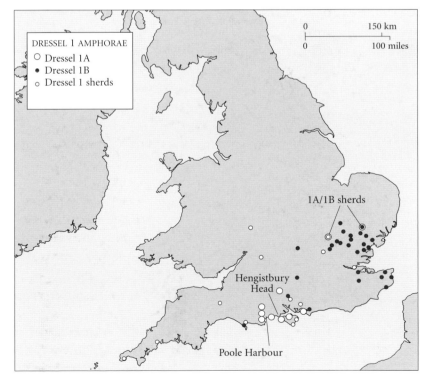

CAESAR

In the mid-50s BC, Gaius Julius Caesar was at the zenith of his career [10]. In 60 BC he had formed the First Triumvirate in Rome with Pompey and Crassus. Essentially a cartel of military dictators, the Triumvirate grew out of the decay of the Roman Republic and the rise of men with colossal fortunes, personal armies and overwhelming prestige. Each was acutely conscious that any one of them might increase his power at the expense of the others, and of the need not to lose any of his own influence.

In 61 BC, the Helvetii began a war of territorial expansion that threatened Roman possessions in southern Gaul, and Caesar was given a special legal dispensation to command an army. Three years earlier he had set out on what evolved into a war of conquest across Gaul, lasting nine years. The war not only provided Caesar with enhanced standing, but also gave him the military muscle to pursue his ambitions in Rome. Nevertheless, the campaign in Gaul was risky and dangerous, during which the invasion of Britain seems to have been more of a curious indulgence than a necessity. But Caesar had a variety of reasons for invading Britain. Firstly, it helped sustain at least an illusion of military momentum. War provided him with prestige, so it was essential to keep fighting one to justify his position. Secondly, Britons had intervened in the Gaulish resistance by offering military assistance and by providing a haven for the fleeing Bellovaci in 57 BC. And finally, Caesar knew that Britain symbolized all that the Romans feared about barbarian wildernesses and chaos. Invading it and confronting a 'hitherto unknown' people would be an enormous publicity coup.[11]

Roman intervention in the region was already becoming decisive. By 56 BC, the Veneti had taken on Caesar's fleet and lost catastrophically. Despite their lack of maritime skills, Caesar's forces improvised and found a way of tearing off the sails and masts from the Veneti ships, enabling them to be easily surrounded and boarded. The impact on the control of commercial traffic in the Channel was permanent. Caesar was also already playing off the Gauls against one another. Having earlier defeated the Gaulish Atrebates, he had installed a man called Commios, presumably an Atrebaten himself, as their king. This anticipated the policy of client kingship, later used to dramatic effect by Augustus and his successors. Commios was sent ahead to Britain to advise the Britons 'to seek the protection of Rome' (a euphemism for capitulation).[12] This time Caesar miscalculated.

Caesar's invasion of Britain in 55 BC was small in scale, and only two legions and cavalry were involved. The dispatch of Commios was supposed to make things go smoothly. They did not. Caesar's plan of using intimidation and manipulative diplomacy was ignored by the Britons,

10. Julius Caesar (b. 100–d. 44 BC). Caesar's invasions might have been militarily inconclusive, but they proved to be a decisive turning point in Britain's relationship with the Roman world.

who immediately detained Commios. When Caesar reached Britain, he was unable to beach his ships, and the troops were coerced into wading ashore. The Britons made a play of suing for peace, but when a storm blew up and wrecked Caesar's fleet, they took advantage of the chaos to evaporate. A stalemate ensued: the Britons could not effectively attack a fortified Roman encampment, but the Romans could not make them fight a proper battle.

Caesar returned to Gaul in a repaired fleet. He had underestimated the opposition, and failed to appreciate the logistical issues of landing a fleet on a tidal beach and fighting an unpredictable enemy. Caesar had no choice but to mount a face-saving follow-up. The invasion of 54 BC was a more organized affair, but the outcome was similarly inconclusive. This time Caesar brought five legions and cavalry, provoking most of the Britons in the southeast to abandon their habitual self-destructive infighting and throw in their lot with the most powerful tribal king, Cassivellaunus. For the Romans, this was a potentially disastrous development. Cassivellaunus ruled lands north of the Thames and was probably king of the Catuvellauni, known to have been a tribe of that area in the lead-up to the invasion of AD 43. Caesar now proceeded inland through Kent, drawn on by the Britons who repeatedly used chariots to harass the Romans.

Had all the Britons sided with Cassivellaunus, the outcome might have been very different. Instead, they allowed their existing differences to confound the confederation. Cassivellaunus had killed a king of the Trinovantes in an earlier dispute, and their heir apparent, Mandubracius, had already fled to Caesar for help. Now the Trinovantes offered their support if Caesar would return Mandubracius to them. Other tribes capitulated as well. In return, Caesar was furnished with intelligence on the whereabouts of Cassivellaunus' headquarters. The occasion was a portent for the future. The Britons always put their own petty disputes first, invariably providing the Romans with a critical strategic advantage, a mistake they continued to make in the invasion of 43 and long afterwards.[13]

By this time, Caesar was dangerously extended. He had brought his forces north of the Thames to confront Cassivellaunus in his *oppidum*, a sprawling settlement loosely defined by woodlands, marshes, ramparts and ditches. Cassivellaunus tried to outmanoeuvre Caesar by organizing an attack on the Roman coastal base. The attack failed, and Cassivellaunus was obliged to sue for peace. He would hand over hostages, and Mandubracius would be acknowledged. Caesar went back to Gaul and never returned. He had 'discovered' Britain for his descendants rather than 'bequeathed' it to them.[14] In 49 BC, the civil war erupted that would bring Caesar supreme power and ultimately his death five years later.

AFTER CAESAR

Caesar's invasions did not result in any permanent Roman occupation of Britain. Indeed, they barely constituted more than exploratory raids. No physical trace of either expedition has ever been found. Sideshows in the conquest of Gaul, they were nevertheless of colossal importance to Britain. Roman power had transformed control of Channel trade. The evidence from Hengistbury is of a marked decline in trade there, perhaps because the Veneti stranglehold on movement had been broken. However, this depends on a very precise dating differential between sub-types of amphorae, and the transition need not have been quite as fast as is sometimes suggested. But change there certainly was, because other trade routes seem to have developed in the aftermath of Caesar's invasions.

Caesar had negotiated a peace deal apparently to his advantage, though the Britons were quite content to break the terms by failing to pay tribute. However, he had started a dialogue. The tribes of southern Britain had now been drawn into a direct relationship with the Roman world in which patronage could play to their advantage, even if it also meant their enslavement. Caesar's description of tribal politics in Britain and Gaul paints a picture of endemic instability. He names certain tribes in Britain that are for the most part never heard of again. Tribal identities, it seems, were little less durable than the lives of their rulers. Tribal ruling houses depended on prestige, which itself depended on control of land and resources. Late Iron Age peoples were increasingly successful in their exploitation of the landscape, resulting in bigger populations and pressure on available resources. The Trinovantes, the only tribal name that survived, had spotted the advantage of having powerful friends. But Roman interference in Britain was not one-way. In the age-old game of power politics, self-interest is everything. Like today's politicians, tribal leaders had no interest in the long term. In a similar manner to the Gaulish tribes, some of the British tribes started to adopt the symbols and imagery of prestige in a more Roman idiom.

Caesar had shown the Roman world that Britain was accessible and negotiable, an essential ingredient in recreating Britain in the Roman mindset. It was already normal for Roman traders to settle on the fringes of the Empire or beyond, creating mercantile centres. One may have existed at Braughing-Puckeridge (Hertfordshire), in Catuvellaunian territory. This site has produced a great deal of high-quality early imported Roman tableware. But more importantly, the discovery of graffiti and *mortaria* (used only in the preparation of Roman food) suggests that some of the people living here were Roman, rather than native. A place like this must have been founded on maritime trade coming up the Thames.

No wonder then that with routes like this open, Roman goods appeared in a variety of rich graves on the Hertfordshire and Essex border over the next century, for example at Baldock and Welwyn Garden City. Baldock, dating to *c.* 100–50 BC, is the earliest known, and, characteristically for these graves, featured 'feasting equipment' in the form of a cauldron and firedogs, as well as a Roman amphora. The Welwyn grave seems to have been deposited in a timber vault around 50–25 BC [11]. It contained several Italian wine amphorae, 30 pottery vessels and a silver Italian cup. Such graves point to something subtler than trade. Their contents may well reflect Roman patronage, which reached its climax in the client kings established by Augustus at the end of the first century BC. The Lexden grave, buried after 17 BC, was even more elaborate. At least 16 amphorae were represented, along with metal-bound chests, silver and gold, and iron mail. It was traditionally thought that such graves must represent tribal aristocrats, but this is a judgment based solely on the grave goods, not on the burial rituals.[15] If the occupants were less significant individuals, this may mean that access to these goods in late Iron Age Britain was slightly easier than previously thought. Along the south coast, Fishbourne Harbour could have offered an equally amenable location for Roman traders. Not only have Roman imports of pre-conquest date been found here, but a case has also been made for the establishment of a pre-43 Romanized settlement. Further west, Poole Harbour now seems to have become the main port of entry in the southwest, supplanting Hengistbury Head.

11. Welwyn Garden City (Hertfordshire).
This cremation burial included wine amphorae and a silver cup of Italian manufacture, and other personal items. The location of the grave strongly suggests that the occupant was a wealthy member of the Catuvellauni, with strong trade or diplomatic links to Rome. Late first century BC. (British Museum).

12. Eppillus of the Atrebates.
King of the Atrebates around the time of Augustus, Eppillus struck coins with legends that describe himself as *Rex Callevae*, or 'King of Calleva', and *Commi F(ilius)*, 'son of Commios'. (British Museum).

13. Augustus (27 BC–AD 14).
Cameo portrait of the first Roman emperor. Augustus maintained a policy of buffer states along the Empire's borders, and offered patronage and protection in return for loyalty and stability. Britain's tribal leaders soon realized that the Empire would have a decisive influence on their future. (British Museum).

When Commios fell out with Caesar in 52 BC, he fought once more with the Gaulish Atrebates until he was defeated, and fled to southern Britain.[16] Here he seems to have founded a dynasty, known to us initially through coinage. Since later rulers in his line struck coins at *Calleva* (Silchester), this was probably where he established his stronghold. Begun originally as an Iron Age *oppidum*, by as early as 20 BC Silchester may have had a street grid, identifying its ruler as someone with a precocious sense of self-improvement on a Roman model. The kings in the dynasty Commios founded, like the ruling houses of the Trinovantes and the Catuvellauni, used Latin words and Roman iconography on their coins [12]. After the invasion of AD 43, Silchester was made the regional capital and named *Calleva Atrebatum*, 'Calleva of the Atrebates'.

Although the Claudian invasion was a dramatic historical event, Roman influence and patronage had started to play a very important role in southern Britain since at least Caesar's time. During this period the Roman Empire ceased to be a state ruled by military dictators and became a monarchy in all but name, with imperial prestige invested in the person of the emperor. Augustus, Caesar's nephew, became the first emperor in 27 BC [13]. Augustus deliberately and continually intervened in frontier politics, deposing and imposing rulers in territories on the Empire's fringes. He cultivated submission to Roman interests and the adoption of Roman customs and expectations, and brought the sons of ruling native families to Rome to educate them in Roman ways. Britain was simply another component in a chain of frontier territories that stretched to the Middle East. By the time of the Claudian invasion, the tribal élite of southern Britain no longer had any meaningful concept of their power in a non-Roman context. They used Roman goods, accepted Roman gifts, adopted Roman titles, fled to the emperor for help when they felt under threat, and defied him when they felt powerful.

CHAPTER 2

THE CONQUEST OF BRITAIN:
AD 43–142

In or around the year AD 142, the emperor Antoninus Pius (138–61) ordered the construction of a turf and timber wall between the Forth and the Clyde in Scotland. Known today as the Antonine Wall, it marked the northernmost frontier of Roman Britain. It had taken almost exactly a century after the Roman army arrived to reach the point where permanent control of even the Southern Uplands of Scotland could be contemplated. What may have started out as a limited attempt to invade southeast Britain evolved into a seemingly endless series of campaigns. No wonder Tacitus called Britannia 'the warlike province'.[1]

THE CLAUDIAN INVASION
Of all the pieces of bad luck that have afflicted Roman Britain's history, the gap in our text of Tacitus covering the time of the invasion is one of the most unfortunate. All we have today is what Dio Cassius wrote (or, at any rate, a synopsis of his work) around 160 years later. Dio did, however, have access to original records. So while he is short on facts and geographical detail, his account can be treated as essentially reliable. To this we can add other historical references, such as Celtic dynastic tribal coinage and, of course, the archaeological evidence.

Claudius had reputedly ordered the invasion because 'Berikos', according to Dio, had fled Britain as the result of an uprising. We can identify Berikos from Celtic coins as Verica, a king apparently of the Atrebates and thus perhaps a descendant of Commios, the Gaulish Atrebate and erstwhile ally of Caesar in 54 BC. Of course the invasion was a pretext for war. Rome, after all, had nothing to fear from Britain.

There was a subtext. Claudius had come to power in AD 41 as the result of peculiar circumstances. So far there had been just three emperors: Augustus (27 BC–AD 14), Tiberius (14–37) and Caligula (37–41). Augustus had brilliantly restored the Roman Empire to order after decades of civil war. He had used showmanship, military acumen, cynicism, political guile and diplomacy to rebuild the state around himself, but in such a sufficiently institutionalized way that it survived his death. His position was almost indistinguishable from that of a monarch, but since the concept of kingship was anathema to the Romans, the fiction was perpetuated that it was the Senate that remained in power. By virtue of his prestige and qualities, Augustus held a unique portfolio of offices within that system. Power was legally transferred by appointing an heir to appropriate positions, but in practice it was transferred to the closest Augustus had to a son, his stepson and son-in-law, Tiberius. But by AD 37 Tiberius had degenerated into a perverted, half-crazed and hated recluse. And by 41 Caligula, Augustus' great-grandson, had degenerated into a perverted, half-crazed and hated megalomaniac.

It was remarkable that the office survived the murder of Caligula in 41 at all. Claudius [14] was the grandson of Augustus' sister, Octavia, nephew of Tiberius and grandson of Augustus' wife, Livia, by her first marriage. He had survived the murderous intrigues of previous years thanks to his reputation as a buffoon, something he probably cultivated in the interests of survival. He was made emperor because he was available to the Praetorian Guard who had just murdered Caligula. But Claudius was more than equal to the position.

Claudius managed to remain in post because he knew he needed to prove himself. Britain had proved too much for Caesar. Now it offered Claudius the prospect of a military triumph, an essential qualification for a Roman emperor, and of exceeding his esteemed ancestor's achievements. Conquest lubricated the wheels of power. It provided more land, people and resources to appropriate and exploit, and – more subtly – the opportunity for Rome's magnanimous donation of Roman ways to other parts of the world. Of course, this involved exploitation, but it also satisfied a commitment to promoting a way of life the Romans genuinely believed benefited others. The Victorians, who busily exploited the British Empire, also brought innovations in communications and other public facilities, and this was equally true of the Romans. The benefits they brought might have been through the mechanisms of enslavement, but many people 'enslaved' in this way seem to have been prepared to put up with the hardships. In this manner, so the Romans believed, their conquests were legitimized and morally justifiable. In Britain, the consequences of Augustus' diplomacy were dynastic ambitions in which Roman backing was decisive. Strabo reported that several British rulers had solicited the friendship of Augustus by sending envoys and gifts.[2] No wonder two British kings felt they could flee to him for support around the year AD 7, as part of the routine comings and goings of supplicants more than happy to sacrifice a little independence to hang on to a powerful friend. Tincomarus and Dubnovellaunus are listed in Augustus' *Res Gestae*, along with several other rulers that had sought refuge at Rome.[3] Coinage shows that Tincomarus was a ruler of the Atrebates, and Dubnovellaunus of

14. Claudius (AD **41–54**). Bronze head of the emperor, found at the River Alde at Rendham, near Saxmundham, Suffolk. (British Museum).

the Cantiaci, in Kent. Tincomarus claimed to be a son of Commios, either Caesar's Commios or a son of his with the same name. Why either Tincomarus or Dubnovellaunus should have fled is unknown, but factional politics within each tribe are no less likely a reason than the machinations of more powerful neighbours. The important point is that these kings owed their positions to Augustus. What Augustus had effectively done was to initiate and encourage the creation of states ruled by dynasties, whose members focused their attention on consolidating and maintaining dynastic interests.

15. The conquest.
The progress of the conquest between 43 and *c.* 87 can be only approximately reconstructed from historical sources and inscriptions. Evidence from Alchester has been used to argue that the campaign in the south may have been directed from further north than hitherto thought, but this is based on a single tombstone of a veteran of the II legion.

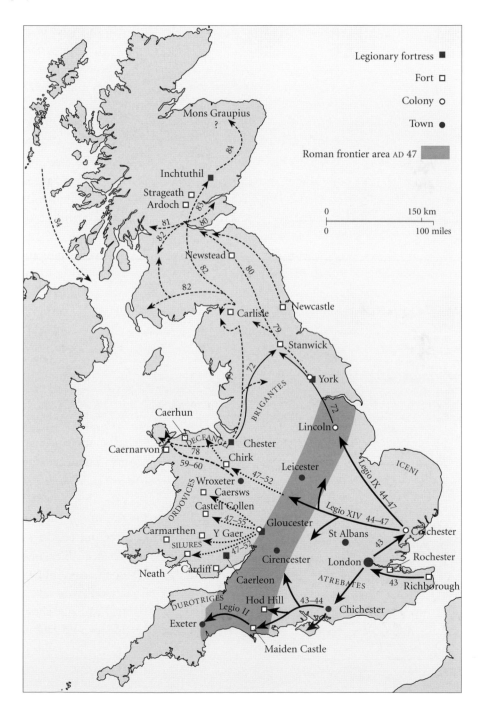

Verica provided Claudius with a reason to invade Britain. It was no more than a reason, because Verica is never heard of again. One thing we can be certain of is that the tribe to the north of the Thames, the Catuvellauni, ruled by Cunobelinus, had grown in power since Caesar's time. Britain was of little intrinsic value to Augustus or Tiberius; indeed, Tacitus called this the period of 'long oblivion' for Britain.[4] But stable tribal politics in Britain helped the Romans secure coastal Gaul.

The status such men enjoyed in life was transferred to the grave. The Folly Lane burial, close to the *oppidum* at *Verlamion* (later the Roman *Verulamium*, and later still St Albans) and dating to the early AD 50s, produced not only evidence for organized destruction of grave goods by fire, but also for the sheer quantity of imported goods and bullion [16], dwarfing finds at other nearby sites. Coins of Cunobelinus include depictions of the king wearing a Roman-style helmet.[5] Other types show a variety of classical items and symbols. Latin words and abbreviations feature in their legends. By the late 30s, the Catuvellauni controlled most of the land immediately north of the Thames. They had spread out from their Hertfordshire homeland to take control of the Trinovantian territory and its capital at Colchester to the east, and were also exerting influence over the Atrebates in central southern Britain [17]. It is inconceivable that the Romans neglected to attempt to draw Cunobelinus and the Catuvellauni into their diplomatic net.

However, Cunobelinus showed signs of having become too powerful. In 39 Cunobelinus had exiled one of his sons, Adminius, who crossed the Channel and asked Caligula to invade Britain in retaliation. Recognizing Britain's vulnerability, Caligula ordered preparations for an invasion, including the raising of two new legions, *XV Primigenia* and *XXII Primigenia*.[6] But his plans came to nothing. It would have been difficult for Claudius to disband the new legions without provoking a mutiny, but now the garrison on the German frontier was dangerously large. An ambitious governor might take advantage of the forces available to try and seize the throne. On the other hand, the new legions and preparations meant that Claudius had all he needed to invade Britain.

By 43 Cunobelinus had died, leaving his kingdom to his sons. The legacy of his territorial aggrandizement was political instability, but there is no doubt that his prestige had been very great. Suetonius called him 'King of the Britons', which means that from Rome's perspective, Cunobelinus was the only significant player.[7] His death may well have created the political chaos that provided Rome with a key opportunity to invade. Whatever the background, great events – and the invasion of Britain was a great event – normally turn on such accidents of fate.

16. St Albans (Hertfordshire). This knob made of elephant ivory was found in the burnt remains of the first-century burial at Folly Lane, and was probably used as the finial of a piece of furniture included in the grave goods. Its exotic origins suggest that the deceased was a wealthy and influential tribal leader. (St Albans Museums).

In the late summer of 43, the Roman fleet arrived off Britain's coast. Filled with reluctant heroes, the ships had been troubled by adverse currents and winds. Only the timely appearance of a lightning bolt to point the way had given the notoriously superstitious troops the courage to carry on. They might have been wondering why they were there.

At this time, Britain's population was divided into dozens of different tribes. In the south, society was sophisticated enough to organize major tribal defensive installations and settlements such as Maiden Castle and Danebury, and to maintain productive agriculture and diplomatic contacts with Rome. Meanwhile, concepts like coinage and literacy were being absorbed from the Continent. Britain was not, as Virgil put it, 'entirely segregated from the whole world'.[8] The closer a tribe was to the Roman Empire, the stronger its political, commercial and cultural influence in a society that stored wealth in coins and manufactured goods. Those tribes bought or were given Roman goods, and these often survive in the record. The visibility of British tribal culture in the archaeological record is a result of its proximity to the Roman Empire.

Caesar's potted account of Britain in 55 BC presents the Britons as a sequence of progressively less 'civilized' communities, starting with the coastal districts facing Gaul. These were the 'most civilized', farming the land and living in densely packed homesteads.[9] Of course, Caesar was highly influenced by his own fairly narrow idea of what constituted civilization, and also by his own lack of any detailed information. Caesar described the inland Britons as being definitively less civilized because of their lack of arable agriculture. In fact, the archaeological evidence from northern Britain suggests that he was quite wrong. But Caesar had a vested interest in reinforcing a stereotype. In our own time we crave more order, reliability, security, money and display of status through possessions. There is no reason to assume the Britons were significantly different. Given the choice, and before 43 there was a choice, those who could had increasingly opted for the visible trappings of Romanized civilization.

The underlying dynamic amongst these tribal communities was the control of territory. The more the population grew, the greater the pressure on resources. Tribal leaders fabricated territorial disputes, creating a permanent sense of tension that gave them the environment in which to consolidate their prestige. We might have guessed this from the proliferation of hillforts and *oppida*, but Caesar's accounts confirm it. The run-up to the invasion of 43 is a mixture of spin and fact, but it shows us that Rome's imperial politics, and the tribal machinations in Britain, were already closely linked.

17. Colchester (Essex).
Gold *stater* struck for Cunobelinus at *Camulodunum* (Colchester). As the most important tribal capital in Britain, its capture was a key objective in the Roman campaign. (British Museum).

None of this would have been of any particular interest to the soldiers off the south coast of Britain in the late summer of 43. The letter written by Cicero to his brother, Quintus, during the invasions by Caesar a century before, gives us an idea of what went through some of their minds. Cicero's excited reply to his brother's letter shows that Quintus had already told him about the sea and the coastline.[10] Cicero anticipated news of natural features, the people and their customs, and the battles to come. The invasion of Britain was an adventure for participants and armchair travellers alike. For officers and aristocrats, the expedition was the thrill of a lifetime. It was a chance to win military and social respect, to do something that would echo down through a lifetime of anecdotes [18].

For a ranker, war meant the prospect of money in the form of loot and donatives, and the suspension of garrison drudgery. It also meant the prospect of absolute terror, a sense that probably also preyed on the minds of many of the officers. To the ordinary man in the mid-first century AD, being asked to go to Britain was like someone today being asked to embark on a mythical journey into Middle Earth, with all its attendant terrors. At the time, most people believed Britain to be little more than a legend, isolated in fabulous obscurity beyond the sea, and a home to magic and superstition. Being sent to Britain was, in short, a bowel-emptying experience that will have left most soldiers half-paralyzed with fear, while they tried to keep their footing on the heaving decks. Given half a chance they would never have embarked, and indeed the invasion nearly foundered for that very reason. The troops had refused point blank to set foot on the ships, until Claudius sent a freedman called Narcissus to speak to them. The sending of an ex-slave was such an unmitigated insult that to avoid humiliation the soldiers gave in and obeyed the orders of their general, Aulus Plautius, and set out for Britain.

The only thing the soldiers had to fear was the dangerous crossing itself, because the landing in Britain was unopposed. Exactly where this took place is anyone's guess. Dio says the landing occurred in three waves, which could mean three different places, or a staggered arrival in one place. Much scholarly energy has been expended on trying to decide where that place was. Claudian military features at both Richborough [19] and Fishbourne Harbour make either a legitimate candidate. But the nature of military invasions, especially successful ones, is for more landings to be made in short order as a campaign progresses. It is possible that Richborough and Fishbourne were each used in the same year, as well as other, unknown locations. It is equally possible that they were used in successive years, as and when required. Archaeology unfortunately will never be good enough to determine an exact sequence. The main argument in favour of Richborough being the first landing place is the combination of its location on a main route to the Thames, the Claudian military buildings, and a later triumphal arch erected at the ceremonial entry point into Britain. In favour of Fishbourne is the security offered by a pro-Roman tribal area, including the Atrebatic territory around Silchester.

Dio tells us nothing about the size of the force. In the *Agricola*, Tacitus says 'legionaries and auxiliaries' were sent.[11] The only unit definitely involved was *II Augusta* along with its commander, the future emperor Vespasian [20], mentioned in a retrospective account of Vespasian's career by Tacitus.[12] It is normally assumed that the legions *II Augusta, IX Hispana, XIV Gemina* and XX and their auxiliaries invaded Britain, because these four are testified in Britain by the year 60. If they all arrived in 43, then the combined force of legionaries and auxiliaries would come to roughly 40,000. However, legions often operated in detachments, called vexillations, so it is quite possible that the invasion was made up of these rather than whole legions. The invasion force probably also included vexillations from several other legions. Honours won by the centurion Gaius Gavius Silvanus of *VIII Augusta* suggests that at least part of that legion was involved as well.[13] Clearly it is impossible to say for certain how many soldiers or exactly which units actually took part.

The Britons retreated into woodland to avoid a battle, but Aulus Plautius defeated Caratacus and Togodumnus, the sons of Cunobelinus. Thus Catuvellaunian prestige was permanently damaged. Lesser tribes that had been subject to them began to capitulate to the Romans, allowing Plautius to consolidate the advance by building a fort and garrisoning it. No fort of such an early date has ever been found. The claim that Syndale, near Faversham (Kent), is the prime candidate is unsubstantiated. Unlike the Claudian ditches at Richborough, Syndale has failed to produce anything conclusively diagnostic of a fort, let alone a military presence.

The Britons then made a tactical mistake, assuming that by fleeing across a river they could camp in safety and watch the Romans' frustration. Only the Thames or the Medway are legitimate candidates for this river. The hoard of 34 gold *aurei* found at Bredgar, near Sittingbourne (Kent), is sometimes interpreted as a Roman officer's hoard, buried before the battle, and thus evidence that the Medway was the river the Romans reached. In reality, this is false logic. It is impossible to know exactly when, or in what context, the coins were buried. The latest coin date is 42, making 43 a possibility, but so also is any time in the next decade.

The Britons were wrong in thinking they were safe. An auxiliary unit of 'Celts' forded the river and took the Britons by surprise, killing their horses.[14] Vespasian led more Romans across the river to kill the

21. Claudius (41–54).
Gold *aureus* depicting one of the triumphal arches erected in Rome to commemorate the invasion of Britain. (British Museum).

immobilized Britons. However, the battle was more evenly matched than Dio described. The Britons did not try to flee, and even remained overnight for more fighting the next day. This time the outcome was more decisive, though it could have gone either way until the efforts of Gnaeus Hosidius Geta swung the battle in the Romans' favour. He was later awarded the *ornamenta triumphalia* for this achievement. By sitting across the river, the Britons had provided the Romans with the best chance to make use of their more disciplined and coordinated tactics.

The Britons then fled, falling back on the Thames to cross where 'it form[ed] a lake at high tide', probably somewhere in the vicinity of today's central London.[15] Once again, 'Celts' forded the river while the rest of the Roman force crossed a bridge upstream. This was probably a pontoon bridge set up by Roman military engineers at a point where the river could be easily crossed. This could have been a different stretch of the Thames to the one where the earlier battle had just been fought, but it does imply that the first battle had been fought on the Medway. A more radical suggestion is that Dio assumed two separate river battles were involved, when in fact he had used different accounts of the same battle.[16] The progress is similar: both involved 'Celts' fording the river, and other forces crossing at a different point to rout the Britons. The point is an important one, and reminds us of the dangers of assuming our literary sources are invariably reliable.

Crossing the Thames took the Romans into Catuvellaunian territory. The stakes were now far higher for the Britons, made worse by the sudden death of Togodumnus. The Romans struggled in marshland by the north banks of the Thames, but Plautius halted the advance and waited for Claudius. Dio said the fighting worried Plautius, but the reality was more likely political expediency. Claudius needed his chance to blaze across the Roman firmament. Given that the invasion had come late in the summer, and it would take several weeks for news to reach Rome that the army was waiting for him, Claudius cannot have arrived until the late autumn of 43. But arrive he did, replete with elephants in his train, and proceeded to enjoy a series of formal capitulations by tribal leaders. Crossing the Thames, he 'led' the Roman army into battle against the Britons, though this presumably means that he was merely present, before entering the Catuvellaunian capital at *Camulodunum* (Colchester) and establishing a military base there .

Claudius had achieved his prime purpose. In theory he could now have withdrawn the army, and, like Caesar, claimed to have conquered Britain without having the trouble of actually ruling it. But surpassing Caesar was a more tempting prospect. Moreover, Caratacus had retreated to western Britain where he reappeared in alliance with the tribes of south Wales. So the Catuvellauni remained undefeated. Perhaps

Caratacus unwittingly drew the Romans further into a longer war, or perhaps this had been his intention all along. Meanwhile Claudius, after 16 days in Britain, went home to Rome and held a victory parade [21]. The cult of the British Victories was established as far afield as Corinth.[17] Roman historians were less impressed. Suetonius thought the campaign was 'average', and Tacitus noted that Britain's reduction to a Roman province was 'gradual'.

THE ROAD TO REVOLT

On the eve of the Boudican revolt in 60, few of the soldiers who took part in the invasion were still serving. For those that were, the previous 17 years of campaigning had taken Roman forces north, west and south-west. The tribes made and broke alliances as seemed convenient, and denied Rome a single cohesive target. Instead, she was presented with elusive enemies who flitted in and out of woodland and marshes, and avoided set-piece battles. No wonder then that Tacitus could say the only region of Britain that been controlled was 'the nearest part'.[18]

Meanwhile, Vespasian had led *II Augusta* along southern Britain, fighting 30 battles and capturing the Isle of Wight and more than 20 native towns.[19] He can thus be linked personally to the evidence of vicious fighting at Maiden Castle (Dorset), the Claudian fort huddled in the corner of the Iron Age hillfort at Hod Hill [22, 23], and the Roman military occupation of the hillforts at Ham Hill (Somerset) and Hembury (Devon). Since Vespasian must have been supported by naval forces, it is obvious that the Romans would have established various landing points along the south coast as the campaign progressed. The military activity identified at Fishbourne is as likely to have belonged to this campaign as to the initial invasion, if not both. However, recent excavations of a fort built in the mid-40s at Alchester (Oxfordshire), and the discovery there of a first-century tombstone belonging to a veteran of *II Augusta*, suggest that the legion may in fact have spent a significant part of this time fighting further north than previously believed.

By now the Fosse Way had been established, running from Exeter right up into Lincolnshire. As a line of communication it was obviously of enormous importance, but whether or not it was intended as a frontier is unknown. The road was not fortified, although there were some forts and fortlets scattered along it. If there was ever any plan to halt here and make a province out of the more compliant (or so it might have been thought) south, it was shelved.

The mid-first-century fortress at Exeter, founded by *c.* 50, was probably *II Augusta*'s. With its vaulted legionary bathhouse, Exeter symbolized the impact of classical culture on a place where nothing like it had ever existed before. To the north, *IX Hispana* had possibly already reached as

22, 23. Hod Hill (Dorset).
Aerial view and plan of the Iron Age hillfort. The Claudian fort has been built into the northwest corner, utilizing the Iron Age defences for two of its sides.
A = Commandant's house
B = Headquarters

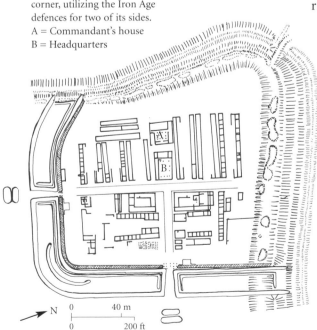

far as Lincoln, a strategically vital location, much closer to the sea then than it is today. Behind it the legion left a variety of vexillation fortresses along with Ermine Street, which carried communications back to the river crossing at London. *XIV Gemina* was heading towards the Welsh Marches. The road network fanned out from London, provoking the spontaneous development of a trading centre which was evolving into a significant town. Linking all of these sites was the Roman navy, which controlled much of Britain's coastal waters and provided a means of supplying bases at Exeter and Lincoln, and elsewhere.

By 47, much of southern Britain had technically capitulated, giving Rome the vital allies she needed. Amongst these must have been Togidubnus, who was awarded 'certain cantonal areas' to rule. An inscription from Chichester locates him in the area, and it has long been assumed that he owned the remarkable palace at nearby Fishbourne.[20] Whether he did or not, or whether or not it was the governor's residence, does not alter the fact that parts of central southern Britain showed astonishingly rapid Romanization in this period. We know nothing of Togidubnus' origins, but the geographical location makes it likely that he had some connection with the Atrebates, and indeed may even have been the dynastic beneficiary of Verica's appeal to Claudius.

Further east, resistance increased when Plautius handed over control to Publius Ostorius Scapula in 47. Ostorius moved rapidly to disarm tribes in an area 'on this side of the Trent and Severn', meaning much of central, eastern and southern Britain.[21] The Iceni of East Anglia objected. Being disarmed was more than a humiliating public castration; it cut right to the very heart of their existence. Nevertheless, their revolt caught Ostorius unawares, illustrating how little initiative the Romans had in this war. The known vexillation fortresses at Longthorpe, Great Casterton, Osmanthorpe and Newton-on-Trent all lay well to the west of Iceni territory.

Ostorius suppressed the rebellion with auxiliaries. Even so, the Romans were continually abandoning the task in hand to deal with more pressing problems. In Wales, Caratacus was organizing resistance amongst the Silures [24]. This was extremely dangerous. The Welsh tribes' total lack of interest in Roman comforts meant they were alienated from everything that Rome stood for. Their lack of cohesion might have compromised the natural advantages their remote and difficult territory gave them, but Caratacus was unifying them.

Ostorius marched against the Deceangli in north Wales. He was almost bound to do this. Had he failed to conquer additional territory, he would have looked like a failure, and his personal reputation as a general demanded a more conspicuous result. The attractions of defeating Caratacus by cutting him off must have driven him on, and he may also have had half an eye on Anglesey. Anglesey was the Druid centre, from which the Druid priesthood helped organize resistance to the Roman conquest.

Ostorius ravaged Deceangli territory, but failed to force them to a battle. The idea was to discourage Welsh tribes from supporting resistance in southern Britain. Whether or not there was any plan to hold Wales permanently is unknown, though by 49 the Romans were smelting lead and extracting silver (a by-product of lead) in the Mendips. The invasion of Wales was not just a punitive conquest; there was also gold in those hills. But Ostorius had acted too hastily, and failed to cover his rear flank. The Brigantes of northern Britain had officially capitulated to Rome, but not all the Brigantes agreed. An armed coup erupted and Ostorius had to withdraw to put it down, before returning to Wales to deal with the Caratacus problem. Ostorius took more precautions this time. The fortress at *Camulodunum* was given up and made into a colony of veterans, and the legion, probably XX, was released for war.

24. Caratacus of the Catuvellauni. Despite Caratacus' role as the leader of the resistance against Rome, this silver coin bears the head of Hercules and, on the reverse, the thoroughly Roman device of an eagle, copied from Roman coins. (British Museum).

At this time, Caratacus enjoyed matchless prestige. He retreated, but avoided selling out. He exploited the narrow valleys of south Wales to lead the Romans further in, and eventually to Ordovician territory. But he was running out of places to pull back to, and made a crucial error. Caratacus consolidated his forces for a last stand, giving the Romans exactly what they wanted: a set-piece battle. He established himself behind ramparts overlooking a river. Behind him, steep hills covered the rear flank. In Tacitus' description, the Romans were hankering for the chance to fight. This is unlikely, despite their frustration with Caratacus. Strategically, there was no advantage. They were exposed in every direction, and they faced a highly motivated enemy. Ostorius had been initially confounded by the obstacles, heightening the tension, and had to spend time looking for a suitable place to cross the river. At this stage, sheer numbers and hardware started to tell. The Britons had little hope in close hand-to-hand fighting, and the physical structure of their ramparts was too feeble to stand up to Roman demolition work. Both auxiliaries and legionaries were used in the battle, showing how tough the fight was. Caratacus was defeated but escaped, leaving his family and brothers behind to be captured.

Now Rome's policy of patronage paid off. Caratacus fled for protection to Cartimandua, queen of the Brigantes. She handed him over and he was carted off to Rome, where in 51 he appealed to Claudius' imperial magnanimity to spare his life. Duly reprieved, Caratacus was pensioned off in Rome and disappeared into obscurity. Claudius celebrated the climax of his conquest of Britain by erecting a triumphal arch in Rome. Part of the inscription survives, recording the 'submission of 11 British kings' and the first successful campaign to bring 'barbarian tribes beyond the Ocean into the dominion of the Roman people' [25].[22] It was, like most victory boasts, premature. The capture of Caratacus opened a destructive decade that climaxed in the virtual annihilation of the province.

Ostorius set out on an orgy of revenge. Stories spread amongst the Silures in south Wales that he had publicly announced they would be slaughtered or enslaved. This gave them nothing to lose. Legionary cohorts building forts in Silurian territory were quickly ambushed. The best troops were killed, along with eight centurions and their camp prefect, before help arrived. Other troops foraging for supplies with a cavalry escort were wiped out. Ostorius was forced to bring in auxiliaries and legionaries, but even then the battle only petered out as night fell. The Silures escaped with few losses, and continued to maintain a concerted guerrilla campaign. Their success began to encourage other

25. Claudian inscription, Rome. Only fragments of the dedicatory inscription on the arch erected by Claudius in AD 51 to commemorate the campaign in Britain survive, but enough can be read to record the date and the submission of '11 British kings', as well as the emperor's proud claim that he had been the first to bring the remote island under Roman control.

tribes to consider rebellion. Then Ostorius suddenly died in post, and the Silures took the opportunity to rout the legion.

Aulus Didius Gallus arrived to replace Ostorius in 51 or 52. Tacitus thought Didius Gallus magnified the Welsh problem to exaggerate his own success at dealing with it, but there seems little doubt that things had quieted down. Like Ostorius, Didius Gallus found Wales had to take second place to the Brigantian problem. Cartimandua's estranged husband, Venutius, was considered to be the finest British exponent of war. Not only did the divorce occasion a Brigantian civil war, but Venutius turned against Rome, too. Didius Gallus had to intervene to restore stability.[23] Roman goods found at Stanwick, long thought to have been the principal Brigantian stronghold, indicate that Cartimandua welcomed Romanization, even if the price was the loss of independence. Like the client kings further south, she knew that her power depended on Roman support.

Tacitus accused the aged Didius of being content to let his legionary commanders organize the war while he rested on his laurels. The death of Claudius in 54 and the accession of Nero certainly diverted imperial attention from Britain. If Tacitus was correct, perhaps Didius Gallus was partly responsible for the disastrous events of the next few years. He left in 57, only to be replaced by Quintus Veranius Nepos, who died within the year, thereby escaping having to deliver his promise to conquer the whole of Britain within two years.

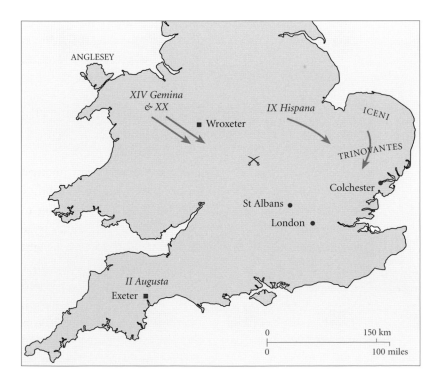

26. The Boudican revolt.
This map shows the progress of the Boudican revolt across East Anglia towards the cities of Colchester, London and St Albans, which were destroyed, thwarting the initial effort of the IX legion to stop the rebel forces. The XIV and XX legions on campaign in Anglesey marched southeast to meet and defeat the rebels somewhere in the Midlands. The II legion at Exeter failed to mobilize to provide assistance. (After Jones and Mattingly).

The governorship of Gaius Suetonius Paullinus (57/8–61) was probably the most decisive in the history of Roman Britain. Suetonius Paullinus, an experienced general, set out to destroy the Druid stronghold in Anglesey. It had been well known since Caesar's time that the Druids operated apart from the tribal leaderships as a separate social caste. In an island politically fragmented by petty kingships, the Druids provided a vital cohesive force. They controlled law and order, and used excommunication to enforce their power. They were also literate, a fact that enhanced their control over an illiterate society. Anglesey's pivotal role behind the resistance cannot have gone unnoticed, but it may have taken the work of Ostorius and Didius Gallus before a campaign could be undertaken.

Soldiers from the XIV and XX legions and auxiliaries [27] crossed the Menai Straits to face a frenzied crowd of women and armed men, whipped up by Druids uttering strange incantations. The intention was to create intimidation and fear in a theatrical display of barbarian hysteria, and the soldiers were effectively transfixed with terror. Under pressure from Suetonius Paullinus, the soldiers recovered themselves, and the outcome was a foregone conclusion. The crowd was annihilated and the Druids' sacred groves wiped out.

Britain was heavily garrisoned by Roman standards, but any campaign into Wales or the north meant leaving the south and east dangerously unguarded. The Iceni saw their chance, and this time the rising was devastating. The story pivots around Boudica, widow of the king of the Iceni, Prasutagus. Prasutagus foresaw what might happen to his kingdom, and took the precaution of naming Nero as one of his heirs. When he died in or around 59, things went horribly wrong. Boudica was flogged and her daughters raped. Centurions, presumably detached to the region as part of the governor's staff, ransacked the kingdom, while imperial slaves working for the procurator took what they wanted from the royal household [28]. The centurions and slaves competed against one another to wring the region dry. Since this treatment gave them nothing to lose, the Iceni rebelled.

There was another agenda. Some of Britain's tribal élite had accepted substantial cash donations from Claudius, and had also taken out loans from speculators like Nero's tutor, Seneca. The loans were probably offered in part so that the Britons could pay the taxes imposed by the governor and garrison of the province to pay for their 'protection'. The procurator, Decianus Catus, now demanded the donations back, and Seneca called in his loan, perhaps because payments had been defaulted on. There was, presumably, no chance of any of the Britons being in a position to repay their debts, though it is not clear if individuals regarded as more reliable – like Togidubnus – had also been told to repay their loans.

27. Wroxeter (Shropshire).
Tombstone of Marcus Petronius, a *signifier* (standard-bearer) with *XIV Gemina*. The lack of the titles *Martia Victrix* may mean that Petronius died before the legion's triumph in the war against Boudica. About 50–65.

As Suetonius Paullinus was on the other side of Britain he was power-less. Indeed, it would have been several days or weeks before he even heard about the uprising in the east. By that time the Icenian revolt, led by Boudica, had swept out of East Anglia into the south, wiping out Roman settlements as it went. An uprising on this scale was unusual by Roman standards. The colonists at *Camulodunum* had failed to build defences. This was unfortunate: the colony was a focal point of local resentment because of the imperial cult housed in the Temple of Claudius [29]. The Trinovantes, who had benefited from the Roman invasion by the destruction of Catuvellaunian power, had been badly treated as well. They were driven out, and their territory appropriated and given to colonists in land grants.

An appeal was sent out for help, but Decianus Catus (who was probably in London) sent only 200 troops to reinforce the small resident garrison. The colonists took refuge in the temple precinct, but after a two-day siege *Camulodunum* fell and its population massacred. A vexillation of the IX legion, probably based at Lincoln, was routed on its way to the colony [30]. Realizing that things would get worse before they got better, Decianus Catus fled to Gaul. Suetonius Paullinus reached London with an advance guard, but the fate of the IX legion persuaded him to withdraw and leave Colchester to its fate. The rebels went on to destroy London and St Albans, and then headed out to meet the Roman army. The II legion was not in a position to flee the province, so it did the next best thing and stayed in camp. The legion seems to have lacked a com-manding officer at the time. It was Poenius Postumus, the camp prefect, who weighed up the odds and decided that prudence was the better part of valour.

Tacitus and Dio both describe Boudica as the principal leader of a rebellion that at its climax included the Iceni and some of the Trinovantes. Few of them had a sophisticated political and legal reason for joining the rebellion. Many were attracted by the prospect of plunder, and the chance to settle scores that had long-standing, pre-conquest origins with other tribes. Boudica exists only in the Roman record, and we have no idea

28. Colchester (Essex). Tombstone of Marcus Favonius Facilis, a centurion of the XX legion, probably erected *c.* 43–47 before the legion was relocated to the west and a colony established at Colchester. A number of centurions took advantage of their positions to exploit the Iceni after the death of Prasutagus. (Colchester Museums).

29. Colchester (Essex).
The Temple of Claudius as it might have appeared in the first century.

30. Lincoln (Lincolnshire).
The east gate of the colony at Lincoln (*Lindum*) contained traces of the timber gate of the legionary fortress of the 60s and 70s. The timbers are modern replicas.

what the Britons thought of her. For both Tacitus and Dio, Boudica served as a perfect literary foil for Nero. They both wrote after Nero's reign, and his collapse into narcissistic self-indulgence. Nero was in every sense the opposite of the ideal Roman leader. Boudica, in contrast,

was attributed with all the virtues Nero lacked, made doubly paradoxical by the fact that she was a woman. It is possible that Boudica was a minor player, whose role was exaggerated by the historians for literary and moral effect. They had to show the foe to have been sufficiently dramatic a threat to warrant the level of the disaster. Thus they magnified the Roman achievement in defeating her, and told a moral tale. Britain's rebels might have compromised the Empire, but they had the qualities that had made Rome great. For many of Rome's commentators, the irony was that wealth and success were sending Rome spiralling into decadence and corrupted values.

Somewhere in the Midlands, Paullinus, now with his full army, faced the rebels. A set-piece battle was exactly what he wanted, and it was the first time that things had gone his way. Boudica had lost the initiative. The defeat of the rebel horde was utterly decisive for southern Britain. Tacitus claimed that 80,000 Britons were killed at a cost of just 400 Romans. The figures are bound to be exaggerated, but probably reflect the imbalance. The rebels were routed because they were weighed down with baggage, loot and their dependents. Boudica might have inspired them, but judgment was poor and the outcome inevitable. She was said by Tacitus to have committed suicide, and by Dio to have grown ill and died. This confusion alone ought to make us wonder just how important she really was. She may have been a peripheral component of the revolt, or a figurehead whose personal reputation grew rapidly in local and Roman lore because of her exotic, even erotic, appeal. The reality was that the revolt had presented the Britons with nothing more than chaos. Crops had not been planted, and hungry people have little stomach for rebellion.

Togidubnus might have been a quisling, but he and his kingdom survived intact and prospered. He and Boudica symbolize the split in British feelings about the Romans, and the consequences of picking the wrong side. Togidubnus was one of those tribal leaders who accepted Roman power and what it could do to validate and support his own position. Such power might have been totalitarian and absolute, but men like Tacitus could, and did, articulate criticism of the Roman state, and the legal system provided recourse to justice. Bad emperors were murdered, and bad governors were prosecuted. Roman culture was, by ancient standards, occasionally surprisingly liberal. Boudica represented another variety of tribal leadership, one that sought to deny the broader population access to the very things so many tribal leaders had been taking advantage of for decades.

No wonder then that no tribe of southern, central or eastern Britain ever rebelled again [31]. To begin with, they had little opportunity. The army was reinforced, and kept mobilized building forts throughout the

31. Nero (54–68).
A brass *dupondius* struck at Lyons, *c.* 64–68. The reverse depicts *Securitas*, an important quality for a Roman emperor. In the aftermath of the Boudican revolt, the basic stability of the Roman state proved an important part of settling Britain. It was the end of tribal rebellion in southern Britain.

region. Far to the southwest, Poenius Postumus fell on his sword in shame for depriving *II Augusta* of the chance to share in the victory. Nero celebrated the efforts of the XIV legion that had formed the main body of the army, and thereafter it rejoiced in the titles *Martia Victrix*, 'warlike and victorious'. Two thousand legionaries arrived from Germany to bring the IX back up to strength and make good other legionary losses, together with eight auxiliary infantry cohorts and 1,000 cavalry. The real harm was to the rebels, because they had failed to take care of any agriculture and had spent their time looting instead.

The most intriguing development was the appointment by Nero after the Boudican revolt of a new procurator, Gaius Julius Alpinus Classicianus [32]. A Gaulish aristocrat, his forebears had been made Roman citizens and his wife was the daughter of a pro-Roman tribal leader, Julius Indus. Indus had pursued his own tribal ambitions within the Roman system, and had sided with the Romans to suppress a regional Gaulish revolt in AD 21. Classicianus was therefore more inclined to reconciliation than revenge, and his appointment must have been made in that spirit. Tacitus believed that Classicianus allowed his personal distaste for Suetonius Paullinus to obstruct *bonum publicum* ('the public good'), by recommending that anyone who had played a part in the rebellion should wait for a new governor.[24] Suetonius Paullinus had come close to losing Britain, so he was scarcely the man most likely to let sleeping dogs lie. Classicianus objected to the punitive measures being

32. Trinity Square (London). Tomb of the procurator, Gaius Julius Alpinus Classicianus, who restored the credibility of the Roman government in Britain after the Boudican revolt. It is the most important surviving relic of the period of the rebellion. About 65–70. (Restoration of wording by R. S. O. Tomlin).

imposed by the governor, believing they would only foster resentment. Nero sent a freedman called Polyclitus to investigate, to the bewilderment of the Britons who found it incredible that an ex-slave could be in such a position. Polyclitus recommended that Suetonius stay in post, but the loss of a naval force provided a face-saving pretext to withdraw him.

POST-BOUDICAN RECONSTRUCTION

In Rome there was no triumph. The rebellion was so humiliating that little public acknowledgment of it was made. The new governor, Publius Petronius Turpilianus (61–63), deliberately avoided doing anything that would provoke a violent response. Marcus Trebellius Maximus (63–69), a man with no military experience, succeeded him. Tacitus regarded both men as ineffectual because of their lack of further conquests, but they were ideal for the circumstances.

Rome's civil war of 68–69 had repercussions for Britain as legions started to take sides after Nero's suicide. Four emperors (Galba, Otho, Vitellius and Vespasian) battled it out. Only with the accession of Vespasian in 69 did the crisis subside. In Britain, the XX legion mutinied, and either forced Trebellius Maximus out, or came to some sort of settlement with him. The XIV legion spent some of the period actively fighting on the Continent. A new governor, Marcus Vettius Bolanus (69–71), sustained the policy of appeasement. The main problem he encountered was the scandal in the Brigantian royal house. Cartimandua, who 20 years before had handed over Caratacus to Rome, took her husband's aide, Vellocatus, as her lover, thus prompting another Brigantian civil war. Vettius Bolanus had to pull out Cartimandua in the first instance, but then had to face the disappearance of Rome's northern ally in Britain while Venutius was still active.[25]

The Brigantian problem revived more active military conquest in Britain, though the Roman army may well have been in the region supporting Cartimandua. Forts at Rossington Bridge and Templeborough (both in Yorkshire) were established by the 60s. Quintus Petillius Cerealis became governor in 71, bringing with him a score to settle. In 60–61 he had commanded *IX Hispana* when Boudica routed it, and in 70 he had suppressed the revolt of Civilis in Gaul. Now he started a war to take northern Britain for good. Since Vespasian had withdrawn the XIV legion, it was probably at this time that *II Adiutrix Pia Fidelis* arrived to replace it. It was certainly at Lincoln by 76, suggesting that the IX had probably led the advance north by establishing the new fortress at York [33].

33. Lincoln (Lincolnshire). Tombstone (cast) of Titus Valerius Pudens of *II Adiutrix Pia Fidelis*. The legion replaced *IX Hispana*, which moved to York, but was withdrawn from Britain by the late 80s. About 76–85.

34. Samian bowl, South Gaul.
Bowls like this Form 29 mould-decorated example flooded into Britain during the commercial boom of the post-Boudican reconstruction period. About 70–85. (British Museum).

The campaign against the Brigantes was no walkover. Tacitus says that there were many battles, and that many of these were bloody. Castleford (Yorkshire) was established by the 70s, providing a key stronghold on the road into the north. By the same date military building was under way at Carlisle, showing that although the war was difficult, the Roman command of logistical and engineering problems enabled an infrastructure to be created across Brigantian territory in short order. The Brigantes might have had the upper hand when it came to the remoter hills, but they had been contained within a Roman framework.

The new governor, Sextus Julius Frontinus (73/4–77/8), instead of consolidating the north, found his hand forced by events in Wales. He embarked on a war that silenced the Silures permanently, and it is probably at this time that the legionary fortresses at Caerleon (for *II Augusta*), and Chester were established. Frontinus succeeded in cementing Roman control more or less permanently in Wales. Despite continuing warfare in the north and west, vast quantities of Roman goods were pouring into towns in the south [34].

AGRICOLA

The *Agricola* of Tacitus is a eulogy to his father-in-law, Gnaeus Julius Agricola. Britain features because it was where Agricola spent some of his earlier career as a military tribune and legionary commander, before becoming governor in 77 or 78, so its inclusion is a lucky chance for us. Tacitus' accounts of figures such as Cerealis and Frontinus were coloured by his desire to maximize Agricola's achievements. Enough other evidence exists to show that his basic chronology was correct, as was his description of Agricola's achievements. In fact, much of the general picture is reliable, though Tacitus credits Agricola personally wherever possible, rather than general imperial policies.

Agricola remained in post for around six years, until 83 or 84. The exact dates are uncertain. This was an exceptionally long term of office, and there is no obvious explanation other than that he was engaged on a protracted campaign, and his tenure overlapped the deaths of Vespasian in 79 and Titus in 81. The latter death in particular was unexpected, and probably discouraged any unnecessary changes in the remote provinces.

Tacitus provides a detailed account of Agricola's conquest of northern Britain. Of late a more critical approach has been taken to the text, and more attention paid to artifactual and dendrochronological evidence. But pottery types and tree-ring dates are not the conclusive evidence their advocates sometimes claim. Archaeology cannot resolve issues involving a very few years. But the evidence, together with Pliny the Elder's cryptic reference to the fact that 'for nearly 30 years now Roman armed forces have extended knowledge [of Britain] not further than the Caledonian forest', does suggest that the Roman army had reached the north by the early 70s.[26] Pliny's text was dedicated in 77, suggesting that Cerealis and Frontinus may well have taken Roman troops further than Tacitus implies.

Even so, it is clear that the Roman army moved steadily north throughout Agricola's governorship, surveying, garrisoning and building forts, such as Elginhaugh [35], near Edinburgh, and Fendoch, near Perth. One of the most important bases was the fort at Newstead (Borders) at 4.28 ha (10.58 acres), with a major supply base to the rear at Red House, near Corbridge (Northumberland). Newstead would go through four separate phases of occupation during the late first century. By 80 or 81, Agricola's forces had reached the Forth and Clyde isthmus. More than 50 years later this would become the setting for the Antonine Wall frontier, and Tacitus acknowledged that it was an ideal location. But, cryptically, he says that the army's zeal and Rome's glory precluded the possibility of staying there. This might mean that Agricola realized it was the ideal place to stop, but was ordered to carry on, perhaps by Domitian, who acceded in 81. Or it might be that Tacitus was trying to justify Agricola's decision to continue.

Eventually the Caledonian tribes were pushed back far enough to provoke more drastic retaliation. Until then they had fragmented into factions, with some trying to ingratiate themselves with Agricola to further their own ambitions. Evidently they were galvanized into cooperation by the prospect of permanent occupation. For the second time in its existence, the IX legion was nearly wiped out by a surprise barbarian attack, and was saved in time by reinforcements. The culprits escaped by disappearing once more into the forests and marshes.

The following year, 83 or 84, the campaign came to its inevitable climax. The battle of Mons Graupius became another historical set-piece, in which Tacitus uses Agricola and the tribal leader, Calgacus, as mouthpieces for rhetorical speeches. The most revealing parts are attributed to Calgacus, who calls the Romans 'robbers of the world', creating 'devastation and call[ing] it "peace"'. That this was written by a Roman shows that some of the Empire's commentators were sophisticated enough to appreciate the complex problems associated with imperial power and conquest. Tacitus was not condemning the Roman Empire, but he was condemning the manner in which Rome had abused her advantages. Appropriately, he blamed Agricola's withdrawal on Domitian's jealousy. There were no coin issues explicitly celebrating the conquest.[27]

Agricola's campaigns can be identified from some of the marching camps along the east coast of Scotland, while in northern England many of the later forts can be attributed to this period. However, the best-explored fort of the period is the short-lived legionary fortress at Inchtuthil (Perthshire), given up around 87 or 88 when it was systematically demolished, even to the extent of burying nail stocks deep in a sealed pit to prevent the enemy from using them. Its plan, reconstructed from careful and selective excavation, is an almost textbook example of the Roman legionary fortress [36]. Other forts were also dismantled, including Fendoch and Elginhaugh, the latter yielding during excavation a hoard of unused nails weighing 160 kg (353 lb). On a much smaller scale, the recent discovery at Carlisle of a wooden writing tablet recording a debt of 100 *denarii* owed by Quintus Cassius Secundus to Gaius Geminius Mansuetus, both soldiers of the XX legion, is a reminder that Agricola's campaigns were a real historical experience for thousands of men. The document is dated 7 November in the year 83, which places it either the winter before or just after the battle of Mons Graupius.[28]

35. Elginhaugh (Lothian).
Plan of the Flavian auxiliary infantry earth-and-timber fort. (After Hanson).
A = Commandant's house (*praetorium*)
B = Headquarters (*principia*)
C = Granaries (*horrea*)
D = Probable workshop (*fabrica*)

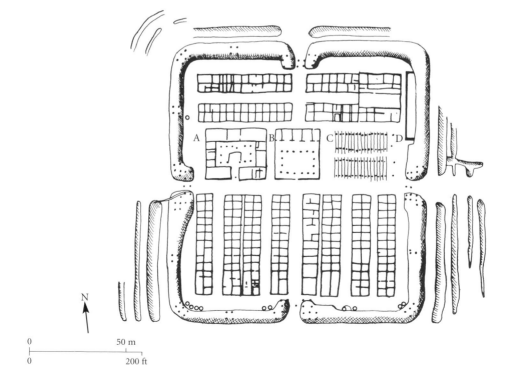

0   50 m

0   200 ft

Another document from Carlisle names an auxiliary cavalry trooper of the *ala Sebosiana*, serving on the governor's staff, and also names Agricola.[29]

Northern Scotland might have been given up, but southern Scotland was a different story. Inchtuthil and Strageath were amongst the forts in the north abandoned by the late 80s, but Newstead was reconstructed on an even larger plan by the same date and covered 5.78 ha (14.28 acres). Big enough to accommodate an auxiliary cavalry wing and a legionary vexillation, Newstead was designed to enforce Roman interests in southern Scotland. Dalswinton to the west was one of several other forts that were also remodelled and enlarged, while at Glenlochar a new fort was built.

The legacy of the campaign was the incorporation of northern England and southern Scotland into the Roman province. Agricola had himself circumnavigated Britain while chasing mutinous soldiers. While it was already well known that Britain was an island, this seemed to consolidate Roman psychological control. Nevertheless, Britain was still essentially of marginal interest. The Rhine and Danube frontier was far more important to Domitian because if that fell, Rome was vulnerable. He had lost two armies there, and could not afford the resources to hold Scotland as well.

36. Inchtuthil (Perthshire). Plan of the Agricolan legionary earth-and-timber fortress. The headquarters building (H) is unusually small, and, had the fort remained in use, would probably have been replaced. The fortress plan is important evidence for the use of double-centuries in the first cohort. About 83–87. (After Richmond).
G = Granaries (*horrea*)
W = Workshop (*fabrica*)
H = Hospital (*valetudinarium*)
HQ = Headquarters (*principia*)

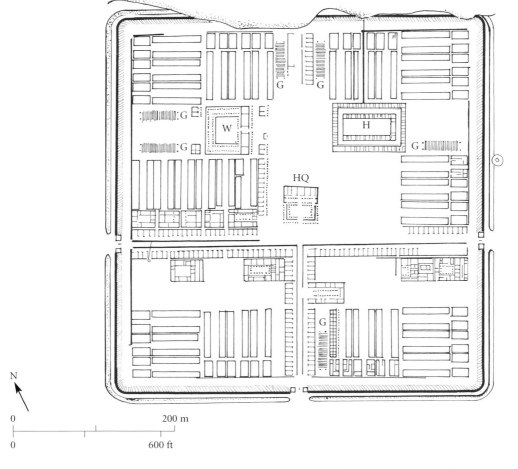

Richborough's monumental marble-clad arch probably belongs to this period [37]. Enough fragments survive to show that it must have been of late first- or early second-century date. Domitian was fond of triumphal arches and of displaying his achievements,[30] so it seems more than likely that, despite abandoning Scotland, he was content to build or accept the gift of an arch commemorating the conquest of Britain.

By 84, the south had been quiet for a generation. Since the year 60 urban development seems to have been more coordinated, especially under Agricola, whom Tacitus credits with encouraging individual Britons and communities to build temples, forums and houses. Roman goods and coinage started to reach comparatively remote rural establishments. This is an extremely important social change. Before 43 trade was on a small scale, enjoyed by only a few in Britain. By the 70s and 80s this had altered out of recognition.

One of the methods Agricola used was educating the tribal élite in Roman ways. Today it has become fashionable to question the extent of Agricola's real contribution, but, ironically, Agricola is the only governor attested on any of the few inscriptions that record civilian public building in Britain. The St Albans forum inscription suggests that Tacitus was right about Agricola's achievements, even though he also observed that

37. Richborough (Kent).
Reconstruction drawing of what the triumphal arch built at *Rutupiae* to commemorate the conquest of Britain may have looked like. The hypothetical inscription shows a dedication to the deified Claudius, but the arch was probably erected under Domitian (81–96) and usurped by his successors Nerva (96–98) and Trajan (98–117).

DIVO·TI·CLAVDIO·DRVSI·F
CAESARI·AVGVSTO·GERMANICO·
PROVINCIA·BRITANNIA·F

the Britons mistook cultivation for enslavement.[31] But it is facile to assume that Tacitus was singling out the Britons for being gullible. One of Tacitus' main themes was that the decline into decadence was a disease that had afflicted Roman imperial culture. What was happening in Britain was merely what had already happened in Rome.

The visibility of Roman goods in the archaeological record is our best clue as to why the end of the Boudican revolt was the end of rebellion in the south. This was a region where for generations tribal leaders had been aware of the classical world and what it had to offer, but from which ordinary people had been largely excluded, even in the pro-Roman enclaves. The reasons would have included ending the élite monopoly of trade, but the episodic warfare and territorial disputes that had so characterized pre-Roman society had been ended. Disarmament might have emasculated the tribes of southern Britain, but in another, paradoxical sense it liberated them from the costs of freedom.

BUILDING FRONTIERS

After the mid-80s, the story has to be pieced together from brief entries in other histories, and reconciled with the archaeology. Monumental inscriptions are rare until well into the second century. When the names of governors turn up in these sources, we often know nothing else about them. Only archaeology can fill the gap, but it cannot create history.

Agricola's efforts marked a watershed in Roman Britain's history. There was no attempt to consolidate or hold on to the remoter territory he had won over six or seven hard years of campaigning. But had he ever really won it? The network of roads and forts in the Southern Uplands of Scotland suggests fairly comprehensive control. Further north, the line of advance marked by forts like Cargill, Cardean, Inverquharity and Stracathro suggests that Agricola had only a tenuous hold on the eastern coastal strip. Most of northern Scotland was untouched by the campaign, and it remained that way for the rest of the Roman period. Even in the Southern Uplands many of the new or remodelled forts, like Newstead, were destroyed in the first decade of the second century, probably by the army as it pulled back. The withdrawal of *II Adiutrix Pia Fidelis* by the late 80s reduced Britain's legionary garrison permanently to three. Trajan had bigger fish to fry in the East and in Dacia. Britain, in short, was a sideshow.

If Rome ever had designs on conquering all of Britain, this was when they ended. The period 84 to 122 covered the last 12 years of Domitian's reign and that of the short-lived, elderly emperor, Nerva (96–98), the whole of the reign of Trajan (98–117), and the first five years of Hadrian's reign (117–38). It saw the transition from dynastic rule to an age in which emperors chose their heirs from suitable candidates and adopted them as sons. The Empire reached its greatest extent under Trajan with the conquests of Parthia and Dacia, before Hadrian abandoned some of the latest additions and consolidated the frontiers.

We have occasional glimpses of Britain in this period. Suetonius mentions a governor of Britain under Domitian called Gaius Sallustius Lucullus. Lucullus had invented a new type of spear, but was foolish

THE VINDOLANDA WRITING TABLETS

The stone fort visible today at Vindolanda [40], near Hadrian's Wall, was not built until the 220s, replacing an earlier stone fort, built around a century earlier under Hadrian (117–38). Before that there had been a series of turf and timber forts, dating back at least to c. 90. Thanks to the sensational discovery of wooden writing tablets in waterlogged deposits associated with the timber forts, Vindolanda is now one of the most important Roman military sites in the Empire. Such wooden tablets rarely survive, and they provide a priceless

window into the bureaucracy and correspondence that kept the Roman world functioning.

The tablets date mostly to the period c. 90–105, when the Ninth Cohort of Batavians and the First Cohort of Tungrians were stationed at Vindolanda. They include work rosters, letters both official and private, and the celebrated strength report of the First Cohort of Tungrians. 'I have written to you several times', complains Octavius, in a letter concerning money needed to pay for grain.[34] In another, Florus seeks the urgent

loan of an axe [38].[35] Much the most moving, however, is the invitation from Severa to her friend, Sulpicia Lepidina, the wife of Flavius Cerealis, who commanded the Batavians [39].

Another letter discusses the thorny problem of how many wagons would be needed to transport stone.[36] It is certainly not the only one to mention the transportation of commodities by road. The letter from Octavius mentions wagons and the memorable observation that he is not prepared to risk injury to his

38. *Left.* **Vindolanda (Northumberland).** Letter from Florus to Calavirus concerning a sealed box and the loan of an axe. (British Museum).

39. *Below left.* **Vindolanda.** Letter from Claudia Severa inviting Sulpicia Lepidina to her birthday party. About 100. (British Museum).

To Sulpicia Lepidina (wife) of Cerealis, from Severa:
Claudia Severa, greetings to her Lepidina On the third day before the Ides of September, sister, for the day of my birthday celebration, I give you a warm invitation to make sure that you come to us, to make the day more enjoyable for me by your arrival, if you are present. Give my greetings to your Cerealis. My Aelius and my little son send you their greetings. I shall expect you, sister. Farewell, sister, my dearest soul, as I hope to prosper and hail.[38]

enough to name it the *Lucullean*.[32] The paranoid Domitian promptly had him executed. Lucius Neratius Marcellus is named as a governor of Britain on a military diploma of 19 January 103, and also turns up in Pliny the Younger's letters, as well as on one of the writing tablets discovered at the fort of Vindolanda (Northumberland).[33] The Vindolanda writing tablets are an immensely important resource, but they represent

animals *dum viae male sunt*, 'while the roads are bad'.[37] Another letter (*c.* 180–200) from Martius asks Victor to write to him at *Bremesio* (probably Piercebridge), and if that is not possible to leave the letter at

Cataractonium (Catterick). Victor seems to have been heading south from Vindolanda along Dere Street, perhaps on his way to York, or even to London.

40. Vindolanda.
Aerial view of the third-century fort, near Hadrian's Wall. In the foreground, the civilian settlement (*vicus*) clusters around the road. The late first-century timber forts that produced the writing tablets lie at much lower levels.

only fragments of archives held at a single fort site on the northern frontier around the end of the first century. None of these references, however, tell us what military policy Marcellus conducted in Britain.

The Roman army maintained a considerable presence in northern England. The pivotal installations were at Corbridge and Carlisle to the west, with a road (today called the Stanegate) running between them [41]. Forts were dotted along the Stanegate and throughout northern England, administered from the legionary fortresses at York and Chester [42]. The Agricolan lead pipes of 79 at Chester show that the fortress there was certainly in operation by that date [43]. By 107, the IX legion was erecting stone gates at its fortress at York and installing monumental inscriptions. Building work was piecemeal and could stretch out over a very long period of time, depending on the legion's other responsibilities. Chester's construction was seriously disrupted. During the late first century this was probably due in part to being garrisoned by *II Adiutrix*, while the XX legion was in Scotland with Agricola. By *c.* 89, the XX had taken over, but also had other responsibilities on the northern frontier. It was certainly engaged on Hadrian's Wall in the 120s.

Conquest had been replaced with consolidation. To the south, towns were developing, along with a Romanized countryside, though it is a moot point as to what extent urban life pervaded indigenous culture. The former fortresses at Gloucester and Lincoln became colonies, probably under Domitian.[39] It is likely that Lincoln became a colony after the IX legion moved on to York and once *II Adiutrix* had pulled out, sometime before 89. In the north, the infrastructure of a permanent military zone was being established, though it extended into the south as well. The Vindolanda tablets paint a picture of a world of intermittent skirmish warfare in which the Britons were irritants, not a strategic threat. Officers and their families indulged themselves in hunting and social events. Soldiers were being permanently detached to duties on the governor's staff at London, where a fort had been built to house them. They administered police duties throughout the province, and along with their supplies formed a major part of the traffic that moved about the road network.

THE WALLS

The withdrawal from Scotland created a rather vague state of affairs, in which the auxiliary garrisons of forts like Vindolanda on the Stanegate maintained a status quo. The arrangements lacked a clear purpose, and also meant that large numbers of troops were scattered across the north. They spent much of their time guarding against minor incursions by bands of opportunists, or policing normal tribal activities, including trade, cattle movements and passage to seasonal settlements. The tombstone of Titus Pontius Sabinus, a centurion with the North African legion *III Augusta*, records that he had commanded vexillations of three other legions on a 'British expedition' between 117 and the late 120s.[40] Hadrian's biographer said that when the emperor came to power in 117, 'the Britons could not be restrained under Roman control', and coins struck *c.* 119 depict Britannia.[41] So it seems that the endless frontier skirmishes may have developed into more serious warfare.

By 117, the practical costs of conquest had become unsustainable. Trajan's wars in Parthia and Dacia had stretched the Empire too far. Hadrian decided to consolidate the frontiers and bring an end to expansion, though he was largely formalizing what was already the case. Hadrian arrived in Britain in or around 122, and instituted what is today the most visible evidence of Rome's presence in the island. He had

41. *Opposite above.* Corbridge (Northumberland).
A short stretch of the Stanegate at Corbridge (*Coria*) is visible on the site today. This road played a key role in maintaining Roman military control of what is now northern England under Trajan (98–117).

42. *Opposite below.* Chester (Cheshire).
Plan of the legionary fortress at Chester (*Deva*), which included the unusual 'elliptical building' (E), headquarters (H) and baths (B). The fortress was begun *c.* 76 by *II Adiutrix*, but occupied by the XX, which completed it, from *c.* 87.

43. Chester (Cheshire).
This section of lead pipe from the fortress at *Deva* names the governor, Agricola, showing that building work had begun by the early 80s. The lead had probably been extracted from the lead mines in northern Wales.

44. *Below.* **Wallsend (Northumberland).**
Reconstructed view of the fort at *Segedunum*. Wallsend, and the stretch of Wall leading to it from Newcastle, was an addition designed to guard a long stretch of the Tyne. The garrison was the 500-strong part-mounted Fourth Cohort of Lingones.

45. *Opposite.* **Housesteads (Northumberland).** Hadrian's Wall, looking west. Milecastle 37 (see p. 54) is visible in the foreground. The Wall builders exploited the landscape so that the frontier commanded the high ground, overlooking steep drops to the north.

arrived from Germany where he had seen at first-hand the consequences of complacent frontier troops with nothing but routine garrison work to do: lax discipline, corruption, self-indulgence, and a lack of military standards. In Britain the position must have been similar, but Hadrian ordered the construction of a permanent frontier [45]. Britain was not the only place where he did this, but it was the only place where the frontier was to be in stone. The line chosen, a little north of the Stanegate, was short enough at 80 Roman miles (119 km, or 74 miles) for this to be manageable, though to begin with only half was built in stone. The Wall was supposed to 'divide' Romans and barbarians.[42] Of course, it was more complex than that. A major military project would revive a sense of purpose in the British garrison, and would help compensate for the uneven distribution of forces amongst scattered forts. The design of the Wall shows that it was not an impenetrable frontier, but allowed supervised movement [44].

HADRIAN'S WALL

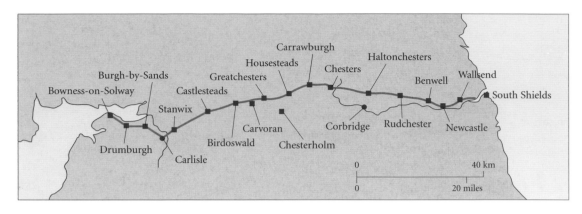

Hadrian's Wall was begun in the early 120s under the command of the governor, Aulus Platorius Nepos (*c.* 122–26). Inscriptions show that the actual work was carried out by all three legions then in Britain: *II Augusta*, *VI Victrix* and *XX Valeria Victrix*, along with a detachment from the fleet, *classis Britannica*.

On the evidence of the Ilam pan (see p. 167), the Wall may have originally been called *Vallum Aelium* ('The Aelian Frontier'). Like Newcastle, which was called *Pons Aelius* ('The Aelian Bridge'), its name commemorated Hadrian, whose full name was Publius Aelius Hadrianus.

The Wall was designed to be 10 Roman feet (3 m) wide and probably around 15 Roman feet (4.5 m) high. A berm of 20 Roman feet (5.9 m) separated the Wall from a forward ditch. It would stretch from *Pons Aelius* to the River Irthing in stone, and then on to to *Maia* in the west in turf and timber, a total distance of 118 km (74 miles).

Roughly every Roman mile there was to be a fortified gateway, or milecastle, with accommodation for a dozen or more soldiers [47]. Between each milecastle were two watchtowers at around one-third mile intervals. The Turf Wall had turf milecastles, but stone turrets.

46. Hadrian's Wall.
The Wall and the northern forts.

Plans change
Even while the Wall was being built, plans were changing [48]. The Wall was reduced to eight Roman feet (2.4 m) or less in width. This new Narrow Wall was built on foundations prepared for a 10-foot wall, and joined to milecastles and turrets already prepared with 10-foot 'wing walls' (see p. 120). The ditch was abandoned where the rock was too hard to excavate. It was also decided to build forts right on the Wall itself, and 14 were laid out and built, despite the ensuing demolition of newly-built wall and turrets. An additional section of wall was added to the east between Newcastle and Wallsend.

47. *Left.* **A Milecastle on Hadrian's Wall.**
Reconstruction drawing showing what the milecastle might have looked like with the forward ditch. The details are partly based on those found at milecastle 37, near Housesteads, but the heights of the Wall, gate tower and crenellations are hypothetical.

48. *Right.* **Willowford (Cumbria).**
Turret 48a was built in expectation of the Broad Wall, but the change of plan to the Narrow Wall resulted in the offset.

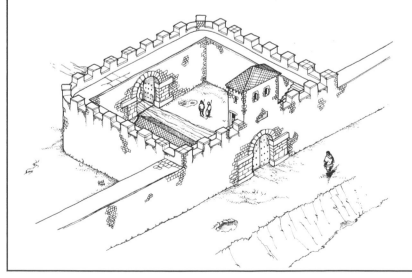

Hadrian's Wall Forts (east to west)

Wallsend	*Segedunum*
Newcastle	*Pons Aelius*
Benwell	*Condercum*
Rudchester	*Vindobala*
Haltonchesters	*Onnum*
Chesters	*Cilurnum*
Carrawburgh	*Brocolitia*
Housesteads	*Vercovicium*
Greatchesters	*Aesica*
Birdoswald	*Banna*
Castlesteads	*Camboglanna*
Stanwix	*Uxelodunum*
Burgh-by-Sands	*Aballava*
Drumburgh	*Coggabata*
Bowness-on-Solway	*Maia*

Forts behind the Wall (east to west)

South Shields	*Arbeia*
Chesterholm	*Vindolanda* (between Housesteads and Greatchesters)
Carvoran	*Magnis* (between Greatchesters and Birdoswald)

Once the forts were built, the Vallum was added. The Vallum was a flat-bottomed ditch, 20 Roman feet (5.9 m) wide, with flanking mounds. It ran parallel to the south of the Wall along its length, diverting to go round forts. Its purpose was probably to create a protected military zone, and to control access from the south. But before the end of Hadrian's reign a fifteenth fort was added at Carrawburgh, and the Vallum was filled in at that point. The forts varied in size, but were usually large enough to accommodate a mixed milliary unit.

What was the Wall for?

Despite the claim by Hadrian's biographer that the Wall was intended to 'divide' the Romans and barbarians, it was obviously not a barrier, as the milecastle and fort gates prove. Instead, it seems to have been originally conceived as a fortified way of controlling movement. So the most likely use of the Wall was to defend against incursions by raiders, and to create secure crossing points over the Vallum where traffic could be searched, taxed, and split up before being allowed to continue.

Once the Antonine Wall had been abandoned in the 160s, Hadrian's Wall became the permanent frontier. Later in the second century, the Turf Wall was replaced in stone. Some of the milecastle gates had been blocked up, and some of the turrets were derelict. By the early third century, many forts needed restoration, and by the end of the fourth century, much of the Wall and its forts had fallen into disrepair.

The new governor of Britain, Aulus Platorius Nepos (122–26), administered the great project, and brought with him from Lower Germany a new legion for Britain's garrison, *VI Victrix*. The IX legion had gone by this time, but whether it had been withdrawn several years before for other duties, or was simply changing places, is unknown. What is certain is that IX more or less disappears from the record. The old idea that it had been lost in Britain is no longer considered credible.

The construction of the Wall involved many of Britain's legionaries throughout the 120s. Most of the initial work was carried out under Nepos, though it is possible that work extended into the governorship of Lucius Trebius Germanus, who was in post by August 127. Despite the fact that modifications were clearly being made in the 130s, by the time Hadrian died the Wall was an operational frontier. Although the Roman administration regarded the territory beyond the Wall as part of the Empire, it was clear where practical power ended.

Ironically, within a few years Hadrian's Wall was mothballed, and the frontier transferred north to the same Forth-Clyde line that had tantalized Agricola three generations before. In 138, Antoninus Pius succeeded Hadrian and faced trouble in Britain. In or around 139, the governor Quintus Lollius Urbicus was obliged to 'drive back the barbarians' and build 'another wall, of turf'.[43] Inscriptions from the Antonine Wall confirm that this was the wall he built, and inscribed stones at other forts show that building work went on elsewhere, including at High Rochester, Birrens, Strageath and Newstead. Newstead was rebuilt as a major stone fort, with evidence that its garrison was divided, perhaps between a legionary vexillation and a cavalry regiment. The Southern Uplands of Scotland were being reincorporated into the military infra-

49. The Antonine Wall.
The turf Antonine Wall was originally designed to have six forts, possibly of stone and interspersed with fortlets, but the plan was changed to have a turf-and-timber fort every 3.2 km (2 miles), though the total number remains uncertain. No evidence for turrets or towers has been found, and there was no Vallum as on Hadrian's Wall. The Wall was built *c.* 139–43.

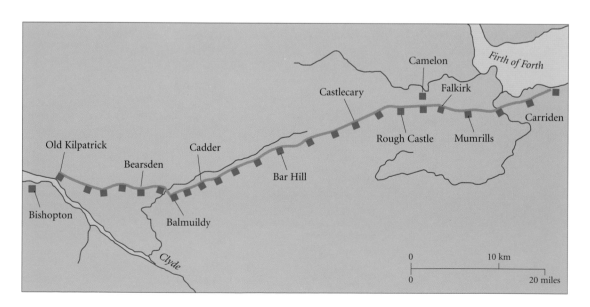

structure of northern Britain. Perhaps the arrangements on Hadrian's Wall had proved overwhelmingly frustrating to tribal peoples who found their way of life unacceptably disrupted, or perhaps they were simply provoked by the appearance of a frontier and its garrison. The other possibility is that the Wall was too unwieldy to garrison effectively.

The Antonine Wall, at 60 km (37 miles), was shorter and simpler than Hadrian's Wall [49, 50]. Although it had a forward ditch, there were no turrets or a Vallum. An important series of coins depicting Britannia was issued, all dating to the year 143 (see p. 85), exactly one century after the original invasion. The new Wall marked the largest formal extent Roman Britain ever reached. It has produced a series of elaborate inscriptions recording the building work by the various legions [51], including a vexillation of *XXII Primigenia*. An enigmatic series of Britannia coins was struck in 154, but it is unknown if these refer to specific warfare or were just distributed as a special issue in Britain, which is where almost all of them turn up. The Antonine Wall was held for around a generation, but in the 160s it was given up and Hadrian's Wall became the permanent

50. The Antonine Wall (Dunbartonshire).
Today only weathered sections of the Antonine Wall's turf rampart and forward ditch survive to mark the short-lived northernmost frontier of Roman Britain.

51. Old Kilpatrick (Dunbartonshire).
Relief from the Antonine Wall, recording completion of 4,411 Roman feet of frontier by the XX legion. About 139–43.

frontier. The forts in Scotland were, for the most part, systematically dismantled and their sites cleared before the army withdrew. The recent exploratory excavations at Drumlanrig, near Dumfries, illustrate perfectly how the installation had been levelled, confirming a picture found elsewhere, for example at Strageath.

The civilian world also provides us with a watershed in the 140s. Brough-on-Humber was a small town on the Humber estuary that thrived on river trade and ferry traffic. At around this time a civic magistrate, Marcus Ulpius Januarius, paid for a new stage for the town theatre, recorded on an inscription, the last of its type from Britain. From now on there were few major public or military building projects. The first half of the second century was the high water mark of Roman Britain's public and military life. The rest of Roman Britain's history would be very different, and no less remarkable.

CHAPTER 3
LATER ROMAN BRITAIN

By the time Marcus Aurelius (161–80) had been emperor for a very few years, Hadrian's Wall was back in operation for good. Although the Wall itself seems to have been completed – in stone, at least – during the later second century, its facilities, like the milecastles and turrets, were in a variable state. Some turrets were eventually demolished, while some milecastle gates were blocked up or abandoned. Crossing points were installed on the Vallum. A few forts beyond, such as High Rochester and Risingham, continued to mark Rome's claim on the immediate territory to the north.

Despite those outpost forts, pulling back to Hadrian's Wall meant that southern Scotland was left *trans Vallum* ('beyond the Wall'), a hinterland that Rome claimed, but which mostly lay beyond her control. On the frontier itself forts housed soldiers, but the natural economic and social activities the troops attracted meant that most established forts supported quasi-civilian communities that clustered around them. These settlements symbolized a uniquely Roman contribution to Britain's landscape.

The continued presence of the army, and military pay, were essential for the continued existence of those northern settlements. To the south, the greater towns, such as the colonies and *civitas* capitals, grew of their own accord within the Roman system. By the late second century, the major towns were all equipped with a suite of public buildings, although exactly what was provided in each varied enormously [52]. Another product of the Roman economy and communications were the 'small towns'. These settlements clustered around road junctions and river crossings, acting as local markets and industrial zones. Characteristically lacking evidence for formal organization, they were an organic product of the infrastructure of Roman Britain.

SETTLING THE NORTH

The withdrawal to Hadrian's Wall did little to settle the remote north. Before Marcus Aurelius had been on the throne for long, news reached Rome that 'a British war was threatening'.[1] A new governor, Sextus Calpurnius Agricola, was dispatched to fight it, and appears on several Wall inscriptions, which unfortunately tell us nothing. This is typical of the problems that face interpretation of the evidence. The biography of

Aurelius mentions the war, but there is nothing from the archaeological, epigraphic, or numismatic record to confirm it. Later in his reign, Aurelius sent 5,500 newly-recruited Sarmatian auxiliary cavalry to Britain, either to replace troops lost in battle or to train them up in a remote province where their loyalty could be tested without risk.[2]

The northern frontier was clearly still an active problem. In about 177, Ulpius Marcellus became governor and remained so for about six years [53]. The death of Aurelius and accession of Commodus in 180 may have delayed his replacement, but renewed warfare made a change of governor undesirable. For once we have a rather more explicit description of the problems: Dio states that tribes had 'crossed the Wall that divided them from the Roman soldiers, doing a colossal amount of damage, even wiping out a legate with his troops'.[3] The loss of a legate was a disaster. An altar of around this period from Kirksteads near the western part of the Wall names Lucius Junius Victorinus Flavius Caelianus, legate of a legion (probably the VI), and describes his exploits as *trans Vallum prospere gestas*, 'successful deeds beyond the Wall'. It shows that legates were probably routinely, and perhaps complacently, engaging in the risky business of fighting in the frontier hinterland. Now the tribes had brought the war into the province. Ulpius Marcellus defeated them, but his long tenure suggests a struggle. The importance of the victory in 184 was enshrined in a substantial issue of *Victoriae Brittannicae* coins struck that year.

Marcus Aurelius had the misfortune of having a surviving son, depriving him of his predecessors' ability to choose the best man for the job of successor. Commodus was certainly the worst man for the job. His decline into vice and violence, and his reckless disregard for the obligations of rule, made a violent coup inevitable. The British legions were infuriated by how Commodus was handing over day-to-day control of the Empire to his praetorian prefect, Perennis. They tried to appoint one of their own legates, Priscus, as replacement emperor, but Priscus declined. Nevertheless, the legions dispatched a delegation of 1,500 soldiers to Rome to tell Commodus that Perennis was

52. Winchester (Hampshire). Fragment of an imperial inscription, probably from the basilica or a major temple at Winchester (*Venta Belgarum*). At 29.2 cm high (11.5 in), these letters make the inscription the largest yet known from Britain. The 'TO' is easily restorable as 'Antoninus', referring to either Antoninus Pius (138–61) or Marcus Aurelius (161–80), who was normally styled 'Marcus Antoninus Aurelius'.

53. Chesters (Northumberland). Inscription recording the building of an aqueduct at Chesters (*Cilurnum*) by the Second *ala* of Asturians during the governorship of Ulpius Marcellus (*c.* 177–84).

plotting to overthrow him. Commodus was terrified by the whole episode, but he immediately handed Perennis to the praetorians for lynching and sent Publius Helvidius Pertinax to govern Britain. Unfortunately, before Pertinax's firm hand turned the British legions against him, they decided he was an even better candidate for emperor than Priscus.

Pertinax fled Britain when one of the legions mutinied, and his ensuing treatment of the culprits was regarded as excessive. In his place was sent Clodius Albinus, who had ambitions of his own and now had the means to fulfil them. On 31 December 192, the praetorians had had enough and murdered Commodus. The Roman Empire was plunged into its worst crisis since the civil war of 68–69, sparking off a catastrophic century of warfare and instability.

THE CIVIL WAR AND SEPTIMIUS SEVERUS

Pertinax was appointed emperor to replace Commodus, but his severe reign lasted just 86 days before the praetorians murdered him, too. Next, they auctioned the Empire off to the highest bidder. Didius Julianus won by offering each praetorian 25,000 *sestertii*. He never paid up and was executed just 66 days later, on 2 June 193. By then several other players had entered the ring. In Syria, the governor Pescennius Niger was pro claimed emperor by his army. In Upper Pannonia the same thing happened to Septimius Severus [54], and in Britain to Clodius Albinus. The process of events was complicated, but initially Severus gained the upper hand by appointing Clodius Albinus as his heir, and set off to defeat Pescennius Niger. With Niger disposed of, Severus turned on Albinus.

In 197 at Lyons, Severus narrowly defeated the army of Clodius Albinus, drawn from Britain's garrison. It used to be claimed that very few of the garrisons of Britain's northern forts in the third century were the same as those in the second, and that this was evidence for the disruption caused by the war of 193–97. Unfortunately, the inscriptions naming auxiliary units at any one fort mainly belong to after the civil war and on into the third century, while most of our evidence for the second century comes from military diplomas, which do not name the forts that units were based in.

The Maeatae, a tribal group in the Wall area, joined forces with the Caledonians further north while Clodius Albinus was absent during the civil war.[4] Septimius Severus sent Virius Lupus (*c.* 197–202) to be the new governor. Lupus paid the Maeatae a subsidy, buying enough time

54. Septimius Severus (193–211). Severus initiated a programme of military works in Britain, culminating with his protracted and inconclusive Scottish campaign (208–11). Soon after the emperor's death, his son Caracalla (211–17) abandoned his father's conquests. (Indiana University Art Museum).

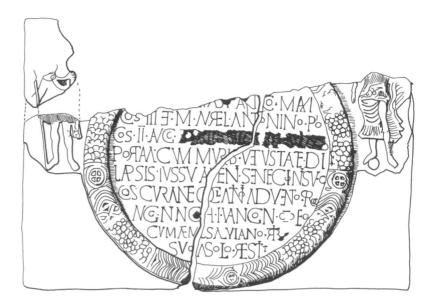

55. Risingham (Northumberland). Elaborate inscription recording the restoration of a fort gate between 205 and 207 at Risingham (*Habitancum*), during the governorship of Alfenus Senecio and the procuratorship of Oclatinius Adventus.

to repair military installations. This was a dramatic change of policy that eventually became routine. Inscriptions record a major programme of rebuilding and restoration work, and often survive because they were reused in later building work at the same sites. One such inscription from Bowes says that the Vettonian cavalry restored the bath-house which had been 'burnt by the force of flames' for the resident First Cohort of Thracians.[5] The cause could have been either an attack by the enemy or an accident. Baths were liable to burn down because of their furnaces. At Brougham, an inscription from around this time records that after the baths had burnt down, they were repaired by replacing the floor supports and conduits.[6]

The building work carried on through the governorship of Gaius Valerius Pudens (202–5), and into that of Lucius Alfenus Senecio (205–8). Usually the slabs simply record dedications, but one from Risingham records that the gate and walls were restored having 'decayed from age'.[7] Such texts were once interpreted as Roman euphemisms for enemy action, but the overall picture is more one of general decay, echoing evidence from Birdoswald and other sections of Hadrian's Wall of a frontier that had never really been finished or maintained rigorously.

An interesting development is that the Risingham inscription records the involvement of the procurator, Marcus Oclatinius Adventus, whose responsibilities were only supposed to be the province's finances [55]. The scale of the work concerned might have made it essential that he was involved, as well as Senecio. Another possibility is that Septimius Severus, who arrived in Britain to reinvade Scotland in 208, had instructed Britain's administrators to begin making preparations for the great campaign he planned.

THE CAMPAIGNS OF SEPTIMIUS SEVERUS

Septimius Severus (193–211) had worked hard to become emperor, and he recognized the risks of holding onto his position. At some point in his reign after defeating Albinus, he made Britain into two separate provinces: *Superior* (the south) and *Inferior* (the north). *Britannia Superior* included the II and XX legions, while the legate of the VI legion governed *Britannia Inferior*. This distinction, together with the recording of soldiers on the staff of the governor of *Britannia Superior* on inscriptions in the north, suggests that *Britannia Inferior* was in some way administratively subordinate. But it split the legionary command, making the possibility of another Clodius Albinus far less likely.

Severus, unlike Claudius, did not need to prove himself. But he had two sons, Caracalla and Geta, who were designated as his successors. He wanted them to earn the prestige of a major campaign without compromising the integrity of the greater Empire. In 208, they arrived in Britain, together with Severus' wife, Julia Domna. One source (Herodian) claims that a governor in Britain had reported a barbarian rebellion, but this goes unmentioned in Dio.[8] If the claim was true, it provided Severus with his pretext. If it was not, it could just as easily have been fabricated to provide a pretext. All the recent military building work could easily be evidence that Severus had planned the war for several years. But it is just as likely that when Severus decided he needed a war, Britain looked like a convenient place to wage it.

Imperial lead seals survive in large numbers from this date as evidence of mass transportation of goods. South Shields, a major coastal fort to the east of Hadrian's Wall, was substantially redesigned to accommodate an unusually large number of granaries. Severus also brought money with him. This, and the need to house an imperial family, is thought to have led to a certain amount of public building. York's defences were remodelled at about this time, and there is some evidence that timber housing was cleared to make way for larger stone buildings. The biography of Severus describes the emperor returning 'to the palace', which must mean his imperial residence in York.[9] The dedication of a Temple of Serapis by the legate of the VI legion, Claudius Hieronymianus, is recorded on an inscription from York, dating to the very late second century, or early third.[10] Hieronymianus is not named as governor of Britannia Inferior, so the inscription must precede the division of Britain. Since Severus and Caracalla both worshipped Serapis, Hieronymianus probably dedicated the temple as a gesture of loyalty. A good case has been made for the construction of a major religious precinct in London at around the time Severus was in Britain, based on the identification of a substantial stone arch, which would have made an appropriate entrance to such a complex.

Severus also brought over legionary vexillations, almost certainly including *XXII Primigenia*, and some of the Praetorian Guard [57]. He was taken aback when the Maeatae and Caledonians offered peace. This was a common spoiling tactic, designed to put the Romans off their guard. Julius Caesar had been tricked in the same way. Determined not to make the same mistake, Severus instead made another. He packed the tribal embassies off and started the war anyway. During the Agricolan campaigns, the IX legion had been ambushed in Scotland, and the culprits had escaped by vanishing into the forests and marshes. Either Severus had not read Tacitus, or he ignored him. Once again, the tribes retreated into a landscape in which they could move and strike as they pleased. They were adept at sustaining indefinite guerrilla campaigns by lurking in swamps. Meanwhile, the Romans were confused and terrified by the terrain, handicapped by equipment, and increasingly compromised by extended supply lines. Efforts were made to cross the swamps by laying down pontoons, but the only way to advance successfully was by sea.[11] There was no chance of a set-piece battle, and every chance of a humiliating defeat. The Romans eventually reached northeastern Scotland. If they flattered themselves that they had fought their way up there, they were wrong. Split up and harassed by guerrilla bands, they were easy prey.

In 210 the tribes offered peace again, and, sick and exhausted, Severus believed them. He announced a victory and commemorative coins were issued, but he had been tricked again [56]. The tribes restarted the war and the fighting extended throughout the winter of 210–11. The process finished Severus off, and he died at York in February 211. His sons Caracalla and Geta succeeded as joint emperors, but abandoned the conquests in Britain. A year later, Geta was killed by his brother.

THE THIRD CENTURY

Loyalty to the person of the emperor was a fundamental requirement of the Empire. Rulers like Antoninus Pius earned it. Caracalla (211–17) enforced it with vindictive paranoia, even murdering a governor of *Gallia Narbonensis* who fell foul of him. Gaius Julius Marcus, a governor in Britain in 213, instituted a building programme at auxiliary forts, recorded on inscriptions that named him and his loyalty to Caracalla. Unfortunately, Julius Marcus must have made a mistake and paid for it, either with his life or imprisonment, and his name only survives on a milestone from Hadrian's Wall that somehow escaped the censors' attentions. Military units also started to adopt appropriate epithets to mark out their loyalty, either because that loy-

alty was genuine, or because it was sensible to do so before it was called into question. Under Caracalla or his cousin Elagabalus (218–22), the II legion became *Augusta Antoniniana*. Both Caracalla and Elagabalus used the official name 'Antoninus Pius', as part of Severus' pseudo-imperial lineage. Inscriptions continued an intermittent record of building activity at forts up to the mid-third century [58], and conveniently provide us with many names of *Britannia Inferior*'s governors.

There was an accumulating sense of insecurity. Between 217 and 251 there were ten emperors, of whom all except one died a violent death. The tenth committed suicide. In contrast, between 98 and 192 there had been five emperors, only one of whom met with a violent end. The increasing pressure on the frontiers was largely responsible for this change. Frontier warfare had a habit of breeding soldiers with ideas above their station, and the kind of troops to help them achieve these ambitions. It also drew the emperor away from Rome and put him into mortal danger. Severus Alexander (222–35) managed a stable reign until 232, when he was forced to fight the Sassanids in the East, before then being called to the German frontier. His troops promptly killed him, and proclaimed one of their generals, Maximinus, as emperor. Valerian (253–60) later rose to power much as Maximinus had. Recognizing the challenging demands on his time, Valerian appointed his son Gallienus to rule with him. Within three years, Valerian set out to fight the Persians in the East, and was captured in 260. He never returned. Gallienus (253–68) ruled in his stead, but was plagued by continuing frontier warfare. In 259, Gallienus' son, Saloninus, was murdered at Cologne by Postumus, commander of the Rhine garrisons. While this roster of emperors might not seem to have much to do with Britain, it had dramatic consequences.

Britain began a long period of transformation. Major towns were now likely to be surrounded with fortifications, if they were not already. The south started to become more overtly part of a military province. Soldiers had always been part of civilian Roman Britain's daily life: they served on the governor's staff and garrison in London, visited the spa at Bath, and took charge of local policing and other official duties. There was a permanent fort at London, and a second-century fleet fort at Dover [59], and possibly Lympne. But military establishments were more incidental than fundamental to this part of Britain until the early third century.

56. *Opposite above.* Septimius Severus (193–211).
Bronze *as* of 208–10 commemorating victories in Britain.

57. *Opposite below.* Birrens (Dumfries and Galloway).
Inscription recording building work at Birrens (*Blatobulgium*) by *XXII Primigenia* and *VIII Augusta*. Probably of Antonine or Severan date, this confirms the presence of Continental legionary vexillations brought over to supplement the resident legions during rebuilding work.

58. Lanchester (Durham).
Inscription from the fort at Lanchester (*Longovicium*), recording the building of a baths-basilica by the First Cohort of Lingones under Marcus Aurelius Quirinus, during the reign of Gordian III (238–44).

New forts were being built, including those at Brancaster (Norfolk) and Reculver (Kent), in commission by the 230s. Another fortified compound at Caistor, on the east Norfolk coast, may belong to the same date. At around the same time, London was surrounded by a massive landward wall [60]. Seaborne piracy had become an increasing problem in the third century. The North Sea and the English Channel provided maritime raiders from northern Europe with a convenient route to provinces such as Britain and Gaul. During the rest of the century and early 300s, Brancaster and Reculver were joined by a series of fortified coastal compounds of uncertain function and character around the south and east coasts. The British forts were matched by another series along the Gaulish coast. Today, these British coastal fortifications are known as the 'Saxon Shore' from their description in the late Roman military document, *Notitia Dignitatum.* On the west coast, other fortifications were built. The Saxon Shore forts have produced little in the way of internal buildings or military equipment. The projecting bastions were defensive rather than offensive, but whether the forts were compounds for hous-

59. Dover (Kent).
One of the two lighthouses (*pharos*) that overlooked the harbour at Dover (*Dubris*), at its present height of 13 m (43 ft) with a medieval upper stage. Its original height was perhaps twice that. Probably built in the second century, along with the fort at *Dubris* housing the fleet, *classis Britannica.*

ing garrisons, refuges for civilians, or simply fortified ports, is entirely unknown. They almost certainly belong to the same initiative that led to the walling of cities, but we have no idea if this was a centralized initiative, or simply different authorities ordering similar facilities at a similar time.

POSTUMUS AND CARAUSIUS

Gallienus discovered that the Roman army had to change. He created a more mobile army by using vexillations, anticipating the type of Roman army used in the fourth century, which could respond quickly and decisively to frontier problems. Before Postumus took power, a vexillation from the XX legion took part in one of Gallienus' wars. In 260, vexillations taken from British and German legions, as well as their auxiliaries, were in Pannonia. None of this stopped Postumus. After murdering Gallienus' son Saloninus, Postumus formed a breakaway regime in the northwest provinces. He knew his support was regional, and that Gallienus needed the stability he could offer. In a climate of military and economic chaos, Postumus restricted his imperial claims to Britain, Gaul and Germany, creating what is now known as the Gallic Empire.

The vexillations may have been unable to return to Britain. The evidence from the fourth century is for a vastly reduced II legion. The XX legion seems to have disappeared at some point in the 300s, though a detachment was on Hadrian's Wall between 262 and 266.[12] Postumus had no need of the forts to protect himself from Gallienus, but he did need to prove to the peoples of the Gallic Empire that he could protect them from external threats, especially from coastal piracy. In any case, the shore fort building carried on, long after the Gallic Empire had ended.

Postumus was excellent at presentation. He adopted all the formal trappings of a Roman emperor, claimed imperial virtues on his coinage, and posed as a restorer of traditional Roman qualities. In the violent and unstable years of the late third century, Postumus realized the importance of appealing to tradition. Far from rebelling against the Roman Empire, he claimed to be restoring it. This would be a mark of most of the usurpers that followed, especially those whose rebellions started out in Britain.

60. Tower Hill (London). Roman London's third-century walls enclosed 138 ha (341 acres), thereby defining *Londinium* as the largest city in Britain. Only the lower section visible here is Roman. The medieval wall-builders incorporated what was left of the Roman walls. Most of Britain's other major towns were equipped with masonry walls by the middle of the third century.

The previous 50 years of chronic instability had had various consequences. One of them was chronically debased coinage, as each successive regime needed to buy the army's loyalty. By the time Postumus came to power, gold was rare and 'silver' coinage was little better than bronze with a silver wash. Postumus produced good quality gold coinage, and tried hard to restore the silver and base-metal small-change coinage that had suffered so badly. The designs were good, and some were innovative and creative [61]. Producing intrinsically valuable coinage was synonymous with imperial prestige. Postumus failed to re-establish silver, the staple bullion used to pay soldiers, but he inspired (or enforced) loyalty in the British garrison. Some of the units styled themselves *Postumiana*. The First Cohort of Aelian Dacians, long-term resident at Birdoswald, and the Sebosian Cavalry at Lancaster both adopted the title.

Postumus was murdered in 268. A brief and violent series of successors culminated in the accession of Tetricus I in 270. In 273, Tetricus capitulated to Aurelian (270–75), who pensioned him off. The demise of the Gallic Empire did nothing to solve the problem of maritime raiders. Portchester, the best-preserved of all the British shore forts, was built in the 280s [62], with Pevensey following in or after 293. There is no doubt about the danger, but there was just as much from within. Britain was still ripe for revolt, but this was an age of imperial usurpers, in which rebels posed as restorers of Rome.

Before he was murdered, Probus (276–82) faced a revolt by an unnamed governor of Britain. Despite this evidence of Britain's potential instability, Probus put the revolt down and then sent prisoners-of-war from Continental skirmishes to Britain. They later joined Britain's garrison, but their loyalty can hardly have been guaranteed. By 285, the Roman Empire emerged from another bout of political and military turmoil, with Diocletian now in power. Diocletian knew Roman government needed reform. He appointed Maximian to be his co-emperor, and divided the Empire in two. He would rule the Eastern Empire, and Maximian would rule the West as the senior emperors, or *Augusti*. They recruited a pair of junior emperors, the Caesars, to assist them. Galerius would rule with Diocletian, and in time would succeed him, and Constantius Chlorus would assist and then succeed Maximian. The idea was to delegate imperial authority and spread the load, while also instituting a programme of smooth successions. This four-emperor system was known as the Tetrarchy.

In 284, a soldier from *Menapia* (roughly equivalent to Belgium), Mausaeus Carausius, excelled himself in a civil war in Gaul. He fought for the Empire against the Bagaudae, a group of landless outlaws whose livelihoods had been amongst the casualties of the disorder of the age. By

61. Postumus (259–68).
A double-*sestertius*, struck over a first- or second-century *sestertius*. Postumus established the Gallic Empire, which ruled alongside the legitimate regime until 273.

62. *Opposite*. Portchester (Hampshire).
Aerial view of the Saxon Shore fort at Portchester (*Portus Adurni*), built under the rebel Carausius (286–93). A Norman gatehouse, and later a 12th-century castle, were built into the Roman fort walls.

286, Carausius had suppressed them, and was appointed by Maximian to lead the Roman fleet in the North Sea against the pirates. Carausius did too well. Stories were put about, perhaps by Maximian, that Carausius let the raiders through, only setting on them as they staggered home weighed down by loot, which he pocketed for himself. It might have been true, but it is no less likely that Carausius had started to acquire the sort of loyalty Postumus had earned for producing results. No emperor could afford a general with that sort of popularity.

63, 64. Carausius (286–93).
A pair of bronze medallions, probably struck as donatives. The letters on the bottom of each reverse represent the initial letters of words from the Fourth *Eclogue* of Virgil, and mean 'the Golden Age is back. Now a new generation is let down from heaven above'.

Carausius moved decisively to confound his critics. In 286, Carausius declared himself emperor. Almost all that we know about the regime has had to be pieced together from a few scattered references in imperial histories, panegyrics and coinage. It is Carausian coinage that above all else demonstrates the regime's flamboyant and imaginative command of Roman iconography and imagery [63, 64]. Utilizing phrases, words and images from Virgilian poetry, Carausius plundered the classical Roman tradition to portray himself as a messianic figure who would restore Rome's golden age.[13] Such use of coinage as a propaganda tool was unprecedented. Although Carausius borrowed ideas from Postumus, he made a much more impressive job of it. No official Roman coinage ever carried such explicit literary references. He styled himself 'Marcus Aurelius Mausaeus Carausius' to manufacture a spurious lineage from the second-century Antonine emperors.

Carausius issued the best-quality silver coins produced for 220 years on which to display his slogans. These were swamped by his abundant bronze coinage that repeated many of these themes and added a host more, including types commemorating legions stationed both in Britain and on the Continent. Some of the coins were produced at London in its first era as a mint town. For a short time, Carausian coinage was also issued at Rouen. The Rouen coinage is so different, and so much less idiosyncratic, that it seems to have been produced by people who knew very little about their new usurper. Carausius is recorded on a single inscription, on a milestone found near Carlisle.[14] Together with the mint at London, it helps show that Carausius had spread himself from one end of Britain to the other.

Some Carausian coinage was targeted specifically at the army. The reformed silver would have gone a long way to consolidating his legitimacy in military eyes. It is also likely that the urban élite and rural landowners regarded his efforts at sea as proof that he was a more useful protector than Maximian. In 286 almost any mature man of consequence whose wealth and property was in Britain would have grown up under the Gallic Empire and seen how effective Postumus had been. Roman Britain's élite seem to have been excluded from the upper echelons of Roman cosmopolitan society. This exclusion, deliberate or accidental, may well have contributed to a sense of isolation, elevating a sense of parochial loyalties. Paradoxically, however, a striking characteristic of the revolt was the way in which Carausius appealed to classical aspirations and themes. There was no attempt to revive ancient tribal traditions or identities. It was a mark of how much Britain had changed in the 230 years since the Boudican revolt. The Carausian mission was an explicit effort to turn back the clock to Augustan Rome, not to the world of Caratacus.

Carausius was a source of monumental embarrassment to the Tetrarchy. Bad weather wrecked their plans to invade Britain in 289. Carausius remained in control, but by 293 he decided to adopt a more conciliatory approach. With breathtaking cheek he issued coins in the names of Diocletian and Maximian, as well as himself. For good measure he added a type that showed the three of them together, with a legend that read 'Carausius and his brothers'. He had, in effect, appointed himself to the Tetrarchy. In the same year, Constantius recaptured Boulogne, causing terminal damage to Carausius' prestige. Before the year was out, Carausius had been murdered and replaced by his finance officer, Allectus. Allectus had none of Carausius' flair. His coinage was produced with greater mechanical competence, but no more silver was produced, and the bronze and gold coins exhibited none of the imaginative panache that distinguished Carausian issues [65].

Apart from the Carausian milestone, only the coinage of Carausius and Allectus survives as a manifestation of the breakaway regime. The fort at Portchester seems to have been begun around 293, suggesting that it was ordered by either Carausius or Allectus, but as a single site in a much more protracted series it would be unwise to attach too much significance to it. Portchester hardly amounts to a major strategic initiative. Massive structural timbers found on St Peter's Hill in London were felled in or around 294, and it has been suggested that their size is evidence for a monumental building, possibly Allectus' headquarters. The connection makes for good archaeological speculation, but the nature of the building, as well as for whom it was built, is unknown. In any case, timbers felled in 294 might not have been used for several years, and by 296 Allectus was dead.

In 296, a new imperial fleet set out in two waves. One flotilla was commanded by Constantius Chlorus, and embarked from Boulogne. The other, commanded by the praetorian prefect, Asclepiodotus, left from the Seine. Asclepiodotus approached the south coast of Britain by the Isle of Wight. Shielded by fog, he landed somewhere in the Solent area and headed north. His arrival ambushed Allectus, who had to flee inland before he had had time to organize his forces. Asclepiodotus caught up with whatever army Allectus was able to pull together, defeating it and killing Allectus. Constantius, meanwhile, sailed up the Thames and seized London to the obsequious gratitude of the population. Or so it was claimed. Britain had been 'restored to the eternal light', as a celebratory gold medallion issued later by Constantius bragged [66]. But it was not the last time Britain would play host to a usurper.

65. Allectus (293–96).
A bronze *radiate* struck at London. Allectus was made emperor after the murder of Carausius, but within three years he, too, was defeated and killed, this time by the army of Constantius I.

66 Constantius I (293–306).
A gold medallion showing Constantius as Caesar, struck at Trier. The reverse commemorates the 'liberation' of London and the 'restoration of the eternal light' after the defeat of Allectus. About 296. (British Museum).

BRITAIN AND THE TETRARCHY

Diocletian reorganized Britain as he had everywhere else. By 312–14, there were four provinces within the diocese of Britain. Administration and control of the army came under separate commands. A *vicarius* administered the diocese of Britain, while four governors took care of the provinces. The garrison came under the control of the *dux Britanniarum*, while one *comes* controlled the Saxon Shore forts and another some mounted units. The reorganization of Britain was undoubtedly part of Diocletian's more general rearrangement of the Roman Empire, but the events of the Carausian revolt must have encouraged his plans. This turned out to be wrong, but Maximian and Constantius were determined to pose as saviours. Oppression and punishment would have been a disaster. So Carausius and Allectus were damned as criminals who had oppressed the Britons. This cannot have been true, or else the revolt would have foundered quickly, and with less trouble.

The mint at London continued in operation, now striking the generic coin types of the Tetrarchy that flooded the Empire. An inscription from Birdoswald on Hadrian's Wall, dated to 297–305, records major restoration work on several of the fort's principal buildings, but probably predates the division into four provinces [67].[15] The text refers to the buildings' ruinous state. It is striking that throughout the third century, after Caracalla withdrew from Scotland, there is no literary reference at all to trouble with barbarians on Britain's frontiers. It is likely that for much of the third century, northern Britain remained relatively peaceable. So it would be no surprise if the forts and other installations in the north had been allowed to run down during that time.

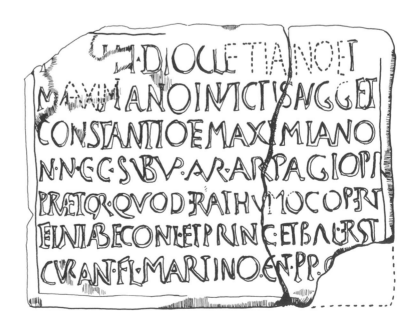

67. Birdoswald (Cumbria). Inscription recording the restoration of the headquarters, baths and commandant's house, under the governor, Aurelius Arpagius, during the reigns of Diocletian and Maximian. One of the latest inscriptions from Roman Britain. About 297–305.

In 305, Constantius Chlorus returned to Britain and began a new campaign into Scotland. We only know about the campaign because it was described in an imperial panegyric that compliments the emperor for his good sense in making no attempt to occupy the territory. There seem to have been no great strategic or tactical consequences of the campaign, and in 306 Constantius died at York.

Diocletian overlooked the dynastic ambitions of his colleagues and their families. Galerius had decided to appoint a relative of his own to succeed Constantius, but at York the soldiers declared Constantius' son, Constantine, emperor. After a succession of wars, Constantine emerged in 324 as the supreme victor. He ruled until his death in 337, when the Roman world was divided amongst his three surviving sons: Constantius II, Constantine II and Constans. In 313, Constantine issued the Edict of Milan, legitimizing Christianity. Constantine recognized that Christianity offered him a tool with which he could recruit men who owed their elevation and power to him, rather than relying on older, established families. That the church was already organized in Britain is plain from the attendance at the Council of Arles in 314 by British bishops from the sees of London, York, and probably Lincoln.

The division of the Empire amongst the sons of Constantine did not go smoothly. Constantine II took the West, including Britain, but went to war against Constans, who held Italy. Constantine II was killed there in 340. Constans arrived in Britain in the winter of 342–43 on a surprise expedition. Making a trip across the Channel in winter for any reason was a risky business, made the more so as it meant leaving his imperial domains exposed. Constans may have come because of barbarian attacks, but the urgency and unusualness of the expedition suggests the reason was more pressing, and may have been news of a plot against him.

Another possible reason was religion. Christianity, now in the ascendant, was institutionally less tolerant than paganism. This had led to increasing legal restrictions on pagan activities. Christianity itself had problems. Inherent differences over liturgical details, or even fundamentals like the divinity of Christ, had been obscured by the centuries of episodic persecution. Now that Christianity had become the religion of power, the overriding question was which brand of Christianity would emerge the victor? The question of Christ's divinity became the most serious issue, because it was a dispute that became synonymous with the power struggle between Constantine's sons. Constans was an Orthodox Christian who believed Christ to be the divine Son of God, while Constantius II [68], ruling in the East, held the Arian belief that Christ was the Son of God, but not divine. While it was possible to be entirely sincere about such things, religious differences could also provide a front for more basic rivalries, posturing and conflict.

68. Constantius II (337–61). A gold *solidus* struck at Antioch. Exotic gold coins like this found their way to Britain, where they were used as a means of storing wealth by the super-rich. The Hoxne treasure hoard included 569 gold *solidi*.

FOURTH-CENTURY REBELLIONS

Britain participated in a series of rebellions during the rest of the fourth century. One of the curious contrasts between archaeology and history is that none of these historical events have any certain manifestation in the ground. The archaeological story of the fourth century is of urban decay and rural wealth in the great villas. In 350, Constans was toppled by a coup in Autun and murdered. Magnentius, an army commander said to have had a British father and a Frankish mother, led the rebellion. For three years, Magnentius ruled a breakaway Empire that included Britain, posing as an Orthodox Christian as a direct challenge to Constantius II's Arianism [69]. In 353, Magnentius was defeated and killed. Constantius II was determined to punish anyone who had supported Magnentius, and an imperial secretary called Paul was sent to Britain to deal with any Magnentian supporters.

Paul overstepped his remit, and charges were trumped up against innocent men. Some were executed, and many were ruined. Amongst them were some of the people who owned the great villas that stand out as the most conspicuous evidence of Roman life in Britain at the time. So desperate was the situation that the vicar of Britain, Martinus, tried personally to kill Paul. Martinus failed and committed suicide on the spot. Perhaps Paul had been ordered by Constantius to indulge in a terror campaign to reassert the regime's power. It is dangerous to link historical events with specific archaeological sites, unless there is some unequivocal piece of evidence to do so. There is no such location, but one major villa site at Gadebridge Park (Hertfordshire) bucked the trend [70]. Despite growing to a substantial size with architectural pretensions, it fell out of use by 360 and was comprehensively demolished. The foundations were buried, and the site returned to agriculture. We will never know the exact context, but it is tempting to wonder if the villa estate was one of those confiscated by Paul.

The Magnentian revolt allowed Britain's élite to exhibit a parochial sense of identity and self-determination. Constantius II now had the problem of managing a fragmenting Empire on his own. In 355, he appointed his cousin, Julian, as commander of forces in Gaul and the northwest. Julian immediately had to deal with officers siphoning off money for private expenditure, and barbarians who were preventing vital grain shipments from Britain reaching the Rhine garrison by blockading sea movements. To get round this, the grain had to be shipped to Gaul and then laboriously transported overland to Germany. By 359 the issue was largely resolved, but Britain's problems had only just begun.

The long peace on Britain's northern frontier was deteriorating. In 360, the Scots and Picts raided the frontier. A general, Lupicinus, was

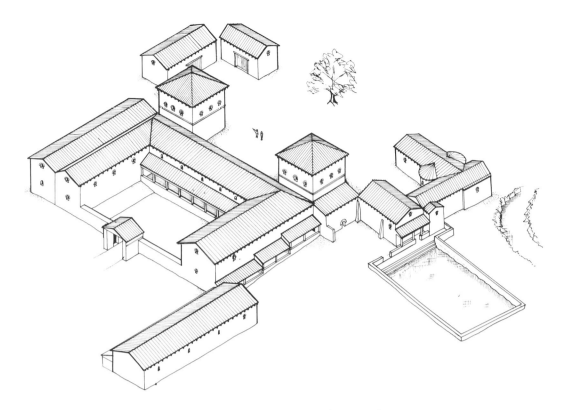

sent to deal with them, but we do not know what he achieved except that it was not permanent. Constantius II died in 361, and was succeeded by Julian II until 363. Julian was a reconstructed pagan, and attempted to reverse the laws against paganism at the expense of the Christians. The attempt lasted no longer than his life. By 364, a new imperial house was in power. Valentinian I (364–75) ruled in the West and his brother Valens (364–78) in the East. Throughout this time, the Scots, Picts, Attacotti and Saxons brought what Ammianus called 'uninterrupted hardships' to the Britons.[16] These difficulties seem to have had little impact on the villa owners in the south, who continued to invest in their houses [71].

The 'hardships' reached their climax in the so-called 'barbarian conspiracy' of 367. In Britain the Picts and Scots wreaked havoc, carting off spoil and prisoners, while the Franks and Saxons attacked Gaul. The barbarians captured the *dux Britanniarum*, Fullofaudes, and killed Nectaridus, 'count of the maritime area' (probably the Saxon Shore). The damage is likely to have been localized. Coordinated and effective widespread destruction is immensely difficult to achieve, but leaving a trail of damage is much more plausible. There is little or no physical evidence to support the story, unlike the Boudican revolt, for which substantial traces of destruction layers have been found. Ultimately, Valentinian sent over a general called Theodosius to restore Britain. Upon arrival in London, Theodosius sent his troops to catch up with the barbarians as they

70. Gadebridge Park (Hertfordshire).
The villa in its final form before demolition, shortly after 350. It is possible, but unverifiable, that the owner was one of the victims of the pogrom instigated after the fall of Magnentius in 353. (Based on elevations by David S. Neal).

71. Lullingstone (Kent).
Mosaic panel depicting
Bellerophon killing the
Chimaera and surrounded by the Four
Seasons. This is one of many
mosaics installed in villas during
much of the fourth century,
suggesting confidence and
optimism in the south, while in
the far north barbarian incursions
caused increasing trouble.

staggered home with their loot. He knew that they were too dispersed to defeat in set-piece battles, and that desertions by the frontier garrisons had reduced the available forces. Frontier scouts, called the 'Areani' and probably hired as irregular mercenaries, were blamed for failing to watch out for barbarians and instead selling them secrets about Roman army movements. Theodosius expelled the Areani from the bases and recovered the deserters by issuing pardons, and then set about restoring the province's infrastructure and administration.

London's landward bastions were added to the city wall around this time, but they could just as easily have preceded 367. Workers seem to have been sent out from the *civitas* capitals to restore Hadrian's Wall, but the inscriptions that record them can be only attributed to the fourth century. Even so, the stones suggest that local government was still functioning in the late fourth century, and could administer the provision of work-gangs to help repair the province's frontier defences. In commemoration of the great event, London was renamed *Augusta* and its province, *Maxima Caesariensis*, was renamed *Valentia*. This information comes from the *Notitia Dignitatum*, but the text is corrupt at this point. It was once thought that it listed *Valentia* as a new, fifth province of Britain, but it now seems much more likely that a word was lost in translation, and that the text should read 'Maxima Caesariensis, now Valentia'.

Britain was still treated as backwater. A Pannonian called Valentinus was exiled to Britain as punishment for an unspecified crime. He promptly used the opportunity to organize opposition to Valentinian, and tried to involve other exiles and the army. Valentinian's death in 375, and Valens' in 378, provided the opportunity for more turmoil. Valentinian's son, Gratian, the ruler in the West, appointed Theodosius I (son of the general of the same name) emperor in the East. In Britain, the garrison decided that one of their own commanders was a better prospect than Gratian. In 383, they declared Magnus Maximus, a Spaniard, as their new emperor [72]. Maximus immediately left Britain to prosecute a civil war against Gratian on the Continent, taking much of Britain's garrison with him. Gratian was murdered by one of his own officers, but by 388, Theodosius had defeated and killed Maximus.

Magnus Maximus had done nothing for Britain except denude her defences. Or so later historians, such as Gildas, said. According to Gildas, Maximus had laid Britain open to attacks by Scots and Picts, resulting in further appeals for help.[17] By 394, Theodosius I had largely settled the fall-out after the Magnus Maximus episode. But he died in 395 and left the Empire to his sons: Arcadius in the East, and Honorius in the West. Honorius would be the last legitimate Roman emperor to rule Britain, but as a child he was emperor only in name. The real power was held by Stilicho, 'Master of the Soldiers'. An imperial panegyric of the year 400 describes in poetically extravagant, but factually uninformative, terms Stilicho's work to protect Britain from barbarians. In fact, in 401 Stilicho withdrew troops from Britain to use against the Visigoths.

The Western Roman Empire had little prestige left. It was now ruled from an imperial court that had withdrawn to the safety of Ravenna in northeastern Italy, where swamps and remoteness gave the place some sort of security. In Britain, there was little sense that her interests were going to be taken care of. After 379, official coinage was distributed in Britain in smaller amounts, but far fewer copies were ever made to compensate, in direct contrast to earlier periods. Something was happening to Roman Britain's liquid economy, though exactly what is very difficult to say. A surprisingly large number of coins dated 395–402 were found at the coastal fort of Richborough [73], but this is totally different from the picture found elsewhere in Britain.

Coinage ceased arriving at all after 402, so Britain's troops were appar-

72. Magnus Maximus (383–88). Bronze coin struck at Arles. The reverse shows Maximus 'recovering' the state. In reality, his rebellion was yet another destabilizing event for the Roman Empire and especially for Britain. (British Museum).

ently not being paid. The soldiers indulged themselves with a series of usurpers in 407. First they deposed Victorinus, the vicar of Britain, and installed Marcus as emperor. Marcus did not live up to expectations, so they replaced him with a man called Gratian, who seems to have been a civilian magistrate. He was equally unpopular. The troops turned to one of their own number, who looked far more promising. Flavius Claudius Constantinus had the perfect name for an emperor. It was also almost exactly a hundred years since the British garrison had triumphantly elevated Constantine I to the purple, and installed a dynasty on the throne. Soldiers like such good omens. Constantine III accepted the position, and gathered up what he could of the British garrison, setting out on a Continental war of conquest. He never came back, and nor did Britain's garrison. By 409, Honorius had had no choice but to accept the situation and appoint Constantine III as joint-consul. This gave Constantine legal authority in the West, but his failure to do anything about the barbarian problem led the Britons to declare themselves independent of Roman rule and to take charge of their own defences.[18] Constantine III's administration started to implode with internal rebellions of its own. In 410, Honorius asked the towns of Britain by letter to do what was necessary to defend themselves. By ceasing the process of reciprocal patronage, Roman Britain was brought formally to an end. Britain, however, clung on to being Roman for several decades yet. Just as Rome's influence had grown steadily before 43, it would wane just as slowly after 410.

73. Richborough (Kent).
Remains of a brick font, probably associated with an adjacent timber church of fourth-century date built within the walls of the shore fort at *Rutupiae*.

CHAPTER 4
GOVERNING BRITAIN

The Roman Empire created the idea of mainland Britain as a unified geographical area. This excluded Ireland, which was never invaded, although Roman artifacts show that trade across the Irish Sea existed. The Romans perceived, governed, exploited, patronized, funded and manipulated Britain as a single entity. This is a critical psychological distinction between the periods before and after 43. It is only through Roman eyes that we have any detailed idea of political and social structure before and during the conquest period. Where the Romans were able to see a political structure that they could understand, they tended to perceive that structure as a tribal dynastic monarchy. The references to Cunobelinus of the Catuvellauni and his sons, Caratacus and Togodumnus, and the fate of Prasutagus of the Iceni and his family, suggest that this notion was broadly accurate, at least in the south and east. The idea of 'dynasty' should not be taken too literally, because if Caesar was correct about the native habit of sharing wives, it is unlikely that a king's sons were all by the same woman. It is also likely that the idea of 'son' was a looser concept than ours. Even in the Roman Empire, adoption was already a well-established device for sustaining a paternalistic society and the transmission of property through a male heir.

Before 43, rulers in Britain won prestige by appropriating territory and other valuables from neighbouring tribal areas. By the first century AD, Roman patronage had become the most decisive factor in maximizing that prestige. It was a power-politics version of the normal Roman patron-client relationship, in which men of status surrounded themselves with associates who performed useful services in return for personal, practical and financial support. The relationship was two-way. The patron (in this case, the emperor) had obligations to his clients, just as the clients had to him. Client kings provided useful administrative and social buffers, helping to stabilize regions by exploiting existing hierarchies and loyalties. But the policy did not outlive the first century. There is plenty of evidence for the treatment of allied kings in the eastern half of the Empire and in North Africa. The Celtic dynastic coinage, with its explicit verbal and visual allusions to Roman titles and attributes, is the best evidence that a similar game was being played in Britain. The flight of Verica took place because he and his associates legitimately expected Roman military support as part of the patronage relationship.

After the invasion, Roman control in Britain depended on maintaining structural continuity. Wherever possible, Claudius allowed approved tribal leaders to remain as client monarchs, providing they swore allegiance to Rome. Togidubnus is the prime example. We know nothing about his background, but with so much indirect evidence for the Roman policy of training and educating the sons of rulers of friendly frontier nations, it is likely that he was a son or relative of a tribe in central southern Britain, who had been educated in Rome prior to the invasion or shortly afterwards. Since Togidubnus is referred to on an inscription at Chichester, he was probably a member of the Atrebatic ruling house. There is more circumstantial evidence from Chichester, and also Silchester, for very early signs of Romanization and imperial patronage. A gold ring, found 200 m (656 ft) east of the Fishbourne palace, is inscribed with the name of Tiberius Claudius Catuarus (see p. 201).[1] 'Catuarus' is a Celtic name, here belonging to a man made a Roman citizen under Claudius, as Togidubnus had been. The ring does not substantiate Togidubnus' ownership of the palace, but it is evidence for the existence of a cabal of his associates, enfranchised along with their king by the Romans in return for their support.

Members of allied dynastic houses sometimes fought in the Roman army. The recent sensational discovery in southeast Leicestershire of a Roman silver cavalry helmet, hoarded together with over 3,000 Iron Age coins, may be evidence that part of an individual tribal warrior's career was spent in the Roman army. Alternatively, it might instead have been a high-value gift from a Roman official, or even the emperor. Catuvellaunian coinage included a type depicting Cunobelinus wearing a Roman-type helmet. The hoard coins, mostly of the East Midlands Corieltauvi, date the deposit to the early first century AD. The helmet is unparalleled in Britain, but chain mail in some early first-century graves, for example at Folly Lane and Lexden, might also have had similar origins.

It has recently been suggested that allied British kings might even have been given auxiliary units detached from the Roman army specifically to support them. This includes the radical, and interesting, idea that the extremely early Roman fort at Gosbecks, near the Catuvellaunian stronghold at Colchester, could in fact have been a base for troops in the garrison of Cunobelinus.[2] Other instances of early Roman military-type installations or buildings, for example at Fishbourne, have also been normally attributed to 43 or afterwards. It is possible that some of these precede the invasion.

74. South Cadbury (Somerset). Bronze plaque found in a guard chamber at the hillfort's southwest gate. The realistic treatment of the hair shows considerable influence from the classical world. This conflation of styles became increasingly common in the years before the Roman conquest. Late Iron Age.

COINAGE IN ROMAN BRITAIN

In the first two centuries AD, Roman coinage adhered to a fairly standard system of denominations, though availability varied at different times and from province to province [75].

1 gold *aureus* = 25 silver *denarii*
1 *denarius* = 4 brass *sestertii* (the double-*denarius*, or *antoninianus*, was introduced *c.* 211–17)
1 *sestertius* = 2 brass *dupondii*
1 *dupondius* = 2 copper or bronze *asses*
1 *as* = 2 bronze *semisses*
1 *semis* = 2 bronze *quadrantes*
1 *quadrans* (the *semis* and *quadrans* are almost never found in Britain)

75. Coinage in early Roman Britain.
Top row (left to right): gold *aureus* of Nero (54–68); silver double-*denarius*, or *antoninianus*, of Elagabalus (218–22); silver *denarius* of Trajan (98–117). Bottom row (left to right): brass *sestertius* of Trajan (98–117); brass *dupondius* of Vespasian (69–79); bronze *as* of Domitian (81–96).

Most coins had on the obverse a portrait of the emperor, or, less often, a member of his family, usually his wife. The reverse carried a seemingly limitless variety of goddesses and female virtues, such as Fortuna, Laetitia (Joy), Libertas, Minerva, Salus (Health) and Victoria. Other reverses included male gods, like Hercules and Jupiter, with some special issues commemorating wars.

Gold is virtually never found other than in hoards. Silver coins are quite frequently recovered, but around half of these are contemporary forgeries (known as 'plated *denarii*'), made of a silver-plated copper core. Such forgeries rarely appear in hoards, suggesting that people were quite aware of which was which. Most site finds in Britain are brass, bronze and copper base-metal coins.

From an early date the imperial authorities had been debasing the silver to make the bullion they had go further. The purity level reached around 50 per cent under Septimius Severus (193–211), and subsequently plummeted. By the late third century, the double-*denarius* (introduced by Caracalla, 211–17) was bronze with a silver wash. At that time, any older coins that were still around disappeared into the melting pot.

Thereafter, emperor after emperor attempted to reform the coinage [76]. In the fourth century, the coinage system was changed completely. A new gold coin, the *solidus*, was the staple bullion coin. Issued in large quantities, it was reliable and accepted everywhere. Silver was only sporadically struck, and Britain seems to have been one of a very few places that preferred it. This may reflect lower levels of personal wealth, but even some of the late treasure hoards (such as Hoxne) were dominated by silver coinage. Vast quantities of bronze small-change denominations were struck, but today we do not know what these were called, or how much they were worth.

76. Coinage in late Roman Britain.
Top row (left to right): silver double-*denarius* or *antoninianus* of Trajan Decius (249–51); bronze *radiate* of Postumus (259–68); *follis* of Constantius I (293–306). Bottom row (left to right): gold *solidus* of Constantius II (337–61); bronze issue of Constantine I (307–37) struck at London, *c.* 307–24; bronze issue of Constantius II (337–61); silver *siliqua* of Julian II (360–63).

The invasion of 43 is so dominant an historical feature that it is easy to overlook the underlying continuity. Once the invasion had taken place, clearly some tribes, like the Catuvellauni, presented significant problems. To begin with, the Iceni and the Brigantes both had factions that were prepared to play the client-king game. But the instability and inherent unreliability of the system was made obvious by what happened in both areas. The Iceni were not all prepared to tolerate any further exploitation after the death of Prasutagus. In the north, Cartimandua proved her usefulness by handing over Caratacus, but resistance from a powerful faction led by her estranged husband, Venutius, provoked a crisis. In both cases, the outcome was costly warfare followed by long-term garrisoning.

Tacitus says that this was the Britons' greatest weakness. Constantly divided by the petty squabbles and ambitions of their chiefs, they never unified under a common banner against an enemy, preferring instead to combine in small, ineffective confederations. Thus 'in this way they fight individually, and are universally conquered'.[3] Had Caratacus been able to count on the support of all of the southern tribes, he might have led a successful defence of Britain. Instead, the Roman invasion was used by some tribes to further their own ambitions.

The genius of Roman power was in delegating authority to existing communities and hierarchies [77]. Ultimately, this was done by force from the outset. But Rome was incapable of supplying the manpower to enforce government at every level. When Roman government worked, it did so through coercion and compliance. Most tribal communities were

77. St Albans (Hertfordshire). The basilica and forum at *Verulamium* as they might have appeared in the second century. The complex was at the heart of Roman urban government. The members of the town council (*ordo*) that met in the basilica here were probably drawn from the local Catuvellaunian aristocracy, thus perpetuating their control of the region, but now within a Roman administrative framework.

based on warrior élites, amongst whom prestige was earned through military prowess, control of land, and so on. From their number, the most prestigious were chosen as kings. These communities were not 'urbanized', and they had no pre-existing institutions that could be adapted into the Roman system, unlike the Greek cities of the East. But the tribes had a social hierarchy and identity. The Roman administrators of Britain adapted these to create regional administrative units, known as the *civitates*. The native aristocracy, from now on, would measure their prestige according to status within their *civitas*.

Some of the tribes of southern Britain were well disposed towards Rome, and had already gained a sufficiently sophisticated way of life to accept this change. But there was no proper tradition of urban settlements and formal infrastructure. These had to be created. In the remote north, the Romans faced communities that had little concept of anything remotely identifiable as an administrative structure. This may well have played a part in the decision to abandon any permanent attempt at controlling Scotland after Agricola's governorship. Scotland would have used up far too many resources in a futile attempt to impose Roman culture on a population that could see no advantage, and had no interest, in complying.

GOVERNING BRITANNIA

Britain was an imperial province, and was part of the emperor's personal domain, like most frontier provinces and unlike the senatorial provinces that clustered around the Mediterranean. As such, Britain was governed according to the principles and policies that affected the whole Roman Empire. Britain was a dominion within a much larger government system, and while that system depended on effective delegation of authority through a hierarchy of government officials, it was still run as a single entity: *Britannia*. Even after the civil war of 193–97 and the subdivision of Britain into two provinces, and then into four by Diocletian, Britain was still treated as a specific region.

Britain was governed by the emperor's delegate, a *legatus*. The legate was in charge of military and civilian affairs, and, like the emperor, also served as a priest presiding over official religious functions and events.[4] Legates were drawn from Rome's senatorial upper classes, those in possession of property to the value of one million *sestertii*. Senators pursued a fairly well-established career of progressions through a hierarchy of magistracies. Each tier entitled them to consideration for administrative jobs. Britons were marginalized from Rome's ruling class presumably because none possessed the appropriate property qualification. Britons were regarded as the inhabitants of a truculent, barbarian and crude provincial outpost, administered by men who came from other parts of the Roman Empire. From as early as the 60s, these could even include men of Gaulish origin, which only emphasizes Britain's social exclusion.

Normally governors had to have served as a *praetor*, granting them propraetorian status. Britain presented a special problem. As a military province with a substantial garrison, she required experienced senior governors. Britain's legates were therefore drawn from men who had gone to the top and served as consuls, giving them proconsular experience. However, a proconsular governor in an imperial province was dangerously close in prestige and status to the emperor himself. So, incongruously, Britain's governors were men of proconsular status in a job officially rated as propraetorian. This is most clearly illustrated on various inscriptions from the military north, naming the governor and abbreviating his title to 'LEG PR PR' [78].

The governor was certainly based in London by the end of the first century, and possibly as early as the 60s. It has often been claimed that the palace at Fishbourne was the residence of the client king, Togidubnus, and repeated so often that the idea has been accepted as proven, though in fact it is completely unsubstantiated. Given the considerable evidence for a Roman presence, possibly military, on the site at the date of conquest, it is just as likely that the palace was built as a governor's residence. The evidence for London being the governor's base by the end of the first century is mostly indirect, but more reliable. A Vindolanda tablet states that soldiers from the garrison were in London, and by the second century the Cripplegate fort had been built to house the governor's garrison.[5] Several soldiers are testified on tombstones from London. The procurator (see table, p. 88) was certainly based there. The monumental palace-type structure at Cannon Street has long been interpreted as the governor's palace, but so far nothing has been found to prove this apart from size and location.

78. High Rochester (Northumberland).
Inscription from High Rochester (*Bremenium*) recording building work by the First Cohort of Lingones, during the governorship of the propraetorian legate, Lollius Urbicus (138–42?).

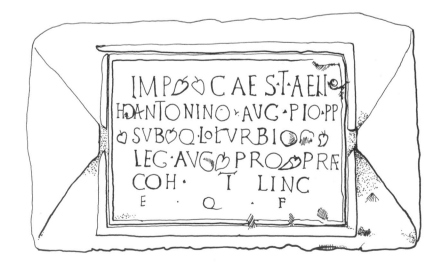

BRITANNIA

The first known representation of Britannia was at Aphrodisias in Asia Minor, where she appears on a mid-first-century marble relief with Claudius, commemorating the conquest [80]. Portraying places and virtues in the form of personifications (usually women) was normal in the Roman world.

Britannia makes no appearance on coinage until Hadrian's bronze *as* of *c.* 119. She is depicted as a warlike female, complete with spear and shield, sitting on a small pile of rocks. Later on in the reign, Britannia was shown in this guise, with Hadrian greeting her with the legend 'ADVENTVI AVG BRITANNIAE' ('the coming of the emperor to Britannia').

In 143, Antoninus Pius (138–61) issued *sestertii* with Britannia reverses, commemorating the war in the north that had led to the building of the Antonine Wall [79]. In 154, a series of bronze *asses* was issued, also with Britannia reverses. Apparently distributed only in Britain, they may commemorate another war and were probably given to troops as a donative.

Britannia's last appearance on coinage was during the reign of the rebel emperor, Carausius (286–93). On a few, very rare coins, the emperor is shown being greeted by Britannia with the legend *Expectate veni* ('come, the awaited one'), alluding to a passage in the *Aeneid* and supporting Carausius' self-

79. Antoninus Pius (138–61).
Brass *sestertius* of 143, depicting the figure of Britannia on the reverse.

proclaimed role as saviour of Britannia. The same coins carry the mark 'RSR', now known to refer to a passage in Virgil's Fourth *Eclogue*, *Redeunt Saturnia Regna* ('the Golden Age is back'), and which also appears on a medallion of the reign (see p. 70).

Britannia was not revived by any of the later rebels, such as Magnus Maximus and Constantine III. She makes a final reappearance at the beginning of the fourth century in the poetry of Claudian, about a

campaign led by the general, Stilicho. Claudian describes Britannia as dressed in a Caledonian animal skin, with tattooed cheeks, and a cloak reminiscent of an ocean's waves.

After the end of the Roman period, the image of Britannia did not resurface until the seventeenth century. The coins of Hadrian were copied for the copper halfpennies and farthings of Charles II, and Britannia has remained a feature of British coinage ever since.

80. Aphrodisias (Turkey).
Marble relief depicting Claudius defeating Britannia. It was important for the emperor to publicize his greatest military triumph in this symbolic fashion, as the campaign validated his right to rule in the eyes of his subjects. Mid-first century AD.

The best evidence for the names of governors comes from Tacitus' *Annals* and *Agricola*. Both sources contain biographical details and descriptions of events and personalities that collectively take us as far as the mid-80s. Thereafter, evidence is generally restricted to occasional references in written histories, inscriptions and diplomas. In the third century, once Britain was divided into two, almost the only names we hear about are the governors of *Britannia Inferior*, thanks to the continuing practice of erecting military inscriptions into the mid-third century. Conversely, we know almost nothing about the governors of *Britannia Superior* [81].

As the emperor's personal delegate, the governor deferred to him when he was in Britain. This must have happened when Hadrian toured the province, but the only time we know it to have occurred was during the campaigns of Severus between 208–11. Severus brought with him both of his sons, Caracalla and Geta. Caracalla accompanied the army into Caledonia, but Geta was instructed by his father to 'exercise jurisdiction over the subject people of the province', as well as to administer the rest of the Empire.[6] Although Geta had been promoted to the position of joint Augustus with his father and brother in 209, he was still only 20 years old, and far too inexperienced to govern Britain, let alone the Roman world. Appropriately, Severus provided a council of his friends to act as advisers.

Britain was a demanding province because of the military obligations. The Flavian emperors created an additional legate, the *legatus Augusti iuridicus* ('imperial judicial legate'), to ease the load. Judicial legates had usually served as legionary legates first, and would go on to govern provinces. If the governor was absent, they could stand in. The late Roman Digest of Law preserves details of a case presided over by Britain's judicial legate, Lucius Javolenus Priscus, in the 70s or 80s, concerning the estate of a helmsman in the *classis Britannica* whose son had predeceased him.[7] The post existed as late as the end of the second century, when it was held by Marcus Antius Crescens Calpurnius. One *legatus iuridicus*, Marcus Vettius Valens, went on to become 'patron of the province of Britain', a position of uncertain responsibilities, possibly honorific.

Governors had usually served at an earlier point in their careers as legionary legates, another position reserved for those of senatorial rank, except briefly under Commodus when equestrians (see below) were made eligible. Even command of a legion could be a propraetorian or proconsular appointment. Tacitus says that the XX legion had proved a handful for proconsular legates, becoming mutinous during the civil war of 68–69 when a propraetorian legate was appointed.[8] Agricola, sent to succeed and punish the offending

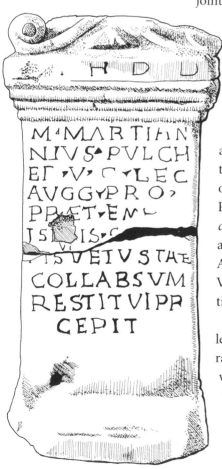

THE GOVERNORS

A. Plautius	43–47	Ulpius Marcellus	*c.* 177–84
P. Ostorius Scapula	47–51/2	P. Helvius Pertinax	*c.* 185
A. Didius Gallus	51/2–57	Clodius Albinus	*c.* 192–97
Q. Veranius Nepos	57/8	Virius Lupus	*c.* 197–202
G. Suetonius Paullinus	57/8–61	C. Valerius Pudens	205
P. Petronius Turpilianus	61–63	L. Alfenus Senecio	205–8
M. Trebellius Maximus	63–69	***	
M. Vettius Bolanus	69–71	G. Julius Marcus	213
Q. Petillius Cerealis	71–73/4		
S. Julius Frontinus	73/4–77/8	***Britannia Inferior***	
G. Julius Agricola	77/8–83/4	[M. Antonius Gor?]dianus	*c.* 213–16
***		Modius Julius	early 200s (*c.* 219?)
G. Sallustius Lucullus	*c.* 84–94	T. Claudius Paulinus	220
under Domitian		Marius Valerianus	221/2
***		Claudius Xenephon	222–23
P. Metilius/Maecilius Nepos	–98	..... Maximus	225
T. Avidius Quietus	98–102?	Calvisius Rusonus	*c.* 225–35
L. Neratius Marcellus	102?–6?	V. Crescens Fulvianus	*c.* 225–35
***		Claudius Apellinus	*c.* 225–35
M. Atilius Metilius Bradua	114–18	[T?]uccianus	237
possibly under Trajan or Hadrian		Maecilius Fuscus	238–44
Q. Pompeius Falco	118?–22	Egnatius Lucilianus	238–44
A. Platorius Nepos	*c.* 122–26	Nonius Philippus	242
(L.?) Trebius Germanus	126–30		
S. Julius Severus	130–33/4	***Britannia Superior***	
P. Mummius Sisenna	133/4–38	Q. Aradius Rufinus	*c.* 225–35?
Q. Lollius Urbicus	138–42?	M. Martiannius Pulcher	*c.* 238, 247–49,
G. Papirius Aelianus	142?–46		or 251–60
***		***	
Gn. Julius Verus	158	Octavius Sabinus	262–66
[..]anus L[.....]	154 or 159	*under Postumus*	
M. Statius Priscus	161–62		
S. Calpurnius Agricola	163		
Q. Antistius Adventus	–177?		

legate in around the year 70, is probably the best example of a senator who followed a British legionary command before later being appointed governor of the province.

Equestrians, whose property qualification was 300,000 *sestertii*, served in a multitude of imperial administrative positions. In Britain, the *procurator Augusti* ('imperial procurator') was the most senior, and provided a check on the governor by having full responsibility for finan-

THE JUDICIAL LEGATES

C. Salvius Liberalis	c. 75–85
L. Javolenus Priscus	c. 85+? (but before 91)
***	
M. Vettius Valens	130s
C. Sabucius Major Caecilianus	170s
M. Antius Crescens Calpurnius	180s/190s

THE PROCURATORS

Decianus Catus	–61
Gaius Julius Alpinus Classicianus	61–
Ti. Claudius Augustanus	c. 78–84
Cn. Pompeius Homullus	c. 85+
C. Valerius Pansa	Some time before c. 150
Q. Lusius Sabinianus	2nd century
Sex. Varius Marcellus	Late 2nd/ early 3rd century
M. Maenius Agrippa	Antonine
M. Oclatinius Adventus	c. 205–8
M. Cocceius Nigrinus	c. 212–17

82. Greenwich (London).
Tile from the site of a roadside temple complex stamped 'PPBRLON' for the 'Procurator of the Province of Britannia at London'. Such tiles were probably used in official buildings.

cial affairs. The procurator, Decianus Catus, was in post in London by the time the Boudican revolt broke out. His successor, Gaius Julius Alpinus Classicianus, is known from a reference in Tacitus, and the remains of his tombstone have been found in London (see p. 40). A variety of items from London, mostly tiles stamped 'PPBRLON', an abbreviation for *Procurator Provinciae Britanniae Londinio*, have been found in the city and surrounding areas [82]. A writing tablet found in London and stamped by the procuratorial office is undated, but it uses a plural verb that suggests there may have been more than one procurator at certain times. One of the most important holders of the post was Marcus Oclatinius Adventus. Named on imperial building inscriptions in the north during the lead-up to the Severan campaigns in Scotland, he seems to have had unusually wide responsibilities. He had started out his career as an illiterate soldier, reflecting the very different conditions of the third century, when promotion increasingly depended on opportunism and merit, rather than class and wealth.

The title 'procurator' was also applied to a variety of lesser administrative posts. An inscription from the villa at Combe Down (Somerset) names Naevius, 'freedman and assistant of the procurators' who had restored a 'headquarters' [83].[9] The context is not clear, but the procurators may have been responsible for administering an imperial estate. Procurators could be placed in charge of almost any imperial property or interest.

Troops were detached to fulfil a variety of administrative and practical jobs, such as policing and tax-collecting. At Bath, Gaius Severius Emeritus was 'centurion of the region', as recorded on an altar found near the middle of the city. It commemorated his repair and reconsecration of a *locum religiosum* ('holy spot'), after it had been vandalized 'by insolent hands'.[10] At Carlisle, Annius Questor was centurion of the region at the end of the first century.[11] In Richard Alston's words, 'the deployment of the centurions in the localities was a very powerful government mechanism'.[12] Other examples from around the Empire make it certain that on a day-to-day basis, the people of Roman Britain would have seen soldiers fulfilling a number of minor administrative duties, as well as undertaking civil engineering and building work.[13]

By 312–14, Britain had been reorganized into four provinces: *Maxima Caesariensis* (the southeast and East Anglia), governed from London; *Britannia Prima* (Wales, the southwest and West Midlands), governed from Cirencester; *Britannia Secunda* (the north), from York; and *Flavia Caesariensis* (northeast Midlands and Lincolnshire), with its centre at Lincoln. Government under the new system was more complicated, and less easy to understand because we have far less evidence for individual careers or specific examples of exercises of authority. Instead, we have to rely on the *Notitia Dignitatum* and occasional references in written histories. The *dux Britanniarum* ('duke of the Britons') held overall command of the army in those provinces which were now organized into the diocese of Britain, under the supreme control of the *vicarius*, or 'vicar'. Each province had its own governor. *Maxima Caesariensis*, as the senior province, was governed by a senatorial *consularis*, while the others

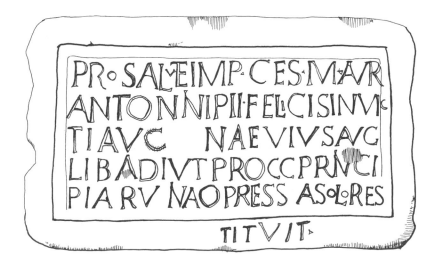

83. Combe Down (Somerset). Inscription recording the restoration of a 'headquarters', perhaps of an imperial estate, under Caracalla (211–17) or Elagabalus (218–22).

were each governed by a *praeses*, an equestrian rank reflecting the post's lesser status. There was therefore a crucial distinction from earlier periods: control of civil and military affairs had been split.

Although the names of many governors and some lesser officials are recorded, we know very little about their careers or activities in Britain [84]. Tacitus is our only detailed source, and he was almost entirely concerned with military exploits of the period 43–84. For this reason, his brief discussion of Agricola's civilizing campaign has been relentlessly dissected and endlessly quoted. Agricola was said to have promoted Latin education and Roman dress, and encouraged the Britons to build temples, fora and marketplaces.[14] However, Tacitus presents this information as an example of his father-in-law's munificence, enlightenment and effective government. By implication, he does not attribute achievements like these to Agricola's predecessors. We are not in a position to contradict him, especially as the only governor mentioned on any civilian public building inscription is indeed Agricola.[15]

Inscriptions from Britain record many soldiers on the governor's staff. The position was called *beneficiarius legati*, literally 'a person

HIERARCHY IN THE FIRST TO THIRD CENTURIES

Senatorial rank

Legatus Augusti: Governor of Britannia, normally who had served as a consul in Rome. During the third century there were two, governing *Britannia Superior* (the south) and *Britannia Inferior* (the north), respectively. The latter was also legate of the VI legion at York, and was therefore probably subordinate to the governor of *Britannia Superior*. The governor was also in overall charge of the provincial army.

Legatus Augusti Iuridicus: Judicial legate, only episodically appointed.

Legatus legionis: Commander of a legion. When Britain was divided into two after the civil war of 193–97, the commander of the VI legion at York also governed *Britannia Inferior*.

Equestrian rank

Procurator Provinciae Britanniae: Procurator of Britain, with financial responsibilities.
Procuratores: Lesser procurators in a host of minor administrative posts.

HIERARCHY IN THE FOURTH CENTURY

Civil

Vicarius Britanniarum: 'Vicar of the British provinces'.
Comes sacrarum largitionum: Controller of provincial finances.
Consularis: Governor of *Maxima Caesariensis*.
Praeses: Governors of *Britannia Prima, Britannia Secunda* and *Flavia Caesariensis*.

Military

Dux: Commander of the entire army in Britain.
Comes: Commander of parts of Britain's army; for example, *comes litoris Saxonici per Britanniam*, 'count of the Saxon Shore in Britain'.

favoured', in this case favoured through exemption from normal duties. Although most testified are known from the north, the appearance of one recorded on an inscription at Dorchester-on-Thames and another at Winchester (both undated) must reflect their travels around Britain, either with the governor or on his business.[16]

Governors must also have had battalions of clerks and slaves, but these are almost entirely absent from the record we have. Thousands of people will have served on the staff of the provincial government over the centuries, administering correspondence, requests for personal favours from friends and peers, court cases, appeals, representations, laws and other matters. One letter from Vindolanda seems to allude to a request that the correspondent's friend appeals to the governor, Lucius Neratius Marcellus, on the former's behalf.[17] A document from London, dated 14 March 118, refers to a dispute over tenure of a wood in Kent called *Verlucionum*, and was probably a case heard by the judicial legate.[18] Since both of these cases refer to trivial, everyday matters, we can assume that vast numbers of documents were involved in governing Britain throughout the Roman period, and that Britain was governed in much the same way as all other provinces.

TAXATION AND FINANCE

Florus said that Britain was valueless to the Empire, but that in possessing Britain, Rome was able to show the extent of her power and munificence.[19] Since the Romans had no concept of an 'economy' and its management, at least in any sense that we would understand it, we have a real problem in assessing how Roman Britain's finances were controlled.

Taxes and tribute were levied to impose punishments and maintain imperial administration and the army, and also by individual communities and cities to fund local administration and projects. Dio attributes to Boudica's pre-battle rallying speech a poll tax grievance.[20] Tacitus says that the Britons were prepared to tolerate paying tribute so long as there were no abuses.[21] The poll tax was levied to pay for the Roman administration and garrison of a province on the basis that the Romans were there to protect it and its inhabitants.[22] Other taxes included a five per cent inheritance tax on estates. Agricola had to reform abuse of the tribute and grain-taxation system. The Britons were theoretically paying their tribute in grain, which was stored in state granaries.[23] The system had been abused by forcing the Britons to travel long distances to locked granaries, where they had to purchase grain with which to pay their taxes. Of course, the grain stayed where it was.

84. Bath (Somerset). Altar recording the restoration of a *locum religiosum* by the centurion Gaius Severius Emeritus after it had been vandalized. Severius Emeritus was one of numerous centurions routinely seconded to administrative duties around Britain.

ROADS & MILESTONES

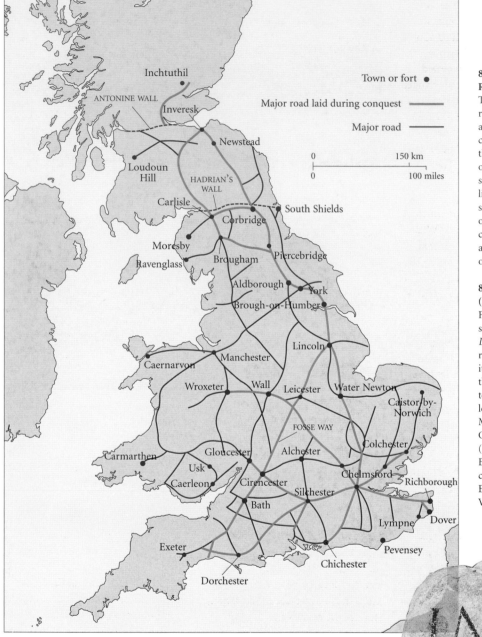

Town or fort ●

Major road laid during conquest ——

Major road ——

0   150 km

0   100 miles

Inchtuthil

ANTONINE WALL

Inveresk

Newstead

Loudoun
Hill

HADRIAN'S
WALL

Carlisle

Corbridge

South Shields

Moresby

Ravenglass

Brougham

Piercebridge

Aldborough

York

Brough-on-Humber

Manchester

Lincoln

Caernarvon

Wroxeter

Wall

Leicester

Water Newton

Caistor-by-
Norwich

FOSSE WAY

Colchester

Carmarthen

Gloucester

Alchester

Usk

Chelmsford

Caerleon

Cirencester

Richborough

Silchester

Bath

Lympne

Dover

Exeter

Pevensey

Chichester

Dorchester

85. The roads of Roman Britain.

The principal roads radiated from London, and were initially constructed to support the military conquest of the province. The social and economic life of Romano-British society came to depend on these crucial communications links, along with countless other roads and tracks.

86. Wall (Staffordshire).

Fragment of a milestone, found near *Letocetum*. Enough remains of the text and its style to show that the milestone belongs to the reign of the legitimate emperor, Marcus Aurelius Claudius II Gothicus (268–70). At the time, Britain was under the control of the Gallic Empire, then ruled by Victorinus.

Road maps and milestones

A Roman road map, known as the Peutinger Table, survived into the Middle Ages. Itineraries were also compiled that listed settlements along a road in a schematic way. The Antonine Itinerary consists of 225 routes throughout the Roman Empire, several of which are set in Britain. These route maps made it possible to proceed along a road, guided by milestones [86], which carried details of distance to a destination.

Milestones were probably mass-produced with imperial titles, with local information painted on once they were installed. Most extant examples belong to the third and early fourth centuries. In some places, milestones were renewed fairly rapidly after a regime change, whereas in others this did not occur. Trajan Decius (249–51), for example, is recorded on nine milestones, three of which are from Aldborough (Yorkshire). The obscure and short-lived regime of Florianus (276) is commemorated on four milestones, two of which come from near Castleford (West Yorkshire). The best-represented period is 305–37, during which 18 record Constantine I, probably because milestones were not renewed after this time.

Some milestones are from very remote areas, and are important evidence for the reach of Roman authority. Five are known from Cornwall, yet little evidence for roads or other Roman settlement in the area exists.

Roman roads?

Watling Street (Kent) and Ermine Street (Lincolnshire) both appear to be characteristically 'straight' Roman roads connecting settlements. But along both roads most settlements had pre-Roman origins, and this was often the case elsewhere in Britain. Most of the major routes must have been well established before 43, even if their alignments were adjusted and their surfaces widened and metalled [87].

The impact of Roman roads

The road system had a dramatic effect on some settlements, Water Newton being probably the best example. Never a formal town, it owed its growth almost entirely to

87. Aerial view of the Fosse Way.
This major road ran from Exeter (*Isca Dumnoniorum*) northeast past Bath (*Aquae Sulis*), Cirencester (*Corinium Dobunnorum*) and Leicester (*Ratae Coritanorum*), to Lincoln (*Lindum*). It intersected Watling Street at High Cross (*Venonis*), in Warwickshire.

its prime location on the main road north. Major and minor settlements now benefited from the flow of passing trade. Shrines and hostelries offered accommodation, sustenance and spiritual reassurance to soldiers, pilgrims and itinerant traders.

Roads were an exacting and expensive necessity. Although it is usually said that the costs of road transport were ruinous compared to water transport, it seems plain enough that people made do with roads, even if they were sometimes difficult. Sometime before 191, Titus Irdas, serving on the governor's bodyguard, set up an altar on Dere Street, at Catterick (Yorkshire), to give thanks to the god 'who devised roads and paths'.[24]

The roads of Roman Britain were not just used by soldiers and officials. They provided countless tinkers and traders with the means to wend their way around the province, offering the local population the opportunity to buy manufactured goods and services on their doorsteps.

BUILDING ROMAN ROADS

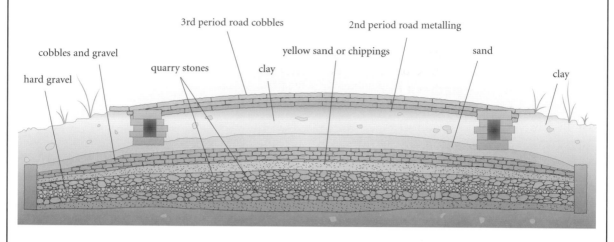

3rd period road cobbles

2nd period road metalling

cobbles and gravel

yellow sand or chippings

sand

quarry stones

clay

clay

hard gravel

clay

88. Layers of Roman roads.
Major Roman roads were built from a sequence of layers that created a solid and durable surface, cambered to allow drainage on either side. Roads were regularly resurfaced throughout the period.

Military surveyors and architects set out road alignments, while the soldiers, together with requisitioned local labour, followed on to build foundations, lay surfaces, and dig flanking ditches. Roads were curved in section to help drainage. The foundations and metalling created a substantial raised surface, known as an *agger* [88]. Rivers were crossed with fords, bridges, or ferries.

Exactly what Agricola did to correct this is not clear. Either the Britons no longer had to travel miles to do this, or they were able to pay with their own grain rather than having to buy it [89]. Such taxes were unavoidable obligations unless the emperor saw fit to grant a community or province exemption, as Nero did in Greece in 66–67. Since payment was unavoidable, it was not unknown for a population to find itself ruined by having to borrow from moneylenders at astronomical interest rates. Tax dues may have lain behind Seneca's loan, and the resentment at its recall in the lead-up to the Boudican revolt.[25] It was a destabilizing state of affairs, since the provincial administration was caught between a resentful population and pressure from lenders to enforce recovery of the debts.

The most important indirect taxes were customs, imposed on goods transiting from one district to another, or sales taxes on transactions like the sale of a slave. They were collected by independent *conductores*, whose fee was a percentage of the takings. By the late second century, *conductores* had mostly been replaced with salaried procurators on the imperial staff. On the evidence from other provinces, it is likely to have been a fixed sum for each commodity. At Zaraï, in Africa, an inscription from the year 202 at an internal customs station recorded the fixed amounts levied on commodities passing through. A typical sum was one-and-a-half *denarii*, imposed on slaves, horses and mules, while a half-*denarius* (2 *sestertii*) was payable for lambs, hides and skins.[26]

The assessment of property and population for tax was made possible by having a census. Two censors are known from Britain. In Colchester, Gnaeus Munatius Aurelius Bassus was censor of the Roman citizens in the colony, probably in the late second or early third century. Somewhere in the remote military northwest of Britain, most likely in southwest Scotland, a man of unknown name served as 'censor of the Anavionensian Britons', probably in the early second century.[27] The tribal region is unknown, but since it was probably fairly obscure, it only emphasizes the fact that all of Britain must have been drawn into the administrative net of provincial government. Like the sporadic appearances of documents, the 'censor of the Anavionensian Britons' must have been representative of numerous other officials maintaining records of population and property on the fringes of the Empire.

Taxation became more onerous under the Tetrarchy. The government had no opportunity to harvest wealth through conquest, but its obligations to defend the frontiers had become much greater. State officials

89. Baginton (Warwickshire). Modern reconstruction of one of the mid-first-century timber granaries at the Lunt fort.

ROMAN LONDON

London is undoubtedly Roman Britain's greatest legacy. At 138 ha (330 acres), it was the largest city in the province, and served as the centrepiece for a system of communication that has shaped the face of modern Britain. London is today exactly what it was in the beginning: an international commercial metropolis. Ironically, the intensive occupation of London since antiquity means that more Roman material has been found here than at any other Romano-British town. Bombing in World War II and the subsequent redevelopment has led to an almost unending sequence of major excavations and discoveries.

Until the conquest in 43, the Thames served largely as a tribal boundary. There is no trace of any significant prehistoric settlement in the London area. After the conquest, the Thames became the most important route into the heart of Britain. By the year 50 a bridge had been built, close to the present site of London Bridge. It was a decisive moment. London's name provides us with no clues as to its origins. But by the time of the Boudican revolt, *Londinium* was a well-known and prosperous trading centre that had developed of its own accord. Yet the city was important enough to make it one of the three key urban targets for the rebellious Britons. It seems that the combination of a vast increase in military commercial traffic under Roman occupation, together with the bridge and roads made London's development into a significant town inevitable. The most likely scenario is that Roman entrepreneurs, servicing the influx of soldiers and administrators, took advantage of the facilities and settled there. Confident and complacent, none of them took the trouble to install fortifications. During the rebellion, London was torched and any remaining inhabitants massacred. The aftermath was equally dramatic, as London was transformed from a frontier-trading town into the capital of Roman Britain, with all the features necessary to make it a major administrative, social and economic centre.

90. Reconstruction view of Roman London.
London in the mid-second century. The Hadrianic forum-basilica was one of the biggest buildings in *Britannia*, and London the largest settlement.

Temporary fortifications were erected and London was rebuilt. The new procurator of the province, Gaius Julius Alpinus Classicianus, was based in London instead of at Colchester. His tombstone has survived, reused in a bastion added to the walls in the late fourth century (see p. 40). His presence marks the time when London emerged as the pre-eminent town in Roman Britain, and we can safely assume that the governor was also based there. A massive building on the site of the present-day Cannon Street station has been tentatively identified as the governor's palace. The fort in the northwest part of the city housed his garrison, and was certainly in existence by the early second century. Its associated amphitheatre had been built by the year 70. The many tiles stamped 'PPBRLON' (see p. 88) show that

the Roman government was behind a number of the major public buildings. The city may have been classed as a colony or a *municipium*, but ironically no inscription has ever been found that specifies its formal legal status.

A crucial part of the reconstruction was the installation of public buildings. London received a modest forum and basilica by 85 at the latest. They were soon replaced by a far bigger version on the same site, with a cathedral-sized basilica begun under Hadrian (117–38), and from which the well-known bronze bust of the emperor (see p. 143) may have come. Public baths on Huggin Hill were begun around the same time as the first forum, but there were several other, earlier baths.

Around these great structures houses and shops proliferated, jockeying for position and street

frontage. Excavations at No. 1 Poultry have produced evidence for a series of tightly-packed wooden buildings along the street, and this seems to have been typical of much of Roman London in the first and second centuries.

During this time the quantity of evidence for commercial activity exceeds any other known settlement in the province. Substantial timber wharfs were being built as early as the year 62, and vast quantities of imported goods started to arrive, including glass, Gaulish samian ware and Italian amphorae. London also became home to artisans and

91. Plan of Roman London.
London's modern streets bear little relation to known Roman streets shown on the plan, though the third-century walls (which incorporated the earlier fort) provided the foundations for the medieval walls.

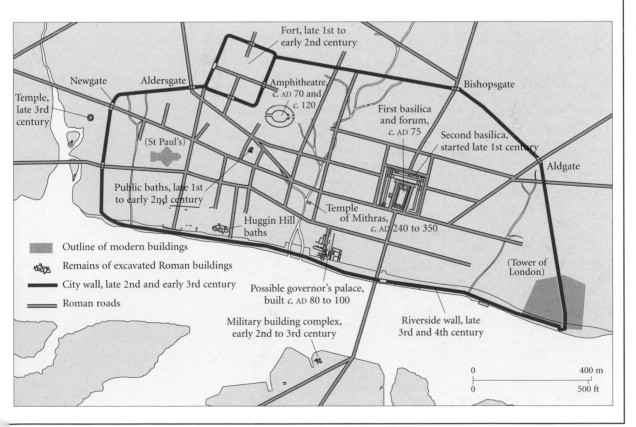

manufacturers of all types, including potters, metalworkers and jewellers.

London's population is known to us from tombstones and graffiti. Its military population, serving on the governor's bodyguard or acting in some other official capacity (such as policing), is as usual more conspicuous than any other group of people. Ulpius Silvanus, a

veteran of the II legion and devotee of Mithraism, is recorded on the marble relief he donated to London's *mithraeum* (see p. 249). Silvanus had enlisted at Orange in Gaul, but London's inhabitants included people from even further afield. Aulus Alfidius Olussa, who died in London at the age of 70, had been born in Athens. Tulla Numidia's tombstone was

93. The Governor's Fort.
Reconstruction of the fort at London, possibly built as part of improvements at the time of Hadrian's visit. The fort housed the garrison of the governor, including detachments from units stationed across Britain.

incomplete when found, but her name suggests that she or her father originated in North Africa.

Religion is another indicator of how closely this early London resembled its modern counterpart. Open only to men and emphasizing the importance of valour and physical resilience, Mithraism was popular amongst soldiers and traders. Its adherents carried the cult around the Empire, as did the

92. Borough High Street (London).
An oil-lamp in the shape of a human foot, found during the digging of the Jubilee Line extension. The wick was placed in the hole in the big toe, and oil would have been poured through the hole in the ankle. Mid-second century.

c. 125–30, London was rebuilt, but the boom had passed. Commerce began slowly to decline over the next hundred years. As with most towns in Roman Britain, a circuit of stone walls was built in the third century, but we have no idea whether this was to meet a specific threat, to control movement, or to simply be a statement of power. The new walls were later reinforced with riverside fortifications. In 286, London became the capital of the independent breakaway regime ruled by Carausius (286–93). Carausius struck the first coins in London, a process continued by his murderer and successor, Allectus (293–96). The female personification of London first appeared on the gold medal struck for Constantius Chlorus (293–306), to commemorate his recovery of the city for the Empire (see p. 71).

The city's latter years were very different. The forum and basilica had been demolished by *c.* 300, and other public buildings were in various states of disuse. The riverside fortifications had a devastating impact on commerce. The cramped commercial quarters of the first and second centuries had been replaced by more widely-spaced housing. Nevertheless, investment in the defences continued, with bastions being added to the walls after 350. London seems to have faded quietly in the way of most of Roman Britain's towns, as the economy that supported them ceased to exist. In the fifth century, settlement seems to have shifted temporarily west to the area now known as Aldwych, but by the tenth and eleventh centuries London was once again a thriving city.

followers of the Egyptian goddess, Isis. Two inscriptions, a first-century *graffito* on a flagon and a third-century altar, record a temple of Isis in London. Such exotic cults sat easily alongside more mainstream religious pursuits. Tiberinius Celerianus, probably a merchant shipper, made his dedication to Mars Camulos and the Imperial Spirits at a temple precinct in Southwark (see p. 176).

London's later history was just as dramatic as its beginning. After substantial damage sustained by fire

94. Monument Street (London).
Tile and stone culvert used to drain water from the city out to the Thames.

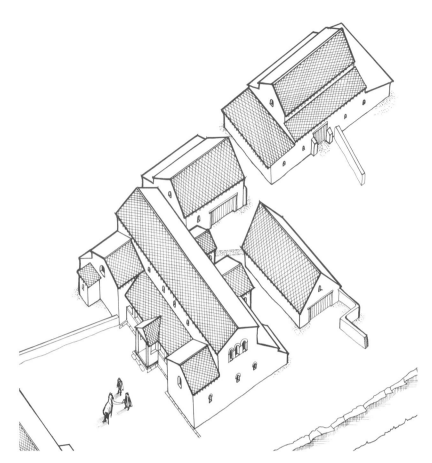

95. Cirencester (Gloucestershire).
This late fourth-century farm at Cirencester (*Corinium Dobunnorum*) was built within the town walls on a virgin plot. Like any such establishment in the late Roman world, its estate, manpower and produce would have been subjected to taxes and tribute based on standard units of measurement.

multiplied as bureaucracy became more cumbersome. Britain's taxes were now handled by a *praepositus*, and submitted to the receiver of revenues, or *rationalis*. The problems with endemic inflation had led to taxation being more commonly paid in kind, as food and resources were often more useful than cash. Land was divided into 0.26-ha (0.64-acre) units, or *iugera*. Each *iugerum* was assessed for its productiveness. The more productive it was, the higher its taxable value. The population was counted. Then the state assessed its needs and set the tax rate payable per head and per agricultural productivity unit. Throughout the fourth century this continually increased, unlike earlier taxation, which had been fixed [95]. The system was unfair and rife with corruption. The main beneficiaries were the local officials drawn from the landowning members of town councils.

CHAPTER 5

MILITARY INSTALLATIONS

The army had a monumental impact on the character of Roman Britain, and was responsible more than anything else for those defining characteristics of Romanization. Its remnants dominate the archaeological record. The army was not a faceless mechanism made up of disciplined and programmed androids executing imperial military strategy. It was also not an exclusively military organization in the way we understand it. Evidence from around the Roman Empire, especially Egypt, shows that soldiers were often behind public buildings and engineering projects. They acted as administrators and policemen, tax-collectors, manufacturers and labourers, and even trapped wild animals for the circus. In other words, soldiers did more or less whatever was required of them by the state.

Units in the Roman army, legions and auxiliary regiments alike, were proud of their identities and loyalties to their respective commanders, and jealously maintained traditions of titles and ethnicity. Those identities were cumulative products of each unit's individual history, and stretched back in some cases over several centuries. The XIV legion left Britain by around the year 70, but for the rest of its existence it basked in the titles *Martia Victrix*, won for suppressing the Boudican revolt. In the same manner, the RAF's No. 617 Squadron is known to this day as the 'Dambusters' after its exploits in May 1943, and will be for as long as it exists.

The identity of a regiment, with its standards and battle honours, provided a solid psychological and social foundation [96]. Where it had been based and for how long, from where its numbers had originally been recruited, and what its duties had been, all helped to create a unique combination of military traditions and external influences. A unit that had been based for generations on a Hadrian's Wall fort, for example, had over the years abundant opportunity to interact with the local population, affecting customs and language. A unit that had arrived in Britain after a period based somewhere else on the imperial frontiers brought its own ethnic traditions, absorbed from where it had been based, and perhaps soldiers born to women there.

96. An auxiliary cavalryman. A modern re-enactor poses as a second-century auxiliary cavalryman near the earth-and-timber Antonine fort at Drumlanrig (Dumfries and Galloway).

The army in Britain has been afforded much attention in traditional Roman archaeological and historical literature because of its visibility in the record. This is so crucial that its effects cannot be overestimated. Inscriptions provide us with more evidence than anything else for religious activities, individuals and families. In Britain, almost half of all surviving inscriptions come from the Hadrian's Wall area, and most of these are explicitly attributable either to a military unit, or to individual soldiers [97]. The rest are usually attributable to probable soldiers or their immediate civilian associates. Most of Britain's other inscriptions belong to the military zone. Even in the so-called 'civilian' towns of southern Britain, a grossly disproportionate quantity of the few extant inscriptions can be attributed either to soldiers from the military phase of the settlement's existence, or to later soldiers in transit or on other duties. In other words, soldiers were far more likely to commission inscriptions, whether commemorative unit inscriptions, individual religious dedications, or tombstones. This raises the important question of how much soldiers were responsible for other examples of Romanization, such as the use of coinage or building of accomplished architecture, even where we cannot prove their involvement.

Since archaeologists necessarily use surviving physical evidence to understand and assess each community, this visible and tangible bias to the military raises all sorts of peculiar problems. The apparently higher levels of literacy amongst soldiers, testified in Egypt where documents survive much better than anywhere else, correspond with Britain's epigraphic record.[1] In a remote province, where literacy scarcely existed before the Roman invasion, the Roman military may not only have been the principal engine behind Romanization in all its forms, but may have remained so throughout much of the period.

ORGANIZATION OF THE ARMY

Until the end of the third century, the army was based around the legions and their attendant auxiliary troops. Despite the importance of the army, our understanding of how it was organized depends on making sense of a large number of incomplete pieces of evidence. Writing in about the year 23, Tacitus listed 27 legions dispersed around the Roman Empire.[2] They were allocated according to strategic and tactical needs. As a result, the Rhine, one of the most dangerous frontiers, had eight legions, nearly a third of the total at the time. From what we know of other legions at different times, the number seems to have hovered at around 30 for most of the rest of the next two centuries [99].[3]

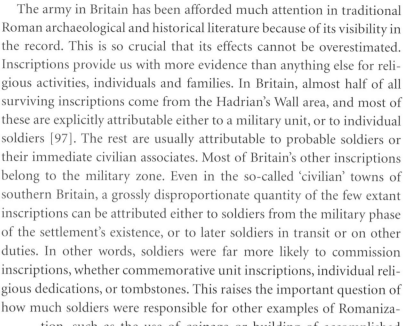

97. Vindolanda (Northumberland).
Altar dedicated to Jupiter Optimus Maximus by Quintus Petronius Urbicus, commander of the Fourth Cohort of Gauls. Early third century.

98. The Roman military in Britain.
The principal military installations of Roman Britain, not all of which were occupied at the same time. The map also shows the main civilian settlements and mineral sources.

Map legend:
Permanent legionary fortress ■
Temporary legionary fortress □
Fort ■
Fleet-controlled iron extraction ✕
Colony ◉
Civitas capital ●
Small town ○

Map labels: Inchtuthil, ANTONINE WALL, Newstead, HADRIAN'S WALL, South Shields, Corbridge, Carlisle, York, Caerhun, Manchester, Lincoln, Caistor-by-Yarmouth, Chester, Caernarvon, Wroxeter, Caistor-by-Norwich, Dolaucothi, Castell Collen, Colchester, Carmarthen, Caerwent, St Albans, Chelmsford, Usk, Gloucester, Caerleon, London, Cirencester, Neath, Canterbury, Cardiff, Silchester, Dover, Bath, Ilchester, Pevensey, Exeter, Chichester, Dorchester

99. Caerleon (Monmouthshire).
Tombstone of Gaius Valerius Victor, a legionary with *II Augusta*, who died at 45 years of age after 17 years' service. He came from Lyons (*Lugdunum*) in Gaul. Gaul, Spain and Italy were the most common sources of legionaries stationed in Britain. Probably late first century. (British Museum).

The Legions

Vegetius attributed Roman military success to the brilliance of legionary organization.[4] The legion was commanded by the *legatus legionis*, a man of senatorial status who was literally the 'delegate' of the emperor. The second-in-command was the senior tribune (of the six allocated to the legion), and like his commander was of senatorial rank. Such a man might proceed to his own legionary command, and indeed this was the course followed by Agricola. The other five tribunes were of equestrian rank, and might have been promoted to the position of senior tribune after commanding an auxiliary unit, or serving in a civilian administrative post. For these five, a career as a procurator, or further auxiliary commands, might follow. The *praefectus castrorum*, 'prefect of the camp', was third-in-command. His duties were varied, and ranged from being sent off with a party of troops on fort-building detail, or looking after tools used for carpentry.[5] During the Boudican revolt, the legate and senior tribune of *II Augusta* appear to have been absent, and the *praefectus castrorum*, Poenius Postumus, was left in charge.[6]

Legionaries were Roman citizens. The basic unit was the *centuria*, or 'century', meaning literally '100', but the term was used loosely. On campaign each century had eight tent parties (*contubernia*), with eight men per tent. This makes 64 soldiers, with another 16 men on guard, giving a total of 80 men per century.[7] In a legionary fortress, all of the troops had accommodation. Each barrack block had ten pairs of rooms, one for each *contubernium* [100]. The same arrangement was usually found in auxiliary infantry forts. Each century had a centurion, together with his assistant, the *optio* ('a helper freely chosen').[8] The century also had its own *tesserarius*, who organized the daily comings and goings of troops in the century, and the *custos armorum*, who took care of its equipment.

The centuries were organized into cohorts. The barracks at the Flavian fortress of Inchtuthil show that nine of the ten cohorts had six centuries, while the tenth had five double-centuries, confirmed on an inscription from Lambaesis, in North Africa, that names five *optiones* in the first cohort.[9] Therefore, nine cohorts consisted of 480 men each (4,320 plus 108 centurions and *optiones*), and one had 800 men (plus ten centurions and *optiones*). The latter was called a *milliaria*, derived from the word for 'thousand' and which was just as nominal a term as 'century'. This provides us with a total of 5,120 plus 128 centurions and *optiones*. The doubling of the centuries in the first cohort seems only to have taken place by the late first century. In the fourth century, Vegetius describes the battle order that started with the first cohort to the right, then the second, and so on to the fifth. The sixth cohort had the most recent recruits, and they fought behind the second cohort. The centurion of the first century in the first cohort was known as *primus pilus*,

and was the legion's pre-eminent centurion.[10] By the late first century BC, the legion had only 120 cavalry, and this remained the case.[11]

So the legion in the late first century AD had around 5,368 men, with an additional number of officers and others (such as doctors), collectively making up a total of around 5,500 men. It is obvious from inscriptions and other references that the actual number on any day varied, due to men on detachment to the governor's guard, sickness, unfilled vacancies and casualties.[12] Moreover, legions were continually being divided into vexillations, or wings. Like almost every administrative unit in human history, the complete legion was usually just a theory.

The Auxiliaries

In his description of the army in AD 23, Tacitus says that the auxiliaries were made up of infantry and cavalry. He added that their total was similar to that of the legions, but that their numbers varied continuously as required, and therefore he could not list them. According to Vegetius, auxiliaries were hired for their range of regional fighting techniques and skills, made vastly more useful to the Romans through discipline and their coordinated use within the Roman army.[13] Auxiliaries were not

100. Caerleon (Monmouthshire). Legionary barrack blocks at Caerleon (*Isca*) in the northwest corner of the province.

Roman citizens, unless a display of special valour had been followed by a grant of status from the emperor.[14] Individual auxiliaries who were honourably discharged after 25 years' service (usually more in practice) were granted citizenship on retirement.

Josephus, referring to the Jewish War in Palestine in the late 60s, provides numbers.[15] The V, X and XV legions had 18 cohorts of auxiliaries attached to them, with an additional five cohorts and six cavalry auxiliary units brought in for the campaign. Ten of the 23 cohorts were '1,000-strong', and the remainder were '600-strong with 120 cavalry'. The numbers were nominal.

Auxiliaries were commanded by equestrians. The cavalry units and infantry cohorts were commanded by a *praefectus*, but the *cohors milliaria peditata* was commanded by a tribune. The *ala milliaria* commander outranked other auxiliary commanders. Centurions and *optiones* commanded individual centuries, and in the cavalry units a *decurion* commanded each *turma*, assisted by a *duplicarius* and *sesquiplicarius*, titles that merely mean 'double pay' and 'one-and-a-half times pay', respectively.

Other auxiliary troops are normally described as 'irregular' because they were hired on an ad-hoc basis in frontier areas, and did not enjoy integrated status. These men were not awarded with citizenship on discharge. Formed into loosely organized cavalry (*cuneus*, meaning 'wedge') and infantry (*numerus*) units, each had its own arrangements. They fought alongside mainstream auxiliaries, and served in a variety of capacities, such as the *numerus Exploratorum Bremeniensium* at High Rochester in the early 240s.[16]

Tacitus says that 'allied provinces' contributed ships (*triremes*), as well as the other auxiliaries.[17] For obvious reasons, once Roman power extended along the English Channel and around the Gaulish coastline, a fleet became a permanent necessity. The *classis Britannica* is known from its fort at Dover, recorded on roof-tiles stamped 'CL.BR'. It also seems to have been involved with iron-working in southeastern England, for example at Beauport Park (Sussex), where similar tiles have been found. On Hadrian's Wall at Benwell, a fleet vexillation built the granary under Hadrian, *c.* 122–24.[18] The fleet was commanded by a prefect who had already commanded land forces. Marcus Maenius Agrippa commanded the British fleet during the years *c.* 130–34, having previously commanded the First Cohort of Spaniards at Maryport (Northumberland).[19] None of its ships have survived in any form.

THE ARMY IN BRITAIN, FIRST TO THIRD CENTURIES

The Legions

Roman historians rarely make references to specific legions, and even less frequently to specific auxiliaries. Only inscriptions can fill in the gaps. However, a tombstone of a soldier who was in a legion does not necessarily mean that his unit was present. Even when an inscription was made in the name of the unit, the whole legion or auxiliary cohort may not have been there at the time. Tracking movements of military units depends on accumulating data, but any sort of definitive account is beyond our reach.

The legionary garrison of Britain from 43 and throughout most of the first century consisted of four legions. Of these, *II Augusta*, *IX Hispana* and *XX Valeria Victrix* were a constant feature [101]. By the end of the first century, they were stationed at Caerleon, York and Chester, respectively. The fourth legion was initially *XIV Gemina Martia Victrix*, but it had left by 70 to be replaced with *II Adiutrix Pia Fidelis*, which started out at Lincoln before going west to Chester, until XX was pulled back from the north. *II Adiutrix* was withdrawn before 89, leaving Britain with three legions. The only further permanent change was the arrival of *VI Victrix* around 122 to replace *IX Hispana*, last heard of at York by 108. The IX legion then vanishes from the record, apart from a single possible appearance in Holland. From the time of the invasion, the army was reinforced as and when required by vexillations from other legions, such as VIII and XXII. The garrison of Britain also contributed vexillations to Continental campaigns, such as those of Gallienus (253–68). Only II and

101. Benwell (Northumberland). Building stone installed by *II Augusta*, naming the unit and showing its mascots of a capricorn and winged horse, demonstrating that the legion had built at least part of this Hadrian's Wall fort. About 122 30. (British Museum).

VI are mentioned in the *Notitia Dignitatum* for the fourth century; XX is omitted either by accident or because by then it had ceased to exist. The *Notitia* places II at Richborough, a place far too small to accommodate it at its original strength. Presumably it was now seriously reduced in size as part of the military reorganization of the fourth century.

Individual legionaries were detached to an unlimited variety of duties in civilian contexts. The most conspicuous in Britain was the governor's guard, but soldiers were also detached to serve the legionary legate or one of his tribunes. Centurions also served in various capacities, both

THE LEGIONS

With four legions in the first century AD, Britain was one of the most heavily garrisoned provinces in the Roman Empire. From *c.* 70 the number was reduced to three.

The original legions in Britain
II Augusta: Last attested in *Notitia Dignitatum* in the fourth century. Permanent base: Caerleon.
IX Hispana: At York until at least 107–8. Fate unknown.

XIV Gemina Martia Victrix: Until 70.
XX Valeria Victrix: Until at least the late third century. Fate unknown. Permanent base: Chester.

The replacements
II Adiutrix Pia Fidelis replaces XIV from *c.* 70 to *c.* 86, then leaves for Dacia.
VI Victrix arrives with Aulus Platorius Nepos, *c.* 122. Last attested in *Notitia Dignitatum*. Permanent base: York.

Vexillations from abroad
VII Gemina: Vexillation under Hadrian.
VIII Augusta: Vexillations in the invasion force, and under Hadrian and Antoninus Pius.
XXII Primigenia: Vexillations in Britain under Hadrian, Antoninus Pius, and Caracalla.

102. Legionaries in the Roman army.
A group of modern re-enactors dressed as legionaries. The soldier in the centre is a centurion. The armour and weapons are based on excavated examples or sculptures, though on a day-to-day basis Roman soldiers were probably much shabbier in appearance.

military and civilian. When Hadrian addressed *III Augusta* in 128 in North Africa, he specifically referred to the fact that 'many widely scattered posts separate you'.[20] Marcus Censorius Cornelianus was a centurion with *X Fretensis*, a legion that so far as we know was never stationed in Britain, but at some point he commanded the First Cohort of Spaniards at Maryport.[21] Normally an equestrian tribune would have commanded the cohort, so Censorius may have been installed as a stopgap leader. As his legion was stationed in Judaea, his career shows just how far individual troops could be dispersed across the Roman world.

Vexillations and detachments

Legions were perpetually being split into vexillations and dispersed as and when required. Vexillations were sent to Britain during the invasion, and during later warfare to reinforce the resident garrison. Detachments were not necessarily organized purely for war. Large components of II, VI and XX took part in building both Hadrian's Wall and the Antonine Wall. Individual soldiers, especially centurions, were liable to be detached for special duties, including commanding an auxiliary unit, serving on the governor's staff, or administering local civil police responsibilities.

The British legions contributed vexillations to Continental campaigns. An inscription from the Tyne of *c.* 158 [103] records vexillations of the II, VI and XX legions either arriving from, or being sent to, the two German provinces as reinforcements.

A bronze roundel depicting and naming vexillations of *II Augusta* and *XX Valeria* Victrix probably refers to the time they were used under Gallienus (253–68), an event testified on an inscription from Central Europe.

Tracking legions

Although Tacitus provides some information about legions, most of what we know comes from inscriptions. But these need to be interpreted with care. Since soldiers were detached as individuals and in vexillations, the location of a tombstone does not indicate the location of a soldier's unit. To be certain we need several tombstones,

or preferably an inscription made in the name of a legion.

Legions in the fourth century

In later years, the legions became a shadow of their former selves. The *Notitia Dignitatum* places *II Augusta* at Richborough, a far smaller site than the old legionary base at Caerleon. *VI Victrix* still seems to have been at York, but the XX legion is unmentioned. By this time the army had been reorganized into smaller mobile units of cavalry and static frontier garrisons. Our knowledge is severely limited by the fact that no military inscriptions were produced after the end of the third century.

103. Newcastle (Northumberland).
Inscription from *Pons Aelius* dated to *c.* 158 under the governor, Julius Verus. Note the error at the end of line four, where the sculptor omitted the word 'LEG' and was forced to created a compressed abbreviation.

The Auxiliaries

Since far more auxiliary units were involved in garrisoning Britain, and their movements and nature far more variable, it is impossible to be sure how many were involved. One estimate, based on Britain's inscriptions and forts, is that the number of auxiliaries may have been around double the maximum number of 20,000-odd legionaries when there were four legions.[22] Inscriptions make it clear that, for example, while the legions built the Walls, it was auxiliary units that provided most of the permanent garrison along the frontiers [104].

The First *ala* of Thracian cavalry illustrates the problem. An inscription on a tombstone from Colchester names a trooper called Longinus [105]. Since we can reasonably attribute the XX legion to Colchester, a legionary fortress between 43–49, this unit was probably attached to XX. The tombstone of another trooper, Sextus Valerius Genialis (see p. 214), from Cirencester, belongs roughly to the middle of the first century, a time when the legion may have been nearby at Kingsholm, near Gloucester.[23] However, a bronze skillet from Caerleon, the base of *II Augusta*, is stamped for the *ala*.[24] The three inscriptions could easily be interpreted as evidence that the First Thracian cavalry wing was stationed with XX at Colchester, before being installed in an auxiliary fort at Cirencester, and then subsequently based at Caerleon with *II Augusta*.

It is impossible to be certain about any of this, even though it fits with the picture painted by Tacitus and Josephus. All we have available to us is a very general perception of how auxiliaries were used. The unit of 'Celts'

104. *Below.* **Rome (Italy).** Section of relief from Trajan's Column depicting auxiliary soldiers of the early second century on campaign. Auxiliaries did most of the campaigning and fighting in the Roman army.

105. *Opposite.* **Colchester (Essex).** Tombstone of the auxiliary cavalryman, Longinus, who served in a Thracian regiment, and probably served in the invasion force of 43. Probably erected *c.* 43–49. (Colchester Museums).

described by Dio in the first battle of the invasion of 43 shows how auxiliaries, because they were disposable, were placed in the forefront of any fighting. Ostorius Scapula, governor from 47–51, used auxiliaries against an insurrection of the Iceni.[25] The battle against Boudica seems to have been a more actively cooperative effort. Legionaries with auxiliary cavalry and infantry fought together. After the war was over, all were correspondingly reinforced.[26] At the Battle of Mons Graupius in 83 or 84, Agricola had all, or most, of the IX and XX legions with him. Tacitus says that he also had 8,000 auxiliary infantry and 3,000 auxiliary cavalry who formed the main battle line, while the legionaries were placed in reserve.[27] This is very useful information. Not only do we have approximately 11,000 legionaries alongside a corresponding 11,000 auxiliaries, but the auxiliaries were the only soldiers in the front line of the battle. The auxiliary cavalry proved decisive at the height of the engagement, and it was never necessary to order the legionaries to take part.

By the time of the Vindolanda writing tablets in the 90s, auxiliary units were dispersed along the straggling line we know as the Stanegate. The Vindolandan strength report shows that the First Cohort of Tungrians were doing more than simply filling out their time at a fort. Forty-six soldiers had been allocated to the governor's staff, and were serving in the office of Julius Ferox, probably the legate commanding *IX Hispana* at York. A few others were at Corbridge and London. Since this is a single instance of the garrison at a single auxiliary fort, we need to be careful. But it is all we have, and it helps to make sense of why some forts have inscriptions from several different units. Once this was thought to represent different garrisons at different times. Even if a fort had a nominal main garrison, on any one day it might be accommodating sections from different units. The arrangements were in constant flux.[28]

The pattern of evidence recording the auxiliary forces in Britain is unbalanced. In the first century, we have almost nothing except references by historians, such as Tacitus, who never specify the full name of the unit. A few contemporary inscriptions, such as a letter from Carlisle, survive, but in general the period for the years 43 to 103 is a blank. For the second century, one of our principal sources is the 'diploma', a tabular record of auxiliary veterans discharged on a specific day. Some soldiers invested in engraved bronze copies of the official record, and it is these that sometimes survive, though they are rarely complete. One of the better preserved was found at Malpas (Cheshire) in 1812, and was dated 19 January 103 in the reign of Trajan.[29] It only records units from which veterans had been discharged, rather than a full list of units, but it does say that the units named were 'stationed in Britain under [the governor] Lucius Neratius Marcellus'. So on that day the auxiliary garrison of Britain included the units listed on the diploma, which were four cavalry wings and a mixture of infantry cohorts. There are several other diplomas known from Britain throughout the second century, and while they provide invaluable information, the one thing they do not do is tell us is where the units were stationed.

The only means of knowing where auxiliary units were based is when inscriptions naming the units turn up at forts, preferably in some quantity and with datable information on them.[30] The *ala Gallorum Sebosiana* illustrates the problem. In around 78–84, the unit was mentioned by one of its number, then attached to the staff of the governor Agricola, on a writing tablet found at Carlisle.[31] Several diplomas, including the Malpas diploma, refer to its continued presence in Britain up to 178. Just one inscription thereafter places the unit at Lancaster in 262–66, during the reign of the Gallic emperor, Postumus.[32] Another inscription from Bollihope Common (Durham) records that the unit's commanding officer was on a hunting trip, while lead seals suggest activity at Lancaster and Brough-under-Stainmore.[33] None of the seals are dated, but we know that creating such inscriptions was particularly popular in the first half of the third century. That is the best we can do. This cavalry wing of Gauls evidently was at Lancaster in the third quarter of the third century, but there is no reason to assume it had always been there.

At the Hadrian's Wall fort of Birdoswald, numerous inscriptions name *cohors I Aelia Dacorum milliaria*, the '1,000-strong First Cohort of Aelian Dacians'. Several carry enough information to date them to the third century. Between 235 and 238, for example, the tribune Flavius Maximian commanded the unit at Birdoswald.[34] For the second century, all we have are three diplomas showing that it was in Britain in 127, 145–46, and 158, but nothing to place it at Birdoswald. One more inscription, again undated, seems to suggest that the unit contributed to digging out the Vallum.[35] Since this can be reasonably dated to the mid-120s, it seems plain enough that the Aelian Dacians spent most of the second and third centuries on Hadrian's Wall, and that their base was probably Birdoswald throughout most of that time.[36] In direct contrast to this we have *cohors I Alpinorum*, which was recorded in Britain in 103 on the Malpas diploma, but for which there is no other reference. We thus have absolutely no idea where it was based, or how long it spent in Britain.

FORTS AND FORTRESSES

Forts and fortresses still provide the most conspicuous structural remnants of Roman Britain. This is partly due to the sheer scale of the remains, especially in the north. Even in the south, the coastal forts like Pevensey and Portchester have survived in far more dramatic form than the villas and towns. But in the north, stone was more readily available, and the remoteness of these areas made them less susceptible to robbing.

THE AUXILIA

There were dozens of different auxiliary units based in Britain at any one time [106]. They were made up of cavalry, infantry and mixed units, and campaigned and were garrisoned with the legions. Roman historians such as Tacitus and Dio said that it was impossible to say how many units there were at any given time because they were always changing. However, most of the forts of Roman Britain were used by auxiliaries. Our knowledge of how the individual units were made up has been compiled from many different sources.

Infantry units

An infantry auxiliary unit was known as a *cohors milliaria peditata* ('1,000-strong cohort of foot'), but this was a nominal term. The strength report of the milliary First Cohort of Tungrians from Vindolanda states that on 18 May in an unspecified year, *c.* 90–100, the unit numbered '752 including six centurions'.[37] That this number included the sick and those on detachment elsewhere shows that the cohort was technically under strength. In theory, this nominal strength of 800 is reflected in the forts that accommodated milliary units. In practice, many auxiliary forts defy attempts to make sense of the accommodation provided, since barracks frequently do not correspond to any known configurations of infantry centuries or cavalry *turmae*.

The 600-strong infantry units make more sense. These are the part-mounted auxiliary cohorts, which Josephus says had 120 cavalry each. That leaves 480 infantry, the same size as a conventional legionary cohort made up from six centuries of 80 men. From this we can work out that a non-mounted infantry unit of this auxiliary class, the *cohors quingenaria*, was 480-strong.

Cavalry units

An *ala quingenaria* ('500-strong cavalry wing') was divided into 16 *turmae*, squadrons or troops of cavalry.[38] Arrian tells us that the *ala quingenaria* had 512 men, or 32 men per *turma*.[39] Thirty-two is also the figure provided by Vegetius for a cavalry *turma*. An *ala milliaria* was divided into 24 *turmae*, instantly presenting a problem as this makes 768 troopers. Either this was right, or perhaps the *turma* in an *ala milliaria* was larger, or there were more of them.

106. Chesters (Northumberland). This inscription, recording the First Cohort of Dalmatians, has survived because it was reused as a step leading down to the headquarters' strongroom. The style dates it to the late second century, when *Cilurnum* was garrisoned by the Second *ala* of Asturians. The Dalmatian infantry may have been temporarily installed in the fort, or shared the accommodation at some point with the Asturians.

The developing interest in Roman antiquities in the eighteenth and nineteenth centuries led to a great deal of excavation, uncovering buildings which were often left exposed. This is particularly evident on Hadrian's Wall, where the central sector has some of the best-preserved forts in Britain, including Housesteads. Paradoxically, the much less well-preserved forts at Wallsend and South Shields have now become home to the more imaginative efforts to reconstruct Roman buildings.

Military bases absorbed a huge amount of resources, ranging from deforestation to generate massive timber stocks, to large-scale stone quarrying. According to one estimate, Caerleon is thought to have used up 150 ha (380 acres) of woodland just in being built, quite apart from the requirements of long-term maintenance. A writing tablet from the fort, dated to *c.* 75–85, refers to the organized collection of wood by troops.[40] The army was a hive of industrial activity, and remains of massive works-depots have been found, such as the mid-first-century vexillation fortress and depot at Longthorpe, near Peterborough, and the works-depot of the XX legion at Holt, near the legionary fortress at Chester. At Caerleon, large quantities of roofing and other tiles made for the II legion have been found, all stamped with the legion's titles and manufactured in the fortress's works-depot on an industrial scale.

Southern Britain was only briefly occupied by the army during the first few decades of the conquest. A variety of relatively short-lived forts and fortresses, including the legionary fortress at Colchester and the vexillation fortress at Longthorpe, were used for variable periods from the late 40s on into the 70s. By the 70s, the bulk of the army's activity was in the west and north. This was where it established its hold by building permanent bases in timber and turf, later consolidated in stone. The only known permanent forts in the south until the third century were at London, built to house the governor's garrison from as the early second century, and Dover.

Some forts were in use only for a year or two, while others were built, occupied, abandoned, reoccupied and rebuilt before being permanently given up. This particularly applies to the south in the conquest phase, where major forts rapidly gave way to towns, for example at Cirencester, and where campaign forts might be used for as little as one or two seasons before being dismantled and levelled. During the Agricolan campaigns in Scotland, many forts were built that became redundant when Roman forces were withdrawn by the late 80s. The timber fortress at Inchtuthil, and the timber auxiliary forts at Strageath, Elginhaugh and Fendoch, were amongst those carefully dismantled shortly after they had been built.

Some of these Scottish forts were rebuilt in the 90s, usually to different plans and configurations to accommodate different garrisons in different circumstances. Newstead had already had four Agricolan phases, and would go on to have two Antonine stone periods before being finally given up. The excavation of many of these bases has shown how difficult it is to be certain about the garrisons, since the numbers of barracks and arrangements almost always varies from 'textbook' plans. The excavators of the Agricolan and Antonine fort phases at Strageath struggled to make sense of what they had found, and their published discussion is a classic example of the problems faced.[41] The plans of the various timber phases at Strageath show that the basic layout survived through several phases, but also show that some of the fort's principal buildings were laid out on surprisingly irregular plans.

Even where new forts were built in stone, construction work was prone to suspension, sometimes for very long periods. This has been observed in the archaeology at Birdoswald, and also in an inscription from Netherby. Occupation was episodic in some cases, while inscriptions show (or at least claim) that major structures in the fort had been allowed to decay to the point of being ruinous before being repaired. At long-term forts, this often results in extremely complicated archaeology. Birrens, in southwest Scotland, started life as a 0.5-ha (1.3-acre) Flavian fort. It was replaced under Hadrian with a 1.7-ha (4.2-acre) fort, as an outpost for Hadrian's Wall. This version was timber, but the main central buildings were made of stone. The Hadrianic fort was demolished when the Antonine Wall was built, and replaced with a 2-ha (4.9-acre) stone fort with turf ramparts, later destroyed by fire. Birrens was rebuilt again in around 158, but the new structures were in some cases built right onto the remains of the earlier buildings.

Buildings from a fort's earliest phases were often altered over time, if not completely demolished. Structural components can turn up reused in later phases of entirely different structures. At Birdoswald, a section of stone screen, probably from the headquarters buildings, was found in one of the granaries, reused as a threshold.[42] Inscriptions usually only survive because they were reused in later building work [107]. An inscription of c. 297–305 from Birdoswald, recording repairs to the headquarters, the commandant's house and possibly the baths, had been reused as a paving slab in a late fourth-century barracks.[43] At South Shields in the fourth century, an impressive new commandant's house replaced third-century barracks.

107. High Rochester (Northumberland). This inscription, dated to 216 under Caracalla, owes its exceptional preservation to its reuse as a cover-slab. The governor for the year, probably Marcus Antonius Gordianus (see table, p. 87) was subjected to *damnatio memoriae* by the emperor and his name has been excised. The same fate awaited the emperor after his death, possibly explaining the stone's early reuse.

The Marching Camp

Marching camps were overnight bivouacs for the Roman army, and were modelled on the same principles as permanent forts. In the second century BC, Polybius provides the earliest detailed account of a marching camp, designed to accommodate two legions and around the same number of auxiliaries.[44] It was square, measuring 2,017 Roman feet (596 m, or 1,955 ft) on each side creating an area about 36 ha (89 acres) in size.[45] Once the spot for the commanding officer's tent had been chosen, the fort was laid out and was based on a regular grid with specific areas allocated for each unit, its officers and troops. The fort's borders were marked with a ditch, and a rampart made from the spoil with a stockade along the top. An internal *intervallum* created a buffer zone between the fortifications and the internal accommodation.

The idea was that when the camp was built, every man knew what his job was. The process was therefore efficient, and could be executed under duress. Internal communications and systems could be repeated nightly, regardless of whether the army had moved on or not. In the third century AD, Hyginus described a marching camp for a large army of around 40,000 men, but the basic principles remained the same, though at 33 ha (81 acres) it was obviously rather more congested.[46] Here, the fortifications included a ditch measuring 1.5 m (5 ft) wide by 0.9 m (3 ft) deep, and a rampart about 1.9 m (6 ft) high and 2.4 m (7 ft 8 in) wide. The

108. Chew Green (Northumberland). The earthworks at Chew Green close to Dere Street, the main Roman road north, are thought to start with a marching camp covering 7.7 ha (19 acres) and built *c.* 80 under Agricola to hold around 3,000 men. This camp is marked by the furthest left ditch, curving round to the foreground. More camps were laid out during later campaigns on the same site, evident from the sequence of overlying enclosures, until finally a permanent fortlet (at centre right, with the multiple ditches) was built, probably in the mid-second century, to defend this major route and to provide accommodation for passing frontier soldiers and officials.

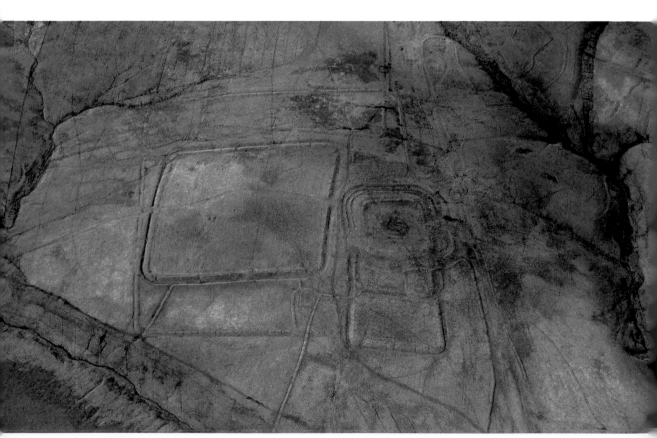

ditches were of two types: the *fossa fastigata*, which was V-shaped, and the *fossa Punica*, which had a steep outer slope and gentle inner slope. Some ditches had square-cut trenches along the bottom, now believed to have been caused by using shovels to clear silt from the bottom of the trenches. Special arrangements were used at fort gateways. The ditch and rampart could curve in or out from the fort to cover an entrance (*clavicula*), a type mainly first century in date, or there could be a small section built outside the fort entrance (*titulum*), a type used from the first to the early third centuries.

Only the defences of a marching camp leave traces, but these are normally only detectable from the air as the army levelled the defences when it moved on [108]. Dozens of camps are now known, with new ones being discovered almost annually. There were endless variations in dimensions and shapes of the defences. The successive camps at Y Pygwn (Powys) show that a 15.2-ha (37.6-acre) camp was followed, on a slightly different alignment, by a 10.3-ha (25.5-acre) camp. On the Hyginus model, these were theoretically big enough to accommodate up to 20,000 men, suggesting that at the very least that one legion and several auxiliary units could have used the bigger one.[47]

Marching camps are almost impossible to date, but those in north Wales probably belong to the campaigns of the first century. Either the II or XX legions could have been responsible, but it is no less probable that vexillations from both, and even from XIV, were involved. Just how difficult it is to attribute these camps to a particular period, let alone a campaign, is evident in Scotland, where two main marches north are known to have taken place: under Agricola (77/78–83/84) and Septimius Severus (208–11). Many marching camps have been detected up the east coast. Testing by excavation has produced the theory that camps with *clavicula* are late first century, those with *titula* are either late first century or Antonine, while the large irregular camps around 48 ha (118.6 acres) in size are thought to be Severan.

The Permanent Fort

The permanent fort was a consolidated form of marching camp. Buildings and troops were distributed within the fort in similar positions, but no two forts or fortresses are the same. Before the mid-first century, forts were often polygonal or irregular rectangles. The 'playing-card' shape then became normal and lasted until the mid-third century. These forts had regular street grids dividing the fort into square and rectangular plots, within parallel ramparts built in a playing-card shape with curved corners and at least one gate in each side. Forts often had annexes, a kind of fortified appendix to the main plan that could be used for a variety of ad-hoc purposes.

Every Roman fort represented a unique combination of factors: location, available materials, the intended garrison, and the preferences of individual fort surveyors and architects. Hod Hill, an early conquest-period fort, was built into the corner of an Iron Age hillfort in Dorset and utilized some of the old ramparts (see p. 32). The Period 2 fort at the Lunt [110], built in the mid-60s, had a very peculiar shape dictated by the reduction of the previous fort's plan, while still accommodating a circular *gyrus* from the earlier fort built *c.* 60.

When permanent forts in stone were built along the northern frontier there were fewer major variants. It is usually possible to predict the main features of fort plans once the basic dimensions have been established. But forts could still buck the trend. South Shields [111], in its third-century guise, retained a stereotypical outline, but was extended and had many of its internal buildings replaced or moved about to accommodate an exceptional number of granaries. South Shields is a conspicuous reminder of the fact that forts rarely (if ever) remained in the form in which they were built. Forts that remained occupied were almost invariably modified in some way, with structures being rebuilt or falling out of use, and ramparts extended or reduced.

Several surveyors and architects are attested in Britain, all in a military context, though in no case can we associate an individual with his work. An inscription from Piercebridge records Attonius Quintianus, a military surveyor (*mensor*), who would have laid out the ramparts and street grid of a fort, and allocated plots for each building.[48] The building work was probably planned by the *architectus*, though in a military context this is better translated as 'engineer', rather than 'architect'. At Birrens, the *arictectus* [sic] Amandus left a dedication to Brigantia [109], and another, Gamidiahus, left one to Harimella.[49] The only other architect we know about is Quintus, at Carrawburgh.[50]

109. *Opposite above.* **Birrens (Dumfries and Galloway).** Carved relief from *Blatobulgium*, depicting the goddess Brigantia and dedicated by Amandus, the *arictectus*. Late second century.

110. *Opposite below.* **Baginton (Warwickshire).** A view across the Lunt fort site with some of its reconstructed features, including a gate, ramparts and a *gyrus*, possibly a horse exercise ring. About 60–65.

111. **South Shields (Northumberland).** View looking northwest across the fort at *Arbeia* towards the modern replica of the west gate. In the foreground is one of the numerous granaries that replaced many of the internal buildings when the fort became a supply-base for the northern frontier and the Severan campaign.

DEFENCES

During the first and early second centuries, rampart construction in earth (or clay) and timber was normal, particularly in southern Britain where the only alternative was laborious construction in flint and mortar, with brick levelling courses. Turf and earth was easy to use, but weathering and decay compromised its durability.[51] Together with excavated remains, sculpted reliefs on Trajan's Column in Rome show that ramparts were built on a platform of logs laid side-by-side on brushwood layers, secured to the ground with stakes. Sometimes a rubble platform was used. The Antonine Wall's rampart was entirely turf, but rubble and cobbling were used as foundations throughout its length. Elsewhere, stone was normally only used when marshy conditions demanded it. Along the top, a timber palisade and walkway provided a defensible fighting platform, reached by steps (*ascensi*) made of timber or stone, or cut into the earth.

It was difficult to build an entirely earthen rampart. Soil dries out unevenly, causing the result to slump. The reconstructed ramparts at the Lunt show this to good effect. The solution was to build a timber frame into the rampart. This braces and contains the earth, just as brick and tile courses were used to create a frame for flint walls. The amount of timber-framing varies a great deal. Some ramparts used little or none, and had raked slopes with turf-facing to help inhibit collapse. Vertically-faced ramparts survived far better with a series of timber verticals and horizontals throughout. However, it is unusual to be able to identify what was actually used at any one fort because of decay. The evidence

112. Poltross Burn (Cumbria). Milecastle 48 on Hadrian's Wall. This section of wall where the Narrow Wall was built on the Broad Wall foundation, abutting the Broad Wall wings of the milecastle, shows both the stone foundation and how the Wall was built. A rubble-and-mortar core was held in place by roughly-dressed facing stones. Although quick to build, the design was equally quick to disintegrate and needed constant maintenance. Most Roman fort walls were built in a similar fashion.

from Britain suggests that raked turf or clay ramparts with minimal timber-framing were preferred, but this may be an illusion based on different excavation techniques used at different times.[52]

Stone ramparts probably reduced maintenance, but building them absorbed colossal amounts of manpower, resources and transportation. Where an earth fort already existed, the rampart was cut back and a stone revetment wall built. The deeper foundations and greater weight meant that external ditches had to be further away to inhibit subsidence. A new fort would have stone ramparts built first, faced on both sides, and then an earth rampart built up behind. At Birdoswald, the fort ramparts were 1.4 m (4 ft 6 in) thick. Here, as at so many Roman sites, the standard of execution was no better than competent compromise. The wall core was simply rubble held together with lime mortar, contained within facing walls that were made of only crudely squared-off blocks. The process was effective, saving labour and time. But the results were prone to erosion since the core was liable to settle. Any damage to the facing stones allowed water and frost to accelerate disintegration.

No Roman fort ramparts survive to full height to confirm what they looked like. Collapsed sections from the fort at Wörth in Germany show that the height to the rampart walkway there varied from 4.2 to 4.8 m (13 ft 8 in to 15 ft 8 in), and that above this was a parapet with merlons (resembling a medieval castle's crenellations). Although dressed stone was used on the facing wall, the wall was 'improved' with plaster and painted red lines to resemble stonework. Something similar was done on parts of Hadrian's Wall. The effect would have created a more imposing obstacle, but it also made damaged sections easier to spot.

Ramparts were built in sections. Carvoran, by Hadrian's Wall, has produced several inscriptions recording rampart construction, giving us an idea of the work done. Here the century of Silvanus *vallavit p cxii*, 'ramparted for 112 feet'. The lengths varied. The century of Valerius Cassianus built a stretch only 19 Roman feet long.[53] At Carrawburgh, the Thruponian century claimed responsibility for 24 Roman feet [113].[54] The inscribed stones were inserted at the end of the completed stretch, and were probably intended as a quality-control device. Vegetius describes the use of ten-foot rods by centurions to inspect the work, followed by the tribunes.[55]

Timber gateways and interval towers built into the ramparts survive almost always only as postholes. Trajan's Column shows a variety of types, some roofed, and some open-framed. Even in stone ramparts, interval towers may have had stone foundations but timber superstructures. Until the middle of the third century, towers remained flush with the wall.

113. Carrawburgh (Northumberland). Centurial stone from the fort walls at *Brocolitia* recording the completion of 24 Roman feet of rampart by the Thruponian century.

114. Birdoswald (Cumbria).
The double-portalled east entrance to the fort at *Banna* is the best-preserved fort gate in Britain, still standing to the height of its arch springers.

Gates were the weakest part of a fort's defences, and thus required the greatest reinforcement. Forts normally had four gates, known as the *portae principales*, but larger forts and fortresses had up to six. Once again Trajan's Column is our evidence for the superstructures. But since the number of postholes varies from gate to gate, several different designs clearly existed, based normally on four or six postholes, and if the gate was single or double. More complicated gates projected inwards and had towers that could be L-shaped.

Stone gates were single or double-portalled. Each passageway required arches, and the stones in the door jambs had to be drilled to accommodate pivots and locking devices. None in Britain survive intact, though in some cases the door jambs survive to the height of the arch springers. Birdoswald had four such gates, and two single-portalled gates [114]. The large number of gates is a mark of how the forts themselves were not primarily conceived of as defensive retreats at this date. Collapsed debris suggests the flanking towers had keyhole windows, but whether the towers were roofed or not, or if there was a walkway over the entrance passages, is unknown. Fragments of sculpture and inscriptions found at many fort gates show that they were used for display and decoration.

The reconstructed west gate at South Shields [115] provides a dramatic full-scale three-dimensional interpretation of a second-century stone fort gateway in Britain. The work is extremely impressive, but it is only an interpretation. It is possible that the original gate did not have two storeys, and that the towers were not roofed. A mosaic from Orange in southern France depicts a gate with unroofed towers, but obviously climatic conditions in Britain were different. However, the South Shields reconstruction accurately portrays the very slight projection of towers at this date, with recessed entrance gates, enabling guards on the tower to look out on any visitors to the fort. During the third century, gate towers were more likely to project significantly, reflecting an increasingly defensive type of warfare. At Vindolanda, around 223, a 'gate with towers' was rebuilt by the resident garrison of Gauls.[56]

INTERNAL BUILDINGS

No Roman fort in Britain has ever been entirely cleared, but excavation, aerial photography and geophysical surveys have recovered fairly complete plans. Since the Roman fort was an Empire-wide phenomenon, there is plenty of supporting information from elsewhere, especially along the Rhine frontier. None of the structures survives to any significant height, so roofing details remain largely unknown.

Inscriptions recording building work provide useful information, but distribution is patchy. There is a bias to auxiliary forts in northern

115. South Shields (Northumberland).
The magnificent replica west gate of the fort at *Arbeia*, built on the original foundations. The height and roofing of the towers is conjectural, but the reconstruction suggests how imposing a Roman fort could be.

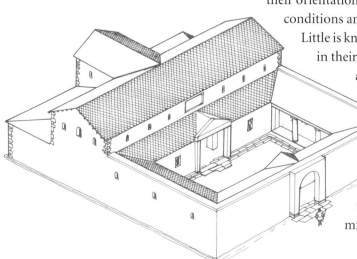

116. Lanchester (Durham).
Inscription from the fort at
Longovicium, recording the
restoration of the headquarters
and armoury by the First Cohort
of Lingones under Marcus Aurelius
Quirinus, during the reign of
Gordian III (238–44).

**117. Housesteads
(Northumberland).**
The *principia,* with its basilican
cross-hall and courtyard, was the
centre of any fort. The basic design
was also used for civilian forum-
basilicas.

Britain in the third century, but the number of texts
compared to potential buildings is minute, and by this
date much of the work recorded was rebuilding or repair
work. The barracks of the seventh cohort of the II legion
were rebuilt at Caerleon between 255–60, while another
seems to have been built afresh at Bainbridge in 205.[57]
These are the only epigraphic references to barracks in
Britain. At Netherby, a cavalry drill hall was completed
in 222, a fact which was recorded on an inscription. The
text is particularly interesting in that it describes the
work as finishing something that had been begun long
before, and which seems to have been suspended.[58]
Although the building is itself unknown, a possible example has been
identified from a geophysical survey of the remains at Birdoswald.[59]
Some time between 238–44 at Lanchester, the headquarters and
armoury were restored by the garrison, the First Cohort of Lingones
[116].[60] Such texts often tell us about buildings we have no remains of, or
that might otherwise defy identification. At High Rochester, two inscriptions refer to *ballistaria* in 220, and in 225–35.[61] Once thought to have
been a platform for artillery, a *ballistarium* seems too unimportant to
merit a monumental inscription. Perhaps the texts refer to a workshop
in the fort that built and maintained artillery equipment.

Excavation has produced the most evidence for fort buildings and,
perhaps more importantly, evidence for how fort buildings changed
across time. It has also shown that predicting fort plans from limited and
selective excavation might overlook local peculiarities. Most of the fort
buildings housed troops in uniform barrack blocks, or *centuriae.* Invariably rectangular, barracks usually had ten pairs of rooms in a row, with a
large suite tacked on to the end that projected slightly. Although barracks
were generally laid out side-by-side in the *praetentura* and *retentura,*
their orientation and numbers of rooms depended on local
conditions and the relative proportions of the fort plan.

Little is known about the facilities available to soldiers
in their barracks, but postholes mark where bunks
and tables stood, and hearths the site of
fires, while the officers' quarters
seem to have been much better-
appointed, with latrines and
drainage facilities.

The central zone of the fort, the
latera praetorii, housed administrative buildings and other facilities. In the
middle was the headquarters building, or

principia [117]. Whereas barracks vary in number according to the size of the fort, the *principia* tended to vary in size depending on the prestige of the fort and its unit. The basic layout, however, remained the same. The *principia* had a cross-hall opening into a courtyard, with portico on three sides. The courtyard lay beside the *via Principalis*, and looked down towards the *porta Praetoria*, where parades, sacrifices and other ceremonies took place. The cross-hall was a rectangular chamber that stretched the width of the building. It resembled the town-hall basilica familiar from many Romano-British civic centres, but was usually much smaller in proportion to the size of the fort. Behind the hall, a range of rooms was built to house the unit's records, with the *sacellum* in the middle where the standards were housed. Valuables were secured in a subterranean strongroom, unless the ground was too difficult to excavate. Next to the *principia* was usually the *praetorium*, the commandant's house, usually built as four wings arranged around a courtyard. The hospital, or *valetudinarium*, has been identified at a few sites, for example at Housesteads [118], where it also consisted of four wings ranged round a

118. Housesteads (Northumberland).
Aerial view of the fort at Housesteads (*Vercovicium*). In the right foreground, three parallel blocks fill out the northeast corner of the fort. In the left foreground, in the corner, is the latrine. Behind these, from left to right, are the commandant's house, the headquarters with hospital behind, and a pair of granaries. The north wall of the fort, on the right, formed part of Hadrian's Wall and replaced a newly-built stretch of Wall and turret when the decision to build forts on the Wall was made. Originally constructed in the mid-120s.

courtyard. Traces of other buildings turn up on a more individual basis, depending on local requirements and survival. Amongst the best known is the latrine complex at Housesteads, complete with tanks, conduits and drains. Others include workshops, and occasionally baths, although more often these were built outside the fort.

The remains of granaries are the easiest to detect in stone forts from their massive walls, raised floors and substantial buttresses to withstand the effects of grain settling. Usually built in pairs to help one buttress the other, they were often the most substantial buildings in the fort. Two granaries normally sufficed. At South Shields in the third century, their numbers were increased at the expense of more conventional fort buildings, presumably to convert the fort into a fortified stores compound, to service both the frontier zone and the Severan campaigns into Scotland. The fort was enlarged from 1.5 ha (3.7 acres) to just over 2 ha (4.9 acres), so that 14 granaries could be built in the northern part by *c.* 205–8. Additions over the next 20 years brought the total to 24.

Legionary fortresses were similar but much larger. Caerleon, for example, covered 20 ha (49.4 acres), or ten times the size of a typical auxiliary fort like Housesteads. The headquarters building was similar in scale to the urban forum and basilica. They also had room for additional prestige structures, such as the monumental legionary baths built at Exeter by the middle of the first century AD. At Chester, the fortress was begun on the basis of a unique master plan in the late first century. Work was disrupted when the XX legion was sent to help build the northern frontier over much of the second century. Chester's original plan included the very unusual 'elliptical building', a structure with an elliptical courtyard and surrounding galleries that has defied interpretation [119]. The building never progressed beyond being laid out. More than a century later the structure was laid out once more, on the same site (but at a higher level) and leaving the earlier work buried. This time it was finished. Clearly the plans had survived from the earlier phase. Only once the frontier work of the second century was out of the way could the soldiers of a much later generation return to those plans and finish the work.

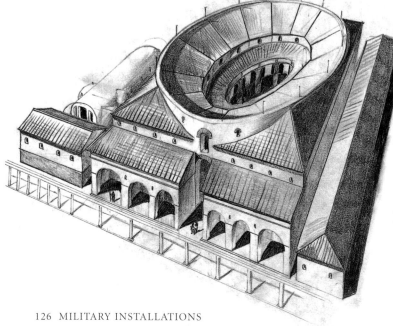

119. Chester (Cheshire).
Reconstruction drawing of the 'elliptical building' at the legionary fortress of *Deva*. Its function is unknown, but it is likely to have been used for honorific occasions, or perhaps virtuoso displays of swordsmanship or horsemanship.

MILITARY AMPHITHEATRES

The legionary fortresses at Chester and Caerleon both had amphitheatres [120], each built just outside the fort ramparts. The only other one known is the London amphitheatre, which was certainly in existence in timber form by the Flavian period before it was replaced in stone. They were mainly used for military displays and ceremonies, many of which were religious in nature, and which commemorated great historical and mythical conflicts. However, the dedication to Nemesis (Fate) in one of the amphitheatre arena shrines at Chester by a centurion, shows that gladiatorial bouts were probably staged there too.

THE *VICUS*

Roman forts that remained established often attracted civilian settlement (*vicus*). Some towns in southern Britain, like Cirencester, had their origins in *vici*. In the south, the army moved on and the forts were abandoned, but the economic and social conditions remained to keep the *vici* viable. In the military north, permanent forts developed some sort of settlement nearby, often covering a much wider area than the fort itself. These were characteristically straggling settlements that included houses, shops, industrial buildings, shrines and cemeteries. Like everywhere else in the military zone, the chance of finding useful inscriptions

120. Caerleon (Monmouthshire). The legionary amphitheatre at Caerleon, built *c.* 90, for *II Augusta*. The arena was created by hollowing out the ground, and seating was built out of stone-revetted earthen banks.

is relatively high. An altar from near Vindolanda records the *curia Textoverdi*, 'the assembly of the Textoverdi'. Evidently the *vicus* community at Vindolanda was organized in a way that imitated the urban constitutions further south.[67] At Old Carlisle an altar recorded a dedication by the *vikanorum magistri*, 'masters of the *vicus* people'.[63] Unlike towns further south, however, most of the *vicus* settlements in the north seem to have declined before the forts. Perhaps they lacked the secure economic base to survive as the army declined, but it also seems that civilian-type settlement moved within the fort walls.

LATE ROMAN MILITARY BUILDING

Until the early third century, existing forts belonged to the 'playing-card' fort tradition that stretched back to the first century. The forts of the Saxon Shore were different, having only tiny ramparts behind massive freestanding walls, and projecting bastions. Burgh Castle shows the evolving design to good effect. Here, the bastions seem only to have been installed after the walls had been built to around half the intended height [121, 122]. Unlike the earlier forts, these shore forts are generally distinguished by a lack of any significant internal buildings, while Pevensey, begun around 295 and one of the last in the series, has an irregular ovoid plan that owes nothing at all to the earlier military building tradition.

In the meantime, the existing forts and fortresses had a variety of very individual fates. At Housesteads in the fourth century, for example, the

121, 122. Burgh Castle (Suffolk). The shore fort defences at *Garriannum*. Built *c.* 275, the fort appears to show a transitional design. The bastions were added after the walls had been partly built, and are only bonded to the upper courses.

barracks were converted into a series of self-contained chalets, rather than strips of contiguous rooms. The ramparts started to disintegrate. Large slabs of masonry from the once-imposing gates were used to repair them, while the gates themselves were shored up with timber. In contrast the commandant at South Shields built an incongruous and well-appointed Mediterranean-style courtyard house around *c.* 300 [123]. About the same time many of the exceptionally large number of granaries there were converted into barracks, and the headquarters building moved back into the middle of the fort. At Birdoswald, by the late fourth century the south granary was used for domestic occupation of some sort rather than storing grain.

New fort building seems to have ended by the mid-fourth century. Although garrisons are attributed to the Saxon Shore forts, there is little or no evidence to substantiate their presence. One of the curiosities of late Roman Britain is the appearance of stones recording building or repair work on Hadrian's Wall by work forces detached from civilian communities in southern Britain. Undated, the stones probably belong to the fourth century and record work by the *civitas Dumnoniorum* and the *civitas Durotrigum*.[64] They might represent forced labour under military supervision, or the need to provide civilian labour in the absence of enough soldiers. The only other military building in the last years of Roman Britain was the series of fortified coastal watchtowers in Yorkshire. Erected either by Count Theodosius or Magnus Maximus, they were designed to keep an eye on any seaborne raiders. Compared to the confident military building of three centuries before, they mark a time when Roman Britain's military infrastructure was on its last legs.

123. South Shields (Northumberland).
A replica of the fourth-century commandant's courtyard house at *Arbeia*, built on the original foundations. The Mediterranean design is a remarkable feature for Britain at any time, let alone at this late date when most forts were steadily deteriorating.

CHAPTER 6

TOWNS IN ROMAN BRITAIN

The towns of Roman Britain are the most important legacy of the period [124]. This has made their study often extremely complicated. London, for example, has produced a great deal of evidence that has largely been discovered through excavations made randomly possible by bombardment in the Second World War, and the equally destructive rate of commercial development since the 1960s. Many urban excavations are conducted in arduous and underfunded conditions. Sometimes the results have been spectacular; London's amphitheatre and the temple precinct in Southwark are particularly good examples. The recovery of vast quantities of evidence from London's wharfs has revolutionized our knowledge of Roman commerce in Britain. Conversely, Roman Britain's second largest town at Cirencester has escaped almost all of these problems, but today has numerous historic buildings that preclude the possibility of excavation.

Urban archaeology is complicated at best, and at worst fragments of layers and buildings are confusingly mixed up with medieval rubbish pits and Victorian cellars. The sheer volume of excavation has shown that the traditional tendency to extrapolate findings from a single site to the rest of the town is unreliable. Ironically, it is the towns that 'failed', or those in which later development gravitated to different areas, that offer the greatest archaeological potential. Silchester, for example, was extensively excavated during the years 1864–78 and 1890–1909. The results were impressive, but techniques of the time meant that timber buildings went unrecognized. Today selective re-excavation is taking place. It is becoming possible to find out more about diet and disease, and the natural environment inside and outside of towns. This means that a broad picture of life in Roman towns in Britain has been constructed, and is evolving continuously.

Rome itself provided the urban archetype and defined the concept. All major towns in the Roman Empire were modelled on Rome, especially those that were new foundations rather than adaptations of existing settlements. London's spontaneous early development before the Boudican revolt illustrates how towns emerged as a direct response to the needs of Roman society and the economy. Town life was as synonymous with Roman culture as speaking Latin, taking baths, and promenading in porticoes.[1] The town was an arena in which everything

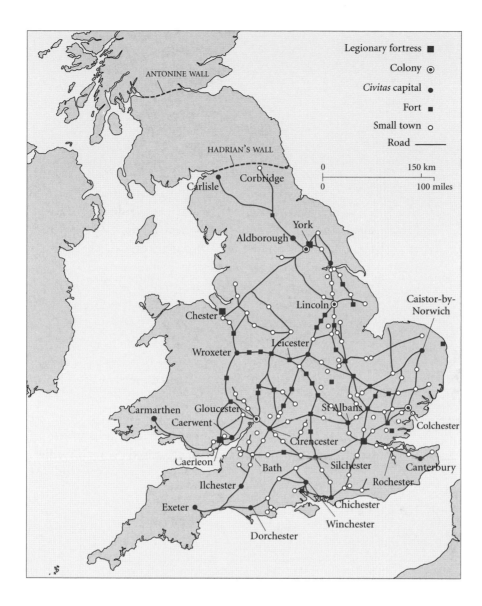

124. Principal towns in Britain.
The colonies (e.g., Colchester) sat in their own territory. The *civitas* capitals (e.g., Cirencester) were the hubs of administrative districts (cantons or *civitates*), based on the old tribal regions. North Wales and northern Britain remained under military control, though some settlements modelled themselves on the *civitates*.

that made the Roman world work came together. The very experience of community living in a Roman urban context created a sense of cooperative security and mutual self-interest, while at the same time generating social and commercial interdependence. Living in towns, or visiting towns for commercial and social reasons, helped promote a sense of shared identity with a Roman context, and reinforced relationships based on patronage within the Roman hierarchy.

There were no towns in Britain prior to 43, but this does not mean that the population had no concept of nucleated settlement. The cooperative work that created Neolithic monuments was an early illustration of community effort, whether by coercion or not. By the late Iron Age, the hillforts had come to represent focal points for communities, as had the sprawling *oppida* (towns), like *Camulodunum*. The use of the term *oppidum* by commentators such as Caesar was the result of trying to find a Latin word for something that had no Roman equivalent. None of these settlements had the key features of towns, such as permanent architecture, clearly defined commercial and administrative areas, or residential zones. Only *Calleva* (Silchester) comes close with its possible street grid from *c*. 20 BC. But otherwise the closest manifestations we have of any sort of related concept are the mint settlements of late Iron Age Britain. *Calleva*, *Verlamion* (later *Verulamium*) and *Camulodunum* all appear in abbreviated form on dynastic issues of the Atrebates and Catuvellauni. Beyond the south and east, there was even less that might be regarded as any sort of proto-town.

The development of towns in Roman Britain ultimately depended on the population's cooperation with and acceptance of the concept, rather than its imposition. In the main this means the native aristocracy. Even if they had enslaved themselves, as Tacitus puts it, they were complicit in the process. The result was a unique variant of the classical idea of a town in a provincial context. It is very easy in our own extensively urbanized culture to overlook the effects on a community of the experience of living within a system of towns linked by roads and a provincial economy.

Urban life produces a different set of social traditions and experiences from rural life. This includes the impact of public buildings, which had never existed in Britain before. In an ever-changing natural world, human beings are always drawn to cities as vibrant but reliable beacons of security. For the native aristocracy, urban government and influence

125. Lincoln (Lincolnshire). The north gate ('Newport Arch') at Lincoln is the only Roman gate in Britain that traffic still passes through, and the only extant Roman arched gate. All major towns had gates, some being built before stone walls. Gates were obviously defensive, but probably also played an important role in channelling traffic so that people and goods could be examined and taxed. Third century.

became the mechanisms through which they received Roman patronage in the form of status, cultivated their interests, and pursued their disputes. For retired soldiers and visitors from elsewhere in the Empire, towns were reassuring bastions of familiarity. For ordinary people, towns provided unprecedented commercial opportunities.

The Empire depended on local communities to operate local and regional government under Roman supervision. This was done through a network of major towns. Their success depended on taking advantage of existing tribal social networks and economic activity. Nevertheless, the far southwest, central and north Wales, and much of the north remained remote and undeveloped. Even within the settled 'urbanized' zone major towns were relatively few, and in some areas, like East Anglia, they were even fewer and more limited in development. At its height, Roman Britain was drastically less urbanized than most other Roman provinces. Moreover, within some of these towns areas seem to have remained undeveloped. The so-called 'small towns' were much more common, but generally lacked most of the definitive features of the major towns, such as public buildings or defences.

FOUNDING FORMAL TOWNS

In Britain, towns had to be created from the ground up. In the Roman world there were several different types of formal town, each with its own legal status. At the top was the provincial capital, followed by colonies of Roman citizens, usually military veterans. After these came the *municipia*, provincial towns whose residents had an intermediate status called 'Latin citizenship', and finally the *civitas* capitals, the regional government centres. There were also innumerable small towns that had no specific legal status, but which, depending on their size, organized themselves in way that often emulated the formal towns.

It was not until the middle of the second century that formal towns were equipped with the necessary facilities. Along the way various obstacles presented themselves, including the catastrophic Boudican revolt, the legacy of which was to ensure that Colchester, London and St Albans had to start all over again. Both London and Wroxeter, where earlier planning problems seem to have resulted in duplicated building work, were seriously damaged by fire in the second century. Each town was affected by unique circumstances, including available funds and manpower, and the level of commercial development in the area. Individuals and interest groups will have had both positive or negative effects that we cannot now know about.

126. Lincoln (Lincolnshire). Altar dedicated to the Fates (*Parces*) and the Imperial Spirits by Gaius Antistius Frontinus, a guild-treasurer (*curator*), in thanks for being appointed to the post for a third time. Many professions were organized into guilds to protect their members' interests. Probably early third century.

Colonies were impositions, created by appropriating land and resources. They provided a means of paying off soldiers by giving them land, rather than risking them degenerating into dispossessed armed bands of malcontents. The colony was was supposed to act as a demonstration of Roman urban life as practised by Roman citizens. With a population of retired legionaries and their dependants, a colony was manufactured in conquered territory by physically laying out a new town together with associated territory. Each veteran held land inside and outside of the town.

Britain's first colony was at Colchester. In or around 47, a legion, probably XX, was withdrawn from Colchester and sent to join the campaign in the west. In its place, a colony of veterans was founded by c. 49.[2] By 60 it already had a senate house, a theatre and a monumental temple to the imperial cult. The temple was particularly significant because it is clear from Tacitus that members of the native Trinovantian aristocracy had become involved in the cult, and thus absorbed into the colony's way of life. This is usually described as having been the result of coercion. Tacitus was being ironic when he said that 'the chosen priests were squandering fortunes on the pretence of religion'.[3] Far from being oppressed, certain individuals were ingratiating themselves with the Romans, as so many Britons had been doing for decades. The Romans had thrown off the Catuvellauni, so being pro-Roman had worked for the Trinovantes. The Trinovantian priests only squandered the money because everything went horribly wrong when the revolt broke out. Had there been no rebellion, the money would have been a sound investment.

Colchester in 60 sounds grandiose, but archaeology in the town has painted a rather more mixed picture. The colonists lived in and around the adapted barracks of the short-lived legionary fortress. Soldiers or veterans must have executed much of the necessary engineering and architectural work. The skills of surveying and laying out a street grid, and then allocating plots for public buildings, would not have been possessed by anyone else at the time.

The other colonies in Britain were at Gloucester, Lincoln and York. Like Colchester, they had all served as legionary fortresses, apart from York, where the colony was established beside the fortress. The bulk of their early populations were made up of ex-legionaries of Italian, Gaulish or Spanish origin and their families. Marcus Ulpius Quintus, then serving in government intelligence on detachment from the VI legion, is named on a tombstone in Rome.[4] He came from Gloucester and was a member of the Nervian tribe. This makes it likely that Gloucester was made into a colony under Nerva (96–98) or Domitian (81–96). Domitian was subjected to *damnatio memoriae* for his various crimes, and his name was routinely excised from monuments and any institution he had founded. His successors then took the credit. Lincoln's foundation is even less certain, but since the fortress had almost certainly been given up by the mid-80s, a foundation under Domitian, or shortly afterwards, is likely. York is named as a colony, along with Lincoln, on an altar of 237 from Bordeaux.[5] The date for its foundation probably belongs to the division of Britain into two provinces, most likely under Septimius Severus (193–211), when York became the administrative capital of *Britannia Inferior*. London may also have been a colony. Although London became the provincial capital, its legal status is unknown. One suggestion is that it was known as a *conventus civium Romanorum*. A *conventus* was the term for a gathering together of Roman citizens with trading and commercial interests in a provincial town.[6]

There were more *civitas* capitals than colonies. Large parts of Britain were organized into *civitates respublicae*, the political communities of local citizens in a district. These represented the formalization of tribal districts into permanent Roman administrative units. Each *civitas* was ruled from the *civitas* capital, but the towns and their districts were each a single unit. Appropriately, their names combined that of the settlement with that of the tribe. Thus, Canterbury was *Durovernum Cantiacorum*, or 'Durovernum of the Cantiaci'. Occasionally it was necessary to fabricate a tribal administrative district. Winchester was founded as *Venta Belgarum* ('Venta of the Belgae'), although Belgae seems to have been a general ethnic identity for peoples of the area, rather than a specific tribe.

COLONIES AND *CIVITAS* CAPITALS

Capitals			
London	*Londinium*	Canterbury	*Durovernum Cantiacorum*
		Carmarthen	*Moridunum Demetarum*
Colonies		Chichester	*Noviomagus Reginorum*
Colchester	*Camulodunum*	Cirencester	*Corinium Dobunnorum*
Gloucester	*Glevum*	Dorchester	*Durnovaria* [*Durotrigum?*]
Lincoln	*Lindum*	Exeter	*Isca Dumniorum*
York	*Eboracum*	Ilchester	*Lindinis* [*Durotragum?*]
		Leicester	*Ratae Corieltauvorum*
Municipia		Silchester	*Calleva Atrebatum*
St Albans	*Verulamium*	Winchester	*Venta Belgarum*
		Wroxeter	*Viroconium Cornoviorum*
***Civitas* capitals**			
Aldborough	*Isurium Brigantium*		
Brough	*Petuaria* [*Parisorum?*]	A number of other towns, such as Corbridge	
Caerwent	*Venta Silurum*	and Carlisle in the military zone, probably acted	
Caistor-by-Norwich	*Venta Icenorum*	as local administrative centres.	

The *municipium* had intermediate status between a colony and a *civitas* capital. The only one known in Britain is *Verulamium* (St Albans). Tacitus describes it as such in the Boudican revolt, but it may not have been given this status until nearer his own time, around 40 years later. It must have served as the *civitas* capital of the Catuvellauni. Citizens in a *municipium* were elevated from provincial status to the privileges of Latin rights, one tier below that of full Roman citizenship. The tribe was recognized by the Romans to have been the most important one in Britain, so the promotion of the town and its inhabitants simply reflected its existing status in the British tribal hierarchy. Recent work has shown how the substantial and prestigious native burial at Folly Lane, dating to the early 50s, was approached by a road leading through the later Roman town and on to the pre-Roman *oppidum*. The road seems to have acted as the focal spine of urban-type development in a 12-ha (29.7-acre) area that later became the centre of Roman *Verulamium*, but which was initially wiped out in the Boudican revolt. Of course, once Caracalla made the universal grant of Roman citizenship, such distinctions between the inhabitants of colonies and the *civitas* capitals and *municipia* ceased to have any technical relevance.

The *civitas* capitals gradually came into operation during the late first and early second century. The process depended on circumstances prevailing in different areas. In some cases, forts were built early in the conquest period close to existing native centres. This was partly for security reasons, but as forts consistently drew commercial activity towards them, they helped sustain local economic activity even if the focus had moved. Cirencester, which became the *civitas* capital of the Dobunni, is the prime example. Close to the native hillfort at Bagendon, the site was chosen for a fort in the mid-40s, which was replaced with another nearby in *c.* 49. It remained in occupation until the 70s. Before long the *civitas* capital had been founded in its place. The forum and basilica had been built by the end of the first century.

In more reliable areas, *civitas* governments were probably in operation earlier. Chichester's town council was in a position to make a dedication to Nero in 59.[7] No public buildings are known of this date there, but if Togidubnus was serving as king, then they may for the moment have been unnecessary. Silchester, in the same tribal enclave, has produced nothing in the way

127. St Albans (Hertfordshire). Mosaic from a townhouse at *Verulamium* depicting the head of Neptune, or Oceanus. The floor is a mark of the development of town life in Britain, and a growing sophistication many decades ahead of most of the countryside. Second century. (St Albans Museums).

of inscriptions to help us, but the discovery of several tiles bearing Nero's titles suggests official patronage of building work by 68 at the latest. A timber forum and basilica were in operation there at least by Flavian times. The forum and basilica at St Albans were apparently dedicated under Agricola in 79 or 81.

Neither Silchester nor Chichester had, or needed, military phases, though military equipment shows that soldiers were present here as everywhere.[8] Further out into Britain, the fort-first, town-second sequence was much more common. Wroxeter started out as the site of an auxiliary fort, probably around the same time as Cirencester, and with a similar security role in view of the hillforts of the area. By *c.* 60 a legionary fortress had been built nearby, probably used intermittently by XIV and XX. The fortress remained in use until the late 80s, or even the 90s, by which time many towns further south and east had already been established as civilian administrative centres.

The Corieltauvi in the East Midlands had at least two native centres, Leicester and Old Sleaford. Leicester was a fort by the mid-first century, benefiting from the military and communications infrastructure. It evolved into *Ratae Corieltauvorum* by the beginning of the second century. Old Sleaford, much further east, has produced evidence of Romano-British occupation, but it waned into insignificance. In the north, the only *civitas* capital was at Aldborough (*Isurium Brigantium*). Here the main Roman military road into the north was the defining factor, rather than any native settlement. Its reach was small, but the military towns at Corbridge and Carlisle are likely to have contributed to regional government along the lines of *civitas* capitals, even though they were not instituted as such. In the civilian zone, some towns, such as Ilchester and Dorchester, were big enough to act as subsidiary *civitas* centres. Caistor-by-Norwich, as *Venta Icenorum* ('Venta of the Iceni'), is the hardest *civitas* capital to explain. No trace of a fort has been found, but in the long-term aftermath of the Boudican revolt it was evidently felt that a regional government centre was necessary. This led ultimately to the establishment of a modest late *civitas* capital as a sort of afterthought in traditionally troublesome territory. The town never grew into anything elaborate, and indeed contracted. Caerwent (*Venta Silurum*) in south

128. Cirencester (Gloucestershire). Mosaic from a townhouse in Beeches Road, depicting a hare surrounded by geometric motifs. The house was built on a virgin plot in the second half of the fourth century. (Corinium Museum).

129. Wroxeter (Shropshire).
The town baths of *Viroconium Cornoviorum* were begun under Hadrian in the 120s, but work was suspended and not completed until the 150s. The view is across the *frigidarium* (cold bath) towards the palaestra (exercise hall), entered through the door in the lare section of standing wall now known as the 'Old Work'. Oddly, the forum and basilica, just across the street, were built on the demolished remains of a late first-century military bathhouse. The sequence indicates the haphazard pattern of public building often found in Roman Britain.

Wales was also relatively late, but represents an upgrading of an existing roadside 'small town' in the vicinity of the legionary fortress at Caerleon.

The only inscription we have which is unequivocal in its content is the dedicatory forum inscription from Wroxeter (*Viroconium Cornoviorum*), one of the last *civitas* capitals to be founded [129]. Its forum was dedicated *c.* 129–30 and honoured Hadrian, who might have commissioned the building.[9] It is unlikely that this was when the *civitas* started to function, though it cannot have been long before. Wroxeter lay in an area where there was little tradition of either the use of coinage or other commercial activity associated with the tribes of the south and east before 43. It may have taken a visit by Hadrian in person to change things during his trip to Britain.

Some important towns grew up independently, and illustrate the urban momentum in the Roman system. London is the prime example. There may very well have been a Claudian fort on the site, but it was not deliberately developed at first into an administrative centre. London did not lie near a major native settlement. If there was a local focus of commercial and communication routes, it probably lay to the west where Westminster is now. However, by 60 London 'was not distinguished by the title of "colony", but was well known for its copious traders and commerce'.[10] While there is extensive evidence for London's commercial waterfront development in the later first century [130], the pre-Boudican port has not yet been found. Despite the Boudican revolt, London was so well established that within a decade it was growing into the largest town in Britain. If not already, London was now home to the procurator, and probably the governor as well, making it the *de facto* provincial capital. The garrison in the Cripplegate fort supports this, and helped provide Roman London with its unique character as a commercial, administrative and military centre. By the end of the first century it, too, had a suite of public administrative buildings, but, unlike most other towns, its business concerned the whole of Roman Britain.

130. Lower Thames Street (London).
Model of the wharfs at London as they might have appeared in the late first century. Behind the docks stood a variety of warehouses. Since the Thames has been progressively narrowed by embankments, the remains of Roman wharfs are usually found inland beneath medieval and later deposits. (Museum of London).

LAYING OUT TOWNS

The establishment of formal towns in Roman Britain lasted until the mid-second century. Most started out in a broadly similar fashion, regardless of whether or not they were founded on sites previously occupied by forts, native settlements, or new plots. It has become fashionable to refute the idea that the army was principally responsible for doing this kind of work. But the Roman army was not a separate social caste, brought out of its barracks only on special occasions to do specific jobs. Soldiers functioned throughout the general community. They were continually detached on an unending series of administrative tasks, and also represented the largest repository of crafts and trades in the Roman world. They are widely attested as civil engineers, architects, labourers, builders and manufacturers. Moreover, many of Britain's new towns were on sites previously occupied by forts.

The forum-basilica complex was the most important building in a major Roman town in Britain. The form of the forum and basilica varies throughout the Roman world. In Britain, the basic archetype resembles most closely the headquarters building of a military fort. Although we cannot be certain, it is very likely that military architects and engineers were probably involved in the design and layout of many civic centres and other aspects of towns in Britain.

In the province of *Mauretania* in the mid-second century, the town of Saldae was engaged in digging out a tunnel through a mountain to bring water to the city. The work had been badly surveyed, and the tunnel, begun from both sides, was out of alignment. The town had to solicit the help of Nonius Datus, a retired military surveyor of the III legion to help out. At the time, *Mauretania* had been a province no longer than Britain. What chance was there in Britain in the 70s of finding all the necessary skills to lay out and build towns without resorting to some military assistance?

FORUM & BASILICA

The basic design

The forum consisted of an open piazza surrounded on three sides by a covered portico, behind which were commercial buildings. The fourth side was formed by the basilica, the most imposing building in Roman-Britain [131]. The basilica had a central nave flanked by one or two aisles, and occasionally an external portico. At one end, a raised dais provided an area for public pronouncements and hearings. The *curia*, one of the rooms flanking the outer aisle, hosted meetings of the town council, and other rooms stored census and taxation archives, and records of judicial decisions. The basic design was later adapted for use in Christian churches.

Surviving fragments show that Silchester's basilica had Tuscan features carved in Bath stone, while Caerwent's had Corinthian ornamentation. A bronze eagle found at Silchester must once have formed part of a statue group, perhaps depicting an imperial figure or deity. The bronze bust of Hadrian (see p. 143) probably came from a full-sized statue that was originally displayed in London's forum. A third-century statue base from Caerwent has an inscription commemorating the legionary legate at nearby Caerleon, and probably once stood in the forum piazza or basilica.

Size

The range of sizes is considerable; each building was usually in proportion to the size of the town it served. Caerwent's piazza was one of the smallest at 1,023 sq m (11,011 sq ft), whereas London's complex was monumental at 27,772 sq m (298,937 sq ft). Its basilica was the largest building in Roman Britain, and towered some 28 m (92 ft) above the ground. Silchester's piazza, at 1,720 sq m (18,514 sq ft), was more typical.

The limits of the settlement were demarcated. Boundaries were extremely important, and played a part in religious ceremonies. They were not necessarily fixed. St Albans outgrew what seem to have been its original boundaries, but monumental arches in stone were erected on Watling Street, marking where it crossed the original boundaries. Street grids were laid out, based on the idea of regular blocks, or *insulae*, covering an area of no less than 15 ha (37 acres), but these invariably exhibit local eccentricities thanks to existing features, such as main roads and

Date

Two forum-basilica inscriptions have survived. St Albans' inscription records a dedication from *c*. 79, during the governorship of Agricola, and Wroxeter's commemorates the dedication under Hadrian in the name of the *civitas Cornoviorum*. Between them, the pair span most of the period in which all Romano-British forum-basilicas were built. However, Silchester had an earlier timber version, later covered in stone. London had a forum and basilica by 75–85, which was demolished when a much larger version was built around it. Erecting these structures was expensive and onerous, as London's second complex shows. Work began *c*. 100 and lasted at least 25 years, with clear evidence of running repairs and cessation of labour. A fragment from an Antonine inscription found in Winchester may be from a basilica. If so, this may extend the period of forum and basilica building in Britain (see p. 60).

Later history

Despite their essential role in the administration of Romano-British towns, the later fate of the forum-basilicas was very different. London's Hadrianic complex, possibly never finished, was demolished by *c*. 300. By the mid-third century, Silchester's forum was being used by metalworkers and other industries, as was Caerwent's before being demolished *c*. 390. Cirencester's remained in use, as did Exeter's, where the basilica was given a new floor after *c*. 378, though it, too, had been demolished within a generation.

Seeing basilicas and fora

Today the best-preserved basilica and forum is at Caerwent, where the remains have been exposed to public view. Part of the rear wall of Lincoln's basilica has survived and is known as 'the Mint Wall' [132]. However, the best impression of a Romano-British basilica can be gained by visiting the late Roman churches in Italy, especially in Rome or Ravenna.

131. *Left.* **Wroxeter (Shropshire).** Reconstruction painting of the forum-basilica at *Viroconium Cornoviorum*. The complex, dedicated *c*. 129–30 under Hadrian, was one of the last major public building projects in Britain and replaced an uncompleted baths. The forum was destroyed by fire *c*. 165–85, but was rebuilt. By the end of the third century, the complex had been destroyed, and commercial activity seems to have removed to the adjacent derelict baths site.

132. *Right.* **Lincoln (Lincolnshire).** The 'Mint Wall' at *Lindum* has been shown to be the rear wall of the colony's basilica, and is the largest remnant left standing of any basilica in Britain. As a colony, *Lindum* was intended to be a showpiece of Roman urban government and civilized living.

rivers. London undoubtedly outgrew its original area, because early cemeteries are found buried beneath areas of the later town. St Albans' grid was laid out roughly parallel to the River Ver, flanking the northeast side of the town. Watling Street, the main road from London, arrives almost from due south, cutting through the grid at an acute angle and creating triangular *insulae*. At Lincoln, the main upper town was joined to the lower town by roads running down the exceptionally steep hill. Since wheeled traffic would have found the hill impossible, a special arrangement of diagonal roads provided much gentler gradients at the expense of a shorter route.

Surprisingly, for a new and unsettled province, none of the new towns seem to have been laid out with fortifications in mind. In some cases, gates seem to have existed across major routes, but generally earth ramparts were not built until well into the late second century, and sometimes later. During the laying out of a street grid, plots were allocated for public buildings, usually occupying several *insulae* in the centre of the town in the most imposing locations. At London, the basilica and forum were placed so that anyone arriving across the bridge from the south entered the town by a road that led up the north bank directly to the forum. The 'governor's palace', with its suite of chambers and outdoor pool, on the site of the present-day Cannon Street station, was terraced into the north bank of the Thames.

Silchester's forum and basilica sat on the highest spot in the town and made the best of limited opportunities. At St Albans, despite the eccentricity in the layout, any visitor arriving from London was led directly towards the south end of the basilica. Nearby, the theatre was built in a setting that coordinated it with the forum and basilica, and a large temple compound. The theatre was not built until *c*. 140, some 60 years after the administrative centre was built. Nevertheless, its plot had remained vacant throughout this time, suggesting that it had been earmarked for the building from the beginning. At Leicester, the *insula* set aside for the forum remained unoccupied until the money and resources were available to build it. At Wroxeter, the Hadrianic forum (see p. 140) was built right over an unfinished bathhouse belonging to the old legionary fortress. Since the town was likely to need a major baths, it seems curious that an existing project was cleared away and built over. This is all the more surprising given that the town then invested in a new bathhouse (see p. 138) across the road from the forum. Civic wastefulness is hardly a modern phenomenon, and disrupted, under-financed and incompetently executed urban building projects occur elsewhere in the Roman Empire.[11] It is also quite possible that in some instances the buildings were never completed. This may have have been the case with the vast Hadrianic basilica in London.

The rest of the land within a town area was allocated to individuals or businesses. The town council controlled what was built and where, and the standards to which it had to comply. The result seems to have been that commercial and industrial districts were created in and around the centre, along key roads. While these might be privately owned, the town could also lease out property for commercial use.[12]

URBAN GOVERNMENT

Towns functioned as organs of Roman local government and administration, each varying slightly according to local traditions, precedents and laws, but all modelled on Rome. The town senate, or council (*ordo*), was made up of 100 representatives drawn from the local community, each of whom had to satisfy a property qualification to serve as a *decurion*. In colonies, this was fairly straightforward. In the *civitas* capitals, it was less so. Since conquest had by definition removed from everyone any right to property, the only way of including members of the local tribal élite was to return it. Togidubnus, as a reward for his loyalty, had 'certain states' handed over to him in his capacity as client king. Small-scale awards of this kind must have made sure that local councils were packed with the right people. As so often in Roman Britain, what we know about local government officials comes from the military north, in this case the colonies. Thus we have Flavius Bellator, the York *decurion*, and Aurelius Senecio, the Lincoln *decurion*. Another is known from Gloucester, so all were probably military veterans.[13] The *decurions* of the *civitas* capitals further south are unknown to us, largely because of the failure of the indigenous population to produce surviving inscriptions.

The council met in the *curia*, part of the forum-basilica complex. Here cases, pleas, petitions and other problems were heard, and decisions made on the erection of public monuments, honorific dedications, and so on. Sometimes the governor and his staff arrived to hear cases that required his judgment. This may explain the reference to a soldier on his staff at Winchester as a *beneficiarius consularis*.[14] There was a constant stream of traffic as soldiers and civilian officials arrived, either to deal with business locally or to pass through to other places. Partly to service their needs, towns had *mansiones*, which functioned as inns or staging posts, where accommodation was provided for travellers on government service. The system was called the *cursus publicus*, and had been created by Augustus to expedite official business. A *mansio* (see p. 156) resembled a very large house, but with extended bathing facilities and accommodation for horses. Wroxeter and Silchester have buildings that can be identified as *mansiones*, but all major and many minor towns had one.

133. Hadrian (117–38). Bronze head of the emperor, found in the Thames at London Bridge, and probably from a statue displayed in the forum-basilica to commemorate the emperor's visit to the province. Under Hadrian's rule, Britain acquired a formal northern frontier in the shape of the celebrated Wall. (British Museum).

Most of the decrees made in the basilica were recorded in council archives that no longer exist. Only very occasionally do the results of their decisions survive. At Caerwent, not long before 220, a decision was made to honour the commanding officer of the II legion, Tiberius Claudius Paulinus, with a statue. Its base survives, preserving the formula of the decision: *ex decreto ordinis respublica civitas Silurum*, 'by decree of the council, the *civitas* administration of the Silures (set this up)'.[15]

PUBLIC BATHS

Baths in Roman culture

Baths represented an important symbolic custom in Roman daily life, and a visit to them was a daily ritual. Clients met their patrons, discussed business matters and exchanged gossip in an environment that provided confidentiality and discretion.

Date

Public bathing was a novelty in Britain, and baths complexes were less of a priority than basilicas and fora. No inscriptions recording baths – except in forts – have survived, so archaeology is our only source of information. At Exeter, for example, the magnificent mid-first-century legionary baths were demolished and replaced with a new basilica on the same site. Unfinished early baths at Wroxeter, probably from the legionary fortress, were also demolished and replaced with a forum-basilica. However, in regions where the tribal leadership had been adopting Roman culture from before the conquest, baths were introduced much earlier. Silchester, St Albans, London and Bath all had public baths by the late first century. Even so, baths remained an optional extra. The St Albans baths complex burned down by the mid-second century, and was left in ruins for at least 50 years.

Design

As physical structures, urban public baths were probably the most sophisticated examples of Roman architecture in Britain. In their first phase, the baths at Silchester consisted of a changing room (*apodyterium*) between the main suite of baths – warm room (*tepidarium*), hot room (*caldarium*) and cold room (*frigidarium*) – and the open exercise yard (*palaestra*), itself surrounded by a covered portico. The design clearly owed much to archetypes found in the Mediterranean, where open-air exercise areas were much more usable than in Britain. The main baths were vaulted, a necessity in an

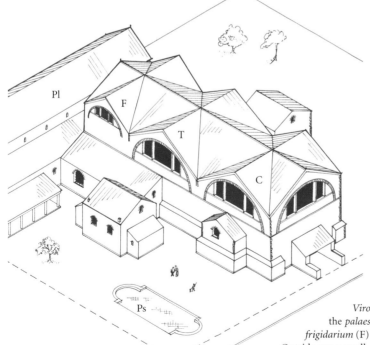

134. Wroxeter (Shropshire).
Reconstruction drawing of the public baths at *Viroconium Cornoviorum*, which were entered from the *palaestra* (Pl) at left. Visitors passed through the *frigidarium* (F) to reach the *tepidarium* (T) and *caldarium* (C). Outside was a small, open-air swimming pool, or *piscine* (Ps).

The town council executed most of its decisions through a variety of magistracies, also based on those at Rome and therefore appointed in pairs to restrict the chance of any one man becoming too powerful or corrupt. The *duoviri iuridicundo* was the senior pair, responsible for the operation of the council, dispensing local justice and organizing religious festivals. The *aediles* were principally responsible for maintaining public buildings and services, and entertainments. The *quaestores* took care of

environment in which constant warm moist air wreaked havoc with conventional roof timbers. This is exactly what happened in the first phase of the baths at Bath, instigating the reinforcement of roof supports and the replacement of the timbers with a vaulted roof. The resulting massive piers are some of the most conspicuous remains on the site. Baths were expensive to operate, requiring a continuous supply of clean water and abundant fuel to maintain the appropriate temperatures in the different rooms.

The baths at Caerwent, Wroxeter and Leicester substituted exercise halls for the more unsuitable open areas. Wroxeter's baths [134] were not operational until the latter part of the second century, perhaps delayed by the necessity of rebuilding the forum that was destroyed in the Antonine fire. The main sequence of baths opened off the exercise hall, with the *caldarium* and the *frigidarium* having individual plunge baths. The hall was 73 x 19.8 m (240 x 65 ft), making it easily comparable in scale

to some of the administrative basilicas. Another, smaller wing of hot rooms was subsequently tacked onto the *tepidarium*. The baths also included a latrine and, rare for Britain, a swimming pool in the courtyard outside. The complex was so large that parts of it remain unexplored. Leicester's baths were comparable in scale, but the design was significantly different; the baths seem to have been arranged as a separate wing from the exercise hall, and were connected by other rooms and corridors.

Later history
The massive masonry required for Roman baths resisted weathering

and decay. Consequently, although its baths and basilica gradually fell into ruin during the late and post-Roman period, Wroxeter has one of the largest upstanding fragments of a Roman public building. The 'Old Work' is the doorway from the *frigidarium* into the baths-basilica. Another large remnant of a baths-basilica is the Jewry Wall, in Leicester [135]. However, the most remarkable remains of all are at Bath (see pp. 158-59), where the baths complex has survived in a miraculous state, thanks not only to its scale, but also to the fact that it was buried by silt and debris when management of the hot springs had ceased.

135. Leicester (Leicestershire).
The Jewry Wall at *Ratae Corieltauvorum*. This massive piece of masonry formed part of the second-century town baths, and survived by being incorporated into a Saxon church.

local taxation and expenditure, using records compiled by the *censitor*. Various lesser officials about whom we know virtually nothing in Britain, but who must have existed because they did elsewhere in the Empire, were responsible for tasks such as repairing and maintaining public buildings.

The evidence for these magistracies in Britain is tiny, but sufficiently random to suggest that the main problem is lack of evidence. Flavius Martius was a senator in the canton of the Carvetii, at Old Penrith, in a

WATER SUPPLY

Thanks to its waterlogged conditions, Vindolanda has yielded an extraordinary collection of artifacts. Among these is a series of massive wooden water mains that were still carrying spring water into the site. Wooden junction boxes and pipes laid under the road have also been found at Carlisle and Cirencester. These finds are exceptional, but they probably preserve evidence for facilities that would have been found in some shape or form at any major Roman military or civilian settlement.

Managing water on an industrial scale was absolutely fundamental to Roman civilization. The accepted method was to locate a source at a higher level than the settlement and divert the water in, either via an architectural aqueduct or, more commonly, by digging conduits into the ground, carefully following contours to maintain the supply. At Dorchester a reservoir was constructed by building a dam, from which a 11-km (7-mile) long timber-lined conduit brought the water into town. At Greatchesters on Hadrian's Wall, a channel around a metre wide carried water 10 km (6 miles) along the contours, even though the source was just 4 km (2.25 miles) from the fort. One of the earliest aqueducts in

Britain was built in timber to service the Neronian 'proto-palace' at Fishbourne.

On arrival at the settlement, the water poured into the *castellum divisiorum* ('dividing reservoir') at the highest point where sediment could settle. Controlled by sluices, wood or lead pipes then carried the water off to wealthy households, public fountains and baths, and various industries. A small-scale version of this can be seen at Housesteads. Water ran down across the fort to its lowest point, where tanks and conduits controlled its passage into latrines. Like most Roman water systems, the principle was that of 'constant off-take'. Water flowed continuously into facilities, but to reduce the pressure at these outlets the main supply ran first into header tanks on pillars at street corners. The constant flow prevented the header tanks from overflowing and kept the water fresh, while the reduced pressure allowed domestic and bathing taps to work without being blown off.

136. Bath (Somerset).
One of the drains beneath the temple and baths complex at Bath, and still in working order. The Roman management of water was key to draining the site and making it possible to build here.

remote pocket of civilian administration in the military north. His tombstone says that he took this position 'after a quaestorship'. He is the only example of a *quaestor* from Roman Britain. Marcus Ulpius Januarius from Brough-on-Humber is the only instance of an *aedile* serving in a town that was not even a cantonal capital. Appropriately to his position, he had between 140 and 161 dedicated a new stage for the town theatre, which is not otherwise attested [138].[16]

Additional water supplies could be had from wells, but anything beyond modest requirements required major engineering. At Gresham Street, in London, remains of at least two chain-driven water-bucket systems have been found, one of which was in action by the 60s [137]. The wooden buckets were joined together with iron links and shafts, rotating on a massive wooden wheel to lift water from a timber-lined well that was around 6 m (19 ft 6 in) deep. The systems might have been used for light industry or small nearby baths, but neither lasted in use for long and were perhaps abandoned when aqueduct supplies became available.

Supplies at individual houses or villas were more ad hoc. Silchester has produced remains of a hand-operated wooden pump with lead cylinders, capable of shifting 22 litres (39 pints) of water per minute, and possibly used for raising water to a domestic cistern.[17] At Chedworth (Gloucestershire) spring water was diverted into a small pool at the site's highest point, from where it could be piped into the two nearby bath-suites. Stone conduits found near Woodchester (Gloucestershire) probably carried water into the villa complex. Proximity to a river played a large part in choosing a villa site. A series of villas grew up along the Darenth Valley (Kent), all

of which lay only a few metres from the river. The Redlands Farm (Northamptonshire) villa was originally built as a watermill, and two stone-lined aqueducts fed the water in from the nearby River Nene. Subsequently the mill was dismantled, and the house extended and converted into a more conventional villa-type structure.

Disposing of waste water was achieved in different ways. York had monumental masonry sewers, large sections of which have survived intact. Silchester, conversely, seems to have depended on open channels in streets. Such facilities were not necessarily bad. At St Albans, the drains around the forum were maintained throughout the period and only became clogged in the fifth century.

137. Gresham Street (London).
A modern reconstruction of the first-century water-wheel system. (Museum of London).

Civic elections were held for all these offices. Towns were divided into wards, in which ballots were held, supervised by men drawn from other wards who had taken oaths that they would officiate with honesty. Candidates had to be 25 years of age or over, and in the case of a *duovir* could not have held the post for five years. Office holders in towns of provincial status, like cantonal capitals or *municipia*, could sometimes be rewarded with Roman citizenship at the end of their tenure. This was clearly offered as a device to encourage integration into the Roman system.

Elsewhere in the Empire, wealthy men, or men who wished to become wealthier and more popular, commonly endowed their communities with facilities like theatres, temples and entertainments, and recorded their generosity on dedicatory inscriptions. These are common finds around the Mediterranean countries. They show how individuals and their families could dominate local politics and offices. Britain, along with several other northwest provinces, is remarkable for the conspicuous shortage of such evidence. The inscriptions might simply not have survived, but this is difficult to accept. Britain's inscriptions are so biased to the military zone that it seems the indigenous and civilian population did not commission honorific inscriptions. Towns without a military presence, like St Albans, have produced almost no inscriptions of any sort. Conversely, London, York and Lincoln, with large military and veteran populations, have produced inscriptions in relative abundance. Even in these towns, civilian examples, such as Brough's Marcus Ulpius Januarius, are few or non-existent, making him extremely unusual, although his name and location suggest that he was a military veteran or the freedman of a soldier. Perhaps in Britain the resources did not exist for individuals to be quite so generous, and the state had to step in. No member of the indigenous Romano-British population is ever recorded as having accumulated enough wealth to reach senatorial or equestrian status at Rome, even though many Gauls reached this position. However, Britons seem rarely to have commissioned inscriptions for any purpose, even those who lived in other provinces. This either means they rarely held office or, if they did, few of them were inclined to record that fact.

In the fourth century, urban public building had ended, apart from defensive works. At the same time, some of the rural villas had entered a period of extravagant investment in extensions, elabo-

138. Brough (Cumbria). Inscription from *Petuaria* dedicating a new stage (*proscaenium*) for the theatre, provided by the *aedile*, Marcus Ulpius Januarius, sometime between 140 and 161. No trace of the building has ever been found.

rate baths, expensive mosaics and other embellishments [139]. Assuming that villas were lived in by the decurial classes, it seems that the urban élite had turned their backs on the towns, ceasing to contribute to public buildings or any other urban improvements (if they ever had), instead spending their money on townhouses and private country estates. The houses testify to the availability of funds. Alternatively, perhaps the decurial class now controlled urban and cantonal affairs from their townhouses and villas, where ostentatious decoration and facilities provided a suitable backdrop for a new type of local government, based on individual prestige and influence.

COMMERCIAL AND RESIDENTIAL DEVELOPMENT

Most of a Roman town's area was given over to industry and housing. At Malton, a crudely-inscribed slab records a *tabernam aurificinam*, or 'goldsmith's workshop', but this is exceptional.[18] At one of the towns of Roman Britain called *Venta* (there are several candidates), a government weaving factory was in operation in the fourth century.[19] *Collegia*, or 'guilds', turn up on a number of inscriptions, but almost always referring only to their association for religious reasons. However, the Chichester text that names Togidubnus and therefore dates to the second half of the first century, records a 'guild of smiths'. Such guilds are well known in towns throughout the Roman Empire. Resembling modern Masonic groups, they provided a means of taking care of mutual self-interest.

139. Bignor (West Sussex). Fourth-century mosaic from the villa at Bignor, possibly depicting Venus. Villa owners invested heavily in their rural seats, but seem to have spent little or nothing on public works.

THEATRES & AMPHITHEATRES

The function

Theatres and amphitheatres played a fundamental role, both in public entertainment and in religious festivals. St Albans' theatre [140] was linked to the forum-basilica by a special road, while Silchester's amphitheatre lay just outside the town's defences, close to a temple precinct within the walls. Festivals frequently involved processions, as well as performances in public auditoria, so not surprisingly theatres and amphitheatres are also known at rural religious sites, such as Frilford (Oxfordshire) and Gosbecks (Gloucestershire).

Theatres and amphitheatres

Romano-British theatres were architecturally quite simple compared to Continental versions. Those at Canterbury and Colchester seem to have been fairly sophisticated, using radial vaults to create raised auditoria. But for the most part, theatres were built by creating turf embankments and digging out the arena. St Albans'

was a hybrid building that resembled a truncated amphitheatre and used stone revetments to contain earth embankments supporting rows of timber seats facing the arena and stage. Amphitheatres were ovoid auditoria surrounding a sunken arena. Examples in Britain were usually built by raising earth banks, contained within timber or stone revetments. Cirencester's amphitheatre was an adapted stone quarry, and Dorchester's was created by adapting a Neolithic henge monument (see p. 239). This was not only convenient, but may also have perpetuated a tradition of local religious activity.

Public games were arranged as routine parts of religious festivals. Gladiatorial contests might have dominated the proceedings, but evidence for these is extremely limited. They were certainly known about in Britain, and are depicted on mosaics at the villas of Bignor (West Sussex) and Rudston (East Yorkshire).

Date and locations

Colchester had a theatre by the time of the Boudican revolt. Remains of theatres have also been found at Canterbury (c. 80–90) and Cirencester. Silchester's amphitheatre seems to have had a timber phase dating to between 55–75. However, the town never acquired a theatre. Wroxeter had neither, but a rectangular enclosure next to a temple precinct may have been used instead. St Albans had a theatre with some features of an amphitheatre, built c. 140 on a site set aside for it around 50 years earlier. London's amphitheatre is so close to the fort that it was probably built for it. No London theatre has yet been found, though it is inconceivable that there was not one. The only inscription we have is from Brough, dating the installation of a *proscaenium* to 140–61 (see p. 148).

Temporary wooden auditoria were commonplace in antiquity, and this may explain the imbalance. Even Rome had no permanent

140. St Albans (Hertfordshire). Aerial view of the theatre at *Verulamium*, built in the mid-second century. Various alterations took place before it was substantially enlarged, c. 300. By the end of the fourth century, the theatre was in ruins, made redundant by the collapse of paganism and the temple precinct with which it was associated.

141. Lincoln (Lincolnshire).
Carved stone relief from a tomb depicting a boy charioteer. It perhaps records an actual event in the colony, or is simply an allegorical representation of the deceased in an idealized pose.

amphitheatre until Vespasian (69–79) ordered the construction of the Colosseum. In Roman Britain, these ceremonies and performances are just as likely to have taken place in such temporary structures, and may explain artifacts like the pottery face mask found at Baldock (Hertfordshire), perhaps used by a band of strolling players.

Later history
Silchester's amphitheatre lasted into the fourth century, and Cirencester's was still in use by the early fifth century. St Albans' theatre had become a rubbish dump by the late fourth century, probably thanks to anti-pagan legislation. Cirencester lay in an area most notable for sustained interest in paganism in the fourth century, possibly helping the amphitheatre remain in use for longer. London's amphitheatre was a rubbish dump as well by the mid-fourth century, and by 367 it was being robbed for stone.

Seeing theatres and amphitheatres
Remains of amphitheatres can be seen at Carmarthen, Chichester, Cirencester, Dorchester, London and Silchester. Some fragments can be seen at Canterbury. However, the most instructive – and visible – site is the theatre at St Albans.

142. Colchester (Essex).
The remains of a stadium, used for chariot-racing and other games, found during the winter of 2004–5. It is the only one yet found in Britain. Probably first century AD.

Stadiums
Very few stadiums, or circuses, used for chariot-racing are known in the northwestern provinces of the Roman Empire, and until 2005 none had been found in Britain. Hairpin-shaped, they usually ranged from 250 to 500 m (820 to 1,640 ft) in length, and consisted of a track running down both sides of a central barrier (*spina*). Banks of seats ran all the way round, except at one end where the starting gates were. In the winter of 2004–5 it was realized that massive walls found on an excavation site just south of the colony at Colchester represented the likely remains of a stadium [142]. Probably built in the first century, the structure would have provided chariot-racing entertainment for the colonists, and is the largest known public building in Roman Britain, at 250 m (820 ft) long. Until the find, chariot-racing was only testified in Britain in the form of a sculpture of a charioteer found at Lincoln [141], on a mosaic found at Horkstow (Lincolnshire), and on a variety of moulded glass beakers depicting the sport. But given the tradition of chariot warfare in pre-Roman Britain, it is likely the activity was popular in the new province. Throughout the Empire chariot-racing provoked pathological rivalry between teams, and elevated victorious charioteers to a level only matched by movie stars today.

Urban populations depend on surplus rural food production. To buy this surplus, these populations have to provide services, but cannot be so large that they exceed the capacity of the rural population to feed them. This is a self-regulating economic phenomenon. The principal towns of Roman Britain were therefore evenly distributed in the most agriculturally productive parts of the province. The clustering of villa estates close to the major towns, particularly on or near the major routes in and out of those towns, demonstrates this close relationship. Many of the richer estates probably belonged to members of the decurial class in each town, but in no instance do we know the name of any villa owner in Britain.

The principal commercial centre in a major town was the forum [143]. The well-known Piazza of the Corporations at Ostia (Italy) preserves mosaics depicting images associated with the individual businesses involved. Nearby were warehouses for storing the goods. In London at Regis House, an early second-century riverside warehouse storing samian pottery burned down, thus preserving remains of its stored stock. Across the river at Southwark, waterlogged conditions preserved part of a storage building in the thriving commercial suburb.

As forums were usually maintained, there is little chance of finding evidence of commercial activity, but the fire of *c.* 165–75 in the forum at Wroxeter was followed by backfilling and repair that buried some of the scattered and burned merchandise. Gaulish samian, Romano-British *mortaria* and whetstones were found in the forum gutter where they fell from stalls around the piazza. The piazza served as an open-air market and thoroughfare, where everyday social and commercial transactions were conducted. The forum could be supplemented by a *macellum*. Examples have been identified at Leicester, Wroxeter and *Verulamium*. Leicester's was so big it matched the forum in scale and was erected in the early third century, perhaps because existing market facilities had proved inadequate.

Evidence for other commercial establishments has been found in most towns. At Pompeii, householders created self-contained, street-frontage apartments, presumably let to traders and craftsmen.[20] A house in St Albans, close to the town centre, seems to have been arranged along these lines.[21]

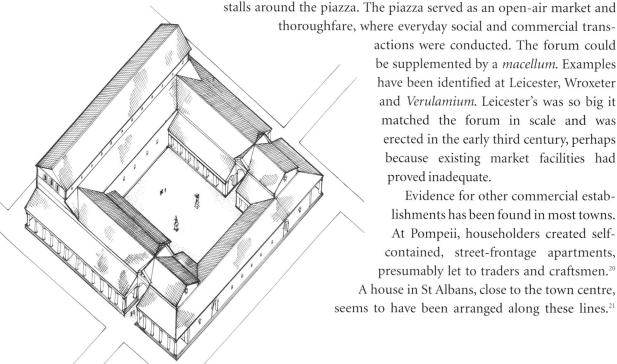

143. Lincoln (Lincolnshire). The forum-basilica complex at *Lindum*, as it might have appeared in the late second or early third century. It replaced the headquarters of the first-century legionary fortress, but there may have been an intermediate timber basilica and forum. Part of the basilica's rear wall, known as the 'Mint Wall', survives today (see p. 141).

A public latrine and an eating house were amongst the businesses that seem to have been let along the roadside. From the mid-first century, towns such as London, and even military *vici*, had streets lined with rectangular buildings made of timber and wattle-and-daub. Their narrow ends faced the street, jostling for frontage space, where light industrial and commercial businesses could take advantage of passing traffic. At St Albans, *Insula* XIV contained a row of timber shops and other businesses that were operating by the time of the Boudican revolt. Traces of crucibles and other debris show that metalworking was one of the activities. Timber-framed buildings were quickly and cheaply erected. There was nothing unusual about building like this, and some of the establishments were comfortably fitted out. Timber housing in Gutter Lane, in London, had painted wall plaster and tessellated flooring. In this respect, towns were more advanced than rural housing, which took much longer to catch up. However, these structures were susceptible to fire, and *Insula* XIV was razed in the Boudican revolt. It was redeveloped, but burned down again in *c.* 155.

By the second century, commercial growth had settled down and there seem to have been the time, money and skills available to start investing in better-appointed townhouses, not least because of the risk of fire. Silchester's *Insula* IX saw its first-century timber houses replaced with stone housing, though oddly a subsequent period saw a new building in timber. Most of the new stone houses consisted of one or two wings with a row of rooms and flanking corridor in each, and were often embellished with mosaics and wall plaster.

St Albans has produced several late second-century mosaic floors, themselves evidence for the existence of mosaic industries in towns (see p. 136). No mosaic workshops have been identified, but premises must have existed where designs were available for examination and prefabricated panels were manufactured. Late second-century mosaics at Cirencester are amongst the most accomplished from Roman Britain, and must reflect the region's wealth by this date. Even houses in Aldborough, beyond York, had mosaics by this time. Fourth-century mosaics installed in villas continue to show very specific regional differences, and almost certainly were made by mosaicists based in major towns.

By the late second century, urban housing was less dense, perhaps because of catastrophic fires at Wroxeter, St Albans (*c.* 155), and London during the reign of Hadrian. The town councils would have issued legislation, demanding that houses be built of more fire-resistant materials and be further apart. This may also be why very few townhouses ever seem to have had baths, since these presented an obvious fire risk. Most townhouses remained in use into the fourth century [144], a time when Cirencester saw the appearance of new farmhouses within the walled

144. Dorchester (Dorset).
Townhouse at *Durnovaria*, built
originally as a small structure in
the third century. It was
substantially enlarged in the fourth
century, and may have remained in
use until the fifth century, albeit in
a run-down state.

area on virgin plots. Whether these represent a response to external
threats by elevating food production in a safe environment, or just the
exploitation of unused land, is unknown.

TOWN WALLS

All major towns in Roman Britain were eventually equipped with walls,
and so were some of the small towns. We do not know why this happened when it did, but they represent the last phase of public building
works in towns, and came well after the construction of public buildings.
Colchester fell easily to Boudica's rebels precisely because the colonists
had levelled the old legionary fortress defences. Not surprisingly, at the
other colonies of Gloucester and Lincoln, the legionary defences were
retained and even strengthened, even though by the late first century
there was no obvious threat to these or any other town. Consequently,
the other towns were left without any walls.

Nevertheless, by the late second century major towns were increasingly being kitted out with circuits of earthen ramparts, incorporating
existing monumental gates. By the middle of the third century, these
were generally faced with stone revetments, providing a much more
imposing façade. It is tempting to link the new defences with testified
historical events. But there really is no evidence to support that. However, the third century was also the time when, as we have seen, the
fortified compounds known today as the Saxon Shore forts were built.
These are generally attributed to the appearance of maritime pirates, but

it is difficult to see how land-locked towns like Cirencester or *Verulamium* would have seen walls as essential. Walls rarely corresponded to the settled area. Caistor-by-Norwich ended up with walls that enclosed a considerably smaller area than that originally laid out. The same occurred at Silchester, though the difference is less pronounced. Conversely, at Cirencester significant areas within the walled area remained apparently unoccupied.

It is more likely that town walls came about for a variety of reasons. Nebulous fears may have helped move town councils to issue decrees in a context where fortifications were being built elsewhere. Town walls also had the capacity to be impressive statements, as well as helping to control the movement of traffic. There may have been local fears that itinerant bands would enter towns and rob householders. In late third-century Gaul, a group of landless malcontents, the Bagaudae, created havoc until an imperial military initiative put an end to their brigandage. Over time, defences were themselves augmented. At Caerwent, a series of prominent bastions were added around the mid-fourth century to walls that had probably been originally built as much as a century before. Similar additions were certainly made elsewhere, for example at London.

It was thought until recently that London's walls might have stifled its commercial base. But recent discoveries have shown how difficult it is for us to interpret town walls, since the circumstances from case to case were very different. At Shadwell, about 1.6 km (1 mile) east of the walled city, a monumental bath-house was erected at around the same time London's stone walls were being built. It remained in use until the late fourth century, spanning a period in which even London's riverside was fitted with a defensive wall, thereby cutting off the wharfs that had played so important a role in London's growth. The new baths complex, and the other buildings around it, may have been part of a new downriver port that allowed trade to continue while London's residents and administrative facilities remained protected behind the walls. At any rate, the idea that London's walls would have stifled the settlement is no longer tenable.

THE 'SMALL TOWNS'

Few 'small towns' have been explored in detail, and many lie under modern developments. Their success reflected the economic and social processes at a local level that had promoted the growth of their more formal cousins. Categorizing small towns is impossible because they lacked the public buildings and substantial townhouses of the principal towns. They did not usually have regimented street grids, and only some had fortifications. Some did have one or other of these features, for example Alchester (Oxfordshire), which had a street grid. Excavations have been limited, which means that in many cases even the area occupied is

145. Wall (Staffordshire).
The baths of the *mansio* at the roadside settlement of *Letocetum*. Establishments like this along major routes serviced the needs of official travellers, traders and individuals, providing food and shelter, stabling and bathing. The baths here reached their final form by the late third century, but fell out of use by the fourth century.

unknown. Water Newton (*Durobrivae*), in Cambridgeshire, was one of the best defined. Its third-century walls enclosed 18 ha (44.5 acres), but aerial photography shows that settlement was, or certainly had been, more extensive. The walled area of Great Casterton (Rutland) covered 7.3 ha (18 acres), but such figures can be misleading. Occupation debris at the unwalled settlement of Baldock (Hertfordshire) has, for example, been traced across 30 ha (74.1 acres). Bath, one of the most specialized small towns, had walls enclosing around 12 ha (29.7 acres), but it is clear from finds in the area that Roman settlement was much more extensive. At the other end of the scale, Dorn (Gloucestershire) on the Fosse Way had walls enclosing just 4 ha (10 acres), though here, too, settlement was evidently more widespread.

Overall, the small towns had entirely individual histories that reflected their unique circumstances. These included road and water communications, being a convenient day's journey or more from a major town, natural resources (for example, the lead mines at Charterhouse), the presence or lack of a local shrine and *mansio*, whether or not there had been a fort on the site, and so on. Towns grew because the economy and society of a Roman province depended on their existence. Wherever men gathered to exploit a location, such as a river crossing or road junction, the resulting settlement often grew into a town. Small towns seem to have thrived in fourth-century Britain, in contrast to other northwest provinces. Even so, at this time those that were fortified, such as Ancaster and Horncastle, both in Lincolnshire, and Dorn seem to have had walled areas that represented much smaller zones than the settlements once covered.

Small towns usually exhibit strip development along street frontages on major routes. But unlike major towns, they did not noticeably progress further, unless singled out for special treatment. Caerwent was like any other small town until it was made a *civitas* capital. This transformed its character by providing all of the features of an administrative centre, though it never grew very large. Springhead's location in Kent favoured the development of a small town. The settlement had a small temple precinct with several Romano-Celtic temples in it, suggesting that there was a pre-Roman cult in existence when Watling Street was consolidated as a major Roman trunk route through it by the mid-first century. Springhead lay an easy one-day journey west from the large town at Rochester on the road to London, making it an ideal place to break the trip. The setting, though ruined today by development, was clearly once convivial and attractive. Wall (Staffordshire) had once been a fort, but its development into a small town depended on the fact that it lay on the main road from London to Wroxeter and Chester. A *mansio* was built here to service the constantly passing traffic [145].

Ancaster not only lay on Ermine Street between London and Lincoln, but also on an east-west route that cut through a gap in the Lincolnshire Wolds between Sleaford, the old Corieltauvian settlement, and the Fosse Way to the west. The shrine of an otherwise unknown deity called 'Viridios' was located somewhere in the settlement that must have grown up around the crossroads, and which probably had Iron Age origins. The road south from Ancaster forks, but both routes rejoined at Water Newton on the River Nene. Water Newton lay very close to the major early vexillation fortress at Longthorpe, but it rapidly developed around the road junction, largely because of the natural resources that made a pottery industry possible [146]. By the third century, Nene Valley pottery was one of the dominant ceramic industries, and Water Newton was an imposing small town with its own walls.

We know almost nothing about the administration of small towns. But the evidence of administrative structures in the *vici* that clustered around the northern forts makes it likely that all of these places had local governments. If assemblies of magistrates were possible on the edge of the Roman world, then the small towns in southern Britain must also have had their own administrative assemblies, even if they had no public buildings that we can identify. These were probably created on an ad-hoc basis and were perhaps only intermittently in operation, as and when enough people had the time or inclination to maintain them.

146. Water Newton (Cambridgeshire).
Beaker with white painted decoration made in the local Nene Valley potteries. Good road and river communications ensured *Durobrivae*'s growth on the back of the pottery industry. The wares were widely distributed, but especially in an area covering most of East Anglia, Hertfordshire, London and the East Midlands. Height 20.8 cm. Third century.

ROMAN BATH

Bath is the most remarkable Roman site in Britain, and was known to the Romans as *Aquae Sulis* ('The Waters of Sulis') and *Aquae Calidae* ('Hot Springs'). The settlement had no formal status, but it did have some of the most extravagant architecture in the province and one of the most cosmopolitan populations. The centrepiece, dominating the town, was the massive temple and baths complex that surrounded the sacred hot-water spring of the local deity, Sulis, conflated with classical Minerva [147]. Sulis-Minerva is attested on numerous inscriptions and 'curse' tablets found in and around the complex.

Bath lies on the Fosse Way, laid down by the Roman army in the late 40s. A fort is likely to have been established here early on, but to date only auxiliary cavalry tombstones substantiate this. There seems to have been no native settlement, or any kind of physical shrine. By the late first century, engineering and structural work had begun to convert the site into a full-scale religious, healing and leisure complex [148]. The spring was contained within a wall to create a pool, with the overflow channelled into the River Avon. The spring became the central feature of the temple precinct. Nearby was the altar where sacrifices and offerings were made, overlooked by the temple of Sulis-Minerva, of which much has survived.

The temple's pediment sculpture is a remarkable conflation of styles in acknowledgment of this hybrid cult. The central disc, depicting Oceanus with serpent hair, echoes the image of the Gorgon Medusa on the medallion Minerva wore on her breastplate (see p. 236). However, Oceanus has taken on a wildly provincial form contrasting with the classical building. A recent, though unsubstantiated, theory suggests that Togidubnus wielded so much power across the south that he may have been responsible for developing Bath as a Romanized shrine. The army is known from the Continent to have had an active interest in developing spa sites, and it is equally likely that it was their efforts that lay behind the work.

Certainly soldiers from around Britain and their personal entourages continued to frequent Bath.

On the other side of the sacred spring from the temple lay the monumental baths, dominated by the Great Bath [149], flanked at either end by conventional baths suites. In the early part of the period the Great Bath seems to have had a timber roof, which rotted and had to be pulled down by the late second century. At around this time the sacred spring itself was enclosed beneath a vaulted building, creating a suitably steamy and mysterious environment. By the early fourth century, the vault had caused the building to begin collapsing, and it was reinforced with buttresses. The new buttresses created an architectural façade that overlooked the altar and was mirrored by an architectural screen on the other side.

One of the 'curse' tablets found at Bath shows that there was certainly a temple to Mars in the vicinity. Curved architectural fragments

147. *Left.* Bath (Somerset).
The temple precinct as it might have appeared in the fourth century, looking towards the temple of Sulis-Minerva. The building to the left, echoed by a blind façade opposite, covered the sacred spring.

148. *Opposite above.* The temple complex at Bath.
A reconstruction drawing of the temple and baths complex that dominated the centre of *Aquae Sulis.*

149. *Right.* The Great Bath.
The superstructure of the Great Bath is nineteenth-century work.

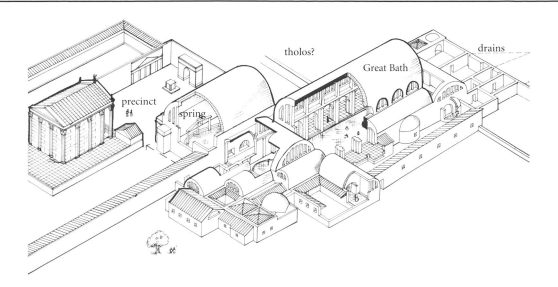

precinct

spring

tholos?

Great Bath

drains

show that either a theatre or a round classical temple of Greek origin (*tholos*) stood nearby. Curiously for a place that must have had a reputation as a healing cult, there is little or no evidence of this from the various inscriptions that have been found. Perhaps the most interesting is the rededication by the 'centurion of the region', Gaius Severius Emeritus, of a sacred spot after it had been 'wrecked by insolent hands'. Bath, it seems, also attracted rowdy pleasure-seekers, a reminder that the healing cults of the Roman Empire were also plagued by quacks and charlatans, only too happy to relieve the gullible and sick of their funds.

Nevertheless, there is no doubt that the temple and baths complex matured into what must once have been one of the most beautiful places in Roman Britain. The spring in the end would be its undoing, and also its preservation. As Roman Britain decayed, and as Christianity supplanted paganism, maintenance evaporated. The pool silted up and overflowed, and the site became awash with mud. The buildings themselves eventually collapsed into the mire, from which so much has been recovered from the eighteenth century to the present day.

CHAPTER 7

INDUSTRY, COMMERCE & PRODUCTION

There was no Roman concept of an 'economy' as we understand it. Instead, there were countless local economies and industries that functioned without any recourse to balance sheets or accountants. Virtually no records have survived to show how the Roman version of an economy worked. All we have are occasional references in ancient texts, and the physical materials recovered from sites. We would need to know where these goods were made, the quantity in which they were produced, how they were transported, who they were sold to, and so on. Generally, this information is not available.

Writing at the end of the first century BC, Strabo believed that the Britons' enthusiasm for trade meant that they had effectively Romanized themselves without any need for an invasion. He says that Britain exported grain, cattle, hunting dogs, slaves, gold, silver and iron. The Britons imported from Gaul ivory chains, necklaces, amber, glassware and 'other trinkets', and did all this despite the onerous customs duties imposed in Gaul on commerce.[1] Diodorus Siculus added his description of the export of tin to Gaul.[2] So, trade was well established long before the Claudian conquest. Britain exported basic resources in exchange for manufactured goods, benefiting a very limited upper tier of society. The process resembles that seen in Third World countries today. Strabo's picture probably did not change much for the first two centuries of Roman Britain, although the quantities grew enormously. There is no comparable description of Britain's imports and exports in later years, but it probably remained an exporter of staples. Imperial panegyrics of the late 290s praised the importance of Britain's abundant harvests [150]. In or around 359, the emperor Julian is said to have built new granaries in Gaul to store grain imported from Britain.[3]

There was a considerable change in how the land was organized. Britain has traditionally been perceived as having highland and lowland zones. The lowland zone, roughly to the area south and east of the Fosse Way, is the most agriculturally productive. By the late Iron Age, the population and its agricultural output were producing enough of a surplus to sustain the trade Strabo describes. The highland zone was capable of some agricultural production, and was the source of most of Britain's minerals.

150. Lullingstone (Kent).
Mosaic panel depicting Autumn with attributes invoking the harvest. Britain's agricultural produce was of vital importance to the Roman Empire in the west when this floor was laid, *c.* 360.

A more sophisticated model has been devised recently, in which the southeast and East Anglia are an Eastern Zone, and Wales, the northwest and the southwest peninsula form a Western Zone [151].[4] Both zones essentially maintained a form of continuity in rural land usage from the Iron Age into Roman Britain. Between the two lies a Central Zone running all the way from the extreme northeast down through Lincolnshire, the East Midlands, the Mendips and Cotswolds, Somerset and Dorset. The Central Zone corresponds approximately to the area in which Roman villas were most densely distributed and with a high proportion of the major towns, and thus was the area that changed the most in the Roman period.

Communications linked the military establishments with major towns and small towns. This infrastructure also joined Britain to the rest of the Empire. Towns were markets and sources of production, and attracted imported goods, as did the forts. Villa estates and small farmsteads were linked into this network. Since rural sites represented at least 90 per cent or more of the population, this was extremely important. The level of industrial and commercial activity in Britain is reflected at almost every settlement of Roman date. The Vindolanda tablets have provided us with unparalleled evidence for the types of goods moved about in Roman Britain. Many provide detailed lists of commodities, quantities and costs, including goods that rarely survive in the archaeological record. The very triviality of the material shows that this kind of record-keeping must

151. Rural zones in Roman Britain.
Roman Britain can be divided into three zones of rural settlement. The Central Zone is characterized by more intense settlement and farming, and is where the majority of villas are concentrated. To the east and west, settlement was more dispersed. In the remote southwest and northwest, and in north Wales, settlement is more native in style. (After Hingley and Miles, in Salway).

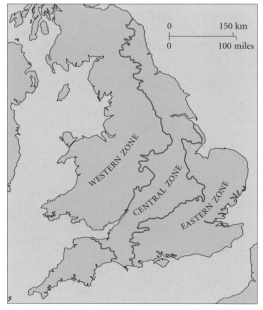

have been widespread and routine, resembling the abundant similar material found on papyri from Roman Egypt. They show that even remote places had access to the Roman trade network.

MINING

Mineral resources have often been regarded as a possible motive for invading Britain. Since metals were already being exported this is unlikely, but exploitation certainly increased after 43 to satisfy the needs of fort-builders, town development and commerce. To begin with, minerals were controlled by the *procurator metallarum*, 'procurator of mines', who was probably responsible for an iron punch found in London bearing the letters 'M.P.BR' for *Metalla Provinciae Britanniae*.[5] The best evidence for metal extraction comes from lead-mining, mainly from lead pigs stamped with date of production and source. Other metals were probably treated the same way, but since these were either bullion, or prone to corrosion in pure form (mainly iron and copper), for obvious reasons little survives. There have been occasional finds of tin and copper ingots, vital to the production of bronze used to make coins, brooches, jewelry, instruments, decorative fittings and vessels [152].

Little is known about the process of extraction of lead, largely because Roman lead mines were used after the Roman period, often destroying evidence of earlier mining [153]. At Charterhouse, the lead ore was laboriously hacked out along natural faults in the rock. Lead deposits are sometimes associated with silver, which was important to the Empire, as bullion was used to pay its soldiers and officials. A number of the lead pigs from Britain are accordingly stamped 'silver works', but it is almost impossible to identify any silver obtained this way. Silver is very rare in ingot form, and the only silver ingots found in Britain are much later in date and are not even demonstrably British.

Stamped lead pigs record mining mostly in the Mendips (Somerset), Derbyshire and Flintshire, and belong to the mid- to late first century [154]. They show that the government maintained careful supervision of the movement of lead. Pliny the Elder, writing in the mid-70s, said that Britain's lead ('used to make pipes') was abundant, and so easily extracted compared to deposits in Gaul and Spain that a law had been passed to limit its production, presumably to prevent the price being driven down.[6] A Mendips pig was stamped with Claudius' titles for the year 49. Evidently the frontier zone mining was already underway within a few years of the invasion, probably under the army's control. An undated pig is stamped *Britannicum Aug Le(g) II*, 'British (lead) II Legion Augusta'. However, most metal extraction was leased out. By the year 60 in Nero's reign, Gaius Nipius Ascanius was operating a mine in the Mendips and another one in Flintshire, at Carmel. His stamped pigs

152. Bronze key handles.
These key handles are typical of a huge variety of cast bronze artifacts manufactured in Roman Britain. The iron shanks of the keys have completely disappeared.

reflect the coordination and transport infrastructure that made multiple interests like this possible.[7] Lessees could also be cooperatives. One pig is stamped *Socorium Lutudarensium Britannicum ex argentariis*, 'Product of the Lutudarensian Company, from the silver works' in Derbyshire.[8] Some of the lead was certainly used in Britain. Lead pigs from the Flintshire field and marked *Deceanglicum* for the tribal area have turned up in Chester, where lead pipes bearing Agricola's titles as governor have also been found.[9] Three pigs, all bearing the name of Vespasian (69–79) and marked 'from the British silver works at VEB…', were found in a pit within a warehouse in London.[10] 'VEB' is thought to be the prefix of the unknown name of the Mendips lead works. The lead had been brought to London either for use there, or for export to other parts of Britain or the Continent. Several British lead pigs have been found in Gaul, confirming that it was exported. A pig was found at St Valéry sur Somme, one of several found in Gaul, stamped *Britan(nicum)* by the II legion under Nero.[11]

Lead's natural malleability made it ideal for use in plumbing, though of course wood and ceramic pipes were extensively used as well. Lead typically found other uses as waterproofing for roofs, tanks, weights, pewter (when alloyed with tin), bronze (when alloyed with copper), 'curse' tablets sold at shrine sites, seals and packaging labels. The labels are particularly useful as evidence for the movement of goods which themselves do not survive.

Lead extraction continued in Britain, but it became of less interest to the authorities whose real concern was the silver. By the fourth century, some lead mines were under local government control. The *civitates* of the Brigantes and the Iceni are named on lead pigs found in a wreck off Brittany. Pewter had become popular in the third and fourth centuries. It was made at many places in Britain into a second-grade silver-substitute fine tableware [155], and was also used extensively for coffins.

If lead was the plastic of the Roman Empire, iron was its steel. Iron was the automatic choice for use in weaponry, armour, vehicle fittings like linchpins, spindles for millstones, ploughshares, cramps used for securing stones and flue tiles in buildings, and tools and utensils of all sorts, in every possible application. Iron was even used for manufacturing some jewelry. Iron artifacts are well known from Britain, but corrosion has usually severely degraded them.

153. Lead mining.
Lead ore specimen from north Derbyshire.

154. Hints Common (Staffordshire).
Lead pig bearing the titles of Vespasian and Titus for the year 76. The pig is also stamped 'DECEANG' to denote its origin in the lead mines in northeast Clwyd. Weight 68.3 kg (151 lb). The base is 57.2 x 14.6 cm. (British Museum).

155. Dottery (Dorset).
Fourth-century decorated pewter plates, part of a hoard found at Dottery, near Bridport. Pewter became a popular second-grade tableware in fourth-century Britain, used by those who could not afford silver. It was widely manufactured in Britain, supplanting to some extent fine pottery in this role. Diameter of the largest dish 37.4 cm.

Britain has extensive deposits of iron ore. The primary ancient sources were the Weald of Sussex and Kent, and the Forest of Dean. Wealden iron was the most important natural resource industry of lowland Britain in the Roman period. Like early lead extraction, the military seem to have been involved, though the evidence is largely indirect. The *classis Britannica* is attested at a number of ironworking sites, such as Beauport Park and Cranborne, from stamped tiles. Since soldiers were commonly used in a wide range of jobs, it is quite feasible that the fleet had been allocated iron extraction for the state. Alternatively, its responsibilities might only have been transporting iron across the Channel and to the military north.

Mining was labour-intensive and continuous. Settlements grew up around mines. One developed around the Charterhouse lead mines very early in the Roman period, with a street system and even a small amphitheatre. Traces of slag show that the ore was smelted on site. A small Claudian fortlet may have housed a garrison, but at only 2,750 sq m (29,600 sq ft) it was little more than a fortified compound, and was probably used as a storage area for finished pigs. Charterhouse was well placed, and was occupied into the fourth century. A spur road from the Fosse Way joined it to the main road network, and the sea lay about 16 km (10 miles) to the west. Another ironworking settlement developed at Weston-under-Penyard (Herefordshire), in the Forest of Dean. Such places probably resembled frontier towns in North America that developed rapidly when new sources of minerals were discovered, such as Silver City, in South Dakota.

METALWORKING

The proliferation of manufactured metal goods in Roman Britain is the most conspicuous archaeological feature after pottery of the period. These range from weapons and tools to personal dress items, which themselves range from simple iron or bronze rings and brooches to elaborate gold and silver items. However, for obvious reasons, most surviving material is bronze [156], copper, or iron. In spite of how common these items are, the vast majority originally made will have been recycled, so metalworkers spent a great deal of their time reusing old metal goods. Much of what survives are brooches or similar items that were lost or deliberately deposited as grave goods or ritual offerings, and scrap pieces that were accidentally discarded before being recycled.

All urban, military and village settlements, as well as many villas, have produced evidence of metalworking, usually in the form of furnaces, crucibles and scrap. Crucibles themselves provide evidence of the level of production. As early as the late first century, the largest known had capacities in excess of 2,000 g (70 oz) of bronze, enough to manufacture 60 or more brooches. However, the bronze measuring-vessel found at Carvoran (see p. 177), probably used for grain and bearing an imperial inscription from 90–91, weighs just under 11.8 kg (26 lb) and is one of the largest bronze items known from Roman Britain.[12] At Castleford, around 800 pieces of clay moulds used in the manufacture of spoons have been found.

Forts and fortresses usually had a *fabrica*, or workshop, where the unit's weapons and armour were manufactured, along with iron nails and cramps used in building, and various fittings, such as washers, needed for artillery. The *fabrica* at the short-lived Flavian fortress of Inchtuthil has produced traces of smelting and other debris, but the most remarkable find was around a million unused iron nails, sealed in a pit by the withdrawing army to prevent them falling into the hands of the enemy. An *armamentaria* is recorded at Lanchester,[13] and an armourer called Julius Vitalis, serving with the XX legion, is attested at Bath [157].[14] Men like Vitalis were responsible for manufacturing and servicing the iron strips that formed legionary armour and its various fittings. It was labour-intensive work. It has been calculated that one mail shirt, destroyed in a fire of *c.* 300 at South Shields, would have been made of around 54,000 iron rings, taking an armourer many months to make.

Metalworking went on in almost every settlement. A goldsmith was working close to the so-called 'governor's palace' in London in the late first century. At York, a stone relief depicts a smith at work with his hammer, tongs and anvil. The goldsmith's workshop recorded on an inscription from Malton, and the various traces of metalworking in the towns, such as the St Albans *Insula* XIV shops and the Silchester basilica

156. Lullingstone (Kent).
Bronze jug found in the mausoleum just behind the villa at Lullingstone. Height about 21 cm. Third century.

157. Bath (Somerset).
Tombstone of Julius Vitalis, an armourer with the XX legion, who died at 29 years of age after nine years' service.

metalworkers, were mentioned in Chapter 6. In towns there were manufacturing firms with slave staff, but metalworking was also an everyday craft skill that virtually every settlement would have had someone reasonably competent in. A villa estate, for example, could not have functioned without its smithy. One of the rooms in the villa at Gadebridge Park (Hertfordshire), for example, has produced various traces of ash, iron slag and tools, as well as normal occupational debris, suggesting that this was where the villa blacksmith both worked and lived in the early fourth century.

The Snettisham and Thetford treasure hoards both seem to record work-in-progress belonging to jewelers. The Snettisham hoard [158] was buried after 155, but includes 83 silver coins, carefully selected from those of Domitian struck between the years 85 and 96, when silver coins were 93.5 per cent fine, an optimum combination of purity and hardness. The Thetford treasure includes a number of brand new gold rings set with much older gemstones that had evidently been recycled.

Found in relative isolation, the Thetford and Snettisham hoards are reminders that metalworking could just as easily be an itinerant activity, as well as one based in town premises. Brooch-making equipment, consisting of two-piece bronze moulds and various unfinished blanks, discovered at Old Buckenham (Norfolk) seems incongruous in such a remote context, unless it was simply an accidental loss by a travelling craftsman.[15] Since brooches are the commonest metal finds in Roman Britain, apart from coins, this sort of equipment must have been in prolific use, though it scarcely ever survives.[16] Other metalworking industries grew up in small settlements. Shrine sites were often focal points of small metalworking industries, because pilgrims expected to be able to purchase souvenirs in the form of votive statuettes, post metal votive letters or feathers on walls in the shrine area, or leave messages for the god secured with small bronze seal-boxes.

158. Snettisham (Norfolk).
A jeweler's hoard including finished rings and a collection of unmounted gemstones, and silver and brass coins for melting down into more jewelry. (British Museum).

The Fossdyke Mars [159] is an exceptionally fine piece of Gallo-Roman art that was probably made in Britain, but possibly by an immigrant craftsman. The pan from Ilam (Staffordshire), which names a number of forts along Hadrian's Wall, is one of three vessels probably produced as souvenirs of the frontier [160].[17] The maker of the Ilam pan made effective use of coloured enamel inlaid in a band around the bronze vessel, a particularly regional technique. The range of skills supplied the Romano-British market with a variety of choices, doubtless reflected in the prices. Some of the finest material was probably made abroad, possibly including the Mildenhall Treasure and monumental bronze statuary like the bust of Hadrian from London. But as we know so little about where this kind of material was made, it would be very unwise to rule anywhere out. The skills, after all, were as portable as the man or woman who possessed them. Some of the material in the early fifth-century Hoxne hoard is so rare it is impossible to say where the pieces were made.

By the fourth century, pewter, made from lead and tin, had become an increasingly popular substitute for silver tableware. But as it was an easily recyclable metal with a low melting point, relatively little survives. A number of sites have produced evidence for pewter manufacture, such as the former temple site at Nettleton (Wiltshire), which was also a small village settlement astride the Fosse Way. Like any such place there was an iron forge, complete with furnace and flue, as well as evidence of iron slag dated to the late fourth century. At another building, clay crucibles and traces of bronze slag used for bronze smelting were found. The pewter manufactory was established in the remains of a third-century house around 340, where several fragmentary limestone moulds used for casting dishes and bowls were found.

In antiquity, doctors enjoyed considerable veneration, although Pliny the Elder thought the general public was gullible and paid far too much respect to a profession dominated by quacks and charlatans. In Britain, Greek doctors are recorded in military contexts, such as Antiochos, who made a dedication to Asklepios, the god of medicine, at Chester.[18] More common, however, are the engraved stone dies used by itinerant practitioners to press into their patent eye salves, sold as solid blocks of medicine [161]. Eye disorders were common, and feature in the strength report from Vindolanda, which refers to ten men off-duty thanks to eye inflammations.[19] From Chester we have 'the anti-irritant salve of Quintus Julius Martinus' on a stone die, and from Cirencester 'Atticus' mild salve for all pains after the onset of ophthalmia'.[20] It is unlikely that the oculists named actually used the stamps. They had probably

159. Fossdyke (Lincolnshire).
Bronze statuette of Mars made by Celatus the coppersmith for the brothers Bruccius and Caratius Colasunus, who paid 100 *sestertii* for the work. Probably second century. (British Museum).

160. Ilam (Staffordshire).
Bronze pan, inlaid with enamel. The inscription names some of the Hadrian's Wall forts 'according to the course of the frontier'. Probably *c.* 130–200. (British Museum).

produced patent-branded eye salves, later sold on by middlemen. Several such stamps have been found at villas, probably because practitioners toured the province touting their patent remedies. Britain was even a source of medicine. At Haltern, in Germany, a lead bung from a jar bears the inscription *ex radice Britannica*, and probably refers to a medicine derived from a root (*radix*) found in Britain.

FOOD AND OTHER NATURAL PRODUCTS

Food scarcely survives at all in the physical record, but imported amphorae provide useful clues. London has produced many amphorae used for shipping wine, olive oil, olives and fish sauce (a kind of fermented paste), from as far away as Turkey and Lebanon. They were arriving as early as the 50s, reflecting Tacitus' description of London as a thriving mercantile centre before 60. Fish sauce was a product widely imported from the Mediterranean, and also closer to home. One amphora from the Thames still contained its 6,000 olives. Another from Chester is thought to describe its contents as 'flavoured fish-tail sauce,

matured for the larder'.[21] Others list wine, olives and brine amongst their contents. Collectively, the evidence points to a substantial trade in goods, particularly up to the mid-second century, and especially from Spain. It then tailed off, more or less disappearing by the third century. Exactly what happened thereafter is not very clear, because later amphorae are less common and do not carry inscriptions. It is likely that trade became more regional. Waterlogged deposits have preserved remains of wooden barrels that probably carried similar products. Occasionally foodstuffs like grain were carbonized by fire and turn up in excavation. One sample from London, destroyed around the time of the Boudican revolt, had been imported from the eastern Mediterranean area.

As so often it is the Vindolanda writing tablets that supply us with information about foodstuffs used in Britain, and the ability of the Roman system to transport it to the northern frontier. Barley, *cervesa* ('Celtic beer'), wheat, honey, cumin, pork fat, beans, ham, venison, chickens, geese and pickling are all amongst the goods recorded. Naturally, however, most trade in food took place within Britain. The large numbers of fowl bones found, for example, at the shrine of Mercury at Uley, could have come from animals reared in the immediate vicinity or from the more general area, as well as being brought by some of the pilgrims.

Pastoral farming, of course, produces more than just meat. It also produces wool, for example, but this has little chance of surviving, contributing to the distorted picture in the archaeological record. Fortunately, the *birrus Britannicus*, a kind of woollen coat, was listed on Diocletian's Edict of Prices. It must have been a familiar commodity, though the reference may have been to a style rather than to a product specifically 'made in Britain'. British wool rugs (*tapete*) are also listed as high-quality products, suggesting that by the beginning of the fourth century Britain had a well-developed textile industry.[22] Under exceptional circumstances leather goods can survive. Vindolanda has produced a large number of shoes, ranging from utilitarian boots to elaborately decorated sandals. In general, however, objects made of bone, including weaving frames, pins, combs, hinges, and gaming pieces are more likely to survive.

The circumstantial evidence of town and villa distribution suggests that the rural surplus was transported to nearby towns for sale and dispersal into a wider market. But we should never underestimate the potential for long-distance movement of food, even within the province. London's wharfs have shown that food was traded over hundreds of miles by sea. Ultimately, the archaeologist has to rely on the movement of more durable materials like pottery to identify the degree to which commodities were traded in Roman Britain.

STONE AND SCULPTURE

The only easily available stone in southeast Britain is flint. Found in irregularly-shaped nodules, it has to be carefully compacted in lime mortar to be of any use for building. The Central Zone coincides with a band of Jurassic limestone that stretches from Somerset right up through Lincolnshire. Easily worked, the limestone was widely used and exported, usually by sea, to the south and east.[23] The late third-century fort at Bradwell-on-Sea, for example, was built partly from Clipsham pink stone, transported from quarries northwest of Water Newton (Cambridgeshire), and must have been taken on a journey by river and sea over 300 km (190 miles).[24]

In the north, abundant local varieties of sandstone made the construction of forts and the manufacture of thousands of carved architectural details, altars and inscriptions possible. Since sources of stone have generally remained useful, evidence of quarrying is fairly rare. However, many quarries have been identified in the Hadrian's Wall zone, some of which have

161. *Opposite above.* **An oculist's stamp.**
This stamp records a variety of salves attributed to Marcus Julius Satyrus. One such salve, based on myrrh, was to be applied 'after the onset of ophthalmia'. Reproduced from an old engraving.

162. *Opposite below.* **A Roman kitchen.**
Foodstuffs are replicated in this reconstructed view of a Roman kitchen, but normally these do not survive in any recognizable form. (Museum of London).

163. Richborough (Kent).
North wall of the third-century coastal fort, showing a clear join between two working parties using completely different styles of laying stone.

POTTERY IN ROMAN BRITAIN

Pottery is a vital source of information about trade and industry in Roman Britain, especially the movement of food.[25] Easily broken, pottery's tendency to absorb traces of foodstuffs meant that it was routinely dumped in huge amounts. It was also used as containers for cremations and grave goods, and for storage, especially of coins in hoards. Most pottery vessels found are recovered from graves or hoards.

The Roman army established its own potteries to produce kitchenware and occasionally more sophisticated material. They bought in from local suppliers, introduced new forms, and helped stimulate production. Early military sites like Longthorpe and Usk have produced sherds that include imported wares and such specialized Roman forms as *mortaria* and lamps [164, 165].

These forms rapidly became widespread, especially in towns where demand was serviced by imports and local industries. A shop stocking imported samian and a clay oil-lamp factory in West Stockwell Street were part of an extensive ceramics industry based in and around Colchester from the mid-first century. Large-scale pottery production tended to be the preserve of more rural areas, such as the massive Oxfordshire industry of the second century and later. A notable exception was the Nene Valley industry, which promoted

164. Grantham (Lincolnshire).
A *mortarium* found at Grantham, but produced at the Hartshill-Mancetter industry, a major force in Romano-British ceramics that dominated the market in central and northern Britain.

the growth of the large 'small town' at Water Newton.

The vast majority of pottery used in Roman Britain was 'grey kitchenware', manufactured in astronomical quantities, usually very close to where they were used. Only under exceptional circumstances were such pieces transported over longer distances. At a local level small potteries, such as the 'Sugar Loaf Court' potter in late first-century London, serviced no more than a few farms or a neighbourhood. Other kitchenware industries, such as the black-burnished potters of the southwest and Thames Estuary area, were on a much bigger scale. Analysis of the wares and plotting of find-spots can pinpoint an industry's market reach, making it clear that water transport and army contracts could have had a dramatic effect on how far these products travelled.

Some specialized classes of pottery were more widely distributed. Normally made by potters who made nothing else, *mortaria* were produced in a number of different forms, all retaining the distinctive gritted bowl for mixing foodstuffs. Early examples were imported, but by the late first century a number of Romano-British industries, like the

165. Pottery lamps.
The two larger, first-century lamps were probably made in Italy or Gaul. The smaller, wheel-thrown lamp was designed to imitate bronze. Found at Billingsgate, it was probably made in London and was discarded after the loss of its handle.

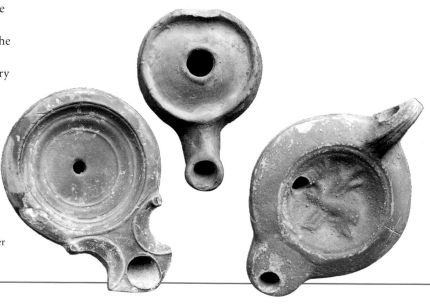

Brockley Hill potteries, had begun to produce them. In the second century, *mortaria* were being made in Hartshill-Mancetter (Warwickshire), Colchester and the Nene Valley. Amphorae, as they had been since the Iron Age, were almost invariably imported for their contents, which ranged from wines to fish sauce and olive oil. Some carry legible traces of writing that record what was inside and occasionally the city of origin.

Fine wares in the western provinces were dominated in the first and second centuries by the Gaulish samian industries. The origin of the term 'samian' is uncertain, but possibly comes from the red-slip wares manufactured on Samos, or the Latin word *samiare*, 'to polish'. The regional version of red-slip samian wares popular in the Roman Empire was produced in south Gaul in the first century and central Gaul in the second century [166]. In the late second century, East Gaulish samian took advantage of the demise of Central Gaul, but was usually inferior in quality. A Romano-British samian industry started up at Colchester *c.* 160, but the project was soon abandoned, apparently unable to compete with Gaulish samian. In the third century, the quality of East Gaulish samian deteriorated further until the industry collapsed altogether. Samian is found on almost all sites of early Roman date. Forts tend to produce the largest range of forms, but even modest farmsteads are likely to produce fragments of samian cups.

166. Alcester (Warwickshire). A mid-second-century samian bowl found at Alcester (*Alauna*), imported from central Gaul. Small towns, just like their larger counterparts, had access to goods imported from across the Roman world.

Samian's value to us lies in the use of distinctive decorative styles and potters' name-stamps. Because samian has been recovered in large amounts from levels of known date, it has helped date associated wares that lack identifying features. Samian imports peaked in the late first century, but continued to enter in substantial quantities until the early third century, when the industry fell into terminal decline and effectively disappeared. Other fine wares were shipped into Britain in far smaller quantities, including the Gallo-Belgic wares Terra Rubra and Terra Nigra, and a variety of beakers decorated with a trailed slip, which survive as the most

conspicuous remnants of a massive North Sea trade into eastern and northern Britain. They started to arrive in the late first century as seaborne trade in London reached its climax, and were still arriving nearly two hundred years later.

During the second century, Romano-British pottery industries became increasingly significant. Hand-made black-burnished kitchenware (BB1) manufactured in the Poole Harbour area was transported in vast quantities to the northern frontier from the second through the fourth centuries, supplemented by the wheel-thrown BB2 wares of the Thames Estuary. The Colchester and Nene Valley

167. Pottery fragments from London. A group of pottery pieces from the London wharfs gives an idea of the prolific range of wares found in the provincial capital, and reflected to a varying extent throughout Britain.

POTTERY *continued*

industries were producing fine wares that resembled Lower Rhineland material. Since Colchester had also been the location of a short-lived attempt to establish a samian industry, clearly derived from prototypes originating in East Gaul, it is quite possible that the Colchester potteries developed in part from the arrival of immigrant potters from the Rhineland. Colchester's samian might have failed, but its colour-coated cups and beakers were widely used until the middle of the third century.

The Nene Valley pottery industry had been around since the army

passed that way in the mid-first century. To the west, a widely dispersed group of potters in Oxfordshire was producing *mortaria* and bowls that copied samian forms. By the third century, the Oxfordshire and Nene Valley industries controlled much of the market for fine wares in Britain. Some imports still arrived, but in very reduced quantities. Alice Holt, near Farnham, was the centre of a substantial kitchenware industry that monopolized the market in the late third and fourth centuries in the southeast. Distribution of the material shows that proximity to the Thames and its tributaries

played a major role in dictating which sites these wares reached.

One of the abiding enigmas of Roman Britain is, given the extent that pottery production had reached by the end of the fourth century, how quickly pottery ceased to be made. Although some fifth-century pottery production continued, along with limited importation of Mediterranean fine wares to western Britain, neither the demand for pottery nor the skills to make it seem to have survived the disruption of the period. There remains no easy explanation for this.

168. Limestone Corner (Northumberland).
Close-up of an abandoned block in the forward ditch of Hadrian's Wall.

produced inscriptions left in the stone face by the military masons. It has been estimated that 3.7 million tonnes of stone were needed to complete the Wall.[26] Much the most dramatic evidence can be found at Limestone Corner [168], between the forts of Carrawburgh and Chesters [169]. Here, the forward ditch of the Wall was cut from the living rock by chiselling out holes for the insertion of wooden wedges. Soaked in water, these expanded and split the rock. Eventually, the work proved too much and it was abandoned, leaving a number of the blocks *in situ*, still with their wedge holes.

More exotic stone was sometimes imported from the Continent. The monumental Trajanic inscription found at Caerleon seems to have been carved from marble quarried in Tuscany. It may even have been carved at the source in the year 98, since when it arrived the text was clumsily altered to adapt Trajan's titles to those of 99–100. Fishbourne Palace was fitted out with veneers made of marble shipped in from the Pyrenees, Haute Garonne, Skyros and Turkey, showing that if the money was available, stone could be obtained from effectively anywhere in the Roman Empire. Given the practicalities, however, such material was usually only imported in very small quantities, though the Carrara marble cladding used for the monumental arch at Richborough is an exception.

Sculptors are known by name on a few pieces, for example, Sulinus the *scultor* [sic] on an altar at Bath. Another Bath altar names a *lapidarius* (stonemason) called Priscus.[27] Carving stone was not restricted to people who did it for an occupation. This much is obvious from some of the

most clumsily executed examples. The Jurassic limestone that crops up so much in the Central Zone is so soft when freshly quarried that it is easier to carve than wood. Private individuals with a reasonable amount of dexterity were quite capable of producing their own carved reliefs, like Juventinus, who carved a figure of the god Romulus in a gabled relief and proudly recorded his own name on it.[28] In the remote north, the relief from High Rochester depicting Venus [170] is a marvellous combination of classical content and amateurish execution.

169. Chesters (Northumberland).
The Hadrianic cavalry fort at *Cilurnum* straddled Hadrian's Wall, not visible here apart from a short stretch between the River Tyne and the fort's east wall. Most of the internal buildings and defences remain buried. The detached baths lie close to the river bank for drainage reasons, and to reduce the risk of fire. Like all of the Wall's facilities, the fort and its buildings were built from locally quarried stone.

170. High Rochester (Northumberland).
Carved stone relief depicting Venus with her handmaidens. Despite the classical subject matter, the exaggerated features and wooden postures are hallmarks of an inexpert sculptor. Height 67 cm. Third century.

TIMBER

Timber was so fundamental in the Roman world that its name, *materia*, has become our general word, 'material'. Timber was used in enormous quantities in the forts and fortresses of the first century, and also in towns, for housing and for the first phases of some public buildings, like Silchester's basilica and forum. It was also used for the construction of ships and carts, as well as for tools, writing tablets, and even sculpture. As fuel it kept bathhouses going, as well as the furnaces that smelted ores into metal and pottery kilns.

Prehistoric communities were already adept at exploiting and clearing woodland. If Roman exploitation was on a grander scale, a new programme of woodland management must have been begun quickly. Just how much effort was involved is clear from a mutiny that broke out in the army on the Rhine in the year 14, caused in part by the work.[29] By 75 to 85, the legion at Caerleon was gathering timber for a fortress calculated to have needed wood from at least 150 ha (371 acres), with additional stocks needed for replacements and maintenance.[30] The contemporary fortress at Inchtuthil is estimated to have consumed over 16,000 cubic m (650,000 cubic ft) of wood, though all that survives are postholes, trench slots and iron nails.[31] A phenomenal 5,500 ha (13,591 acres) of managed woodland has been estimated as the minimum to service the later masonry legionary baths at Caerleon.[32] These measurements are impressive but meaningless, since their significance depends entirely on whether or not they resulted in the exhaustion of stocks, leading to the consolidation of forts in stone, or if demand was met from managed woodland.

References by ancient authors to carpentry, and the evidence of timber surviving in waterlogged deposits, show that carpenters' skills varied as much as those of sculptors. In large-scale, heavy-duty applications like wharfside timbers, the joints were crude. Large iron nails were used indiscriminately to hold the framework together. Conversely, evidence from structures like the Southwark warehouse [171] and early military buildings at Carlisle show that Roman carpenters were quite capable of producing neat dovetailed joints.[33] Trenails were used for dowelled joints when necessary, and remains have been found at, for example, the Blackfriars and County Hall ships, found in London, as well as at Frocester villa. The limited survival of wood means that we have no idea how roofs were constructed, except that they were strong enough to support heavy ceramic tiles.

171. Southwark (London). Waterlogged conditions preserved part of a timber warehouse that had been built into a specially dug pit, accessed by a ramp. This means it was probably designed to store perishable foodstuffs. The floor was made of planks laid on sill-beams. Probably late first to late second century.

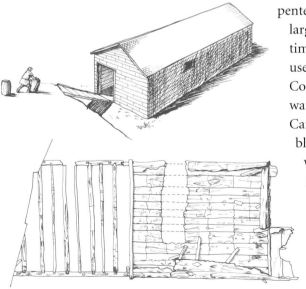

TILE AND BRICK

So long as the resources (suitable clay and water) were available, tile and brick could be manufactured on-site or nearby. The legions and fleet manufactured their own tiles, usually stamped with the unit's titles. The best known are the tiles made by the XX legion at their works depot, located close to the fortress at Holt (Clwyd), and those made for the fleet, *classis Britannica*. Tiles were also produced in London for the procurator, while some of the major towns like Gloucester also had their official tileries. Private and commercial tile production gives us a better idea of the market. The Ashtead villa seems to have been run as a commercial tiling concern. A tilery sited nearby produced distinctively decorated flue-tiles, used at other locations, such as Cobham and Walton Heath, in the region. Other tileries have been found at Chelmsford and London, which seem unrealistically distant for freighting such heavy and fragile goods, so the Ashtead tilers may have built kilns closer to where the tiles were needed.

The Kent tiler, Cabriabanus, used a roller-die to impress his name on his tiles, thus identifying his work. It also produced a relief surface that helped the tile adhere to mortar and was invisible during the tile's functional life span. His work has been found at several places in Kent, including the Darenth and Plaxtol villas, so he must have been a jobbing tiler, taking commissions as and when they arose.

Flue-tiles were often distinctively marked. Usually a tile-comb was used to create diagonal and crossed strips that have no significance beyond creating a roughened surface for mortar. The Ashtead tiler decorated his work with animal scenes [172], even though these were invisible once the tiles were installed. Most roof- and other tiles carry no marks at all, except occasionally for numerals now interpreted as batch-marks; one brick from Woodchester carries the numerals 'XXXXIIII' and 'XXXXVI'. The tile-kiln at Great Cansiron Farm, Hartfield (East Sussex) is not specifically associated with a villa house, but its most probable function was serving that market. One of the *tegulae* found here was inscribed with the numbers 'CCXV' and 'CCXIIII', probably referring to

172. Ashtead (Surrey).
Box-flue tile from the kiln on the villa estate. The distinctive animal chase pattern distinguished the products of this factory, which have been found at several other sites in the area, including Beddington, 13.5 km (9 miles) to the east.

kiln-loads.[34] In general, similarities of tile-comb patterns and other design details at individual sites suggest that most villas were serviced by a kiln built nearby and operated by a single team.

MERCHANTS AND TRADERS

London, also lying on a major tidal river opposite the Continent, started out its life as a home to traders and commerce. Not surprisingly, it has produced unparalleled evidence for trade in the Roman period in Britain. A sensational discovery at Southwark in 2002 could not have been more appropriate. This was a dedication to the Spirits of the Emperors and the god Mars Camulos by one Tiberinius Celerianus, who came from a north Gaulish tribe called the Bellovaci [173].[35] He tells us that he was a *moritix*, or *moritex*, and a Londoner. *Moritix* seems to be the colloquial Celtic term for a merchant seafarer, where Celtic and Latin both used the same root for the word for 'sea' (in Latin, *mare* and in Welsh, *mor*).

Lucius Viducius Placidus was a negotiator, or merchant, from Rouen. In 221, he paid for an arch at York that was probably an entrance to a temple precinct, and possibly a shrine. Placidus also left a dedication at the shrine of the goddess Nehalennia at Colijnsplaat, near the mouth of the Scheldt across the North Sea.[36] What Placidus was trading in can only be guessed at, although pottery is likely, but he evidently dealt in goods that came from the Rhineland. Marcus Secundinius Silvanus also left a dedication to Nehalennia on the other side of the Scheldt estuary, at Domburg, recording his occupation as a *negotiator cretarius Britannicianus*, 'pottery merchant on the Britannia trade'.[37] Another variant was the *negotiator Britannicianus moritex*, Gaius Aurelius Verus, who made a dedication to Apollo at Cologne.[38] Cologne is known to have been a source of goods that ended up in Britain. Pottery was certainly among them, along with glass and pipeclay figurines, some stamped by the manufacturer Servandus of Cologne.[39]

At Vindolanda, Gavo was responsible for supplying some of the food and textiles used at the fort. He is recorded on an account that lists the goods and their prices. Atrectus worked as a brewer (*cervesarius*). He was probably a civilian trader who serviced the market for beer in the fort.[40] Such individuals are freak survivals from what must have once been a very large number of men who made a living out of the cross-Channel and North Sea trade, or who serviced demand on a more local scale. The sea merchants took financial risks in shipping goods across waters that were not only susceptible to major storms, but also to piracy. The results of their collective efforts are clear from the large quantities of ceramic material in particular that was

173. Southwark (London). Inscription from the temple precinct dedicated to Mars Camulos and the Imperial Spirits by the *moritix*, Tiberinius Celerianus. The inscription is incomplete, but parallels from the rest of the Empire suggest that Celerianus had been honoured as *Primus Omnium*, 'first citizen of all Londoners'. (Museum of London).

shipped into Britain. The Vindolanda tablets exemplify how impossible it is to have any really meaningful idea of trade and commerce in Roman Britain. Gavo's account includes wool, beans and honey – substances that have virtually no chance of surviving in the archaeological record.

COINAGE AND UNITS OF EXCHANGE

Coinage made the sophisticated levels of trade in the Roman period possible. Rome also introduced standards of lengths, weights and measures, making exchange more reliable and consistent. The Carvoran dry-measure [174], for example, is thought to have been used for measuring corn. Its stated capacity is 17.5 *sextarii*, about 9.5 litres (16.7 pints). Since it carries an imperial inscription for the years 90 to 91, it may have been used for assessing tribute or for doling out official rations to military units.

The so-called 'Celtic' tribal coinage was largely silver and gold, but the weights, denominations and purity of issues varied immensely. Celtic coinage was demonetized after the invasion and generally disappeared, though very occasionally some pieces appear in hoards of Roman date.[41] In the Roman world, currency was based on intrinsic value. Debased silver, for example, was worth less than purer silver, even if the denomination was the same. Throughout the period, the purity and weight of silver and gold coinage fluctuated either because silver was debased, or because gold and silver was struck in smaller weights. A range of brass and copper small-change coins was issued for everyday circulation. Soon after the invasion, Roman coinage became the only circulating coinage in Britain. To begin with, soldiers were probably the most prolific users of coin. Barter is likely to have dominated transactions in the early part of the Roman period, and probably remained a significant factor in how the economy worked. Nevertheless, all communities had access to coinage, and all of them used it to some extent. Roman coins found their way into hoards in Scotland, showing that even beyond the frontier tribal peoples had become accustomed to coinage as a means of storing wealth.

The government spent much of its time trying to recover the gold and silver bullion paid out to its employees. The coins were of high value, so the recipients either chose to save or hoard the bullion, or exchange some of it at a moneychanger for brass and copper coins [175]. Since taxes had to be paid in bullion, taxpayers had to take base-metal coinage to the moneychanger and exchange it. The moneychangers, naturally, took a cut on the exchange rate. So, in practice, gold and silver always circulated at a premium.

There was a continual loss inherent in the system. Hoards that

174. Carvoran (Northumberland). Bronze dry-measure from the fort at Carvoran (*Magnis*), bearing the name (deleted) and titles of Domitian for 90–91. *Magnis* was not built before Trajan's reign (98–117), so the measure was probably lost then or later.

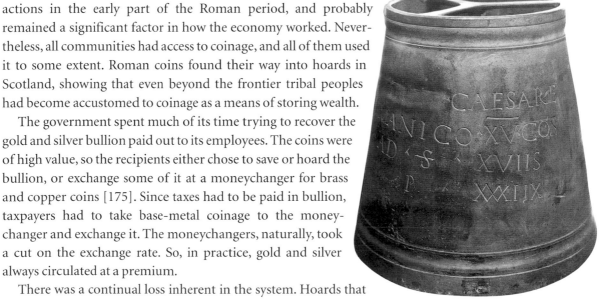

were never recovered (the ones which survive today) resulted in permanently lost bullion. Some was used to manufacture jewelry or other precious metal products. Other bullion found its way out of the Empire, being used to buy goods or buy off barbarians. Strain was put on available bullion stocks and suppliers when emperors chose to offer their employees, usually soldiers, substantial pay-rises or donatives, particularly once the Empire's expansion had been terminated and new sources were no longer available. Under these circumstances, the government debased the silver to make it go further. Unfortunately, the average member of the Roman Empire was sophisticated enough to tell the difference, and promptly hoarded any old silver he had. This only put a further strain on the system through a simple rule of coinage: bad money drives out good.

By the end of the third century, apart from the efforts by Carausius to issue good silver in Britain, Roman silver coinage was a bad joke. Bronze coins issued with a silver wash masqueraded as silver, but fooled no one. The result was steady inflation. From the late third century on, there were numerous attempts to reform the coinage with a variety of new coin types. Silver was coined on and off in the fourth century, but it was no longer produced regularly. Instead, gold dominated late Roman coinage, along with abundant bronze issues that individually represented tiny fractions of the gold coins. The Romans had discovered the difficulties in maintaining dual standard coinage, since the bullion value of gold and silver can never be maintained in an exact relationship. Different factors affect the supply, and therefore the price, of each. The same problem would recur in eighteenth-century England, with a similar result until the coinage reform of 1816. Very little silver was struck between 1715 and 1816, and instead Great Britain, then one of the most powerful nations in the world, used gold denominations and copper fractions of those gold coins.[42]

Throughout the Roman period, these problems were exacerbated by the erratic production and distribution of coinage. Britain suffered from periods when official coin was in short supply, and this was usually made good by bouts of copying or forging generally base-metal coins. This is useful evidence that Britain was dependent on coinage. The most notorious phases were between 43 and 64, when the army seems to have been responsible for issuing copies of official base-metal coins [176], the late third century, and episodically in the fourth century, when copying was so prolific and so variable in quality that many people must have been engaged in its production. However, forging to some degree always took place throughout the Empire. In late eighteenth-century Britain, shortages of copper halfpennies and farthings were made good not only by the forging of official issues, but also by the manufacture of tokens. These

175. Hadrian (117–38) and Commodus (180–92).
Brass *sestertii* of Hadrian and Commodus. During the second century, the *sestertius* was the most important base-metal denomination. Many *sestertii* remained in circulation until the late third century, when inflation meant that they were worth more as metal. Consequently, the coins were melted down to manufacture goods or to make copies of the debased silver issue.

forgeries were also sold as commodities in their own right. Since the copper was worth about half the face value, they could be made and sold at a profit. Unscrupulous employers and merchants bought the counterfeit coins and used them to pay wages and bills. It is both possible and likely that the same activities went on in Roman Britain. The government in the 1770s and 1780s tolerated the forgeries because the economy could not function without them, and doubtless the provincial authorities of Roman Britain felt the same way.

Until the late third century, official coinage used in Britain was struck mainly at Rome, and occasionally in the first century at Lyons. Thereafter, coinage was produced at a variety of provincial mints. These included London between 286 and 325, but most coinage came from Lyons, Arles and Trier. Coinage entered Britain through pay for soldiers and officials, payment for goods and services, and as loans. The London mint, founded by Carausius, produced the first official coinage in Britain, along with the 'C' mint (its exact location is unknown). The 'C' mint was closed in 296, but London's remained in use under the Tetrarchy and Constantine. After *c.* 325, any coinage produced in Britain was unofficial, and circulated alongside the legitimate issues.

We know nothing about the process of supply, but studies of hoards, coin types and die-links (coins struck from the same physical dies) have shown that bullion coin moved freely about the Empire. However, base-metal coin tended to circulate only in the provinces in which it was distributed. Two *as* types of the year 154 are usually only found in Britain, suggesting that the issues were sent to Britain for use rather than to anywhere else. Relatively few official base-metal coins of the early third century seem to have found their way to Britain, in contrast to other areas, such as Italy and North Africa, where they were abundant. Britain continued to make use of second-century coins, which became increasingly worn and which often turn up in late third-century contexts.

Variations in coin-supply and inflation meant that the number of coins lost varied enormously. Since earlier coins had higher intrinsic values and, in the case of base-metal coins, were larger and less easily lost, they usually remained in circulation longer. Base-metal coins from the 270s on were of trivial individual value, and were produced in abundance. Until this was recognized, density of occupation was often assessed according to the number of coins found on a site. Nowadays special mathematical formulae have been devised that help to compensate for this problem. Archaeologists and numismatists alike now know that a site occupied more or less continuously will produce dozens, or even hundreds, of third- and fourth-century coins for every first- and second-century coin.

176. Claudius (41–54).
Copy of a copper *as* of Claudius. Distinguished by poor style and ragged appearance, these copies were manufactured in Britain, probably by the army, after the conquest of 43 to make good the lack of official coinage. The recoinage of Nero (see p. 39) made the copies redundant and they fell out of use.

177, 178. Constantine II (317–37) and Crispus (317–26).
Bronze coins of Constantine II and Crispus as heirs designate of Constantine I. Both coins were struck at London, indicated by the letters 'PLON' on the reverse, and were found in the Langtoft (East Yorkshire) hoard, discovered in 2000. Diameters about 2 cm.

Causes of discontent before the Boudican revolt were 'the confiscation of money given by Claudius to leaders of the Britons', and the recall of loans by others, including Seneca.[43] Seneca's loan was equivalent to 40 million *sestertii*, enough to pay the annual wages of seven legions. It is unlikely that much of this money was in circulation. Either it will have been hoarded by the Britons, melted down and converted into other items, spent on buying goods from the Empire, or used to pay taxes. Whether or not any of this money was ever recovered is unknown. Cash also trickled into general circulation through casual expenditure by soldiers and other officials, and when the state made payments for goods and services. This increased greatly after 64, when Nero started to produce base-metal coin in abundance. Coins of this date and later are far more common in Britain. Perhaps one of the most evocative deposits is the sacred spring of Sulis-Minerva at Bath. Unlike a hoard, which was the property of a single person, the coins deposited here were thrown in by thousands of different pilgrims over many decades. Ever mindful of the value of coinage, most of the pilgrims took care to make offerings from extremely worn base-metal coins, or even forgeries. Each of these coins had clearly spent many years in active circulation.

The supply of coin, or production of copies to make good shortfalls, continued throughout most of the fourth century. But from the 380s there was a tail-off, and, unlike earlier periods, copying seems to have declined as well. The last official coins to reach Britain were struck around 402. Thereafter, any other coins that arrived came in such small numbers that they must have been brought by individuals, rather than as part of official consignments. The cessation of the coin supply, and the failure to make up the difference with local copies, had dramatic implications for Britain's trade and economy. Coinage would not be used so much in Britain again until the seventeenth century.

CONCLUSION

This chapter has only touched on a few aspects of the Romano-British economy, although the subject inevitably recurs throughout this book. There are many different factors that provide us with vivid evidence for the existence of a thriving economy, but it is impossible for us to know which of those factors stimulated others, and vice versa. The army's role is evident in the distribution of goods, such as black-burnished ware, and it probably also played a large part in determining the availability of samian ware. Although samian was abundantly available in towns and smaller settlements, this availability may have been a side effect of military trade in the commodity. If so, then any changes in military buying patterns could have been responsible for the decline in the whole industry by affecting margins.

Coinage was clearly used in considerable quantities, and made the exchange and storage of wealth easier. Its availability probably helped provoke economic activity, but the extensive bouts of copying in the third and fourth centuries show that such availability cannot have been the only factor. Coinage was available in greatest abundance during the late third century and into the fourth, mostly in the form of small bronze coins of indeterminate intrinsic value. But the greatest intensity of identifiable economic activity was in the first and second centuries, the period when the army was at its most active, and when the major towns in particular were experiencing intensive periods of development. Part of the reason for the discrepancy is that the buying power of individual coins at this time was much higher than later on, since the inflationary pressures of debasing bullion silver coinage had not really hit home. It has been suggested though that a conspicuous reduction in coin supplies in the early third century may be linked to the apparent stagnation in urban development.[44] However, the reduction in coin supplies of this period mostly affected base-metal issues, and not those of the silver, which are well represented, for example, in the massive early to mid-third-century hoards. Moreover, this is the period from which we have specific evidence of individuals engaged in the North Sea trade.

These examples illustrate perfectly how difficult it is for us to draw any firm conclusions about how the Romano-British economy functioned. Material from almost every significant Roman site points not only to major levels of imports in the first and second centuries, but also to widespread access to those trade routes. This was the time when towns developed from ramshackle, commercial street frontages into more pretentious places. At the same time, mosaics and more elaborate architecture were very rare in the countryside. But in the fourth century, towns were either stagnating or decaying, and trade with the Continent had declined. Public building was effectively over, though some homeowners were still in a position to invest in improved houses. Conversely, in the countryside, especially in the Central Zone, a significant proportion of the villa estates evolved into expensively appointed miniature palaces. This is so incongruous in the context of the rest of Roman Britain that an obvious explanation is difficult to find. But as rural establishments, villas were generally linked to agricultural production, and it is Britain's grain that we know was of major importance to the Empire at the time. Britain was relatively peaceable and isolated from the major barbarian incursions of the period. This may have completely readjusted the economy, benefiting a particular sector in the community that spent the money on itself.

CHAPTER 8

THE COUNTRYSIDE & VILLAS

179. Rockbourne (Hampshire). Part of the third-century baths suite, in its fourth-century form. The octagonal chamber was the *frigidarium*, and the long room was the *tepidarium*. Although the house never became lavish, its longevity, expansion and improvements reflect a pattern found across southern Britain.

At least 90 per cent of the Romano-British population lived in the countryside. Rural Roman Britain also exhibited the greatest diversity. Some of the rural population lived in caves or remote roundhouse farmsteads that had scarcely changed for hundreds of years. By the fourth century, wealthy people lived in country houses that were architecturally pretentious and surrounded by estates [179]. But even in the lowlands, less than one in six known rural settlements can be classified as 'villas'. Roman types of rectangular houses were commonplace, but the ancient Iron Age roundhouse continued in use almost everywhere. The landscape ranged from the ancient woodlands of the Weald to the bleak moorlands of the north, and from the mountains of Wales to the fenlands of East Anglia. The centre, east, south and southeast were the most densely populated and productive. The Roman world affected everywhere, making all of the countryside integral to understanding Roman Britain.

The descriptions by Caesar, Strabo and Diodorus Siculus create a general picture of Britain as an intensely rural world with a thriving and productive population, even if some of what they wrote is obviously wrong. Tacitus says that the aftermath of the Boudican revolt produced desperation because the participants had recklessly failed to plant crops.[1] This tells us that the tribes involved were accustomed to organizing a cycle of ploughing, cultivation and harvesting. To do this at all meant a systematic approach to life, defined plots of land, and the wealth of empirical knowledge essential to successful agriculture. These traditions stretched far back into the past. The Roman world brought new markets, increased demand from an urban and military population, and improvements in the form of new tools. But the essence of rural Britain probably did not change very much.

In recent years, environmental data has provided evidence for crops and land usage in a wide variety of landscapes and regions. Aerial photography and land surveying have made it possible to identify and plan field systems, and, together with archaeological exploration in advance of road and building work, have shown that rural populations and settlements were denser than previously thought. Villas are no longer interpreted in isolation as architectural phenomena, but as single components of much more complex rural communities.

CROPS AND LAND USAGE

Primeval Britain was mainly wooded. Forest clearance made it possible for Bronze Age peoples to start carving up the landscape into areas for cultivation, while also developing woodland management, allowing timber to be grown for a variety of structural and manufacturing purposes. In the Roman period, woodlands were used for the structural and fuel needs of forts and towns, and also for industries such as pottery and iron-smelting. The Weald of Kent, for example, was a major iron-smelting area and it remained wooded throughout the period. A piece of woodland in Kent, called *Verlucionum*, was the subject of a legal case heard in London in the year 118.[2] Villas of the region were clustered along the northern part of Kent, the River Medway, and its tributaries.

180. Distribution of villas in Britain.
Although villas are known in all three areas, they occur predominantly in the Central Zone. (After Hingley and Miles, and Jones and Mattingly).

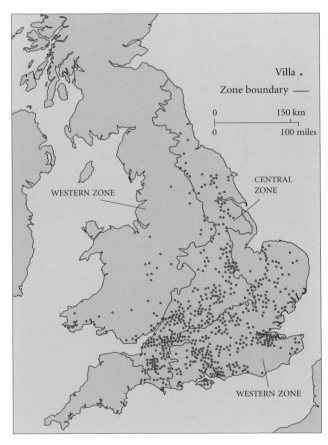

In the areas opened up to agriculture by forest clearance, a number of changes took place after the Roman conquest. Animal bones are ubiquitous finds at Roman settlements, showing that cattle, sheep, pigs, venison, fowl, and even horses were butchered for meat, with cattle and pigs apparently growing in popularity over the period [181]. The need until modern times to drive herds of animals from their homes to places of consumption means that it is impossible to know where they came from. In the eighteenth and nineteenth centuries, it was commonplace for cattle to be driven to London from as far away as Wales. In antiquity, when the roads were if anything better, the same must have happened. Sheep kept for wool were likely to have been clipped with shears, one of the new tools introduced during the Roman period, possibly encouraging the apparent increase in sheep. Field systems were well established in prehistory throughout large parts of Britain, but now they were more likely to be divided up with hedges, or even stone walls, perhaps a reflection of the legal control of land tenure, enshrined in provincial and civic records. Land was reclaimed through drainage, mainly around the Wash.

The Iron Age staples of spelt, bread and emmer wheat, six-row barley, oats and beans were augmented with rye and a range of more exotic plants like coriander, plums and cherries. Working the land itself became easier with the improvement of plough technology. Asymmetric ploughshares were more effective at cutting and turning the soil, helped along by coulters (iron blades fixed in front of ploughshares to cut the soil vertically). Crops were now treated in drying-ovens, a characteristically Roman innovation and found at numerous sites, often with food traces, and stored in granaries instead of Iron Age pits. However, traditional methods remained in use, too.

181. East Coker (Somerset). Fragment of a mosaic panel depicting a hunting scene. Fourth century. (Somerset County Museums Service).

RURAL SETTLEMENT

The countryside varied enormously, from fertile agricultural territory within a day or two's journey from a town, to remote moorland in the military zone. This was reflected in the nature of settlement, of which the villas are the best known. In the Western Zone, which included Wales, the southwest, and much of the north and northwest, rural settlement changed relatively little from the Iron Age. Usually these remoter settlements produce far fewer finds of the material goods so typical of Roman-period settlements further east. But they were not unaffected by Roman contact. Milestones from Cornwall show that provincial administration reached right into the southwest.[3] Even small numbers of characteristically 'Roman' finds suggest that contact did exist, and that the Roman impact on remote rural communities was more significant than is now obvious from the archaeological record.

In the Western Zone and much of the north, villas were generally absent, and native farmsteads usually contained with some sort of enclosure were widespread. These farmsteads had been characteristic of much of Iron Age Britain, but in most of the developed part of the province they gave way to Roman building types. They ranged from the characteristic Cornish 'round', where a handful of dry-stone houses clustered together in a circular or elliptical enclosure, such as at Chysauster [182], to the roundhouses of the north in round, or even rectangular, enclosures. In Scotland, beyond the Roman province, the 'substantial roundhouses', including the brochs and duns, remained. These monumental structures, with walls that could be 5 m (16 ft 5 in) thick, seem to have been the alpha houses of the region. They perhaps reflect a hierarchy in which towns and villas were simply not part of the way status was expressed. In the south and east, for example, Roman building forms, particularly the villas, became the housing type of choice amongst the élite, while Iron Age forms remained lower status. Some Scottish broch residents still had access to Roman goods, like the occupants of Fairy Knowe (Stirlingshire), where Roman coins and glass were used alongside imported fine wares, like samian, and the thoroughly Roman cooking device, the *mortarium*.[4]

Contact probably resulted from a mixture of individual trading relationships and personal choice, rather than general economic trends. In northern Britain, the army was the most influential factor. Here villas are almost non-existent, although there are exceptions, such as the villa at Ingelby Barwick, near Stockton-on-Tees. In the north, the military towns, such as Corbridge and Carlisle, and the *vici* that clustered around the forts were dependent on the army. At the end of the period, the military towns seem to have decayed before the forts, while earlier there is no case of a *vicus* surviving the closure of a fort as had happened in the south. The army imported the goods it needed, while any demands it made locally on produce will have had a marked effect on settlements that were probably only just viable. The economic and social ties that maintained towns and villas were never really established in the north.

In Wales, villas were rare except in the southeast, where the land was more agriculturally productive. Some Iron Age farmsteads, such as at Whitton (Glamorgan), were able to develop into modest villas.

Elsewhere in Wales, settlement became more archaeologically visible, but the difficult landscape prevented this from becoming intensive. Although roundhouses were often replaced with rectangular buildings, the structures remained simple. The land was simply too marginal to support anything better, with the army's demands perhaps making this worse. On the other hand, the villas that did exist must have depended on a military market. In south Wales, most of the villas had been abandoned by the middle of the fourth century. The legionary fortress at Caerleon seems to have been given up, since the II legion is only testified at the much smaller fort of Richborough in the fourth century. The removal of an entire legion is bound to have had a dramatic effect on the economy in south Wales, though the nearby *civitas* capital at Caerwent seems to have survived until the end of the century.

Living on the margin is reflected in the nature of settlement towards the Midlands and Wroxeter. Wroxeter was one of the remoter *civitas* capitals, and it had to wait until Hadrianic times before it was endowed with a forum and basilica. The area was able to support a significant town, but roundhouses remained common nearby and there were very few villas.

182. Chysauster (Cornwall). There were about nine stone roundhouses at Chysauster, each with its own courtyard for outhouses. Little changed here throughout the Roman period, and the village is an important reminder that for much of rural Britain, villas and polite Roman living were unthinkable luxuries.

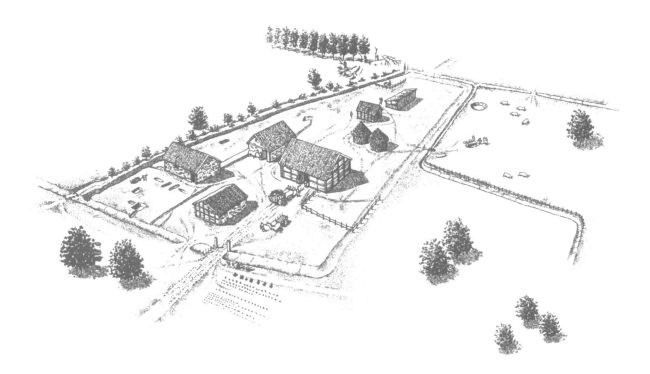

Until the late third century, Frocester, like many other rural sites, remained a simple Romanized farmstead with outbuildings.

In the Peak District, on the border between the 'civilian' south and the 'military' north, some people were living in caves in the Carsington area. However low-grade the places these people lived in, they still had access to the Roman goods that make them identifiable in the archaeological record.

In the rest of Britain, much of the landscape was dotted with villas, but they were interspersed with more basic Roman-type farmsteads or even roundhouses. Frocester Court (Gloucestershire) remained until the late third century no more than a Romanized Iron Age settlement [183]. Roundhouses gave way to timber rectangular houses there, but not until the late third century were the inhabitants able, or willing, to move into a substantial masonry villa. Nearby, at Standish, a similar settlement apparently never reached the villa stage.

Areas without villas include surviving woodland, such as the New Forest and the Weald. On Salisbury Plain, Iron Age traditions seem to have continued almost unabated. Perhaps this was an imperial estate, managed and farmed for the emperor with the economic effect of the removal of the surplus from the local economy. Imperial estates undoubtedly existed, but no evidence to substantiate any in Roman Britain has ever been found, apart from an inscription found reused in the villa at Combe Down (Somerset).[5] It has been suggested that the monumental building at Stonea [184] in the Fens, along with its attendant settlement, may have been the headquarters of an imperial estate established under Hadrian, and administered by soldiers to help supply the northern frontier.[6] Where villas developed they generally did so on the better quality land, and had access to main roads and urban markets. The richest concentrations are in the Mendips and Cotswolds, an area also of relatively high urban density. Cirencester was one of Roman Britain's largest towns, and it lay close to the colony at Gloucester. It also sat on the Fosse Way, which connected it to Bath and Ilchester to the south. The roads joined the major towns to a number of smaller towns, and spurs drew the villas of Somerset [185] and the Severn Estuary into the network.

The individual size and level of architectural embellishment at villas is usually related to location and date. For example, those on the edge of more marginal areas like the Fens or Wales tend to be smaller and less well appointed. Villas are much more common features of the third century and afterwards in Britain, but many had structural histories that stretch back at least into the second century, and sometimes the first. Villas often overlie, or are adjacent to, Iron Age farmsteads, but did not always follow on immediately. The Halstock (Dorset) villa was begun in the mid-second century on an Iron Age site that had fallen out of use a century before.[7] At Park Street (Hertfordshire) an early villa soon followed a late Iron Age rectangular house. The greatest period of villa development was in the fourth century, but by the 380s and afterwards villas were in decline. A few remained in use into the fifth century, but invariably in reduced circumstances (see p. 265).

184. Stonea (Cambridgeshire). Hypothetical reconstruction of the so-called 'tower' that formed the centrepiece of the settlement.

Virtually without exception, villas lay on or close to land suitable for agriculture. This does not necessarily mean that any specific villa's economy depended exclusively on the exploitation of land, but agriculture probably always played an important part. Although the sites chosen vary considerably, villas always had access to water from springs or rivers, and were well-drained. The Darenth Valley (Kent) villas form a prime example, and they parallel another series along the Medway a few miles east. Villas in the Darenth Valley include Lullingstone, Darenth and Farningham, all of which lay a few metres from what was then a wider and deeper river than it is today.

The villa at Great Witcombe (Gloucestershire) could not have been more differently located [186]. The house lies on a steep northeast-facing slope, astride one of the many springs. The location is so beautiful and striking that this must have been the primary attraction. The springs provided water for living and also for the baths, while the slope provided all the drainage needed. The steep hillside meant that the house had to be built along a contour, and its wings terraced into the slope.

Buttresses had to be set up against the walls to prevent subsidence. The water threatened to undermine the foundations, and had to be controlled by being channelled under the house. The buttressing rather implies a detailed appreciation of potential structural problems, but the evidence from other sites collectively suggest that builders took chances, and where problems occurred, remedial measures, assuming there was time, were taken.

WHAT IS A VILLA?

The world 'villa' meant, in theory, a 'farm', but is better translated as a rural dwelling of some pretension, often, but not always, with agricultural associations. A house outside the walls of a city may be a villa, or simply an extramural townhouse. Likewise, a house within the walls, evidently functioning as a farm, may be really a villa, rather than a townhouse (see p. 100). The 'villa' proper means not just the main house, but also all its peripheral structures, such as barns. It follows then that a village a couple of miles away, manned by the villa estate workers, is also technically part of the villa, as are any field systems in the vicinity. Some of the more modest rural houses were perhaps regarded by their aspirant (or downright bourgeois) owners as villas, but seen by their wealthier neighbours as trumped-up hovels. Conversely, there is no doubt that

185. *Below.* **Dinnington (Somerset).**
This villa, which grew to a substantial size in the fourth century, benefited from its close location to the Fosse Way, which enabled it to be incorporated into the provincial communications infrastructure. This geometric mosaic was laid in the villa during the fourth century, and is shown being recorded shortly after its discovery in 2002. Ploughing has damaged part of it.

186. *Overleaf.* **Great Witcombe (Gloucestershire).**
The villa as it might have appeared in the fourth century. The house, which overlooks the same dramatic views that it did in antiquity, seems to have incorporated a water shrine, but this does not mean that its prime function was as a temple.

elsewhere in the Empire the owners of some extravagant villas maintained the conceit that their rural palaces were modest bucolic retreats. Clearly, defining a 'villa' in both our terms and those of the Romans is not an easy task. It is made more difficult because in any one instance we do not know if a villa was owned primarily to make money or to express

status. We do not even know whether the residents owned the premises or were tenants of Romano-British, or Continental, landlords. We also do not know in any one case what the borders of a villa estate were, and whether villages or lesser houses nearby belonged to it.

Although simple stone rectangular houses started appearing before

43, the process was limited, localized and lacking in conspicuous aspiration. In parts of Britain during the late first century, rural villas and simple farmsteads proliferated. The appearance of increasingly numerous rectangular, multi-roomed houses in the south and the Midlands by the late first century is one of the most conspicuous changes of the period. Where villas are known in abundance, the key point is that being made of stone they tend to leave conspicuous traces (even when robbed out). They are easier to identify from the air and as the result of a chance find. Prehistoric housing forms are more difficult to detect, especially when a Roman house was later built on top. They remained in use even in areas where the villas were at their densest, while simple rectangular houses clustered together in villages, probably accommodating estate workers and their families.

Most Roman houses had rectangular plans with more than one room. Wattle-and-daub, timber, thatch and earthen floors could all be features of a Roman-period rural rectangular building. It would be stretching the point to classify a two- or three-roomed rectangular hut as a villa. Virtually all villas are based on wings, with a series of square or rectangular rooms and corridors, with even the largest villa being simply a bigger version of a smaller one. However, Roman-type houses were given to elaboration. This is a crucial distinction from the roundhouse. Roundhouses came and went, and new ones were similar to the old. No one ever extended a roundhouse, installed mosaics or fitted it with a bathhouse.

Roman villas often did change. They were decorated, and grew physi-

187. Plaxtol (Kent).
Reconstruction drawing of what the winged-corridor villa might have looked like from the south in its second-century heyday. The villa does not seem to have remained in occupation into the late Roman period, and may have been absorbed into a larger estate.

cally in size by being extended, replaced by bigger houses, or joining up houses with outbuildings. Rows of rooms were extended, corridors added, thatch given way to tiled roofs, and so on. These 'upgrades' were so common that it was unusual for a rectangular house to remain in its original form, unless it was abandoned. The upgrades appeared at different times at different places, and the contrast between one site and another nearby could be vast, with a century or more passing at one before the other even started to match it. At Boxmoor (Hertfordshire), a first-century timber-framed, winged-corridor house was succeeded in the second century by one built with cob (a mixture of clay, gravel and straw) walls on chalk foundations. This was itself rebuilt with dwarf stone footings to support the cob walls and inhibit damp, with later modifications including a hypocaust, masonry reinforcement and buttresses.[8] The house never became significant, but it illustrates a series of upgrades characteristic of the period.

In the fourth century, the house at Halstock had evolved into a courtyard villa with mosaics and an imposing entrance, from a building that had started life as a much more modest one in the mid-second century.[9] The Lullingstone villa had a long history stretching back into the first century. It never expanded over a wide area, being constrained by its location between a river and a hillside, but it went through many phases of structural alterations. By the fourth century, it had been fitted out with mosaics and an apsidal dining room, but paradoxically the baths at its southern end had been demolished.[10]

Lullingstone is a real exception. For the most part, villas that developed did so by extending their wings. The classic sequence is a row of rooms, to which a corridor was then attached. Since extending in a single line would make one end of the house absurdly far from the other, it was normal for a wing to be built on one or both ends, creating the 'winged-corridor', or L-shaped, villa. If the wings were extended further, they might at this stage start to incorporate existing freestanding bath-suites or barns. Ultimately, a fourth wing could be added, creating a 'courtyard' villa. The villa at Bignor [188] exhibits most of these stages and evolved into a large and impressive building.

The aisled houses were different. Essentially single-chambered houses with a nave and aisles, and a roof supported on pillars, these buildings were used for a variety of purposes, and in some respects could represent continuity from the roundhouse, in which a family and its animals lived under a single roof. But internal room divisions, and even baths, could be added to these houses in what was clearly an attempt to convert them into more prepossessing structures.

Structural changes are often the only evidence we really have for what an individual villa represented to its owners, and what it tells us about its time. The quality of the architectural work varied enormously, and this ought to help us assess the status of a villa in that social context. However, evidence is rarely recovered that tells us what the building really looked like. The façade from the aisled villa at Meonstoke (Hampshire), with its elaborate use of brick to create blind arcading, only survived because the gable end wall collapsed [189]. The preservation of this section shows how brick and tile were used to create a decorative effect with blind arcading. The Redlands Farm villa [190] also suffered collapse, making it possible to reconstruct how the walls had been built. More often, we depend entirely on the excavated plan, remains of carved stonework, and fragments of painted wall-plaster. A place like Bignor, with its exceptional mosaics, was clearly an alpha villa. Lower down the scale, the Minster (Kent) villa was a fairly conventional winged-corridor example, but irregularities in what was an essentially symmetrical plan are likely to have been due to small errors in laying out a wall angle, which became progressively amplified as the rest of the structure developed over the years.[11]

There are some examples of villas that require a little more explanation. The so-called 'villa' at Whitley Grange, Hookagate (Shropshire) is very difficult to accept as one.[12] The complex consists mainly of a courtyard with a bath-suite on the northeast wing, and a symmetrical row of three rooms on the northwest wing. Apart from a portico apparently linking the two wings, and with a corridor that leads off mysteriously to the

188. Bignor (West Sussex).
The villa as it might have appeared in its final form. The original winged-corridor house has been extended to incorporate barns and other outbuildings to create a sprawling courtyard villa.

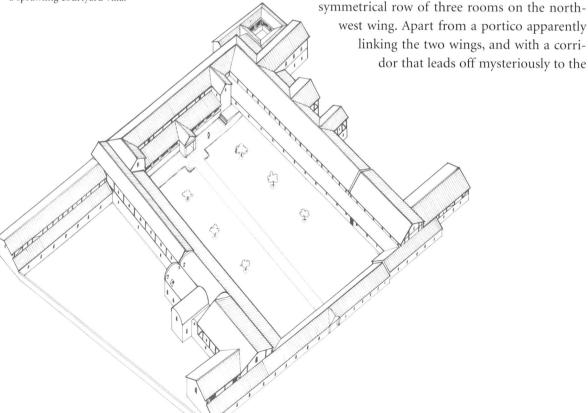

189. Meonstoke (Hampshire).
Collapsed section of façade from the gable end of the fourth-century aisled villa. The preservation of this section shows how brick and tile were used to create a decorative effect with blind arcading.

190 Stanwick (Northamptonshire).
Reconstructed view of the house at Redlands Farm as it might have appeared in its final form. During excavation collapsed sections of walls were discovered, making it possible to be unusually certain about the height and nature of construction.

southwest, there is nothing else. With no apparent provision for living quarters or kitchens, the Whitley Grange site has been recorded as a villa in the absence of any other explanation. At the very most it can only form part of a villa, much of which remains to be discovered, perhaps serving as a remote baths and leisure complex, sited at a favoured spot within an estate. The unusual location and design of the house at Great Witcombe has led to the suggestion that it was a water shrine, rather than a villa. Similar suggestions have been made about other villas, such as Chedworth and Lufton, but the claims are made on tenuous grounds. Great Witcombe had a shrine [191], but this was a normal component of Roman rural houses and their gardens, and not an indication of its prime function. Chedworth's garden *nymphaeum*, estate temple and crude relief of Lenus-Mars are peripheral features of what in every other respect seems to be a large country house.[13]

The concept of the Roman villa was deeply engrained in Roman culture, and belonged to a sentimental myth of Rome's rural origins as a society of 'peasant proprietors'.[14] This emotional self-indulgence is one we find reflections of in our own time, when wealthy people reward themselves by retreating from London to the countryside and boast about their better quality of life. So it was in antiquity, where the pressures of urban life, especially in Rome, encouraged the upper classes to spend as much time as they could in their ancestral rural estates, which were often substantial places. Thus Seneca escaped to his 'place at *Nomentum* … as soon as I left that crushing air in Rome … I noticed an improvement in my condition. You can imagine just how invigorated I felt when I reached my vineyards.'[15]

The best account of villa life was recorded by the younger Pliny in the early second century, in which he discusses his financial, legal and investment arrangements, and also describes his own house near *Laurentum*, a few miles south of Rome's port at Ostia.[16] One of Pliny's letters expounds the various facilities that were appropriate to a man of his position. This was a house of architectural features, of dining rooms, libraries, baths, bedrooms, and colonnades suitable for fine weather and retreats when it was bad. In another letter he speaks of his daily activities, including reading, writing, practising public speaking, entertaining, walking or going riding.

Pliny and Seneca were part of an established literary and social tradition in Roman culture that venerated villa life, and made it an almost fantasy experience. In the fourth century, educated Gallo-Romans, like Ausonius, self-consciously emulated this literary tradition when they

191. Great Witcombe (Gloucestershire).
Water shrine in the south wing of the villa.

192. Brading (Isle of Wight).
Mosaic panel depicting one of the
Four Winds. One of many popular
themes evoking the natural world,
this kind of imagery reflected the
Roman whimsical attitude to the
countryside.

wrote about their own provincial villas. The physical remains of the
greatest villas in fourth-century Britain show that the cultural aspirations to an old and dignified Italian tradition existed in the remotest
parts of the Empire.

WHO OWNED AND LIVED IN THE VILLAS?

Signs of Roman architectural influence were appearing in the south
before the invasion. The people responsible for these and for the early
villas built after 43 may have been an aspirant pro-Roman tribal aristocracy. Fishbourne is the most celebrated for its size, exceptionally early
date, and extraordinary decoration. Fishbourne has been traditionally
interpreted as the home of the client king, Togidubnus, but it is also possible it was built as the governor's residence, or served in both capacities
at different times. Angmering (West Sussex) is more conventional, though
with mosaics and baths it is exceptional for Britain at this date. Such
buildings are so out of context for the period that it is just as likely that
immigrant traders or officials owned them as tribal aristocrats. In any
case, other influential members of the tribes may have resisted the idea of
altering their way of life. Orsett (Essex), in the heart of Trinovantian territory, began life as a significant Iron Age roundhouse in a defended
enclosure.[17] The building was not supplanted by a Romanized farmstead
until the second century, and even then never matched the high status
features of its predecessor. Of course, we do not know why this happened, but Orsett illustrates how exceptional places like Angmering are.

The truth is that we know nothing about villa ownership in Britain,
either in any one case or in general. We do not know whether owners
were descendants of the Iron Age tribal aristocracy, retired soldiers or

administrators (probably themselves of provincial origin, but not 'British'), or immigrants who crossed the Channel in search of new opportunities or to escape the insecurity of the third and fourth centuries. This places us in an unfortunate position, but there is no avoiding it.

Evidence from Gaul and Italy provides some compensation. Here a combination of literary, epigraphic and archaeological evidence paints a picture in which some villas were worked and owned by the families that lived there, while others were operated by people in the owner's employment (or enslaved to him), or leased to tenants known as *coloni*. A *colonus* had traditionally been a free tenant, but by 332 laws were already being passed that effectively imprisoned them on the estates where they lived and worked, in order to make sure that the poll tax could be administered and levied effectively. The massive villa at Chiragan (Haute Garonne) in Gaul was contained within a 16 ha (39.5 acres) estate defined by a wall. High ground to the north and south, and a narrowing valley to the southwest, helps define the available agricultural land within its vicinity. In this area, another four villas and three villages, as well as various other farmsteads, have been identified. It has been suggested that here the landscape helps identify what was probably an estate where the subsidiary villas and settlements were occupied by tenants, workers and slaves of the main villa owner.[18]

If we assume that Britain was broadly similar, then it becomes easy to see that the larger villas like Bignor and Woodchester were the regional equivalents of Chiragan. Woodchester was a very substantial courtyard villa with a long history, though it did not reach its massive size until the late third and early fourth centuries. Within its orbit are a number of lesser sites, including Frocester Court. Since Frocester did not evolve into a villa until fairly late, it is possible that settlements like these were developed by the owners of great villas specifically to lease to *coloni*. Some late third-century villa sites appeared, perhaps for the same reason, at places where occupation had ceased since the Iron Age, such as at Newtown (Hampshire).

One recent study attempted a more sophisticated analysis of use and ownership of villas through an interpretation of ground-plans.[19] The idea was that since larger villas exhibit repetition of room types, this must be evidence for occupation by multiple groups within, perhaps a single extended family. In this context then the villa was a capital asset, held not by any one individual, but by a family-based community. This is an interesting idea, but it is based on evidence so limited in its nature that it is as potentially misleading as assuming similar semi-detached houses of the present are each inhabited by

193. Lullingstone (Kent).
One of two life-sized Greek marble busts of mid-second-century date later sealed in a cellar, although they continued to be venerated. The men portrayed were probably of Eastern Mediterranean origin and may have been father and son, perhaps successive owners of the house in the second century. The style indicates they were men of status, perhaps serving in Roman Britain's provincial government.

similar family units. Since villa ground-plans are very largely made up of square and rectangular rooms, from which we usually have little furniture or any other artifacts used in those rooms, it is not always possible to say what the intended function of a room was, or what it was at any given time later in the house's history.

One instance where repetition is beyond doubt is the pair of almost identical winged-corridor houses at Bradford-on-Avon (Wiltshire), joined by a wall into a single villa complex. The western house was in existence at least by 230, and by 300 the eastern house had been built to such a similar ground plan that it is tempting to see the latter as a house built for a son and his family. But there is absolutely no evidence to support this theory beyond the ground plans and the proximity of the two houses. One could just as easily speculate that the original owner had died, and the first house was sold to a man who invited his friend to build an identical house next door.

Within the villa structure itself, the function of some rooms, such as the baths, kitchens and prominent 'public' rooms, such as the dining room (*triclinium*), is obvious enough [194]. The fittings and decoration ought at least to give us an idea of the kind of person who owned, or lived in, the villa. Prestige installations like the elaborate octagonal bathhouse at Lufton (Somerset), the detached triconch hall with its Orphic floor at Littlecote (Wiltshire), or the massive Orphic floor in the great hall at Woodchester [199], show us that some of the villas were owned by

194. Villa in London.
Reconstructed interior of a townhouse in Roman London, as it might have appeared in the late second or early third century. Although London was Britain's principal commercial and administrative centre, the remains of many houses, from simple strip houses to well-appointed townhouses, have been found. The wealthiest of these houses enjoyed the fruits of a trading network that extended as far as the eastern Mediterranean. (Museum of London).

FISHBOURNE

The discovery and excavation in the 1960s of the first-century palace at Fishbourne [195], just west of the *civitas* capital at Chichester, was a sensation. Although about half the building lay under a road and modern houses, enough remained to show that the palace was the largest villa-type building in Britain, and was of exceptionally early date.

Being so close to the sea, and in an area probably controlled by the friendly Atrebates, Fishbourne was an ideal location for an early Roman base. Military equipment has been recovered from the harbour and vicinity, and at least two military-type timber buildings stood on the site of the later palace in the mid-40s. Within only five years at most these buildings had been replaced by a timber house, complete with painted plaster walls. By the 60s the timber house had gone, and in its place was a much more elaborate masonry house, with such Roman features as baths,

mosaics, marble paving, painted decoration and moulded stucco. This so-called 'proto-palace' would have been extravagant even by the standards of the greatest villas of the fourth century. In Neronian Britain it was revolutionary, but within little more than a decade the palace was demolished.

This, at least, has been the traditional interpretative history of Fishbourne. Recent excavations have uncovered a first-century Iron Age phase beside the later palace, including early imperial Arretine ware, a precursor of samian ware. A fitting from a Roman scabbard was also found, leading to the radical suggestion that Roman development began at Fishbourne well before the invasion. Was this the place from which Verica fled to Claudius for help? Sadly, the dating evidence for this theory is thin, but the Arretine ware otherwise takes a lot of explaining.

There is much less doubt about

what happened later. In place of the proto-palace came the palace proper, begun *c.* 75–80. Sprawling across four ha (10 acres), the new palace consisted of four wings ranged slightly asymmetrically around a central garden. Vast quantities of soil and rubble were moved to level the site. The axis was east to west, with the entrance hall in the middle of the east wing. A path led through the formal garden to the 'audience chamber' in the middle of the west wing opposite. The north wing seems to have been the main residential block, consisting of a range of rooms and enclosed courtyards. The standard of decoration was quite simply beyond anything else in Britain at the time, and it is inconceivable that the workmen responsible had not come from Gaul or Italy. The *collegium fabrorum*, recorded about this time on the famous Chichester inscription that names Togidubnus, may well have worked here. A number of characteristic first-

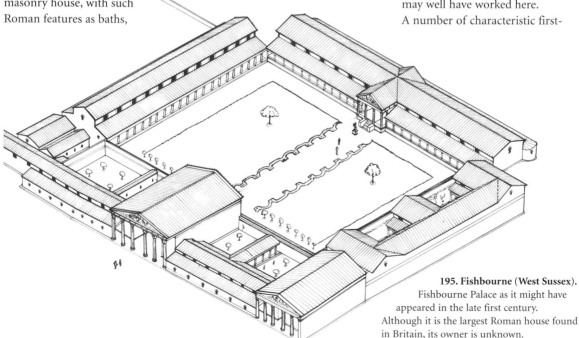

195. Fishbourne (West Sussex).
Fishbourne Palace as it might have appeared in the late first century. Although it is the largest Roman house found in Britain, its owner is unknown.

196. Marble head of a child.
This life-sized bust was found in a rubbish pit in the north wing and is believed to be of Italian or Gaulish manufacture. The subject is likely to have been the owner of Fishbourne or one of his children. Late first century.

Tiberius Claudius Togidubnus, the local tribal king so praised by Tacitus for his loyalty, is the prime candidate. If he had been educated and groomed in Rome, it is easy to see how he could have brought his acquired tastes back with him. Nevertheless, it is equally possible that the succession of buildings were residences built for the governor, who is perhaps even more likely to have had the taste, money and resources to erect an Italian retreat in this remote and barbaric wilderness. The ring found nearby of Tiberius Claudius Catuarus [197], presumably a kinsman or ally of Togidubnus, does not settle the matter, since he could as easily have lost it while making a representation to the governor as visiting his tribal patron.

In the second and third centuries the house was significantly altered [198]. Money continued to be invested in decorations such as new mosaics, but by *c.* 100 structural changes and the installation of new

197. Silver ring.
Found near the palace, the ring inscribed *Ti(berius) Claudius (Ca)tuarus*. The owner is likely to have been an associate or kinsman of Togidubnus.

baths in the east and north wings suggest that Fishbourne might have been divided into separate units. A fire in the late third century destroyed the house, and the site was abandoned. So, ironically, by the time of Roman Britain's Golden Age of villas, the most remarkable villa of them all was in ruins and being plundered for building materials. Some of those materials may have gone to help build the fort at Portchester (see p. 69), constructed at around the same time.

198. Hypocaust system.
Second-century underfloor heating at Fishbourne Palace, installed during a series of modifications.

century black-and-white geometric mosaics were found, reminiscent of those discovered at Pompeii and Herculaneum and buried in 79.

Who owned Fishbourne? The answer is that nothing has yet been discovered to verify who that was. All we know is that he lived in a house that was unparalleled in the northwestern provinces. Obviously,

199. Woodchester (Gloucestershire).
At just under 15 sq m (162 sq ft) this pavement, recorded by Samuel Lysons (1763–1819), formed the centrepiece of the villa's principal room and is one of the largest known mosaics in Britain and northern Gaul. The figure of Orpheus with his lyre and the parade of animal associates is known from several other mosaics in Britain. About 325–50.

persons of the highest status in Roman Britain. These people could be those descended from the tribal aristocrats of the first century, like Togidubnus, now exhibiting social aspirations and tastes that marked them out as thoroughly Romanized. Even the lesser villas, like Sparsholt (Hampshire) with its single geometric pavement, were clearly lived in by people who aspired to the same kind of lifestyle. Of course, it is also possible that villas were owned or lived in by military veterans, or by immigrants from Gaul or further beyond. Some mosaic floors exhibit unusually exotic tastes. Those at Rudston include details of circus events much more characteristic of mosaics found in North Africa, suggesting that either the mosaicist or the residents had lived there once [200].

The disparaging tone adopted towards Britain by fourth-century observers, such as Ausonius, is easier to explain if the owners of some later villas were at least natives, rather than immigrants.[20] A Gaulish provincial himself, Ausonius stressed his own credentials by looking

200. Rudston (East Yorkshire). Mosaic panel (*below*) from the 'Venus' floor at Rudston. Although scenes from the amphitheatre and circus are well known in North Africa, Rudston is unique in Britain, raising an interesting question about the ownership of the villa. The detail (*left*) shows an animal identified as a bull ('*TAVRVS*') that is 'man-killing' ('*OMICIDA*'). (Hull Museums).

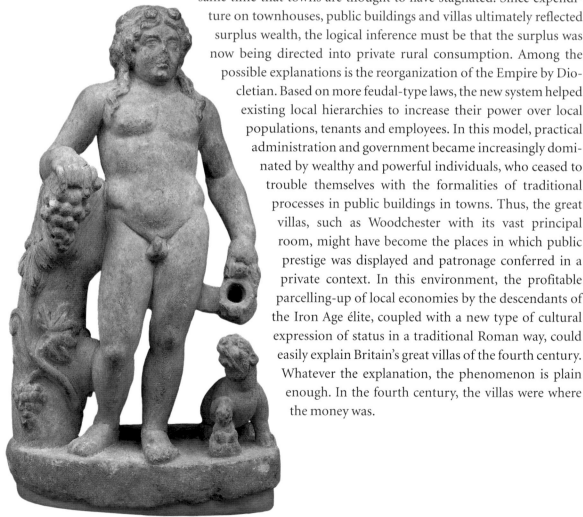

down on Britain. The classical pretensions of Britain's landowning élite were appealed to by Carausius, and serviced by the mosaicists and craftsmen of the fourth century [201], but this might itself be evidence that the villa owners were not British. Villas near the colonies of York and Lincoln must have included some military veterans amongst their owners, and some of these men could have owned villas further south. Serving soldiers and veterans were, for instance, amongst the clientele at the spa shrine of Bath. Many soldiers in the course of their duties spent time on detachment in the south, and with the fortification of the coastline in the third century more would have been accustomed to the area. So the evidence works either way, a state of affairs which is frustrating, but unavoidable.

A theme throughout this book is that the Roman government manipulated patronage through delegation of control to local tribal hierarchies. If this is correct, then it helps explain why villas grew at the same time that towns are thought to have stagnated. Since expenditure on townhouses, public buildings and villas ultimately reflected surplus wealth, the logical inference must be that the surplus was now being directed into private rural consumption. Among the possible explanations is the reorganization of the Empire by Diocletian. Based on more feudal-type laws, the new system helped existing local hierarchies to increase their power over local populations, tenants and employees. In this model, practical administration and government became increasingly dominated by wealthy and powerful individuals, who ceased to trouble themselves with the formalities of traditional processes in public buildings in towns. Thus, the great villas, such as Woodchester with its vast principal room, might have become the places in which public prestige was displayed and patronage conferred in a private context. In this environment, the profitable parcelling-up of local economies by the descendants of the Iron Age élite, coupled with a new type of cultural expression of status in a traditional Roman way, could easily explain Britain's great villas of the fourth century. Whatever the explanation, the phenomenon is plain enough. In the fourth century, the villas were where the money was.

CONCLUSION

The countryside shows a steady and progressive rate of change. Roman architectural designs transformed much of the rural landscape. Even where traditional buildings continued in use, or where Roman building types were modest and few, access to the Roman marketplace seems to have been virtually ubiquitous. The regional variations were enormous, but Roman culture and social and economic pressures were so pervasive that almost every rural settlement was affected in some way. Likewise, where villas were viable they usually existed, and where they were particularly well placed, they were likely to develop into wealthy establishments. Collectively, this creates relatively high visibility in the archaeological record through material such as coins, mosaics and brooches. In some respects, this picture may itself be unbalanced, encouraging us to ignore areas where perhaps communities were so marginal and had so little access to the Roman system that they are rendered almost invisible to us. Likewise, it is impossible to believe that the rural population evaporated in the fifth century, yet by this period the archaeologically visible evidence dwindles to such small levels that this is the impression we are left with.

CHAPTER 9

PEOPLE & PLACES OF ROMAN BRITAIN

The population of Roman Britain was largely indigenous, though many people were descended from immigrants who had arrived during relatively recent prehistory from various places in western Europe. This was a fully hierarchical society that ranged from landowners, administrators and military officials, to peasant farmers, slaves and the urban poor. Members of the urban and military populations from the Continent dominate the literary and tombstone evidence. Intermarriage between all of these groups ensured that Britain's population would always be mixed. Until the third century, soldiers were not supposed to marry, but it is clear that they often had families long before this date.[1] Britain was typical of the Roman Empire in these respects, but the limited evidence available to us means that we have information about only a tiny number of individuals.

Despite Roman influence before the invasion, the conquest had a dramatic impact on Britain, and affected everyone to a greater or lesser extent. Before the invasion, Rome impacted on a relatively small part of the British population. After the invasion, Roman law, money, literacy, access to imported goods, rural economies and the military restructured the very basis of society. Under Rome, the trivial details of individual lives start to emerge. For the first time in British history we can see a period as a human experience, and not as a speculative archaeological or anthropological construct founded on generalities.

Roman Britons existed in a world characterized by change. Industry, although established, reached unprecedented levels, exposing far more people to the risks of accidents or toxic substances. Farming brought innovations in techniques, crop maintenance and animal husbandry. Medical skills improved, although, as infection was not understood, surgeons treated symptoms rather than causes. The people who benefited from such skills were likely to be the rich and the military, whereas the rest of the population probably depended on folk and quack remedies. Certainly there was an active interest in healing, as evidenced by the healing cults and the oculists' stamps used to impress blocks of healing eye salves. But generally evidence for individual medical treatment cannot be identified, unless a recovered skeleton has a healed fracture that has been carefully set, or amputated limbs.

This was also a time when urban settlements brought large numbers of people to live together in close proximity for the first time in Britain, and therefore exposed them to all the risks of infection without immunity. Immigrants arrived from further afield, and in greater numbers, than ever before, bringing new diseases to a population with no natural resistance, while exposing themselves to variant forms and conditions they themselves were not immune to. One possible disease brought from abroad is leprosy, which seems not to have existed in Britain before the Roman period. Pioneering medical research in the nineteenth century showed what happened to rural people first exposed to the infectious environment of towns. However, we also know that Roman Britain was the first time in which washing, personal hygiene, supplies of fresh water and disposal of waste were organized at any level.

POPULATION SIZE

Measuring Roman Britain's population with any meaningful accuracy is almost impossible. There are no census records and no other figures from the period that we could use, though they must have existed.[2] The number of excavated graves is minute compared to the number of people that must have lived at the time, and the numbers of gravestones or other inscriptions referring to individuals is even smaller. All we can do is guess, using what we know about density of settlement, the size of towns compared to their medieval successors, the size of the army, and so on.

In terms of absolute numbers, the population of Roman Britain will have been in a constant state of flux, both seasonally and over longer periods, due to disease and changes in the environment that affected food production and temperatures. Based on the approximate size of the military, including its dependants, and urban populations, the density of rural settlement and its capacity to support people per hectare, and the ratio of rural to urban populations in a pre-modern environment, one reasonable estimate is a population of 3.67 million, where 365,000 of those individuals were urban or military.[3] However, this figure will have varied constantly for a host of environmental reasons.

There is an approximate minimum for the urban population because we know how many people medieval towns could support. This was roughly 150 persons per hectare (about 60 per acre). Cirencester was Roman Britain's second largest city at 107 ha (264 acres), and therefore could theoretically support a population of 16,000. But areas of the city were undeveloped, meaning that a figure of 8,000 to 12,000 is more likely to be representative. In the sixteenth century by comparison, York and Norwich were two of England's premier cities and had populations of 8,000 and

202. Housesteads (Northumberland).
Altar to Hercules, dedicated by Publius Aelius Modestus, prefect commanding the First Cohort of Tungrians. Modestus' name indicates that he or a forebear gained citizenship under Hadrian, but is otherwise a characteristically anodyne Roman name that provides no information about his homeland.

203. Backworth (Northumberland).
Silver skillet inlaid with gold, inscribed with a dedication to the Mother Goddesses by Fabius Dubitatus, possibly the maker. Length 21 cm. (British Museum).

10,000 respectively. Assessing the rural population is much more difficult, because the figures are based on a more incomplete idea of the extent and density of settlement. The Domesday Book counted a population in 1086 of around two million. Roman Britain's population could easily have ranged from around two million to perhaps as high as five million. During the period it may very well have fluctuated quite considerably within this range, making it futile to speculate further.

The graves excavated from the period therefore represent a tiny proportion of the population. One recent survey of excavated cemetery sites was based on just 5,716 burials, most of which were inhumations and thus belonged to the second half of the period.[4] Death rates are difficult to compute for obvious reasons, but before the plague of 1665, London's population suffered a very approximate death rate of three to four per cent, based on 14,000 deaths per annum in a population of about 400,000. In a population of four million, that means around 140,000 deaths per annum, or, over the 367 years that Britain was a Roman province, about 51 million. Those 5,716 graves therefore potentially represent just four per cent of one year, or a little over one-hundredth of one per cent of all the deaths in the period – a minute sample. If Cirencester had a population averaging 8,000 over the 330 years from its foundation to the end of the Roman period, then the estimated 320 annual deaths should have produced a little over 100,000 graves. The 362 graves excavated at the town's Bath Gate cemetery represent a little over one-third of one per cent. Since of the 337 graves where sex could be identified, 71 per cent were male, it is obvious that the sample is biased and so small as to be not reliable.

These tiny proportions show how wrong it would be to assume that the evidence from any one cemetery is automatically representative of the fort or settlement to which it belongs, let alone the population in general. There is a subtle implication in some of the published detailed discussions that somehow estimates and other calculations are leading us to more reliable conclusions. Since any estimate is impossible to substantiate, and the evidence is founded on unlimited variables about which we know nothing, this can be misleading.

204. Ancaster (Lincolnshire). Inhumation grave of an elderly man of late or post-Roman date. Oriented east-west, the grave appears to be Christian, but contained reused blocks, including one naming a local god, 'Viridios'.

Instead, cemetery excavations present us with a range of practices and evidence of disease, as well as sometimes an indication of ethnicity, either based on grave goods or physiological evidence [204]. This sort of evidence is, of course, extremely important and very useful. A large proportion of Roman burials were cremations, particularly in the first and second centuries, and these can show evidence for disease in the teeth, malformation of bones (hypertrophy), or damage to bones (atrophy). Where disease or damage was followed by healing, it is clear that the person survived, at least for a while. However, it is known from modern medical examinations that of two people suffering from the same infection, one person's skeleton may exhibit damage while the other may not. So an excavated skeleton with no apparent damage may still have belonged to someone who died from infection, rather than, for example, a heart attack. Other problems arise because the evidence is widely scattered in the published (or unpublished) record, and in the storage of excavated skeletons.

205. Old Penrith (Cumbria). Tombstone found near the fort, recording the death of Marcus Cocceius Nonnus, aged six years. The child was probably the son of a soldier, but no further details, including cause of death, are given. (British Museum).

LONGEVITY

Human beings have always been capable of reaching advanced ages, and the maximum potential life span has not really altered for millennia. One need only glance through the pages of a seventeenth-century diary to see the extraordinary variation in life spans a single family could experience, and the random factors that affected their chances of long and healthy lives. The diarist John Evelyn (1620–1706) and his wife reached the ages of 85 and 74, respectively. Of their eight children, four sons died in infancy. Two daughters died from smallpox at 20 and 18. One son reached the age of 44, but the youngest daughter reached 85. Of the ten individuals, three attained ages that would be considered respectable today, yet the family's average age at death was 33.[5] The modern tendency to focus on minimum averages at death has created the widespread impression that everyone in the past inevitably died young.

The only difference is that today people have a better chance of reaching old age. The problem in archaeology is measuring actual age at death, because certain skeletal developments require a minimum age to be reached, followed by relatively little subsequent change. Dental wear, being progressive, can sometimes suggest that an individual lived 30 or more years longer than the minimum age indicated by the skeleton. Today, many specialists in this field have come to realize that estimated ages at death of many excavated skeletons may be far too low.

Tombstones provide us with what we must assume is reasonably accurate data, however limited in quantity. In Lincoln, Claudia Crysis reached the age of 90, but at Caerleon a veteran called Julius Valens reached an impressive 100. His wife, Julia Secundina, was still alive to erect the tombstone, although she herself later died at the age of 75.[6] Obviously these individuals were as exceptional then as they would have been 30 or 40 years ago, even if such advanced ages at death were approximations, rather than precise figures. Other tombstones from Caerleon record the deaths of soldiers at the ages of 27, 28, 40, 45 and 65, while women are recorded as having died at the ages of 30, 35, 60 and 65 [206]. Other tombstones from around the province record deaths from infancy to old age. Tombstones are a self-selecting sample. Not only are they usually associated with military sites, but they are also biased to men, and also to people able and inclined to invest in them. In addition, the tombstones almost invariably lack any information about the cause of death. Flavius Romanus, who died at Ambleside aged 35, 'killed in the fort by the enemy', is an exception.[7]

DISEASE AND HEALTH

The Roman period, like all pre-modern times, was a time when physical activity was a much more important aspect of everyday life. Even the affluent will have spent more time walking, while being transported on horseback or in carriages is more physically taxing than being moved around in cars. While this brought its own risks in terms of accidents, it also meant that basic levels of fitness and tolerance of hard work were far higher than today. This is reflected in the low incidence of osteoporosis, where bones, usually in older women, become brittle and fragile. Osteoporosis is associated with a lack of exercise and deficiencies in calcium and protein. In our own time, the condition has become common for obvious reasons.

During the Roman period, there was a significant increase in dental caries. Whereas one in 33 of the Iron Age population had been affected, in the Roman period it rose to as high as one in eight amongst women.[8] The increase, along with a slight increase in dental abscesses, is attributable to sugars in cereal crops that were being consumed in larger quantities. The evidence for diet suggests that the population had access to enough iron to prevent anaemia under normal circumstances. The fact that anaemia had affected around a quarter of the adults, and more than a third of the juveniles, at the Poundbury cemetery at Dorchester requires another explanation than iron deficiency. The most likely cause is infectious disease, conditions of the digestive tract, or high lead levels, though of course the latter

206. Caerleon (South Wales). Tombstone from the legionary fortress at Caerleon, commemorating Tadia Vallaunius, aged 65, and her son Tadius Exuperatus who died at the age of 37 'on the German expedition', perhaps as part of a vexillation sent to fight on the German frontier in the third century.

may have been as a result of very local conditions. Infection can cause damage to the bone, and this is found in more Romano-British skeletons than in those of Iron Age date. An almost unlimited range of bacteria and viruses can cause infection. Thanks to mutation and natural selection, many ancient varieties will no longer exist, complicating our interpretation of disease and infection. It is usually impossible to know which bacteria or viruses had been responsible, even if they were detectable. Nevertheless, bone damage associated with specific diseases suggests that tuberculosis and leprosy were certainly introduced during the Roman period. However, most cases of tuberculosis do not lead to skeletal damage, and therefore would be archaeologically invisible. In other instances, sinusitis, caused by a nasal infection, is easily identifiable from damage to the nasal bones.

Poliomyelitis in Roman Britain could have resulted from improved civic water supplies and hygiene. The explosive growth in poliomyelitis infections in the USA in the early twentieth century is largely attributed to the growth of hygiene and decline of breast-feeding, reducing infant exposure to the endemic disease. Previously, children benefited from ingesting antibodies from their mothers through breast-milk. By failing to develop immunity in protected conditions, children grew up susceptible to infection. This led to polio's perverse appearance in epidemic form in civilized, hygienic communities. Polio has been identified in a handful of Romano-British skeletons, including, interestingly, four from Cirencester, though even here this was only regarded as the most likely explanation rather than a certain diagnosis.[9] But whether this represents an endemic disease, as polio usually was in antiquity, or a local epidemic caused by reduced resistance as a result of improved hygiene, illustrates perfectly how difficult it is for us even to make educated guesses about what happened in any one place or time.

Romano-British men seem to have been taller than their prehistoric predecessors, reaching an average 1.7 m (5 ft 6 in), though women dropped a little to an average of 1.6 m (5 ft 3 in). However, most of the Roman evidence comes from urban cemeteries, which sometimes had disproportionately large numbers of men, who probably benefited from a more predictable and better diet than their earlier counterparts. Moreover, such figures are derived from so small a sample of the total population that there is little chance they are reliably representative.

Being well fed was not necessarily an advantage. Gout, caused by rich food, first appears in Britain in the Roman period, manifested in conditions of the big toe bones. If people were better nourished, fitter and more likely to have access to clean water and medical treatment of sorts, then they were liable to live longer and therefore be exposed to more accidents and general wear and tear. This may be the reason why

Romano-British skeletons have high levels of injury and joint disease, with as many as 14 per cent having the latter. When it comes to evidence for injury, 14 per cent of the adult skeletons in which sex could be determined (a total of 505 out of 3,620) showed signs of bone trauma. Not only is it impossible to know how common this was, it is also impossible to know whether the trauma was the result of a casual accident, a work-related accident, or due to violence of any kind. Even when damage to bones seem to have been caused by weapons, this could just as easily have been the result of a tavern brawl as of warfare.

DEATH & BURIAL

Tombstones are one of the most important sources of information about the Romano-British population. Unfortunately, we have only a few hundred, out of a population that must have numbered between three and five million for the best part of four centuries. Of those that we have, the bias is very distinctly to the military, their families and associates. At Bath, for example, of the 11 tombstones recorded in *RIB*, five are of soldiers. Although a fort probably stood in the vicinity in the mid-first century, these tombstones are mostly attributable to visitors to the shrine and spa. In settlements like Lincoln, a fortress for around 20–30 years, about half the tombstones can be fixed to that period alone. Places like St Albans, never a military settlement, produce virtually no tombstones.

Tombstones have three features: the inscribed text, decorative funerary imagery, and occasionally a depiction of the deceased. Many have survived because they were reused in buildings. One of the best examples is the large number of tombstones from the legionary fortress at Chester, found reused in the fortress walls. This provides us with a very useful series of tombstones, but, of course, none is in its original location, or associated with the deceased's mortal remains. Reuse like this also means that many tombstones are incomplete, with damaged texts or decoration.

Like most Roman epigraphic monuments, tombstones were formulaic. They feature stock funerary phrases usually, but not always, abbreviated to their initial letters. Depictions of the deceased in a decorative panel usually conformed to a stereotyped representation with appropriate attributes. In many cases, the fact that the funerary text does not fit neatly into the panel suggests that the tombstone was a prefabricated off-the-shelf purchase. The text would include the name and often the age at death. More expansive texts add details such as occupation, family members, hometown and province, and the details of those who had erected the tombstone, usually the heirs (*heres*), the wife (*coniunx*), or the deceased's freedman or freedmen (*libertus* or *liberti*).

Tombstones never carry dating information, though the deceased's name and occupation can sometimes provide a clue. Although tombstones are typically conformist, there are several instances of decorative flair and of the allusion to very personal and intimate experiences. However, even details of the name can be a little misleading. It was not unusual for very conventional Roman names to be adopted by people of

Tombstone abbreviations
DM or DMS *Dis Manibus*: 'To the spirits of the departed'.
AN or ANN *Annorum*: '[Number] years of age'.
M *Menses*: 'Months', where added to years of age, usually where children were involved.
D *Dies*: 'Days', where added to years and months of age, also usually for children.
FC *Faciendum Curavit*: 'Took care of the work', sometimes translated as 'had this set up'.
HSE *Hic Situs Est*: 'Is buried here'.
STTL *Sit Tibi Terra Levis*: 'Let the earth rest lightly on you'; much rarer.

PEOPLE AND ETHNICITY IN ROMAN BRITAIN

When it comes to analyzing the ethnic and social make-up of the Romano-British communities, we are dependent on tombstone and literary evidence, though this is necessarily a limited and self-selecting sample. A name on a tombstone is not much use unless some information is provided about birthplace and family. Sextus Valerius Genialis is a classic instance of how misleading his tombstone could have been if it had only partly survived, or the text had been less expansive [208]. With its three components (*tria nomina*), 'Sextus Valerius Genialis' is the

obscure provincial origin, or to be acquired either by recruitment into the army or by citizenship. Such names tell us nothing about a person's true origins unless the tombstone provides the details.

A tombstone from York

This text is unusually detailed and seems to record the deaths, probably not simultaneously, of a legionary veteran's family [207]. The occasion was probably his wife's death, with the opportunity taken to commemorate the earlier deaths of the children. The decorative panel on the stone depicts much older children, suggesting it was purchased off-the-shelf, an impression reinforced by the clumsy insertion of the text.

DM FLAVIAE AVGVSTINAE /
VIXIT AN XXXVIIII M VII D XI
FILIVS / SAENVS AVGVSTINVS
VIXIT AN I D III / […] VIXIT AN
I M VIIII D V G AERESIVS /
SAENVS VET LEG VI VIC
CONIVGI CARI- / SSIMAE ET
SIBI F C

To the spirits of the departed, Flavia Augustina, who lived 39 years, 7 months and 11 days; Saenus Augustinus who lived 1 year and 3 days; and […] who lived 1 year, 9 months and 5 days. Gaius Aeresius

Saenus, a veteran of the Sixth Legion Victrix, took care of the work for his beloved wife and for himself.

207. York (Yorkshire).
Tombstone erected by Gaius Aeresius Saenus to his wife and children. Probably late second or early third century.

name of a Roman citizen. Valerius Genialis served in a Thracian cavalry unit based at Cirencester in the mid-first century, but the text tells us that he was an ethnic Frisian, something we could not know from his Roman name.[10] Adopting a Roman name seems to have been part of the enlistment routine for some auxiliaries.[11] Such military identities could submerge a person's origins.

The military population was endemically transient, though by the third and fourth centuries movement was more limited. Officers, who could even include future emperors, were appointed to one command before being transferred to another, in a different province. Vespasian (69–79) served as commander of the II legion during the invasion, and his son Titus (79–81) served as a legionary tribune in Britain, probably during the 60s [209]. Decimus Junius Juvenalis, from *Aquinum*, in Italy, and probably the man known to us as the poet Juvenal, spent part of his military career in Britain as tribune commanding the First Cohort of Dalmatians.[12] Sometimes men specialized in careers involving Britain. During the Hadrianic period, Marcus Maenius Agrippa, from *Camerinum* in Italy, commanded the *classis Britannica* and the First Cohort of Hispanians at Maryport, before ultimately becoming Britain's procurator. Another of his earlier commands was of the Second Mounted Cohort of Britons, styled the Flavians.

At Lincoln, two members of the IX legion came respectively from *Heraclea*, in Macedonia, and *Clunia*, in Spain. Members of *II Adiutrix* came from Lyons and *Savaria*, in *Pannonia Superior* (modern Hungary). Lincoln's civilians include a Greek called 'Flavius Helius', an interesting conflation of Roman and Greek names in Latinized form, and Sacer of the Senones, a tribe in *Gallia Lugdunensis*. Where no place name is mentioned, the individual, such as Claudia Crysis the nonagenarian, could be local, or at least British, but this is not guaranteed. Marcus Laetilius Maximus served in the first cohort of a legion, and was buried at Lincoln in a legionary communal tomb (*columbarium*).[13] His tombstone states only his name and cohort. The monument on which it was displayed would have carried a main text that identified the legion. Marcus Aurelius Lunaris served as a *sevir Augustalis* (an administrator of the imperial cult) at both Lincoln and York, but he is recorded on an altar he left at Bordeaux, dated to 237. We have no idea

208. Cirencester (Gloucestershire). Tombstone from the first-century auxiliary fort of Sextus Valerius Genialis, who died at the age of 40 after 20 years of service. (Corinium Museum).

which of these three places, if any, he came from, but men of his status were usually freedmen. In Lunaris' case, he had perhaps been freed after the Caracallan edict of universal citizenship, and had adopted part of the emperor's official name, 'Marcus Aurelius Antoninus'.

Auxiliaries were typically distinguished by their units' ethnic titles, but these have traditionally been interpreted too literally. The names generally commemorated the area in which the companies were first formed, but units moved on, and the titles might even have been fictional from the outset.[14] It can never be assumed that a member of, for example, a Gallic unit was a Gaul unless his tombstone says that he was, just as Sextus Valerius Genialis was not an ethnic Thracian despite serving in a Thracian cavalry wing. The longer a unit was in a province, the more inevitable it became that recruits would include the soldiers' offspring by local women, or recruits drawn from the local population or almost anywhere in the Empire. Even the most authentically ethnic unit was unlikely to remain so. Ethnic titles were also adopted simply for the image. Dio describes how a cavalry unit was formed with the title 'Batavians', purely on the basis that Batavians had reputations for being 'superb horsemen'.[15] There is no indication that any actual Batavians belonged to it. The First Cohort of Aelian Dacians, at Birdoswald, was stationed there from Hadrianic times. By the middle of the fourth century, it is extremely unlikely that anyone in the unit had ever been to Dacia, let alone been born there. The Second Cohort of Asturians, a Spanish unit, is attested at Greatchesters in 225 [210]. The *Notitia Dignitatum* names the First Cohort of Asturians there in the fourth century, though this is probably an error for the Second. Either way, few of the fourth-century Asturians are likely to have been ethnic Spaniards by then.

The appearance of African-type ceramics at York in the early third century from North Africa has been postulated as evidence that legionary reinforcements arrived after the civil war of 193–97.[16] This is an interesting idea, but identifying movements of peoples from artifact evidence is not always reliable. There are, for example, no tombstones or other inscriptions from York identifying individuals from North Africa. None of this precludes the possibility that many reinforcements were indeed sent to Britain, merely that pottery is not a reliable verification of it.

Likewise, it has been argued that ethnicity can be identified from grave goods. Excavations at Brougham (Cumbria) recovered an array of burial evidence from a third-century cemetery. It was concluded that the graves contained specific goods that reliably indicated the age and sex of the occupant, and reflected the unit's origins on the Danube frontier area.[17] This may be correct, but there is no epigraphic evidence from

209. Titus (79–81).
Like his father Vespasian, Titus spent part of his military career in Britain. Men of senatorial status, with an eye on a military reputation, benefited from spending a period in Britain, one of the most exacting provinces in the Empire.

Brougham to confirm it. The only units named on inscriptions from Brougham are a cohort of Gauls, a unit of cavalry from Stratonicia, in Macedonia, and the VI legion.[18] None of the three tombstones from the fort specify any ethnic identity at all, and while some of the names are 'unashamedly barbarian', none can be pinned down to any one location conclusively.[19] Moreover, it ought to be obvious that while grave goods might be all that is visible to an archaeologist, they form just one tiny element of the defining features of an individual's life, most of which we know nothing about. Perhaps one of the most defining features of the Roman world was the synthesis and adoption of different cultural attributes and behaviour. This is seen in every province. In Egypt, for example, immigrant people of Greek and other Mediterranean stock adopted mummification, along with other aspects of traditional Egyptian burial practices, but used mummy portraits that were classical in style.[20] The Brougham graves may indeed exhibit 'imported' practices, but it is equally possible that those customs were adopted by those who made use of them whilst stationed in the Danube area, or from their immigrant fellows at Brougham. There are, by the same token, several instances of attested mummification in Italy and other provinces.[21] So it is obvious that conclusions based on artifacts alone are both subjective and simplistic.

210. Greatchesters (Northumberland). Altar from the south gate at Greatchesters (*Aesica*) from 225 recording the presence of the Second Cohort of Asturians. Asturians were still here in the fourth century, but by this time the unit's original ethnicity had probably been heavily diluted by foreign recruits and marriage with local women.

Soldiers, of course, also retired into civilian communities. Gaius Aeresius Saenus was a veteran of the VI legion, but remained with his family at York, where he buried his wife (see p. 213).[22] Ulpius Silvanus, a veteran of the II legion, invested his time and money in a temple of Mithras in London.[23] Publius Aelius Bassus, however, was a veteran of the XX legion, and was buried in a substantial tomb at Watercrook, in the Lake District. The fact that it was a centurion of the VI legion who had organized the burial, illustrates perfectly the fluidity of relationships and distribution of individual soldiers in the military community.

Lincoln, as a legionary fortress and later a colony, is in the best possible position for producing an archive of tombstones and inscriptions. It is simply a fact that soldiers and foreigners were far more likely to commission inscriptions than indigenous Britons. London, being an international trading centre as well as an administrative and military base, has produced the broadest range of individuals, although most of the inscriptions tell us nothing about personal origins. The most important of these was Gaius Julius Alpinus Classicianus (see p. 40), a post-Boudican procurator and husband of the daughter of a Gaulish tribal chieftain. The Athenian, Aulus Alfidius Olussa, died in London at the age of 70, as did a slave of unknown origin called Anencletus on the provincial government staff.[24] Only his position made it possible for him to be commemorated in this way.

We have no other epigraphic evidence of slaves, except in the form of freedmen or women. Of the latter, the best known is the celebrated Regina, freedwoman of Barates the Syrian, at South Shields [211].[25] Her tombstone is the most elaborate from Roman Britain, but its exotic design and the skills used to produce it reflect the resources available in the military zone where an epigraphic tradition was well established. Barates may or may not have been a soldier or veteran, but he commissioned a stone that drew on architectural styles familiar in the Near East and even added a second, condensed version of the funerary text in Palmyrene. What makes Regina so interesting is that she was a Catuvellaunian, and thus Romano-British by birth. When or where Barates bought her we do not know, but he evidently freed and married her, only for Regina to die at the age of 30. The key point is that we only know about her because her non-Romano-British husband commissioned such an explicit tombstone.

For the most part individuals like Regina are lost to us. Even in the rest of the Roman Empire, ethnic Britons in the army, or in any other capacity, are virtually unknown. Either few of them ventured very far, or those that did were unlikely ever to commission tombstones or be recorded in any other way. A very few turn up in military posts, such as Lucco the Dobunnian, from the Cirencester region, who served in an infantry cohort of Britons in Pannonia in 105, and Aemilius the Dumnonian, from the Exeter region, serving in the *classis Germanica*.[26] The latter is interesting as his naval post might reflect a personal background on the southwest coast in Britain.

Identifying indigenous Britons is even more difficult in civilian areas. At towns with no military phase, such as Silchester and St Albans, there is very little evidence. St Albans has produced no legible tombstones at all, and Silchester just one. Interestingly, the latter records the burial of a woman called Flavia Victorina, buried by her husband, Titus Tammonius Victor. Since the name 'Tammo-

211. South Shields (Northumberland).
Tombstone from *Arbeia* of Regina, the Catuvellaunian freedwoman and wife of Barates the Palmyrene. Early third century.

nius' is unknown from anywhere else, the dedication at Silchester to Hercules by a Titus Tammonius Vitalis, son of Saenius Tammonius, is too much of a coincidence for them not to be related. The name is probably British, and local to Silchester.[27] If so, this is an unusual instance of a family that had subscribed to the epigraphic tradition.

Some villas, such as Keston [212] and Lullingstone, are associated with mausolea and a very few graves, but nothing is known about any of the individuals since inscriptions from villas are rare. An exceptional instance of a rural tombstone, found on an unexcavated rural settlement at Wool (Dorset), is too incomplete to be restored. But the formation of its letters suggest that the stonemason had copied a handwritten note, and was accomplished and practised at the task.[28] Since just three tombstones are known from Dorset, it may well be that the rarity of inscriptions from villas is also partly due to stone-robbing in later periods. However, most of those that have been found seem to be reused stones, like the appropriated milestones found at Clanville and Rockbourne. One cryptic exception is Quintus Natalius Natalinus, whose name appears on a fourth-century mosaic found at Thruxton, in Hampshire [213].[29] This is extremely unusual, making it difficult to know if he was the villa owner, his patron, or even the mosaicist. The text adds the words 'ET BODENI', which can either be read as 'and (son) of Bodenus' or 'the Bodeni', perhaps a father and son. One suggestion is that the room and

212. Keston (Kent).
Tombs in the small villa cemetery at Keston. The larger mausoleum is nearly 9 m (29 ft 6 in) wide, and may have been up to 6 m (19 ft 8 in) high, and probably accommodated the bodies of the villa owner and his family. Third century.

its mosaic formed a self-contained Bacchic chapel for the use of a religious guild.[30] Natalinus, with his eminently Roman name, seems to be telling us that his father had an unequivocally British name, which only serves to illustrate how essentially uninformative a Roman *tria nomina* can be in unqualified, isolated form.

If Natalinus was a villa owner, then he was one of the *honestiores*, the landowning upper-classes. Whoever these people were in Roman Britain, indigenous or not, they liked to see themselves in the classical Italian tradition. This is obvious from some of the possessions they left behind, such as the Lullingstone mosaic busts, or their mosaic floors. However, it is almost impossible to know what the personal significance was of the imagery. Subject matter was potentially of religious significance, but also served simply as manufacturing trademarks and as symbols of status. Rudston has its extraordinary 'Venus' floor with panels containing a variety of circus animals and appropriate epithets, such the 'man-killing bull' and the 'fiery lion' (see p. 203).[31] Such panels are common in North Africa, but Rudston is unique in Britain. Where something so unusual is concerned, it is reasonable to suggest that the owner had North African interests, or may have come from there. At Brading (Isle of Wight), a mosaic figure may represent the owner as he liked to see himself [214].

Thruxton, Rudston and Brading take us into the fourth century, when the epigraphic tradition was virtually dead in Roman Britain, partly explaining the lack of inscriptions at villas. Soldiers had virtually ceased

213. Thruxton (Hampshire). Fourth-century mosaic floor recording a possible owner, Quintus Natalius Natalinus.

214. Brading (Isle of Wight). Mosaic depicting the so-called 'astronomer' or 'philosopher', perhaps reflecting the villa owner's image of himself as an educated and inquisitive man. Fourth century.

to produce inscriptions, or at least in any form that survives. The same seems to go for officials. Even now, the individuals we hear about are rarely of Romano-British origin. Even the ultimate patriot, the reckless usurper Carausius (286–93), was a Menapian and came from the coastal regions of the Low Countries. Magnentius (350–53) purportedly had a British father, but also had a Frankish mother and was born at Amiens, in *Gallia Belgica*. His coup took place on the Continent, and he may never even have come to Britain. Magnus Maximus (383–88), fondly remembered in Wales in Dark Age kingship lineages as Macsen Wledig, was a Spaniard in the British garrison. Pelagius was a remarkable exception, but he only became notorious when he left Britain.

GRAFFITI AND CURSES

The appearance of graffiti is one of the most striking differences between the Roman period and what came before and afterwards. Almost all Roman sites produce some sort of graffiti, even if limited to a few scratched symbols on potsherds. The Vindolanda tablets, and isolated examples found at other places like London and Carlisle, show that handwriting, given the abundant written communications and records, must have been a routine part of military and official life. We know from Roman Egypt that soldiers and veterans were more likely to be literate than other groups, so reading and writing must have become familiar to at least a portion of the indigenous population in Britain. The graffiti suggest this simply because of their very ordinariness. The graffito from London, recording the absence of Austalis for 13 days on some mysterious business, is the most remarkable. Inscribed on a tile before it was fired, the writing must have been done by a tiler who not only knew his Latin, but was also sufficiently adept to compose a metrical text.[32]

The panel as written:	Read as:
AVSTALIS DIBVS XIII	*Austalis dibus tredecim*
VAGATVR SIB COTIDIM	*vagatur sib cotidim*
	'Austalis has gone off by himself daily for the last 13 days'

Whatever else one might think about the Roman control of Britain, literacy is ultimately liberating. Since there was no normal written form of Celtic,[33] Latin provided the only route into literacy. It may also have had a unifying social and economic effect on a population that had probably used a variety of similar, but not identical, Celtic dialects. Towns and forts have produced the most graffiti, reflecting density of occupation, and also the level of excavation or casual finds. It is interesting that towns like Silchester and St Albans, which have produced so few inscriptions, have yielded respectable numbers of graffiti on pottery. Remote rural sites have also produced a variety of graffiti, usually just numerals. Alphabets, probably produced as writing exercises by children or their teachers, have turned up in several towns and forts, as well as in the villa at Binsted Wyck (Hampshire), and at Scole (Norfolk).[34] At Irchester (Northamptonshire), a storage jar was used by the potter to make a record of what had been stacked in one kiln load.[35] More often, the graffiti consist of just a personal name, such as 'Vitia', whose name was scratched on a fourth-century jar at Darenth. A samian dish, dated to *c*. 180–260 and found in a grave at Ospringe (Kent), had a series of names inscribed on it, suggesting that it was shared [215]. One of the most unusual must be '[…]mantios the mule-physician', written in Greek on a jar of Romano-British manufacture, found in the Thames at Amerden

(Buckinghamshire). This man, presumably a Greek vet, is a reminder that the Roman world introduced Greek as well to Britain. A small number of stone inscriptions have been found composed in Greek, usually in military or urban contexts.

The 'curse' tablets from Uley [216] and Bath provide an unparalleled insight into the day-to-day trivia that preyed on Romano-British minds. The tablets were hurled into the sacred spring from the second to the fourth century. They were generally written by, or for, victims of theft or those who had some other grievance, and are mainly concerned with revenge. This theme seems to have been the main priority at Bath, and on most of the other curse tablets found in Britain. The practise continued well into the 'Christian' period, which is not surprising given the evidence for paganism in Britain at the time.

Many of the texts are incomplete, or barely coherent. Among those that can be read are inscriptions that record Docimedis and his stolen gloves, Docilianus and his stolen hooded cloak, and the suspects Senicianus, Saturninus and Anniola in 'the case of the six stolen silver coins'. Civilis, whose ploughshare had been filched, was sufficiently aggrieved to make the trip to Bath, since it can scarcely have been stolen from him while he was there. Such victims promised that the stolen item would be given to the goddess (metaphorically, no doubt) if she would get it back for them.

A few refer to the information having been copied for a fee, suggesting that scribes composed curses on behalf of clients who provided them with details.[36] The range of competence in handwriting shows that the writers responsible for the tablets

215. Ospringe (Kent).
Samian bowl from a grave inscribed: *LVCIVS.LVCIANVS.VLI. DIANTVS.VICTOR.VICTORICVS. VICTORINA.VAS COMMVNIS*, meaning 'Lucius, Lucianus, Iulius, Diantus, Victor, Victoricus, Victorina, their communal dish'. About 180–260. (British Museum).

216. Uley (Gloucestershire).
Lead 'curse' (*defixio*) tablet by Saturnina, seeking restitution for her stolen linen in return for a one-third share to Mercury and another third to Silvanus. Dimensions 8.3 x 6 cm. (British Museum.)

ranged from the barely literate to accomplished scribes. Many ordinary people were probably either illiterate, or relied on a functional literacy that allowed them to read and write names and other basic information, without having either the need or ability to do anything more. A number of the names are obviously Celtic in origin, such as 'Severianus, son of Brigomalla', useful evidence for the involvement of the indigenous population in the cult. Unfortunately, none of the tablets tell us where each individual came from, but, like finds of samian and coins in rural sites, the Bath tablets are just another aspect of how the invasion of Britain led to a situation that affected everyone in some way.

PLACE-NAMES OF ROMAN BRITAIN

Most of the smaller towns and settlements are completely anonymous. Even some of the larger small towns are absent from inscriptions, writing tablets and ancient texts that include historical accounts and route itineraries. Those towns that do survive provide evidence for a variety of traditions that included Roman, indigenous and mixed names. Not a single Roman villa identified on the ground has produced evidence of its name in antiquity.

Most names we have belonged to forts, major towns, and some of the small towns. Some cannot now be identified, but inscriptions and distances given on route itineraries, and places where ancient names have been fossilized in later names, have made it possible to identify many of them. *Londinium* is the most obvious, but its source is shrouded in mystery. This suggests that it had remote pre-Roman origins, but there is no evidence for a significant pre-Roman settlement in the area. In the fourth century, for a while at least, it was awarded the honorific name of *Augusta*, but it is unlikely that this ever came into normal usage. In a similar manner, Colchester retained its pre-Roman name of *Camulodunum*, despite being awarded the formal Latin name *Colonia Claudia Victriciensis* after the invasion. *Camulodunum* preserved the name of a Celtic god, 'Camulos' (usually associated with Mars in the Roman period), while –*dunum* was a common name component that meant 'hill' or 'fort'.

At towns such as Silchester and St Albans, the survival of a pre-Roman name is self-evident from the evidence of Celtic coinage that names the mint sites of *Calleva* and *Verlamion*, respectively. *Calleva* seems to have come from a Celtic word for a wood that has survived into modern Welsh as *celli* ('grove'), thus meaning 'town in a wood'. In the Roman period, *Verlamion* became *Verulamium*, but its origins are very uncertain, and had perhaps even been forgotten by then.[37] Canterbury's name of *Durovernum* is more easily explained. *Duro* is the first part of several Romano-British and Gaulish place-names, and was a Celtic word used for a fort, or fortified town. *Verno* was the Celtic word for alder swamp, surviving in Welsh as *gwern* (alder tree). The combination of elements makes it less likely that the name was used for the place before the Roman period, since there was no town here, but once established, the 'town by the alder swamp' was named using vernacular terminology.

Chelmsford (*Caesaromagus*) and Chichester (*Noviomagus*) were hybrid names. *Caesaromagus* has a blatantly Roman prefix in *Caesaro–*, much in the same way a modern town like Kingston incorporates a reference to the monarch. The second part, *–magus*, is a well-known British and Gaulish Celtic term for a field or marketplace, surviving in Welsh as *maes* (field). This created Chelmsford's hybridized 'market-place of Caesar'. Chichester's prefix, *Novio–*, is a Celtic word for 'new' that comes from the same root as the Latin *novus*. Thus Chichester's name is simply 'New Market'. Bath was given wholly Latin names in *Aquae Sulis* and *Aquae Calidae*, 'springs of Sulis' and 'hot springs', supplanting whatever it was called before the invasion.

The northern frontier shows that even new military installations could have Latin or Celtic names. Benwell (*Condercum*) took its name from the Celtic words for 'with' and 'looking around', clearly a reference to its hilltop location. Risingham (*Habitancum*) is not obviously Latin, but the prefix can be identified as an adaptation of the Latin name, *Avitus*. The suffix is less certain, but it has been suggested that this means something approximating 'property', thus 'the property [or estate] of Avitus', where Avitus is likely to have been a Briton with a Latin name. *Luguvalium* (Carlisle) was derived from a Celtic personal name, *Luguvalos*. *Arbeia*, known to be the fort at South Shields, has defied easy explanation. One suggestion is that it preserves a reference to the so-called Tigris boatmen, listed as the garrison at South Shields in the *Notitia Dignitatum*, by alluding to an Arab population.[38] But other suggestions are that it may have had something to do with a river-name. A reconstruction of a corrupt part of the Ravenna Cosmography has recovered a reference to *Horrea Classis* ('Fleet Granary'), which may possibly be another name for South Shields, since the fort was used as a major grain store.

THE ROMANO-BRITISH AND THE ROMAN EMPIRE

Accounts like those of Caesar and Tacitus dominated the popular image of Britain in Roman eyes. The tales of the assault on Anglesey and the Boudican revolt paint a vivid picture of a volatile place where violent and explosive tribal warfare threatened disaster. Although Britain changed almost out of recognition during the first century AD, the Romans regarded the transformation of this frontier wilderness into a Roman

province as never more than a veneer. From a Roman or Gallo-Roman perspective, Britain was permanently on the margins and was depicted as such. Britain was, said the historian Florus, a place retained as a province only because its very worthlessness exhibited Rome's munificence.[39] Since the trappings of Roman civilization were the same as those of slavery, as Tacitus described them, perhaps the Romans always felt ambivalent about Britain. When Britain's tribes rebelled, there was a sneaking admiration for the sheer bravado and leadership involved, and a nostalgic sense that this was what Rome had once been. The Britons who became 'civilized' lost the very virtues that the Romans believed they themselves had lost, and thus denied themselves the chance to be admired.

We would recognize this attitude today as prejudice based on a derogatory stereotype, and it lasted throughout the period. One of the Vindolanda tablets refers to the *Brittunculi*, 'wretched Britons', in a context that is ambiguous.[40] The writer either means Britons serving in the Roman forces, or the local tribal Britons that he and his companions were fighting. Either way the term is derogatory, but it is doubtful if the writer would have used the same word for the Britons further south, many of whom would have been indistinguishable from most other people in the northwestern provinces.

Or would he? In the fourth century, the Gallo-Roman poet, Ausonius, wrote a ribald series of verses about one of his critics, Silvius Bonus. Ausonius was annoyed at being criticized, especially by a Briton, and in his verses poured scorn on the idea that a man could be called 'The Good' and be also a Briton.[41] Ausonius' venom was trivial compared to

217. **Brantingham** (**Yorkshire**). Figure of a nymph from a villa mosaic floor. However remote this part of the Roman world, men with the means to commission mosaics aspired to classical imagery and tastes. Despite this, Britons were generally looked down on by the rest of the Empire, especially by educated and wealthy Gallo-Romans who regarded themselves as truly classicized.

the bile fired at the heretic, Pelagius. Pelagius rejected the Augustine idea of an elect amongst the community of Christians, and preached the idea that any man could earn a path into heaven through his own actions. Pelagius was born in Britain or Ireland, but took his views across the Empire at the end of the fourth century. Declared a heretic, Pelagius was subjected to a stream of invective that he was a porridge-stuffing, bloated Celtic yokel by such church establishment figures as Jerome and

SLAVERY IN ROMAN BRITAIN

Slavery was a normal part of life in the classical world, and once Britain became part of the Roman Empire, it became a much more integral part of life within Britain itself. Society was completely dependent on slave labour and as Rome grew, the demand for slaves steadily increased. That demand was met by war and conquest, but people could also be enslaved because of debt and crime, or simply by birth. Freeing slaves was a common practice in the Roman world, and was often a reward for loyal service. Until that time a slave had no rights and no independent identity.

Freedmen are found almost everywhere in Britain, but having once been a slave was still something of a social stigma. The Claudian army was furious when the emperor sent his freedman Narcissus to encourage them to drop their opposition to the invasion. When Nero sent his own freedman, Polyclitus, to sort out the differences between the governor and procurator after the Boudican revolt, the Britons were said to be stunned that Roman senior administrators should have to obey an ex-slave.[44] Before the revolt, the Iceni had been subjected to exploitation by official slaves on the procuratorial staff, adding insult to injury.[45]

There can be no doubt that thousands of Britons were enslaved during the conquest, though we know nothing about individual cases. The speech composed by Tacitus for Calgacus, leader of the Caledonian tribes in the war against Agricola, stated that slavery was the consequence of defeat. In it, Calgacus encouraged his men to fight so that they could escape the prospect of 'tribute, the mines, and all the other penalties of slavery'.[46] Tacitus also used the term metaphorically, as he regarded defeated peoples, or those who had accepted Roman ways, as effectively 'enslaved'.[47] In the same way, the Carausian regime was accused by the legitimate Empire of having 'enslaved' the children of the Britons.

Not surprisingly, we have very few instances of individual slaves in Britain since they were unlikely to be in a position to record themselves. However, a recently discovered document, dating to c. 75–125, concerns the sale of a slave woman from Gaul called Fortunata.[48] She had been bought for 600 *denarii* by an imperial slave, Vegetus, who was himself owned by a senior imperial slave, Iucundus. There is no certainty that the transaction occurred in London, where the document was found, but

another tablet from London famously records the intention 'to turn that girl into cash'.[49]

Most slaves in Britain led anonymous lives, engaged in endless cycles of toil that could have involved anything from turning the water-wheels in London to tilling the soil on the wind-blown agricultural terraces beside Housesteads fort on Hadrian's Wall. At Caistor-by-Norwich, leg-irons have been found. Slaves who were unruly or unreliable were routinely shackled into chain gangs for their work and then chained in prisons at night.

Life for any slave could be hard, but especially so was that of the rural slave, who was lumped together with farm animals and tools as a means of cultivating the land.[50] Even worse was life in the mines, which was short and vicious. In the first century BC, Columella, in his book on agriculture, recommended that a villa estate consist of the residential house, the farmhouse and the storehouse. He declared that the farmhouse should be where the slave staff lived in individual rooms, unless they worked as shepherds or herdsmen, in which case they should occupy part of the animal buildings. The Gorhambury (Hertfordshire) villa is just one of many instances where

Orosius.[42] Others were gentler, but still regarded Britain as irremediably barbarian. Claudian, in his panegyric for Stilicho at the beginning of the fifth century, depicted Britannia as a woman with tattooed cheeks, and dressed in a blue cloak and skins from 'some Caledonian beast'.[43] It was as whimsical as foreigner's image of Britain today as a land of castles and half-timbered houses.

this pattern seems to have been followed. At Hambleden (Buckinghamshire), nearly a hundred infant burials were discovered. Possibly the offspring of slaves on the estate, they recall Columella's suggestion that female slaves be encouraged to bear children, and to be exempted from work if they had three sons, or even freed if they had more.[51]

This sexual side to slave life could occasionally work out for the best. Along with that of Regina, the wife of Barates, the other remarkable tombstone from South Shields is of Victor, the Moorish tribesman and freedman of Numerianus, a young trooper in the First Cavalry Regiment of Asturians [218]. It has been suggested, based on the tombstone's affectionate nature, that Victor and Numerianus had had a homosexual relationship, which led to his freedom and the expensive tombstone.

Freedmen are in fact the best evidence for the existence of slaves in Britain, particularly the freedmen of soldiers. At Bath, Aufidius Maximus, centurion of the VI legion, benefited from a dedication to the goddess Sulis, made on his behalf by his freedman, Marcus Aufidius Lemnus. Lucius Manius Dionisias made a similar gesture to his former master, Gaius Javolenus Saturnalis, a standard-bearer with

the II legion.[52] Freedmen also included prominent individuals in Romano-British civic communities. Marcus Aurelius Lunaris, the *sevir Augustalis* at Lincoln and York, was probably a freedman since the post was normally held by one.

218. South Shields (Northumberland). Tombstone from *Arbeia* of Victor the Moor, freedman of Numerianus, a soldier in the First Cavalry Regiment of Asturians. Victor may have been a spoil of war, or perhaps simply an unfortunate sold into the slave trade. Early third century.

CHAPTER 10
RELIGION IN ROMAN BRITAIN

219. *Below.* **Carrawburgh (Northumberland).**
This vessel, possibly a clay incense burner, is inscribed *Covetina* [sic] *Augusta Votu(m) Manibus Suis Saturninus fecit Gabinius*, 'Saturnines Gabinius made this for Cove(n)tina Augusta with his own hands'.

220. *Opposite above.* **Horse-and-rider brooch.**
This brooch would originally have had coloured enamels in the recesses. Such objects may have been souvenirs of visits to temple sites. Diameter 3.2 cm.

221. *Opposite below.* **Blackfriars (London).**
Carved relief of, unusually, four mother goddesses. Found reused in the fourth-century riverside wall.

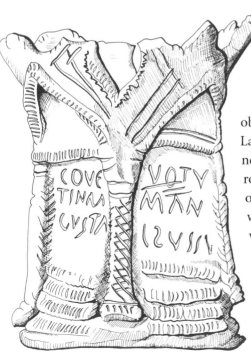

The Roman period differs from all others in Britain's ancient past in the sheer quantity of goods, structures and written evidence. Material with a religious association monopolizes many parts of the record. More temples and shrines are referred to on inscriptions from Britain than any other class of building, and altars and tombstones account for the vast majority of inscribed stones found in the province. Some shrine sites that have been explored, such as the spring at Bath and Coventina's Well at Carrawburgh, on Hadrian's Wall, have produced abundant quantities of votive finds [219], including large numbers of coins and the so-called 'curse' tablets.

Romano-British culture was a unique conflation of Roman and provincial customs, tastes and characteristics. This reaches its most idiosyncratic and conspicuous height in the cults, for which prolific evidence has been found. Although some purely classical cults were worshipped, most cults in Britain were either Celtic in origin, or were adapted by conflating Celtic and Roman archetypes that were perceived as equivalent or complementary, such as Mars and Cocidius, and Sulis and Minerva. The adoption of Roman-type representations and attributes of deities mirrored how the Romano-British had accepted Roman patronage and symbols of status in other parts of their lives. The gods of Britain had taken their own places in a Romanized hierarchy.

Normally we only know about ancient gods, however obscure or localized, because their names are recorded in Latinized form on inscriptions and dedications. The Roman need to visualize these gods in a familiar form meant they were routinely presented in the guise of classical deities. And, as is so often the case with Roman Britain, the context in which those written and visual forms of the names, powers and attributes of various gods have come down to us is a military or urban one.

From the beginning, Britain was also home to imported gods, such as the German goddess, Garmangabis, who was transplanted to the fort at Lanchester (Durham) by the garrison. Others, such as Isis and Mithras, were the consequence not only of a sophisticated and cosmopolitan world, but also of a continual interest in exploring new spiritual directions. Of these, Christianity would emerge as the most decisive religious innovation of antiquity.

Religion was an intensely personal experience for the devotee, as it is for the archaeologists and historians who interpret it. The result is a picture of Romano-British religion that is often compelling, but equally unclear as to what is based on fact, and what is based on interpretation. There is no better example than the boar brooches worn by the Aestii tribe in Germany. Were it not for Tacitus, the probable conclusion would be that that these brooches somehow represented masculine, warlike virtues of bravery, prowess and hunting skills. But Tacitus tells us that they were worn as a symbol of the Mother Goddess.[1] The connection might not seem immediately obvious to us, but the large number of teats female boars have emphasizes fertility. Having this sort of verification is extremely rare. More often than not we have no idea what the symbolism of a particular object was, though there is usually no shortage of ideas. Some scholars believe that mosaic imagery can be interpreted as evidence for the presence of Gnosticism, an interest in spiritual truths, but others are less convinced.[2] The only clear impression this ought to leave the more critically-minded reader is that religion in Roman Britain is a subject we barely understand.

CHRISTIANITY

Christianity, until the fourth century, was essentially just another eastern mystery cult, although with certain key differences. It was inclusive in the sense that anyone could join, but exclusive in that true disciples accepted the Christian god and no other. This latter requirement flew in the face of traditional Roman and Celtic attitudes, and in fact was ignored by some who happily added Christ to their personal list of favoured deities. The most important evidence for the existence of Christianity in Britain is not archaeological, but literary. The presence of British bishops at fourth-century church councils shows that an Episcopal hierarchy had been created by at least 314. The popularity of the Pelagian heresy in 429 and the pleas for help from the church in Gaul demonstrate that the hierarchy was functioning, and that it was still in contact with the Continent.

The physical evidence for British Christianity is significant, but often ambivalent. The most definitive group of Christian artifacts is the third- or fourth-century Water Newton treasure, which was found in isolation and nowhere near any sort of structure that might, however tenuously, have been interpreted as a church. While many of the items carry unequivocal Christian symbols and wording, some of them are votive plaques of a type known from pagan cult sites. Such plaques were usually nailed by pilgrims to walls in temple precincts, and represented the fulfilment of a pagan vow. The Water Newton pieces seem to represent the transfer of that process to a Christian context, but exactly how or why is not clear. They could, for example, represent a Christian cell whose members were reluctant to abandon their old ways of worshipping, or a cult for whom

Christ had been adopted as an associate deity with pagan gods already being worshipped there.

In any case it was the enduring pagan habit of votive goods that makes Water Newton such a visible record of Christianity, and therefore so typical of pagan Roman culture in any archaeological context. Christianity is relatively invisible in the record. Christian graves are 'defined' by an absence of grave goods and by the east-west orientation of the body. The lead baptismal fonts, of which several are known, are the only really

222. Hinton St Mary (Dorset).
The figure depicted in this mosaic panel is apparently Christ, although it is also possible that it represents the rebel emperor, Magnentius (350–53). Magnentius appeared bareheaded on his coins, and the reverses of one issue included a large Chi-Rho (see p. 74). Mid- to late fourth century. (British Museum).

223. Lullingstone (Kent).
This restored wall-painting from the villa's 'house-church' shows a number of figures with their hands raised in the conventional manner of Christian prayer in the Roman period. Late fourth century. (British Museum).

conspicuous traces of Christian rites, and were probably used for bulk baptisms by travelling priests. Pewter found at the Appleshaw (Hampshire) villa, marked with the Chi-Rho, could conceivably have been used in a house-church. The word-square found on a fragment of wall-plaster at Cirencester can be unravelled to reveal Christian slogans. Word games like this were undoubtedly popular, but it is impossible to know what their significance was.

The very small number of buildings identified as possible churches due to their shape and location have produced absolutely nothing that would confirm their function. The Colchester extra-mural 'church' can be tentatively identified as such only because it is surrounded by east-west graves. The Silchester 'church' has much to recommend it structurally as a church, except that its orientation is reversed from what subsequently became normal for churches. Only some innovative reinterpretation of the excavated evidence has shown that the building was probably bigger than originally thought and enclosed a baptismal font. At Richborough, the church within the fort walls was built of timber and escaped the notice of the excavators. Only the identification of a font beside some postholes has shown that a church probably stood there. More recently, probable churches have been identified at Vindolanda and Housesteads, based purely on suggestive structural traces. The single exception to these is the house-church at the Lullingstone villa. In the late fourth century, a self-contained suite of upper rooms at the villa's eastern end was decorated with wall-paintings that include the Chi-Rho and praying figures [223]. There can be no real doubt about what the rooms were used for, but this conclusion could only be reached because the shattered wall-plaster was laboriously recovered and restored. At the time, Christian worship was frequently conducted in private homes, making it even less likely that we would find archaeological evidence of it. The mosaics at Frampton and Hinton St Mary [222] both bear Christian symbols, the latter including possibly the earliest representation of Christ. Both also have a number of pagan mythical elements, which were habitually used by Christians (and pagans) as allegorical symbols. The Lullingstone mosaic, for instance, depicts among other motifs Bellerophon killing the Chimaera. Christians used this event as a symbolic representation of the triumph of good over evil. With the evidence for a house-church on site, a good case can be made for the mosaic having been installed for its Christian symbolism. But without the wall-painting, the evidence would be a good deal more ambiguous.

THE DRUIDS

One of Caesar's most important observations was about the Druids. Since they have no recognizable manifestation in archaeology and are silent in the written record, the Druids exemplify the problems inherent in interpreting cult activity from archaeology. We are left only with Caesar's account and a few other references.[3] Caesar described the Druids as a special caste that had total control over all religious activity and justice, and were exempt from taxes and warfare, and the petty inconveniences of tribal boundaries. The Romans recognized the Druids as a major political and territorial threat to their consolidation of power in Britain, and believed them to be the driving force behind organized resistance. In this sense, the Druids were as inconvenient as the church was to medieval monarchs. Human sacrifice also revolted the Romans, and Caesar and Strabo, among others, made the most of the Druids as symbols of the ultimate barbarian nightmare. They seem to have been annihilated by the campaign against Anglesey, and it is not impossible that some of the Britons welcomed this outcome. After their disappearance, religion in Britain appears to have taken on a largely Roman flavour. As ever, this is an impression created by the high visibility of 'Roman'-type activity, as it is in every other aspect of Romano-British history and society.

THE GODS OF ROMAN BRITAIN

In the pagan pantheon, anything could be venerated in divine form. At its most extreme, this included deities attributed to the various components of a door, but in general places, regions, plants, buildings, springs and trees could all be regarded as the home of a spirit, whose good auspices needed to be sought and whose wrath needed to be placated. This concept was as familiar to the Britons before the conquest as it was to the Romans.

Purely classical gods were rare in Britain. Usually when such gods do appear, it is in an early or politicized context. Chichester, in the Atrebatic enclave and probably the tribal capital of Togidubnus, has produced several inscriptions from very early in the province's history, including the dedication of a temple to Neptune and Minerva. Another slab is early in style, and names Jupiter Optimus Maximus, the most politicized of all the Roman gods.[4] Honouring the head of the Roman pantheon was as much a political as a religious gesture. This was a ritual part of reinforcing loyalty to the state, something any pro-Roman tribal leadership was very well aware of.

Dedications to Jupiter are among the most numerous of all religious offerings in Britain because the annual religious calendar demanded that he be honoured on the day the current emperor came to power, as well as on 3 January. Most dedications are from the military zone, usually offered by the commanding officer in the name of the unit. A series of

224. Bath (Somerset).
A gilt-bronze head of Minerva, probably once part of a life-sized cult statue in the temple of Sulis-Minerva. Late first century. (Museum of Bath).

altars at Maryport may be from a temple to Jupiter outside the fort, or may represent annual revisions of the unit's loyalty. Another series is known from Birdoswald, almost always in the name of the First Cohort of Aelian Dacians, the long-term resident garrison. The calendar of festivals was rigorously observed in forts across the Roman world, and the events that took place at Maryport would have been mirrored at every other military establishment. Jupiter was often worshipped in tandem with the imperial *numen,* or 'spirit of the emperor'. Interestingly, although almost all inscriptions come from the military zone, two were found on a temple site at Greenwich and a dedication to Mars Camulos was recently discovered at Southwark. Both inscriptions appear also to be to the imperial spirits, reflecting the nature of the provincial capital.[5]

Although London probably had a temple to Jupiter, the closest we get to the classical pantheon in epigraphic form there is the dedication to Mars Camulos. The temple precinct at Southwark, where at least two Romano-Celtic temples were built, was probably laid out in the late first or early second century. Evidence for a variety of statue and column bases around the temples suggests an array of sculptural dedications, perhaps to other deities as well. The habit of conflating classical gods with Celtic equivalents venerated long before the conquest is particularly characteristic of Roman religion in Britain, and reflected a pattern found throughout the Empire. The temple of Sulis-Minerva at Bath is the best-known classical temple in Britain, and the gilt bronze bust of Minerva [224] is one of the most overtly classical pieces of British religious sculpture. The Roman epigraphic record of these conflated cults is very often the only reason we know anything about them.

Roman culture resulted in cults becoming more visible because the physical representations of these gods were named on accompanying inscriptions. The Fossdyke Mars (see p. 167), found to the west of Lincoln, was manufactured for a pair of brothers, Bruccius and Caratius Colasunus.[6] To the east of Lincoln, an inscription from Nettleham records the donation of an arch by Quintus Neratius Proxsimus to Mars Rigonometos. *Rigonometos* can be translated from its Celtic roots, producing 'king of the grove', suggesting that the arch records a much older sacred plot of woodland with which Mars had now been associated. Mars was one of the classical gods most frequently connected with cults in the northwest provinces. He was associated with Lenus in the healing shrine in the Altbachtal precinct at Trier, and turns up in this guise at Chedworth and Caerwent. These healing properties made him ideal for conflation with Nodons (or Nodens) at Lydney Park (Gloucestershire), where the pilgrims not only had their dreams read, but, judging by the finds of bronze dogs (associated with healing as far as back as Ancient Greece), also came for medical reasons. There was therefore, not surprisingly, a temple to Mars himself at the healing spa of Bath. It was recorded on one of the curse tablets, but has not yet been found.

Mars was more usually associated with local hunter or warrior gods. At Barkway (Hertfordshire) there was a shrine where Mars was worshipped as Mars Alator and Mars Toutatis.[7] 'Alator' is believed to mean 'huntsman', and Toutatis was a Gaulish god to whom human sacrifices were offered, described by the Roman poet Lucan as 'dreadful Tuetates'.[8] In the north, Mars was often combined with the Celtic warrior god, Cocidius, usually depicted in a similar manner to Mars in military costume with spear and shield. The same pattern is found for many of the other classical deities, but there was nothing rigid about the combinations of gods. Cocidius, for example, was also conflated with the Italian woodland god, Silvanus, at Housesteads, but at Colchester, a coppersmith dedicated an offering to Silvanus Calliriodaco.[9]

Without the known attributes of the classical god involved, it would often be hard to have any idea of the Celtic deity's nature. Mercury Andescociuoucus is only recorded once, on a marble slab at Colchester.[10] 'Andescociuoucus' is thought to mean 'great activator', which perhaps has something to do with Mercury's role as the ambassador of the Roman pantheon. At Nettleton (Wiltshire), Apollo was worshipped with Cunomaglos, a name that probably meant 'hound prince'.[11] This is not as incongruous as it sounds. Conflation of deities was founded as much on complementary qualities as on those that were similar. Apollo Cunomaglos, like so many of these classical-Celtic conflations, is an example of the infinite flexibility inherent in paganism.

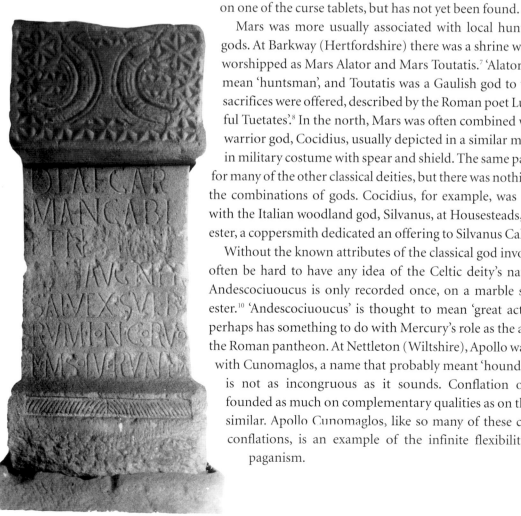

225. Lanchester (Durham). Altar from near the fort at Lanchester, dedicated to the German goddess, Garmangabis, by the vexillation of Suebians, during the reign of Gordian III (238–44).

Sometimes the Celtic deity was venerated in his or her own right, but the manner of worship had been adapted into a characteristically Roman one. Coventina was interpreted by her Roman admirers as a water nymph, and depicted as such on a relief dedicated by the prefect of the First Cohort of Batavians, at Carrawburgh. Two of the inscriptions from the spring name her as 'Nympha Coventina'.[12] Antenociticus, also known as Anociticus, was worshipped in a small temple just outside the fort at Benwell, further east along the Wall. The head of the cult statue was found in the temple, and represented a young male with horns in his hair, possibly linking him to Cernunnos, a god with a stag's head. The cults of these Celtic deities are only visible to us through Roman media, and we know nothing about the gods who were not recorded.

Some Celtic deities were imports. Garmangabis seems to have been introduced by the Germanic vexillation of Suebians, who erected an altar to her at Lanchester during the reign of Gordian III [225].[13] The Roman habit of personifying geographical areas into quasi-religious figures also generated new British deities. Another goddess, Brigantia, represented the Brigantian tribal region, and was depicted in the guise of Minerva on a carved relief from Birrens (see p. 118).

The so-called mystery cults introduced an exotic and unprecedented component into the Romano-British pantheon. Mainly originating in the Eastern Empire, cults like the worship of Isis had started to become fashionable in Rome long before the conquest of Britain [226]. Their veneration in the Roman world was a typical consequence of an international society in which soldiers, officials and traders travelled widely across Europe, North Africa and the Near East. By the late first century, there was a temple to Isis in London recorded on a *graffito* on a first-century flagon. Its presence reflected the cosmopolitan nature of the provincial capital. Either this or another temple of Isis was restored in London in the middle of the third century.[14]

Also becoming popular in Rome long before the conquest of Britain was Cybele, the Phrygian mother goddess, readily associated with the classical Ceres and Juno. Cybele's lover, Atys, castrated himself in a ritual declaration of remorse for an act of infidelity. Her most extreme adherents castrated themselves, and a pair of clamps found in the Thames was decorated with figures that make it certain it was connected with the cult. At Carvoran, by Hadrian's Wall, the prefect had an altar carved with a prayer in the form of a metrical poem to

226. Dendera (Egypt). Relief from the temple of Isis at the shrine of Hathor, built by Augustus. The cult of Isis proliferated throughout the Roman Empire, carried from Egypt to places as far away as London by traders and soldiers.

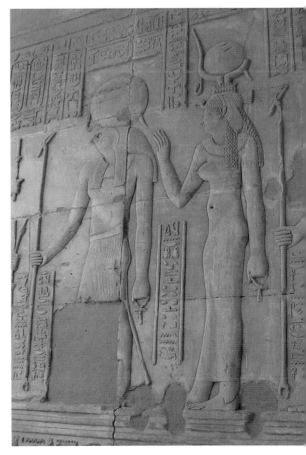

'Ceres the Syrian Goddess'.[15] Serapis, an Egyptian god, originated in the sacred bull, Apis, and had been created as a new cult in late Egyptian times under the Ptolemaic Greek rulers. As a favourite of Septimius Severus and Caracalla, Serapis became particularly popular in the late second and early third centuries. Appropriately a temple was built at York at around the time the imperial household was based there by the legate of the VI legion, Claudius Hieronymianus [227].[16]

The renewed interest in paganism in fourth-century Britain has always been very difficult to interpret, partly because of the ambivalent use of pagan myth and allegory. The very late temple at Maiden Castle produced a strange, small bronze figure group of a tri-horned bull with

CLASSICAL TEMPLES

Very few classical temples are known in Britain. Colchester's temple to the deified Claudius, rebuilt after the Boudican revolt, is the largest yet discovered, but only its foundations survive. Not only was the site adapted for use as a Norman castle, but the temple seems to have been substantially remodelled in antiquity, possibly into a church. Like the slightly later Fishbourne Palace, the Colchester temple's appearance in Britain so early was a revolutionary innovation. It was a massive

structure, and the remains of its podium beneath the castle still stand almost 3.5 m (11 ft 6 in) above the Roman ground level. Its overall size must have been at least 32 x 24 m (105 x 79 ft). Based on these proportions, it has been estimated that the façade had two rows of eight columns, with another sixteen around the *cella*, where the cult statue and valuables were stored. The temple was seen by the Boudican rebels as the ultimate symbol of Roman oppression, and, appropriately

enough, it became the site of the last stand of the colonists c. 60–61. Following the revolt the temple must have been rebuilt, but did not survive in its original form to the end of the period.

As the principal, or at least original, centre of the imperial cult, the size of the Colchester temple is only to be expected. Something similar must have stood in London, but nothing has ever been found. Such temples played an extremely important part in the annual cycle of official religious festivals. At St Albans, two classical temples of indeterminate form stood on the south side of the forum, but the five-odd other temples known in the town were all Romano-Celtic in design – even the prominent temple in its large precinct next to the theatre. At Wroxeter, a small classical-style temple seems to have been squeezed into a street frontage after a late second century fire had

228. Bath (Somerset).
The Gorgon pediment sculpture from the temple at Bath. Minerva wore a Gorgon medallion and was conflated with Sulis, the deity of the sacred spring. Late first century.

destroyed a house formerly on the site.[17] But this is an unusual find. Silchester, where most of the masonry structures are known, had no classical temple at all.

The only Romano-British classical temple known in any detail is the temple of Sulis-Minerva at Bath. Although the building lies deeply buried, with large parts inaccessible, the recovery of pediment sculpture, significant parts of its columns and other architectural details make its original appearance virtually certain [229]. It undoubtedly went up in the Flavian period as a fairly standard tetra-style temple, although the hybrid elements of the pediment mark it out as a building with a very idiosyncratic flavour and iconography. By the fourth century it seems to have been significantly redesigned. Flanking shrines were built on either side of the temple steps, and some sort of covered ambulatory may have been built around the *cella*, creating a structure that had elements of both classical and Romano-Celtic design.

Fragments of other possible classical temples have been found elsewhere, but usually in a context that makes any sort of visual restoration impossible. A small fragment of a massive inscription in Winchester of Antonine date can only have come from a major classical temple or administrative building. The temple of Diana recorded on an inscription found at Caerleon is a good candidate for a classical temple, but no structural remains are known. A large section of entablature, very possibly from a classical temple, was found built into the late Roman southwest gate at Lincoln, acting as a chamfered plinth block in one of the flanking towers. Evidently the temple, if that is what it was, had been demolished for a long enough period of time for an odd block to be reused by persons unknown who neither knew nor cared where it had come from.

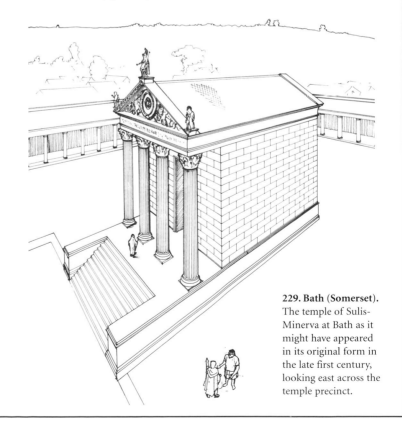

229. Bath (Somerset).
The temple of Sulis-Minerva at Bath as it might have appeared in its original form in the late first century, looking east across the temple precinct.

three women riding on it. The group may represent a barely known Gaulish god called Travostrigaranus, but it seems quite extraordinary that he should have appeared in Britain so late in the day, unless he had somehow been restored by some enthusiast for the old gods. This is not as strange as it seems. The period was an immensely troubled one. The villa owners might have had money and time to spend on the country houses, but the accumulating political insecurity of the age had helped provoke Julian II (360–63) into re-legitimizing paganism. The Christian church was being rent by divisions between the Orthodox and Arian branches. Traditional gods, whether classical or Celtic, might well have seemed like safer and more reliable options. At Lamyatt Beacon, the figures of gods found were conventional provincial representations of old classical gods, such as Mercury, Minerva and Hercules. The Thetford Treasure, deposited at the very end of the fourth century, was unequivocally associated with the god Faunus, an ancient Italian woodland god linked to Bacchus and last heard of in the works of Horace. The appearance of Faunus cult items in Norfolk in the late 300s is confirmed by inscriptions on the silver spoons, without which the very idea would seem totally incongruous.

THE CONTRACT

One of the key characteristics of Romano-British pagan cult activity was the ancient notion of contract. Normally we see the end result of this pact on stone altars in which the abbreviation 'VSLM' appears. The letters stand for *votum soluit libens merito* and means 'he willingly and gratefully fulfilled the vow', where 'he' (or she) is the person responsible for offering the altar. The dedicator had requested a service from the god or goddess, and in return an altar and offerings were promised in exchange. The only context in which we ever usually find evidence for the vows is in the 'curse' tablets found at Bath and Uley, and at isolated, scattered finds. The only traces we normally have of messages to gods made on wooden writing leaves are the bronze seal-boxes that secured any petition made and kept them private. The many seal-boxes found at Great Walsingham (Norfolk) are thought to be evidence for an as yet undiscovered shrine.

What these 'curse' tablets tell us about individuals has already been discussed in Chapter 9, but in religious terms they record the process of the transaction through carefully worded formulae. At Uley, for instance, an unnamed devotee addresses 'the holy god Mercury' to complain about ill-treatment, and requests that the god prevent those responsible from standing, sitting, eating, or drinking, and render them unable to remove the curse unless their blood is spilled.[18] To make sure all potential candidates are covered, the stock phrase *si servus, si liber, si*

230. Dorchester (Dorset).
The amphitheatre (Maumbury
Rings) at *Durnovaria*, just outside
the town walls. It dates to *c.* 70–80
when the Romans adapted a
Neolithic henge monument by
digging out the middle as an arena.
This perpetuated the use of the site
for religious reasons since, like all
amphitheatres, it was used for
games and entertainments
associated with religious festivals.

mascel, si femina ('whether slave, free, man, or woman') is added. Stone
altars usually survive, but offerings could be made and burnt on wooden
or earthen altars (both are attested in ancient literature), or buried in
pits. Altars were deposited in almost any sacred context, and have been
found in water shrines, inside or near temples, at remote open-air rural
shrines, or in what now seems to be total isolation. Although religious
dedications could be made at any time or any place, the sacredness of a
site and the date in the calendar were very important. Much religious ritual was performed according to an annual cycle of special occasions.
Usually some sort of procession came first, depending on the context. In
towns, the theatres and temple precincts were normally connected by
roads, creating a standardized route to be followed for official ceremonies. Private ceremonies may have involved a procession around the
boundaries of a farmstead, a villa estate, or an urban plot.

The offerings preferably involved the sacrifice of a living animal,
together with wine libations and other foods, followed by an examination of the entrails in search of good or bad omens. Not surprisingly, the
physical evidence for sacrifice is almost impossible to identify beyond
the recovery of animal bones at temple sites, where the presence of a particular species may reflect the deity being worshipped. Mercury's
principal associates were the goat, ram and cockerel. Appropriately, of
the quarter of a million bones analyzed from his shrine at Uley, the vast
majority were from these animals, and many must have come from sacrificial animals sold to pilgrims in the temple complex.

Religious activity had to be observed strictly according to ritual to be valid.[19] It was essentially a superstitious approach. If something unpleasant or disastrous occurred, then it would be concluded that the rituals had not been performed properly. Serving as a priest in the Roman world, and carrying out those duties exactly as prescribed, was an integral part of a man's social responsibilities. Priests were not full-time members of a separate caste. The idea of a professional priesthood represented something of a threat to the Roman government, since it diluted the emperor's authority. The emperor was the chief priest, or *pontifex maximus*. Senators served as priests in the course of their other duties, and regarded the position as an honour. Maintaining religious traditions was considered beneficial to the welfare of the state and the community in general. Throughout the Roman Empire, provincial governors and civic officials had responsibilities for observing religious festivals. Other men of lesser rank included priestly duties in their daily routines. Regalia formed an important part of a priest's ceremonial appearance. Priests wore headdresses made of bands or chains, or diadems, and carried staffs or sceptres capped with heads that either represented emperors or deities.

Lucius Marcius Memor was a *haruspex*, or soothsayer, at Bath, the only one known by name in Britain [231].[20] The *haruspex*, who examined a sacrificial victim's entrails, inherited a tradition stretching back to Etruscan times and was a familiar part of Roman religion. Gaius Calpurnius Receptus, *sacerdos deae Sulis* ('priest of the goddess Sulis'), was also at Bath, and another two priests are known on Hadrian's Wall.[21] Marcus Aurelius Lunaris, probably a freedman trader, served as a *sevir Augustalis* at both York and Lincoln, meaning that he was a board member of the imperial cult at both colonies.[22] Another trader, Marcus Verecundus Diogenes, was also a *sevir* of the colony of York.[23] At Greetland (West Yorkshire) in the year 208, Titus Aurelius Aurelianus described himself as a *magister sacrorum* ('master of the sacred ceremonies').[24] Since his altar commemorated a private family offering to Victoria Brigantia and the imperial spirits of Septimius Severus and Caracalla, he may have adopted this rather grandiose title in his capacity as master of his own house, a reminder that the senior man in any context had religious responsibilities to fulfil.

At the fourth century healing cult of Nodons, at Lydney, two rather more unusual religious posts crop up. Titus Flavius Senilis, recorded in an inscription on a now-lost mosaic from the temple, was described as a 'PR REL', for which the only plausible expansion is

231. Bath (Somerset).
Statue base from the temple precinct at Bath, recording Lucius Marcius Memor, *haruspex* (soothsayer).

praepositus religionis, or 'director of the cult', though the term *praepositus* in this context is certainly unusual.[25] The same inscription mentions Victorinus the *interpretiante*, or 'dream interpreter'. The interpretation of dreams as spiritual messages was well established in antiquity, dating back into pharaonic times in Egypt. It was commonplace for people to intensify their sleep experiences by drinking themselves into oblivion first. The physical structure of the temple at Lydney seems to have been designed with recesses for pilgrims so that they could dream their drunken dreams in the vicinity of the god, and wake in the day to have them 'read' by the resident expert. At Bath, a man whose name is lost but who called himself 'son of Novantius', erected his monument, presumably to the goddess, *ex visu*, 'as the result of a vision'.[26]

TEMPLES AND SACRED PLACES

Most prehistoric places were venerated for their natural features, and structures were not integral or necessary to the concept of sanctity. The only pre-conquest buildings identifiable as temples known in Britain were in the southeast, such as the timber circular 'tower' *cella* and enclosure at Hayling Island, in use by the first century BC [232]. They seem to have been yet another dimension of Continental culture already being absorbed from across the Channel before 43.[27] Wanborough (Surrey) had a circular temple by the late first century, but it lay on top of possible earlier structures.[28] The vast numbers of Iron Age coins found on the site make it likely that there had been some sort of pre-conquest temple structure on the site. Wanborough is also an early instance of coins being used as votive deposits, a characteristically Roman habit. Hayling Island's pre-conquest temple was replaced with a Roman version in stone on a similar but much larger plan. The new version had a porch, and was surrounded by a masonry precinct wall and rooms. By the mid-second century, Wanborough had a conventional Romano-Celtic

232. Hayling Island (Hampshire). Reconstructed view of the circular temple at Hayling Island as it might have appeared in the first century. The Roman development of the site represented continuity of use of a much older shrine.

temple. Sacred sites that remained in their natural state were also liable to development. The most conspicuous and exciting example of adaptation was at Bath. Others, like Coventina's Well at Carrawburgh, were left more or less as they were.

Temples in Roman Britain fall mostly into two categories: classical and the much more common Romano-Celtic. The very few classical temples known were in towns. Romano-Celtic temples were built in

ROMANO-CELTIC TEMPLES

Most temples in Roman Britain were of the so-called Romano-Celtic design, a much less elaborate structure than its classical predecessor. The term was coined by Mortimer Wheeler when he excavated the temple at Harlow. Romano-Celtic temples, found throughout the northwest of the Roman Empire, usually consisted of a central *cella* and a surrounding concentric ambulatory. Since a large part of the *cella* of the temple of Janus at Autun, near Dijon, is extant, we know that Romano-Celtic temple *cellas* were tower-like, and that the ambulatory had a pitched roof built into the *cella* walls. However, the proportions must have varied from place to place. In some cases flanking

chambers were built onto the structure, as at Lamyatt Beacon (Somerset), and this modification seems to have been adapted for use at Bath, where flanking chambers and a possible ambulatory were built around the classical temple, creating a very curious hybrid form of temple. Romano-Celtic temples rarely produce any trace of architectural embellishment, even mosaics, although painted wall-plaster is known.

Romano-Celtic temples were built throughout Britain in a variety of contexts, from the relatively isolated temple on Maiden Castle [233] to the urban examples at St Albans and Caerwent. It is rarely clear to whom any one temple was dedicated, especially as many

examples were built on sites that had been sacred in prehistory. At Wanborough (Surrey) there was undoubtedly an Iron Age shrine. By the late first century a stone circular temple had been built, later replaced by a Romano-Celtic temple built beside it in the mid-second century. At Harlow (Essex), Bronze Age burials and numerous Iron Age coins have been found. The Roman-period temple was built in the late first century in one half of a double precinct. By the early third century, Harlow's

233. Maiden Castle (Dorset).
The fourth-century Romano-Celtic temple, sited on the old Iron Age hillfort, as it might have appeared.

large towns, small towns, rural settlements, and in total isolation. In all cases, the temple was the home of the god or goddess. A representation of the deity was stored within the *cella*. Cult activity mainly took place outside in the temple precinct (*temenos*). It was not unusual for several temples, especially Romano-Celtic temples, to be sited within the *temenos*, each dedicated to a different deity. Outside the temples stood altars on which ceremonial sacrifices took place, and over which sacred

234. Caerwent (South Wales).
A Romano-Celtic temple with its precinct. Despite the legal proscriptions against paganism, this temple was built *c.* 330, and remained in use for much of the fourth century.

precinct had been enclosed with stone walls, and additional chambers were built onto the temple. More recent excavations have produced a stone head of Minerva as well as an altar dedicated to the Imperial Spirits. Given the site's history, a now-anonymous Celtic deity must also have been worshipped here. The variety of classical gods represented by statuettes at Lamyatt Beacon emphasizes the flexibility of pagan cult centres.

Such sites help date sequences, but the basic design of the structure itself was so simple it cannot really be dated on typological grounds. Even in the 'Christian' fourth century, new Romano-Celtic

temples were being founded. The Maiden Castle temple, for example, was brand-new in the late fourth century, but was completely basic in form. The town-centre temple at Caerwent, however, was built *c.* 330, but was more elaborate [234].

It was not unusual to build several Romano-Celtic temples in a single precinct. The small town at Springhead had three in one precinct, and at Silchester, *Insula XXX* by the east gate had at least two temples in a precinct that was linked by road to the amphitheatre. Mixing of the Romano-Celtic and classical was very unusual, though this may have happened in the town-centre precinct at Canterbury. Here a classical temple has yet to be

found, though fragments of classical architectural features suggest that one stood alongside the already discovered Romano-Celtic temples. The most curious design of all was the 'Triangular Temple' at St Albans. It occupied a small triangular insula, formed by the intersection of two roads. The main core of the temple was essentially standard Romano-Celtic, but was contained within a triangular precinct.

235. Nettleton (Wiltshire).
The octagonal shrine of Apollo Cunomaglos as it may have appeared before collapsing in the mid-fourth century. The surrounding settlement survived as a centre of light industry, including pewter manufacture. It has been suggested that the ruins were even adapted into an early church, but this has not been proved. The temple and its attendant settlement lay on the Fosse Way between Cirencester and Bath, and in its heyday clearly benefited from and relied on passing trade.

incantations were spoken. The temples provided an attraction to pilgrims and travellers, and formed an integral part of the services provided in towns. Godmanchester (Cambridgeshire), for example, had a temple next door to a building interpreted as the *mansio* (inn).

In some instances, temple-building was ambitious, or at any rate unusual. The shrine of Apollo Cunomaglos at Nettleton [235] probably had Iron Age origins. At its climax, the temple was remodelled as an innovative and ambitious octagonal structure, based on the Romano-Celtic temple concept of internal *cella* and surrounding ambulatory. The octagonal form was apparently beyond the architect's skills, and he failed to recognize that the central lantern of the *cella* would place huge pressure on the external walls. Consequently, no provision for buttressing was made, and the temple eventually suffered partial collapse. Equally unusual, but far more successful, was the probable temple to Victory at Carron, near Falkirk, on the Antonine Wall [236]. Built as a beehive structure with dressed stone, the design allowed the weight of the domed roof to be carried down through the walls. The building was so well executed that it survived intact until the eighteenth century, the only Romano-British structure to do so, until it was dismantled to provide stone for a dam.

In contrast, ritual in the congregational mystery religions of the Roman Empire took place mainly indoors. The temples of Mithras were based on the basilican form of nave and aisles – a form later adapted for use as Christian churches. Not many early Christian churches are known in Britain, although Silchester's fourth-century 'church' beside the civic basilica is one of the most convincing, as is the cemetery 'church' at Colchester [237], with its ground plan of eastern apse, nave and aisles.[29]

The inscriptions from Roman Britain that record temples usually commemorate an individual's endowment of the building or an associated structure, either in a personal or professional capacity. Most come from the north, even if the donor was apparently civilian. At York in 221, the trader Lucius Viducius Placidus built an arch, evidently for a temple precinct, as did Trenico, probably for the precinct of the temple at Ancaster to Viridios, who is named on the slab.[30] At Caerleon, Titus Flavius Postumius, legate of (presumably) the II legion, restored a temple of Diana around the mid-third century.[31] Cooperative efforts are also recorded, such as the building of a temple to the Mother Goddesses somewhere near milecastle 19 on Hadrian's Wall by a vexillation from the First Cohort of Vardullians.[32] The inscription from Chichester recording the client king, Togidubnus, also records the dedication of a temple to Neptune and Minerva by a guild of smiths.[33] And in London, an imperial freedman called Aquilinus probably restored a temple to Jupiter Optimus Maximus, with assistance from three other individuals, probably in the third century.[34]

The renewed interest in paganism in Roman Britain in the late third and fourth centuries, despite the progressive outlawing of pagan practices, was manifested in the countryside where a number of new temples were established, usually as fairly isolated buildings. Urban temples,

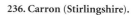

236. Carron (Stirlingshire).
This remarkable 'beehive' temple was probably built by the Roman army as a temple to Victory. Mid-second century.

237. Colchester (Essex).
This 'church' has been identified as such because of the ground plan and clustering of late Roman east-west graves around it. Built about 320–40, with the apse added *c.* 380.

however, generally fell out of use. Lamyatt Beacon (Somerset), begun in the late third century, stood on a ridge with epic views across the Fosse Way to the west. Brean Down, not far away, was begun in the early fourth century. At Maiden Castle, within the old Iron Age fortress, a new Romano-Celtic temple was built on a virgin site after 367, dated by a hoard found under its tessellated floor. Nearby at South Perrott (Dorset), coins of the late third and fourth centuries were deliberately inserted in pits around what is now known to have been a Neolithic or Bronze Age ditched enclosure, probably reflecting a revival of veneration for ancient monuments in the landscape. Similar deposits have been found at many other prehistoric monuments. However, it is extremely unlikely that those who buried the coins had any idea at all of what those monuments had once been used for.

The temple of Nodons at Lydney was originally built in the late third century on a site that must have already been sacred to Nodons, but which had presumably remained undeveloped. Many of these new rural temples were in regions where the most luxurious villas were being developed, often with iconography on their mosaic floors reflecting an intense interest in pagan myth and cult activities. These are characteristically difficult to interpret, or to connect with temples. The triconch hall at Littlecote with its distinctive Orpheus mosaic has been interpreted as the meeting place of an Orphic cult, or as an elaborate summer dining room. Mosaics are virtually unknown in Romano-British temples themselves.

Altars and other votive goods were often set up in the open air. Outside the temple of Mithras, at Carrawburgh, a small stone bench and an altar marked an outdoor shrine to the local Genius and the Nymphs. A few metres to the north, the shrine of Coventina [238] was no more than a stone-lined revetment around the site where her spring rose. Making offerings to a local deity was a way of harnessing that deity's power to Roman ends. Failing to do so might, in the Roman superstitious mind, have risked its wrath. In such a context, building a physical temple was unnecessary, although there is no doubt that one was built at Bath. At Carrawburgh, the shrine to Coventina was left as it was, though now she was offered gifts and portrayed in the Roman way.

This explains the recently-discovered shrine of

238. Carrawburgh (Northumberland).
Relief from the spring at Carrawburgh (*Brocolitia*). Dedicated to the nymph Coventina by Titus D[…] Cosconianus, prefect commanding the First Cohort of Batavians.

Senua, near Baldock, where a quantity of votive gifts, including gold and silver plaques, jewelry, and material deposited by the Spaniard, Servandus, were thrown into a pool. There were probably attendant buildings around the pool to accommodate pilgrims and service the cult. Senua, who is otherwise totally unknown, was probably the Celtic goddess of the water in the pool. Despite the fact that she had been Romanized by being depicted as Minerva, the centre of the cult remained a pool, and not a temple.

Incidental places could become a setting for an act of veneration. On Bollihope Common, near Stanhope (Durham), Gaius Tetius Veturius Micianus, prefect of the Sebosian cavalry wing, hijacked an altar that had already been dedicated to the imperial spirits. He recarved it with a dedication to Silvanus Invictus ('Undefeated Silvanus'), in gratitude for the god's aid in helping him to capture an evasive wild boar.[35] At nearby Eastgate, the prefect, Aurelius Quirinus, made another dedication to Silvanus [239]. To the south, on Scargill Moor, an open-air shrine to Vinotonus Silvanus stood by a stream where several soldiers left other altars in this remote and windswept spot.[36] At Custom Scrubs, Bisley (Gloucestershire), a pair of gabled reliefs depicts Mars Olludius and Romulus, respectively. There is no recorded structural context for either of these reliefs, which were probably displayed in an open-air shrine. Not far from the fort at Risingham, a relief depicting an unnamed warrior god, known locally as 'Rob of Risingham', is still partly visible in situ. All of these altars and reliefs are typical of countless roadside or rural shrines that were scattered across the countryside in every province of the Empire, to which passers-by, travellers and hunters made offerings as a matter of course. In the Christian era, the more obvious and accessible examples were susceptible to destruction, and even 'Rob of Risingham' was partly destroyed in the nineteenth century by the landowner who was sick of visitors. However, anyone passing through Catholic countries in Europe and Latin America will have become familiar with Christian wayside shrines, which preserve a much older pagan tradition.

RELIGIOUS ARTIFACTS

Artifacts with religious associations are well known from Britain. It is not always certain if this religious association represents the object's prime function, or whether it was simply a decorative embellishment. Bronze plaques that record a dedication to a god, like one from Benwell to Hercules by Marus, tribune of the XX legion, are obviously religious. The shield boss of Junius Dubitatus

239. Eastgate (Durham). Altar dedicated to Silvanus by Aurelius Quirinus, commanding officer of the First Cohort of Lingonians at Lanchester under Gordian III (238–44).

of the VIII legion, found in the Tyne, carries representations of a number of gods and mythical figures.[37] Another from Kirkham (Lancashire) depicts Mars preparing his weaponry [242]. Here decoration seems to be the primary motive, but it is no less probable that the images were considered to have totemic protective properties.

THE CULT OF MITHRAS

Mithraism had reached Rome from Persia in the mid-first century BC, one of several exotic eastern cults that rapidly gained popularity as Rome's reach extended further across the Mediterranean world. Like Christianity, Mithraism offered salvation through rebirth, a fundamentally different religious concept from paganism, as well as a communal symbolic meal in a congregational setting within the temple, rather than outside it.

In the Persian legend, Mithras was an associate of the spirit of good, Ahuramazda, and an enemy of the spirit of evil, Ahriman. In this role he was regarded as a powerful force for truth and light, and as a saviour from death. By Roman times Mithras had evolved into the central figure of a mystery cult, characterized by secret ceremonies and initiations. Crucially, Mithraism was an exclusive cult open only to men, making it popular with soldiers and and affluent commercial men, and those to whom its essentially Masonic aspects appealed. Various inscriptions and altars show that Mithras was closely associated with the Sun God, along with other deities like Mercury and Bacchus.

In Roman Mithraism, Mithras fights a bull, created at the beginning of the world, in a cave. He kills the bull with a knife, thus releasing the blood containing the essential life force. Two associates, Cautes and Cautopates, stand by holding torches. The *mithraeum*, based on the basilican architectural form with a nave and aisles, included a *tauroctony*, a relief or painting depicting the killing of the

240. Carrawburgh (Northumberland). The temple of Mithras, just outside the fort at *Brocolitia* on Hadrian's Wall. The mithraeum was built in the second century, but went through several phases of alterations to reach this, its final fourth-century form.

Pottery also performed a variety of religious functions. Clay incense cups, known as *tazze* and resembling chalices, were used in domestic shrines and are occasionally associated with religious sites. Everyday kitchenware jars were often used as cremation containers, while other vessels (typically flagons, beakers and samian dishes) served as grave

sacred bull, at the far end, and was intended to recreate the cave-like environment in which Mithras fought the bull. The faithful took part in a celebratory meal that included wine. Painted inscriptions from a subterranean *mithraeum* found in Rome seem to record lines from hymns that formed part of the ritual.[38]

Several *mithraea* have been found in Britain. All except the London *mithraeum* have been found near forts (Rudchester, Carrawburgh, Housesteads and Caernarvon), while other finds of Mithraic sculpture make it certain that there were more at other forts and fortresses. *Mithraea* were usually small buildings and their congregations were clearly never large, though at 18 m (59 ft) long, London's is one of the bigger provincial examples, and finds from here show that its members could afford to commission works of art of the highest quality.

Joining the cult of Mithras was a complex procedure, involving an opening ceremony that resembled baptism. Thereafter it seems to have involved a sequence of grades: raven, bridegroom, soldier, lion, Perseus, Sun-runner and father. These are mentioned in a letter written by St Jerome.[39] Passing through each of these stages involved tests of endurance in some form. The Carrawburgh *mithraeum* [240] seems to have had an ordeal pit in which, presumably, would-be worshippers were sealed for an

241. Walbrook (London).
Marble relief found near the London *mithraeum*, depicting Mithras killing the sacred bull. It was commissioned for Ulpianus Silvanus, a veteran of *II Augusta*. (Museum of London).

appropriate period of time. At the climax of initiation, a crown was placed on the head of the disciple, and subsequently discarded, whereupon the initiate would announce that 'Mithras is my crown'.[40]

The *mithraeum* at Carrawburgh is the best known. It was constructed in the early third century, but subsequently went through a series of modifications including significant enlargement, and was still in use at the beginning of the fourth century. But before long the temple had been deliberately

desecrated and the *tauroctony* smashed. In London, steps were taken to bury some of the temple sculptures before they too were destroyed, thereby ensuring their survival to the present day [241]. An inscription found in the building is dated to 307–8, showing that destruction took place after this date. In the cases of both Carrawburgh and London, Christian opposition is the most likely explanation.[41] The Mithraic ritual really had no prospect of surviving in the fourth century, not least because the kind of men who had once favoured Mithraism now occupied positions of authority in the Christianized late Roman state. Paganism tended to flourish in Britain's remoter rural areas, never the preserve of Mithraism.

goods, probably containing offerings of food and drink. The flagon with the *graffito* naming the London temple of Isis is of ordinary Flavian type, but in this case had probably been used in the temple itself. A grave at Dunstable (Bedfordshire) contained a standard colour-coated beaker, which carried the handwritten inscription that it was an offering by one Regillinus to the 'branch-bearers', associated with the cult of Cybele.[42] A pottery mould from Corbridge depicts a Celtic warrior god, usually identified as Taranis, with a wheel motif, a standard symbol of the sun. This was evidently used to manufacture identical pottery plaques to be fixed to the sides of jars or bowls, but what the vessels themselves were used for is impossible to say. Religious references did not need to be quite so literal. A Nene Valley beaker from Horksey Toll (Cambridgeshire) depicts an erotic scene involving a phallus [243]. The phallus had potent associations, not just with fertility, but also in its ability to ward off the 'evil eye'. This superstitious side to pagan beliefs played an important part in Romano-British religious activity.

242. Kirkham (Lancashire).
Bronze shield boss depicting Mars, surrounded by military paraphernalia. Diameter 19 cm. (British Museum).

Coinage habitually featured deities, or spiritual personifications, on the reverses. Domitian (81–96), for example, favoured Minerva, and many of his coin types depict the goddess or her attributes and equipage. Coinage played a major role in introducing to Britain the idea of human representations of deities in classical form. But it can be easy to read too much into this. It has been suggested that the Snettisham hoard, evidently the work-in-progress of a jeweler, was really a votive deposit to Minerva because so many of the silver coins depict her.[43]

Almost all of the 82 silver coins were 93.5 per cent fine, a standard only achieved between 85 and 96, although the hoard was buried after *c.* 155. That standard is an optimum balance between purity and hardness, making it ideal for jewelry. The coins are principally those of Domitian and were probably selected for their bullion content, and so the dominance of Minerva types is an incidental consequence, rather than a deliberate selection.

Coins deposited in sacred springs, as at Bath and Carrawburgh, are clear instances of mundane objects being utilized as votive gifts. One possibility is that the dominance of reverse female types at Bath may be a deliberate selection as homage to the goddess of the spring. However, the vast majority of Roman coins carry female reverse types, dominating the mainstream issues that monopolized coins in circulation. Rather more interesting is the preferred use of badly worn coins. In a world where coinage was valued by its intrinsic content, these pieces were bordering on being worth a good deal less than face value, and were therefore cheaply disposable. The recovery of broken or damaged brooches from similar contexts is usually interpreted as evidence for the ritual 'killing' of functional personal items to make them valid votive deposits. This undoubtedly occurred, especially in prehistoric contexts. But it is equally likely that in the Roman period this idea of ritually 'killing' votive gifts survived, but in a form in which already broken or damaged brooches were preferred because they were useless for anything else. The skillets found in the sacred spring at Bath were all worn and old, suggesting that they were only thrown in because they were redundant, or were accidentally lost in the course of a long life pouring libations into the water.

Personal talismans such as rings with gemstones depicting gods, or with inscriptions bearing abbreviated references to gods, were common. The Snettisham hoard includes a number of gemstones ready for setting into new rings, depicting such gods as Ceres, Jupiter, Apollo, Mercury and Minerva.[44] Bonus Eventus ('Good Success'), who watched over the tilling of soil, was the most frequently represented with 27 examples.[45] Ceres, goddess of corn and harvests, was the second most numerous with 20. Perhaps the Snettisham jeweler was targeting people with farming interests. The only two epigraphic records of Bonus Eventus from Britain, however, were found at the legionary fortresses of Caerleon and York, while Ceres only turns up as the Syrian Goddess at Carvoran. This shows how difficult it is to make any conclusions about why any one god or goddess might be venerated on a piece of jewelry. The snake jewelry from the same hoard, made up of rings and bracelets, belongs to a long pagan tradition, in which the snake was a powerful protective amulet as an associate of the healing god, Asklepios. But it is no less true that the snake's physical shape made it a suitable model for aesthetically pleasing jewelry designs. So the end result satisfied both the amuletic and aesthetic functions.

Statuettes of deities, and their associates and attributes, were manufactured in large quantities. Most that survive were made of bronze (although silver and gold were used as well) and in the classical style, but are often relatively crude in execution. Those found, for example, at Lamyatt Beacon and Lydney were probably sold at the shrines to pilgrims, who then deposited them as votive offerings. Others found their way back to private household

243. Horksey Toll (Cambridgeshire). Nene Valley beaker depicting a figure and an oversized phallus. Although the scene has erotic elements, the imagery also had important superstitious and cult connotations. Height about 12.5 cm. Late second or early third century.

244. Below. Plaxtol (Kent).
Bronze figurine of Minerva found in the ruins of a villa in the mid-nineteenth century. Height 19 cm.

245. Opposite above. Biddulph (Staffordshire).
Silver spoon of typical fourth-century style, incised with a Chi-Rho symbol. Length 20 cm. (British Museum).

246. Opposite below. Risley Park (Derbyshire).
Destroyed shortly after its discovery in the 1700s, this silver lanx was reconstructed soon afterwards by soldering together the fragments, creating a mould, and then melting the lanx down to cast a copy. Diameter 49.7 cm. (British Museum).

shrines. One of the finest was the magnificent Gallo-Roman Minerva, found at Plaxtol [244]. Miniature personal shrines made of lead acted as a portable equivalent. One from Wallsend has a figure of Mercury and the remains of little doors, while another from Dorchester shows Minerva in a similar setting. Since paganism was essentially founded on superstition, individuals felt the need to carry protective talismans, including small phallic amulets, which were believed to be able to ward off the 'evil eye' and were manufactured for this purpose.

Silver spoons form a major part of several late treasure hoards, and those from Biddulph (Staffordshire), Canterbury and Mildenhall carry the Chi-Rho symbol [245]. Some of these, along with the pagan spoons found at Thetford, include exhortations to a long life.[46] The Thetford spoons primarily bear inscriptions that refer to the Faunus cult and the concept of heightened awareness through intoxication, suggesting that they were used in the cult's ritual. This raises all sorts of questions about the iconography of the more highly decorated components of other treasure hoards. The Mildenhall Great Dish (see p. 258), for example, features figures from Bacchic revelry surrounding a central motif of the face of Oceanus, recalling the central medallion on the temple pediment at Bath. This would seem to be good evidence that the plate might have been used in Bacchic feasts, but creates a rather ambiguous assemblage considering the Christian motifs on the spoons. Silversmiths, however, used particular themes and mythical figures as their own personal trademarks, and their work was specifically sought after for this reason.[47]

Another theory is that the treasure is evidence for an interest in Gnosticism, expressed through the use of allegorical symbols.[48] The imagery certainly has religious connotations, but it is a moot point whether such material was used for religious reasons. Moreover, such valuable plate was likely to have had several owners in its life, and not all of them need have had a religious use for it, any more than the rich and famous of the seventeenth and eighteenth centuries believed in the pagan mythical figures they posed as in their paintings. The Risley Park lanx [246] shows just how ambiguous this sort of material can be. The lanx, a large rectangular dish, depicts a hunting scene, complete with rural pagan shrine. But an inscription on the reverse states that at some stage in its life the lanx was a gift from a Bishop Exsuperius to the church at an unknown place called *Bogium*. How or when it came to Britain remains unknown.

Cult activity is one of the most significant bodies of evidence that survives from Roman Britain, but it should always be remembered that this significance lies in the fact that the Roman world provides us with written and visual testimony. The overwhelming impression is that religion was a vastly more conspicuous activity than it is today. Shrines of all shapes and sizes proliferated across the landscape, which was itself home to countless numbers of gods and goddesses. They all bear witness to an aspect of life in Roman Britain that was fundamental to everyday existence in every context. The coming of Christianity generated enormous tensions. The destruction of the *mithraea* at Carrawburgh and London has been blamed on resentment of Mithraism's apparent aping of Christian practices. The inscription of Mars Camulos found at Tabard Square, Southwark, seems to have been deliberately buried and carefully concealed at the bottom of a shaft in the late fourth century. Religious affiliations made no difference to what came next, but ironically it was Christianity that would provide the means by which fifth-century Britain could cling to what was left of her time as a Roman province.

CHAPTER 11
THE AFTERMATH

With the benefit of hindsight, Roman Britain's end might seem inevitable. Rome's cultural and military hold on Britain was never total, and in some areas no better than tenuous. The high archaeological visibility of Roman culture dominates what survives to such an extent that anything affecting the towns, villas and forts is bound to have a dramatic effect on the archaeological record. The late treasure hoards look very much like the work of wealthy people desperate to hold onto their valuables. The deterioration of public buildings is symbolic of the decline of the economic network on which the whole of Roman Britain depended. But the end of Roman Britain was no more inevitable than the conquest in the first place. What brought it to a climax were particular events at a particular time, and accidents of fate that meant the key players were the people they were and made the decisions they did.

We have a distorted impression of Roman Britain because building the province at all involved a colossal amount of effort. Since Britain in 43 had none of the infrastructure of a Roman province, it was necessary to create it from scratch. It was not until the middle of the second century that the administrative towns had the facilities they needed, the northern frontier was anything like consolidated, and the legionary fortresses were substantially complete. The effort was vast, the resources used enormous, and the results astonishing. Britain had been dragged from a world of rural farmsteads and dirt tracks, and from a society in which a very few could indulge themselves in manufactured luxuries, into a completely new way of life. The fundamental parameters with which everyone defined their lives had been changed out of recognition, through the unique combination of Roman patronage and the willingness of some Britons to measure their own status in this new context.

The idea of a town is so familiar today that we give it no thought. The Britons, within a few generations, had been exposed to urban institutions and facilities that would have been unthinkable before the invasion. For rural people in parts of the remote north, their world had now become overrun with forts and roads that carved up the landscape, and transformed it into part of an economic and social system that stretched to Egypt and beyond. Even Chinese silk made it to Colchester. The most obscure locations had access to the Roman economic system. In Scotland, Northumberland, Cumbria and parts of the southwest, there would be nothing like this again until the arrival of the railways in the nineteenth century.

This is absolutely no exaggeration. The Roman 'achievement' was unparalleled in the ancient world, and would have been remarkable by any historical standards until electricity and mechanization arrived. Britain in many respects is where the results were most dramatic, simply because there was so little to build on in the first place. That most Britons seem, by and large, eventually to have accepted the change is one of the key points of this book. It was said on a news bulletin after the Iraq war of 2003 that 'the Iraqis care far more about their electricity supply than who rules them'. A matter of opinion, of course, but the point hit on an important truth. The Boudican revolt offered only chaos and disorder, and, not unnaturally, the bulk of the population found it easy enough to accept an alternative that offered stability, security and economic well-being. It is easy to say that the Britons had no choice, but this credits Rome with the ability to impose and sustain brutal oppression without quarter. The Roman army was simply not big enough to do that, however large the garrison of Britain, and nor did the Roman government consider this a desirable way to rule. Inclusion through patronage, however insidious and cynical, was the way Rome maintained her power, not by the sword.

The change in Britain was so significant that it unavoidably creates a dramatic impression in the archaeological record. London is the principal example. Scattered traces of prehistoric settlement are well known in

247. York (Yorkshire).
The 'Multangular Tower', part of the reinforcements made to the legionary fortress defences by Constantius I in the early fourth century.

the London area, but not in any great abundance, and the same is true for after the Roman period. But Roman London in the first and second centuries is the most prolific source of archaeological material in the area until early modern times. Vast quantities of building debris, pottery, coins and innumerable other artifacts bear witness to the sheer explosive impact of the arrival of Rome [248]. As Britain became more Romanized, towns, public buildings, potteries and other industries were established, and imported goods gave way to home-grown products. Therefore, it is easy to gain the impression that Britain's towns had started to decline. There may well have been economic decline, but the lack of new public buildings is not necessarily evidence for it. After all, once a town has a basilica, there is no good reason to build a new one. Evidence for maintenance and repair of the existing structure may not be very evident in the archaeological record. But change in use, like metalworking practices in Silchester's basilica, is perhaps just that: evidence for change, and not necessarily for terminal decline. When the theatre at St Albans fell out of use and became a rubbish dump in the late fourth century, it did so probably because the outlawing of paganism made it a redundant part of town life, and not because that town life had fallen apart.

While the towns had reached some kind of plateau, rural Britain in the fourth century was booming. There is no doubt that expenditure on some rural seats was enormous, and that some of the wealth trickled down into the economy via patronage of the industries and labour that made the luxurious lives of those who lived in the grand villas possible. There was, of course, inequality, but the Roman state was not an egalitarian one, and its whole social and economic system was founded on an institutionalized hierarchy in which land and wealth were qualifications of status. In an economic sense, Roman Britain was certainly more egalitarian than what had gone before. That much is transparently obvious from the comparative quantities, and distribution, of artifacts.

The villas of fourth-century Britain reflected the success with which the Roman way of life had been inducted into the mindset of the Romano-British. The ancient traditions of a tribal warrior aristocracy had been converted into the ostentatious luxury of rural villa culture, with all its self-conscious emulation of older Italian traditions. But judging the villa culture is not really the point. Enlarging a villa and improving it was an inherently optimistic thing to do. No villa owner expected, or indeed wanted, Roman Britain to come to an end. Given this, how is it possible that when Roman control of Britain was given up, the highly visible Roman culture dissipated at all?

248. Billingsgate (London). Fragment of a Trajanic samian Form 37 bowl found in London but made in Les Martres-de-Veyre (central Gaul), depicting a matched pair of gladiators. Made by Drusus I. Early second century.

249. Ancaster (Lincolnshire). Inscription recording the 'holy god Viridios'. Probably from a temple precinct, the slab was reused in a late or post-Roman grave.

THE HISTORICAL BACKGROUND OF THE END

During the fourth century Britain went through political turmoil, but it would be a distortion to imply that she was somehow especially badly off. A series of usurpations meant the garrison was systematically denuded, and was used to support the imperial ambitions of men like Magnentius (350–53) and Magnus Maximus (383–88). There is little evidence that this disrupted normal life in Roman Britain. Indeed, the problems were probably less than in other parts of the Roman world. The various pretenders conducted their fighting in Gaul, not in Britain, and they posed as restorers of Rome, not destroyers. Much of their support came from those who wanted to see Roman values reinforced, not wiped away, even though they did a great deal of damage to Britain's defences. The barbarian incursions that wrought havoc in Britain, like that of 367, are notorious events in the historical record. However, these events were far less damaging than uprisings across the Rhine or in the East, and rebellions led by usurpers. Theodosius I (379–95) had first to deal with a Gothic invasion in the eastern provinces, followed by a war with the British usurper, Magnus Maximus, and then another rebel, Eugenius. In 406, the Vandals led an invasion across the Rhine to devastate Gaul. The complicated events and loyalties of the rebellion of another British usurper, Constantine III (407–11), left Honorius entirely unable to provide any more resources to support Britain [250].

After 410, Britain was formally on her own, but the population was still Romano-British, and it would be another two or three generations before living memory of the Roman province would disappear. The migration of Anglo-Saxons, which had begun when mercenaries were absorbed into the garrison, was important, but involved very small numbers of people. Most of the population was Romano-British, or at least of Romano-British descent. Making sense of what happened is complicated by the very limited archaeological evidence. In a practical sense, the separation made little difference in the immediate short-term. All Honorius had said was that Britain must now defend herself, but this meant no more imperial taxes to pay for troops. It was this lack of funding that made the critical difference, because it totally disrupted the complex cash-based cycle of wages, trade and taxation, and ended patronage through office.

Pelagius was a Briton, but almost all of the significant events of the heresy that he led took place on the Continent. Pelagius rejected the Augustinian view that God had chosen his elect for heaven, and that no amount of good works could undo this predestination. His own beliefs, in an echo of paganism, suggested that men could choose to do good, thereby intervening in divine judgment to decide their own fate.[1] This heretical view caused a ruction in the church, and was popular in Britain.

250. Constantine III (407–11). A gold *solidus* of Constantine III. Constantine's coins were the last to reach Britain before the end of the Roman period. (British Museum).

LATE TREASURE HOARDS

Hoards in Roman Britain

Hoarding was a routine activity in antiquity, and remained so until early modern times. Concealing valuables in times of insecurity, or just for safekeeping, was the best way of hanging onto them. In the normal course of events, hoards were recovered by their owners and do not survive in the record. Those that turn up today, usually found by metal-detectorists or farmers, were left behind, whether through death or forgetfulness.

Thousands of Roman coin hoards have been found all over Britain,

but the most remarkable series are treasure hoards from late Roman Britain, several of which come from East Anglia. They seem to belong to the last few years of Roman occupation, or to the years immediately after. The *Anglo-Saxon Chronicle* even records for the year 418 that the Romans had hidden treasures 'in the earth so that no one afterwards could find them'.

The Mildenhall Treasure

When the Mildenhall Treasure [251] came to light in the 1940s, it was still believed that Roman

Britain was far too much of a backwater to have produced such high-quality silver plate. It was even suggested that American airmen might have brought the treasure back from North Africa during World War II. Since then, analysis of other hoards has shown that individuals in late Roman Britain were not only extremely wealthy, but had access to silver and gold plate manufactured to the highest standards available in the ancient world. The treasure included no coins, but the quality and style of its plate suggest that it could have belonged to any wealthy person in the Roman Empire around the end of the fourth century.

The Hoxne Treasure

Understanding the hoards is very difficult since we have no idea who buried them. The Hoxne treasure consists of a number of personalized items of plate, including five silver bowls, four pepper pots, 78 spoons and 20 ladles, as well as around 15,000 gold and silver coins [253]. The coins demonstrate that the

251. Mildenhall (Suffolk).
Found in 1942, this silver treasure hoard consisted of 34 objects, including eight spoons, several bowls, dishes and platters, ladles, and a pair of goblets. The largest of these is the Great Dish (60.5 cm wide), with its Bacchic figures and Oceanus central motif. Despite the pagan associations, educated Christians in the late Empire were quite at ease with pagan imagery. Probably fourth century. (British Museum).

assemblage, which was closely packed in its deposit, could not have been buried before 408 and was probably buried shortly afterwards. The value in antiquity would have been enormous, so the possibilities are that this was the property of one or more families, stolen loot, or goods seized by the authorities to pay off barbarians. Another hoard, now lost, was found nearby at Eye in the eighteenth century and may have been another part of the Hoxne assemblage, separated for security.

The Thetford Treasure

The Thetford treasure falls into a completely different category. Stylistically the material belongs to the very late fourth century, and coins that may have originally formed part of the hoard date up to 388. Superficially the hoard seems divided into two parts: the gold jewelry and the silver spoons. The jewelry includes a gold belt buckle [252] and 22 gold rings, into which

252. Thetford (Norfolk).
A gold buckle depicting a satyr. Part of the treasure hoard associated with the cult of Faunus.
(British Museum).

much older gemstones had been set. A number of the spoons were engraved with personal names, while other words referring to drinking, along with a wine strainer, suggest that the spoons may have been associated with a late Roman pagan cult of Faunus, an obscure ancient woodland deity. Unfortunately, we have no idea if the original owners buried the hoard, if it had been acquired by someone else, or if the cult was active in Britain or Gaul, which is where some of the items are thought to have been made.

Other hoards

These are by no means the only treasure hoards of this late date. The Corbridge silver lanx is the only surviving piece of a

treasure that was broken up and lost soon after its discovery in the 1730s. The Risley Park silver lanx (see p. 253) has survived, but only as a cast made from the fragments into which it was cut after its discovery. Other treasures include the collection of late Roman silver spoons found at Canterbury.

Overall, the late treasure hoards are an extremely important witness to the quality of material culture available to the élite in late Roman Britain. Their survival is remarkable, but it is probable that the goods themselves were considerably less remarkable at the time. Roman Britain's upper classes had access to bullion goods of outstanding quality that would have compared with the best the Roman Empire had to offer.

253. Hoxne (Suffolk).
Silver pepper pot in the form of an empress and a silver leopard from the early fifth-century treasure hoard found at Hoxne.
(British Museum).

The ecclesiastical hierarchy in Britain was unsettled by the success of Pelagianism. In 429, Germanus and Lupus, bishops of Auxerre and Troyes, respectively, were sent by the church in Gaul to suppress the heresy. This they did with a mixture of spin, miracles and bravado in battle against the Saxons, and even presided over the healing of a tribune's daughter. The account of their visit is a conflation of history, allegory and moral fable.[2] The story reveals that an ecclesiastical organization was operating in Britain and remained in contact with the Continent, and that people still held positions with Roman titles.

Christianity had become the mechanism of order and the unifying factor in international society, and it did so in a Roman idiom. While government links had been broken with Britain, it was the link with the church in Gaul that led to the arrival of Germanus. Many of the administrative terms and offices of the late Roman Empire, such as those of vicar and diocese, were adopted by the Christian church and survive today. St Patrick, who died sometime between *c*. 450 and 493, was born near *Bannavem Taberniae*, a place that has never been identified, but, since he was taken to Ireland after being captured at the age of 16, it was probably in western or northwestern Britain. His father, Calpornius, owned an estate and slaves and held positions as a *decurion* and deacon. This is important because much of what seems to have survived of Roman Britain did so in the west. It is here that the Celtic names of rivers have more frequently survived, and in the southwest where finds from the reoccupied hillforts show that Continental contacts were maintained. In Wales Latin words have survived from antiquity, and Magnus Maximus is remembered as 'Macsen Wledig' and attributed with founding a line of Welsh kings.

The posts Calpornius held suggest that, despite the physical degeneration of buildings and infrastructure, society was still organized in a Romanized manner well into the fifth century. They also remind us of the palpable psychological fear the detachment from Rome provoked. This is hard for us to appreciate, but in the fourth and fifth centuries the prospect of Rome falling created a desperate sense of apprehension, and compromised any sense of security and equanimity. Constantine III had been elevated to power largely because of the historical symbolism of his name, a century after Constantine I had done so much to unify the Roman world under the Christian banner. Continuing to maintain Roman administrative positions was a powerful way of sustaining a semblance not just of normality, but more importantly a sense that the forces of disorder could be kept at bay.

Despite the lack of historical information, we can see that Britain was still attempting to function as she had under Rome. It is evident from the archaeology that things were very different, but the intent to remain

254. Uley (Gloucestershire).
Life-sized limestone bust from the cult statue of Mercury. The statue was carefully buried in the ruins of the temple, probably in preparation for the construction of a fifth-century timber Christian basilica on the site. (British Museum).

Roman still seems to have been intact. It was not until the 440s that there was a dramatic turn of events. The contacts with Gaul this time were used to make a series of direct appeals for help against barbarian attacks in 446. The next 50 years changed Britain forever. Exactly what happened next is not entirely clear, but seems to have involved a British leader, Vortigern, who in 449 called in a warrior force of Angles and Saxons, led by Hengest and Horsa, to repel barbarians. Hengest and Horsa were successful, but soon turned against the Britons and defeated them in a series of battles. More Angles and Saxons arrived, for example, Aelle, who defeated the Britons at Pevensey. The implication is that the Angles and Saxons gradually gained control in eastern Britain. There is much to argue concerning the exact sequence of events, and a definitive chronology has never been produced.

Eventually, the Britons began to reorganize themselves, and, under the leadership of a man of Roman origin called Ambrosius Aurelianus, defeated the Saxons at the battle of Mount Badon in or around 493.[3] The battle ushered in only a temporary period of stability, until the Saxons started up their wars of conquest again. Ambrosius Aurelianus, who was probably a descendant of the Romanized aristocracy of Britain, is the last truly Roman-type figure in Britain's history, and his moment of triumph is a good point at which to leave the story. The chronicler, Gildas, was born in Britain at about the time of the battle. The training and style so evident in Gildas' work shows that educated Latin culture was maintained and still available well into the sixth century, largely through the spread of monasticism. Men like Gildas maintained scholarly links with the surviving classical world. He may have been trained in Gaul, though a monastery in western Britain or Ireland is equally likely. The Latinity exhibited by the composers of fifth- and sixth-century tombstone epitaphs, especially in western Britain, illustrates a significant level of cultural continuity from the Roman period.[4] Some surviving late Roman manuscripts, now stored in the Vatican, may have originated in fourth- or fifth-century Britain, being preserved for a time in Ireland.[5] As far as Gildas was concerned, Ambrosius Aurelianus symbolized the end. He was right. In 577, the Saxons won a decisive battle at Dyrham, and seized Gloucester, Cirencester and Bath. By then any idea that any sort of semblance of Roman Britain could be maintained must have gone forever.

The question of Roman interest in Ireland has often been raised, usually because Tacitus implies that Agricola considered a campaign there, with the assistance of an exiled Irish chieftain. Some Roman material has been found in Ireland, most notably (and controversially) in the 16-ha (40-acre) fortified promontory at Drumanagh, near Dublin. Whether this represents a Roman military base or a trading settlement has never been resolved, not least because Roman material does not seem to have

255. Nassington (Cambridgeshire).
An early sixth-century bronze cruciform brooch. Derived in part from the late Roman 'crossbow' brooch, Anglo-Saxon cruciform brooches evolved into highly elaborate designs. Usually found in burials, they help track the adoption of a new culture across Britain after the Roman period.

filtered out more widely into Irish settlements. Other pockets of Roman material, for example at Leinster, also appear to be self-contained. But if Roman influence was very limited to begin with, by the 500s it had become more conspicuous in, for example, the form of the penannular brooch. In some respects, early medieval Ireland was the unlikely refuge of aspects of Romano-British culture.

THE ARCHAEOLOGY OF THE END OF ROMAN BRITAIN

In the nineteenth and early twentieth centuries, it was believed Roman Britain had disappeared with unnerving suddenness. Pelagian Britain had tribunes, and St Patrick's world had deacons and *decurions*. Such positions invoke the idea of a Roman province enjoying a thriving urban and villa economy, but such a world had ceased to be. Roman Britain's towns and villas fell into disrepair, and then total ruin. The time scale is usually a matter for debate, but the outcome is not. Lullingstone is a perfect example. What had been a house for which someone in the late fourth century had been prepared to spend money on remodelling the structure and installing mosaics, had burnt down by the early fifth century. Houses had always been susceptible to fire, but they were usually rebuilt. Now here, as just about everywhere else, the house was abandoned. Portable villa wealth found its way into hoards like Hoxne, was appropriated by what remained of the provincial government to buy off barbarians, or was simply stolen. The Traprain Law [256] and the Coleraine hoards from Scotland and Ireland, respectively, are *Hacksilber* hoards, meaning that the treasure they contained had been accumulated purely as bullion. Chopped up, crushed and damaged silver plate seems to have been gathered by weight, with no interest or concern for aesthetics, unlike the hoards from Hoxne, Mildenhall, or Thetford, whose pieces were clearly individually treasured. The Traprain and Coleraine hoards, the latter datable to post-410 by coins, represent either booty or bribes.

Meanwhile, coinage in Britain ended with the reign of Constantine III (407–11). The coins bearing his name in the Hoxne hoard were amongst the very last official supplies to arrive before the end. No coins were manufactured in Britain to make good the shortfall. The silver *siliquae* coins that remained available, including some of the Hoxne coins, were often clipped. It was both a reflection of the breakdown in law and order, and the fact that bullion was hard to come by. The only Roman coins that came in now did so in tiny quantities, probably with individuals. The

256. Traprain Law (East Lothian). Fragment of a decorated silver flagon from the hoard of *Hacksilber* found at Traprain Law. Late fourth or early fifth century.

Patching (West Sussex) hoard was made up mostly of coins dating to between 337 and 411. But the hoarder had also been able to get hold of later material. The latest coin was of Libius Severus (461–65), showing that the hoard had not been buried before then. But the hoard is so exceptional that it only emphasizes how the everyday small-change cash economy had ceased to function. The Libius Severus coin is one that would never have entered Britain by any normal route. Either the hoarder was a trader passing through, or someone who had Continental contacts. All the base-metal coins that made casual day-to-day transactions had disappeared.

Even pottery skills were apparently lost within a few decades. The massive industries, such as the Alice Holt potteries, were simply abandoned, presumably because the collapse of a broader town-based economy made them unsustainable. It is of course inconceivable that people ceased to need bowls and dishes, but they either made use of what was left, or turned to wooden vessels, which of course do not survive. There are exceptions. York's calcite-gritted kitchenware industry seems to have continued in operation until well into the fifth century, though the evidence is very limited. But this is unusual and therefore, far from toppling the traditional picture of a general collapse of the Romano-British way of life, the possible survival of part of York's pottery industry only emphasizes how much most of Britain had changed.

Every Roman settlement of consequence saw its buildings deteriorate and eventually fall into ruin. The villa at Frocester Court remained in use, but in reduced circumstances, until it too fell down. The villa at Orton Hall Farm, near Peterborough, was apparently abandoned, but Saxon timber buildings were erected in and around the old villa buildings, suggesting that the estate itself continued in use. A good case has been made for the survival of the villa estate boundaries at Withington (Gloucestershire) into the seventh century. Here the present parish boundaries preserve an estate granted to a convent in 690 by Aethelred, king of Mercia (675–704), which quite possibly included the same land once farmed from the villa.[6] The headquarters building of the legionary fortress at York may have survived until the ninth century, until it collapsed on top of evidence that it had been used for agricultural purposes.

Wroxeter has become the classic modern excavation, where nearly thirty years of work on the baths-basilica site has recovered an accumulation of evidence for the disintegration of the main structure by the fifth century, but not its abandonment.[7] Instead, several timber buildings were erected within the ruins of the old baths basilica [257], and remained in use until some indeterminate time in the sixth century. Then much of what remained of the old Roman building was cleared away, and a new series of timber buildings erected. This has been used to

argue for the maintenance of some sort of centralized authority, very probably ecclesiastical. Since the church is the one organization we have evidence for in the fifth century, the case is a good one but is, as yet, unsubstantiated.

At Birdoswald, the same pattern of physical degeneration of masonry structures, followed by replacement with two successive timber halls on the footings of one of the granaries, was uncovered. Accurate dating is impossible, but occupation stretching into the sixth century is feasible. If so, this may be evidence for continuity of occupation. However, strictly speaking it is also possible that the timber buildings were actually built somewhat later, following a hiatus. In a period when coinage and pottery effectively did not exist, dating spectral traces of occupation and timber buildings is more speculative than substantive. All that can be said with certainty is that the stone floor of the first timber hall sealed coins of the 380s beneath it. However, if we assume that the Birdoswald timber halls do date from the fifth and sixth centuries, then the tradition the fort and its garrison had enjoyed for centuries in the area is bound to have endowed whoever lived there with the resources and prestige to control the region. The most likely context is the survival of authority vested in those who held positions of power with Roman titles, and who commanded some sort of residual respect. Whether these were warrior chiefs, whose antecedents had been officers in a frontier fort, or bishops whose priestly duties were now blurred with those of old town councils, we may never know.

Wroxeter and Birdoswald have shown how occupation may have continued at some Roman sites. However, the picture of dramatic change remains intact: no one at Wroxeter was able, or inclined, to repair or rebuild the baths basilica, or to replace it with anything that matched it either as an architectural work or in its prestige. Those who lived at Birdoswald were unable or unwilling to repair the fort structures, whether or not they erected timber halls in the fifth century or much later. Villas with evidence of continued occupation always show that the people living there were unable to maintain the buildings properly, or to care for mosaics and baths, or anything else that required effort or skills beyond those needed for subsistence. All of the support crafts and the labour needed to maintain towns with complex public buildings, or villa houses and their attendant facilities, had disappeared. We do not have conclusive evidence about who these later occupants were. They could just as easily have been the descendants of wealthy fourth-century villa owners, or people who had simply moved into vacant premises and made of them what they could. Generally described in excavation reports as 'squatters', these ghostly figures lit fires on mosaic floors, executed hamfisted repairs where absolutely essential, and otherwise let the dilapidation continue unabated until the houses were finally abandoned.

Everything that had made forts, towns and villas possible in the visible forms they reached had vanished. In one sense, this is exactly what we

258. Dinnington (Somerset).
The villa remained in use during the fifth century, despite falling into disrepair. In a room in the west wing, this badly damaged fourth-century mosaic served as a threshing floor and was cut through with postholes. The roof later collapsed (indicated by the layer of tile and burnt timber), and radiocarbon dates from grain found on an adjacent floor suggest that the walls fell down no earlier than the 490s, an unexpectedly late date which shows that farming continued even if the resources and inclination to maintain the house no longer existed.

might expect. Since all of these highly visible features were wholly inter-dependent, economically and socially, it is not surprising that they all dwindled at the same time. Towns were part of a burgeoning economy that went along with a developed road communications system, imported goods, coinage and specialized industries. Likewise, the villas evolved as part of that social and economic system, both supplying and placing demands on the market. The army was an important part of maintaining that system, both through its manpower and influence, and also through wages and purchasing. The effects trickled down through the community, and even remote rural settlements had access to modest quantities of manufactured or imported goods. When something changed for the worse, these economic and social interrelationships made widespread dramatic change inevitable.

The result was the disappearance of much of what we define Roman Britain by. There was a demonstrable change in its quantitative charac-ter, and also in the qualitative expectations of its population. The reason for the vagueness about dating the fifth- and sixth-century phases is sim-ply that the evidence itself is vague. There are virtually no coins, datable pottery forms, inscriptions, or anything else that makes the phases of occupation visible to us as historical periods in the way that the 367 years of Roman occupation are. Only where Roman goods or other datable material turn up in a settlement are we on firmer ground.

At York, the collapse of the headquarters building showed that the structure had been used simply because it was conveniently available. When it fell down, it was left in ruins. This is not to say that the people of the post-Roman period did not respect the Roman work, because they did. St Cuthbert, touring Carlisle in 685, was proudly shown a working Roman aqueduct. The Saxons admired the collapsed temple and baths at Bath as the work of 'giants', but the admiration partly stemmed from the awe-struck belief that such things were no longer possible.

Power had probably become the preserve of local chiefs, who may have been warlords or bishops, or a combination of both. This is com-patible with the idea that people with ecclesiastical authority wielded some sort of secular executive power. The positions that St Patrick's father held also illustrate the problems of archaeological and historical evidence. Caesar's invasions have no manifestation in the archaeological record, and were not even recorded or alluded to on coinage issued in his name. St Patrick's world of deacons and decurions may have been vivid to him, but it is invisible in the surviving physical record. We might spec-ulate about chieftain-bishops and deacons at Wroxeter, for instance, but they will probably remain in the realms of speculation.

In pockets Romano-British society continued, albeit in an archaeo-logically less visible form. The fifth-century reoccupation of hillforts like

Cadbury (Somerset), or the coastal stronghold of Tintagel (Cornwall), was undertaken by people who had the inclination to use, and the means to import, goods from the Continent or even further afield. Tintagel has structural remains associated with glass from Spain and ceramics from North Africa and the Near East, dating right into the middle of the sixth century. These finds show that whoever controlled Tintagel not only had the trading and possibly diplomatic contacts, but also the aspirations and taste to sustain a cosmopolitan Romanized existence. The recovery of tin ingots off the Devon coast near Plymouth, and the discovery of nearby coastal settlements with fifth- and sixth-century imported pottery, suggests that the tin trade helped sustain Roman commercial links with Britain. Another possibility is that the Eastern Roman Empire was deliberately fostering contacts with what remained of Roman culture in Britain as part of its programme of patronage and influence. In this respect, Britain had reverted to some extent to the relationship it had had with the Mediterranean world before the Roman conquest. These instances also emphasize our dependence on visibility in the archaeological record. The physical manifestations of long-distance contact might be minimal in the fifth and sixth centuries, but the psychological, social and religious connections might have been very much greater than we can now measure.

CONCLUSION

Making sense of the fate of Roman Britain has taxed the minds of historians and archaeologists for decades. Numerous books and articles have been written that try to unravel the mesmerizing array of complicated, incomplete and contradictory historical information in sources such as Gildas, the Chronicle of 452, the Anglo-Saxon Chronicle, Nennius and Bede.[8] The result is bewildering to any reader, and sometimes impossibly arcane, especially when Latin phrases are meticulously dismantled in the search for lucid chronologies and insights. The results are usually inconclusive because all the sources have significant shortcomings, and in the end it comes down to a matter of opinion. But nothing really alters the fact that the basic procession of events is fairly clear: Roman rule came to an official end in Britain in 410, coinciding with a time when almost everything in the archaeological record that characterizes Roman Britain up till then starts to disappear. Of course, existing coinage, pottery, other artifacts, and some buildings continued in use. The point is that very little new material arrived or was manufactured in the next few decades, so as the items wore out, they disappear from the record. As that happened, Roman Britain unravelled. The process was haphazard and in some places relatively protracted. It remains to a large extent a mystery why the effect was so profound on Roman material culture.

259. Canterbury (Kent).
Painting showing Canterbury as it might have appeared in the fifth century. The ruins of public buildings dominate an overgrown and virtually abandoned site. However, archaeology has shown that occupation continued at many sites, albeit at a much less sophisticated level than before. (Canterbury Museums).

This does not mean that the experience was an entirely negative one. To some extent, the change had more to do with an alteration in behaviour, rather than an explicit sequence of deterioration. We tend to see it as the *end* of Roman Britain, rather than the *beginning* of something new. Nevertheless, the phenomenon that was Roman culture in Britain was devastated by the withdrawal of Roman administration and a fundamental change in the economy. It took generations for Roman culture to dwindle away entirely, but much less time for the effects on material culture to bite. It is always worth remembering that the most conspicuous traces of Romanization in Britain to this day are associated with the military – a force that can never have amounted to much more than 40,000 men, perhaps one per cent of the population. Even with their dependants, this was a small proportion of the whole. In the fourth century, if we allocate 40 people to every known villa, regardless of size, we are still referring to a villa population of around 40,000–50,000. The administrative and economic changes would have had dramatic effects

on these key parts of Romano-British society, and the end of the system that supported its way of life would have equally dramatic effects on the archaeology and the visible Roman record.

Roman Britain was a phenomenon driven by a system, and when that system fell apart, many of the visible signs of what we know as Roman Britain went with it. In the beginning, some of Britain's tribal leaders saw Rome as a vehicle for enhancing their own prestige. In the end, some leaders continued to see her as the source of authority by which they sought to control their communities. But when Rome ceased to fulfil those expectations, or to show any interest in doing so, the nature of power in Britain changed forever. Those who continued to maintain a semblance of Romanized existence found that apart from the church, Rome had ceased to be a source of support. Society in Britain fragmented, creating the building blocks for a different way of life based on regional kingdoms, where patronage and power derived their strength from other sources.

CHRONOLOGY

55 BC Julius Caesar makes his first unsuccessful foray into Britain.

54 BC Julius Caesar makes his second unsuccessful foray into Britain. Caesar does no more than fight a few skirmishes in southern Britain on these occasions, but introduces the Roman world to the Iron Age tribes of prehistoric Britain. This sets off years of diplomatic dealings with the tribes, with Roman influence proving to be a decisive force.

The First Century AD

AD 43 Verica of the Atrebates is ousted, and flees to Rome for help. This gives CLAUDIUS (41–54) the pretext he needs for a military campaign. Aulus Plautius leads the invasion of Roman Britain, and serves as the first governor. He conquers southern Britain and arranges a triumphal march into Colchester for Claudius. The legions involved were probably *II Augusta, IX Hispana, XIV Gemina*, and the XX, as well as part of *VIII Augusta* and some praetorians. Auxiliary troops made up the rest. The force could have been as large as 40,000+ men. The II heads for the southwest, the IX for the north, and the XIV into the West Midlands. XX is based at Colchester.

47–52 Publius Ostorius Scapula becomes governor. Colchester is made the first colony of veteran troops and the XX legion goes west. Scapula marches against the tribes in south Wales, and defeats a rebellion by the Iceni in East Anglia.

52–57 Aulus Didius Gallus becomes governor. He holds the Welsh tribes in check and finds the northern British tribe of Brigantes, Rome's allies, split between the feuding king Venutius and his queen, Cartimandua. NERO (54–68) becomes emperor.

57/8 Quintus Veranius Nepos becomes governor, but dies in post.

57/8–61 Gaius Suetonius Paullinus becomes governor. He sets out to destroy the Druid stronghold in Anglesey, headquarters of the resistance to Rome. In 60 Boudica leads the revolt of the Iceni, joined by some of the Trinovantes. They defeat part of the IX legion, and burn Colchester, London and St Albans.

Suetonius Paullinus marches back with the XIV and XX legions and defeats Boudica, wiping out the rebels and the last tribal rebellion. Suetonius Paullinus keeps the army mobile and garrisons the south. For its role, the XIV is renamed *XIV Gemina Martia Victrix*, and this is probably when the XX became *XX Valeria Victrix*. Paullinus' punitive policy is opposed by the new procurator, Gaius Julius Alpinus Classicianus, who is more concerned with mending fences and building a new future. When a naval force is lost, this gives the government the pretext to withdraw Paullinus.

61–63 Publius Petronius Turpilianus becomes governor. The Roman historian Tacitus accuses Petronius Turpilianus of laziness, but he was probably repairing the damage in Britain and reforming Roman government.

63–69 Marcus Trebellius Maximus becomes governor, and faces a mutiny by the XX legion. In 68 Nero commits suicide and civil war breaks out in Rome. GALBA (68–69) rules briefly. Trebellius seems to have fled to side with VITELLIUS (69) in the civil war.

69–71 VESPASIAN (69–79) is victorious and establishes the Flavian dynasty. Marcus Vettius Bolanus becomes governor. He rescues Cartimandua from the Brigantian feud, and the Brigantes are now drawn into the Empire. By this time the XIV has been withdrawn and replaced by *II Adiutrix Pia Fidelis*. The new legion spends time at Lincoln, replacing the IX which heads off for York. *II Augusta* will soon be at Caerleon.

71–74 Quintus Petillius Cerealis becomes governor. He annexes much of what is now northern England, and may have founded the legionary fortress of the IX legion at York.

74–77/8 Sextus Julius Frontinus becomes governor, and conquers the Silures in Wales. Around this time the spa at Bath is being developed, possibly under the direction of Frontinus, who was later placed in charge of aqueducts in Rome.

77/8–83/4 Gnaeus Julius Agricola becomes governor. He finishes off the Welsh war, conquers northern

Britain as far as the northeast tip of *Caledonia* (Scotland), and circumnavigates Britain. He encourages the erection of public buildings, temples and houses, as well as the spread of the Latin language. He is recorded on an inscription from the new forum at St Albans (*Verulamium*). The historical accounts of Tacitus end, and hereafter we have much less detail. *II Adiutrix Pia Fidelis* moves to Chester while the XX is in Scotland.

79 Accession of TITUS (79–81). Eruption of Vesuvius in Italy.

81 Accession of DOMITIAN (81–96).

84 Domitian recalls Agricola, abandons *Caledonia* and pulls back the Roman army to what is now northern England. *II Adiutrix Pia Fidelis* is withdrawn, and Britain now has three legions: *II Augusta* (Caerleon), *IX Hispana* (York) and *XX Valeria Victrix* (Chester).

96 Accession of NERVA (96–98). Gloucester is founded as a colony, but in fact this probably took place under Domitian, whose achievements were suppressed by his successors after his murder. Lincoln was probably also made a colony at this time.

98 Accession of TRAJAN (98–117). The Vindolanda tablets are written during this period.

The Second Century AD
100s The IX legion is last recorded on an inscription from York, dated 107–8. It was probably withdrawn from Britain and lost in an eastern war. It is very unlikely that it was lost in Britain.

117 Accession of HADRIAN (117–38).

119 Hadrian visits Britain. He orders the building of Hadrian's Wall by the governor, Aulus Platorius Nepos (*c.* 121–24), and encourages public building. The forum at Wroxeter (Shropshire) bears his name. The great basilica of London was built about this time. Southern Britain is now settled with towns, roads, markets, villages, rural farmsteads and pottery industries. The north and west form a military zone with three legionary fortresses: Caerleon (*II Augusta*), Chester (*XX Valeria Victrix*) and York (*VI Victrix*). The latter was brought by Aulus Platorius Nepos.

129–30 Forum and basilica at Wroxeter (*Viroconium Cornoviorum*) dedicated.

138 Accession of ANTONINUS PIUS (138–61). He fights a war in Britain and orders a new wall, made of turf, to be built further north – roughly between where Glasgow and Edinburgh are now – by his governor, Quintus Lollius Urbicus (*c.* 138–42).

140–61 The last known major public building inscription from Britain is set up: Marcus Ulpius Januarius, *aedile* at the town of *Petuaria* (Brough-on-Humber), donates a new stage for the town theatre.

161 Accession of MARCUS AURELIUS (161–80).

163 War breaks out in northern Britain again. The governor Sextus Calpurnius Agricola (*c.* 161–65) is sent against 'the Britons'. Hadrian's Wall is reoccupied and the Antonine Wall abandoned.

170s Marcus Aurelius creates an alliance with the Sarmatian Iazyges. They give him 8,000 cavalry, of which 5,500 are sent to Britain. Whether this was to reinforce the garrison or train them up at a safe distance is unknown. Ulpius Marcellus governs Britain from *c.* 177 to 184.

180 Accession of COMMODUS (180–92).

184 Tribes cross Hadrian's Wall from *Caledonia* and defeat a legionary contingent. The garrison of Britain, outraged by the way Commodus has delegated his power to the praetorian prefect, Perennis, elect as emperor one of their own number, Priscus. Priscus declines, and the garrison sends a 1,500-strong delegation to Rome. Terrified, Commodus allows the praetorians to lynch Perennis. Pertinax is sent to govern Britain and impose some discipline. The British legions eventually mutiny and leave Pertinax for dead. He escapes.

192 Commodus is murdered on the last day of the year.

193 PERTINAX becomes emperor at the beginning of 193, but is murdered on 28 March after 86 days. He is followed by DIDIUS JULIANUS, who lasts 66 days. The new British governor, Clodius Albinus, is one of the candidates to be emperor. In the east, Pescennius

Niger is proclaimed emperor, but is defeated in 194 by SEPTIMIUS SEVERUS (193–211), who has convinced Albinus to be his successor and associate while he eliminates Niger. By 195 Albinus realizes he has been tricked when Severus declares him a public enemy. Albinus takes much of Britain's garrison and sets off for Gaul to meet Severus. In 197, near Lyons, Albinus and his army are defeated. Septimius Severus is the victor.

The Third Century AD
205–8 Much military rebuilding in northern Britain.

208 Septimius Severus arrives in Britain to lead the reconquest of Caledonia with his sons, Caracalla and Geta. The campaign is inconclusive.

211 Septimius Severus dies of exhaustion at York. CARACALLA (211–17) abandons the conquest, kills GETA (211–12), and embarks on a series of campaigns in northern Germany and the East. Britain is quiet now, and undergoes a vast amount of military building on the northern frontier. The rich are beginning to spend money on themselves, and the villas of the southern lowlands start their slow climb to wealth and greatness. In the towns, the age of public building is all but over.

Britain is divided into two to prevent another governor from mounting a rebellion. *Britannia Superior* is in the south, ruled from London. *Britannia Inferior* is to the north, ruled from York.

259 POSTUMUS (260–69) seizes control of Britain, Gaul and Germany to create the Gallic Empire.

268 Murder of Postumus, and accession of MARIUS (268), followed by his almost immediate murder. Accession of VICTORINUS (269–71). In Rome, CLAUDIUS II GOTHICUS (268–70) becomes emperor.

270 AURELIAN (270–75) succeeds Claudius II Gothicus. The Gallic emperor, Victorinus, is murdered in 271 and is succeeded by TETRICUS I (271–73), who names his son, also named Tetricus, as his heir.

273 Suppression of the Gallic Empire by Aurelian.

275 Murder of Aurelian. Accession of TACITUS (275–76).

276 Death of Tacitus. Accession and death of FLORIANUS (276). Accession of PROBUS (276–82).

282 Murder of Probus. Accession of CARUS (282–83).

283 Elevation of Carus' sons CARINUS (283–85) and NUMERIAN (283–84) to the rank of Caesar. Death of Carus. Carinus becomes emperor in the West, and Numerian in the East. Numerian is murdered in November 284. Accession of DIOCLETIAN (284–305).

285 Murder of Carinus.

286 Appointment of MAXIMIAN (286–305) by Diocletian to rule the West. Carausius, commander of the British fleet, seizes control in Britain and part of northern Gaul. This is the first 'British Empire'.

293 Murder of Carausius and accession of Allectus in Britain. Diocletian appoints junior partners (Caesars): Galerius to rule in the East and Constantius I in the West. This system is known as the Tetrarchy.

296 Defeat and death of Allectus by the army of Constantius I. Britain passes back under the control of Maximian (Augustus) and Constantius I (Caesar).

The Fourth Century AD
By this time, perhaps by 296, Britain has been divided into four provinces: *Maximia Caesariensis* (East Anglia and the southeast), *Britannia Prima* (Wales, West Midlands and the southwest), *Britannia Secunda* (the north) and *Flavia Caesariensis* (Lincolnshire and the northeast Midlands). This is also the age of the fabulously wealthy, though by Empire standards Britain remains a backwater.

305 Abdication of Diocletian and Maximian, and elevation of CONSTANTIUS I (305–6) to Augustus in the West, with SEVERUS II (306–7) as Caesar. Constantius I becomes Augustus in the East.

306 Proclamation of CONSTANTINE I (307–37) at York following the death of his father, Constantius I. This disruption of the Tetrarchy leads to protracted feuds involving Maximian and his son, Maxentius.

308 The settlement at Carnuntum passes control of the West to LICINIUS (308–24) and Constantine I,

while GALERIUS (305–11) and MAXIMINUS (310–13) hold the East. The feuds continued as Maximian and Maxentius try to recapture power.

312 Constantine defeats Maxentius at the battle of the Milvian Bridge, using troops partly raised in Britain. The West is now under the exclusive control of Constantine I, while Licinius controls the East.

313 Edict of Milan guarantees total religious toleration.

324 Constantine I defeats Licinius.

337 Death of Constantine I and accession of his sons: CONSTANTINE II (337–40) in Britain, Gaul and Spain; CONSTANTIUS II (337–61) in the East; and CONSTANS (337–50) in Italy, Africa and Central Europe.

340 Murder of Constantine II by Constans. Britain passes under the control of Constans.

343 Constans visits Britain.

350 Revolt of MAGNENTIUS (350–53) in Autun and murder of Constans.

353 Suicide of Magnentius following defeats. Constantius II becomes ruler of the entire Empire.

360 JULIAN (360–63), cousin of Constantius II, proclaimed emperor in Gaul.

361 Death from fever of Constantius II.

363 Death of Julian. Accession of JOVIAN (363–64), formerly commander of the imperial guard.

364 Death of Jovian. Accession of VALENTINIAN I (364–75) in the West, and his brother, VALENS (364–78) in the East.

367 Barbarian conspiracy overruns Britain. GRATIAN (367–83) appointed joint Augustus in the West with Valentinian I. Arrival in Britain of Theodosius, who restores its defences.

375 Death of Valentinian I. Gratian now rules jointly in the West with his brother, VALENTINIAN II (375–92).

378 Death of Valens. Gratian and Valentinian II assume control of the whole Empire.

379 Appointment of THEODOSIUS (379–95) to rule the East.

383 Death of Gratian. MAGNUS MAXIMUS (383–88), a senior officer in the British garrison, is proclaimed emperor in Britain and straightaway invades Gaul.

387 Valentinian II flees to the East.

388 Magnus Maximus defeated and executed in Italy by Theodosius.

392 Murder of Valentinian II.

395 Death of Theodosius. The Empire is divided between his sons: HONORIUS (395–423) in the West, and Arcadius (395–408) in the East.

The Fifth Century AD
407 Proclamation of CONSTANTINE III (407–11) in Britain. He moves to Gaul, taking much of what was left of Britain's already denuded garrison.

408 Constantine III takes Spain.

410 Honorius, with scarcely the resources to defend Italy, instructs Britain to look after her own defences. Around this time the Thetford and Hoxne treasures are deposited, and are not discovered until the late twentieth century.

411 Defeat and death of Constantine III.

429 St Germanus of Auxerre arrives in Britain to deal with the Pelagian heresy.

449 The Anglo-Saxon invasion is reputed to have begun in this year.

From now on Britain continues to maintain a Roman way of life, but this has been gradually fading for decades. The towns fall into ruin and the villas are slowly abandoned. Natural disasters and accidents such as house fires are no longer followed by repair. We know very little about what went on, but it is plain that the end was slow. There was no abrupt disaster.

VISITING ROMAN BRITAIN

For detailed guidance on how to visit Roman Britain there is no substitute for Roger Wilson's *Guide to the Roman Remains in Britain* (2002). This marvellously indispensable pocket-sized volume includes excellent descriptions of sites and museums, made all the more useful with detailed directions on how to get to any one, including guiding the reader through a provincial town or across the hills of Northumberland. The book also provides all opening times and contact details, particularly useful in the winter.

Compared to the rest of the Roman Empire, Britain has relatively unimpressive Roman monuments. The ravages of a northern maritime climate and a lack of durable building stone in the south haven't helped, but it has really been Britain's exceptionally varied history and explosive development that have put paid to so much of what the Romans left behind. Tantalizing descriptions from the Middle Ages and even early modern times can only make us wonder at what we have lost.

However, most of Roman Britain's principal towns are represented by **museum collections**. Undoubtedly the most varied collection is in the **Museum of London**, but other highly recommended museums are to be found at **Cirencester**, **Colchester**, **Exeter**, **Gloucester**, **Leicester**, **Peterborough** (for Water Newton), **Reading** (for Silchester), **St Albans** and **Wroxeter**.

As far as the physical remains of **towns** are concerned the most instructive site today is probably **Caerwent** in South Wales. Small and insignificant in its own time, this diminutive civitas capital today has the only example of a basilica and forum open to visitors as well as a temple, townhouses and magnificent defences. **Wroxeter**'s baths and baths-basilica are some of the most upstanding remains of any Roman town as is **Leicester**'s Jewry Wall, once part of the town baths and now forming a backdrop to the museum. Other sites have their own individual appeal. **St Albans** has its theatre, the only one visitable in any coherent form today, while **Silchester** and **Caistor by Norwich** have the only defences that can be walked round in their entirety. But it is also worth mentioning **Lincoln**'s remarkable basilican rear wall, and city gates, **London**'s amphitheatre by the Guildhall, as well as **Dorchester**'s townhouse.

Despite the fact that Roman Britain is known to have had considerably more than a thousand significant rural houses, most of which might reasonably be called **villas**, little more than a few are exposed to public view today. The most interesting of all is at **Lullingstone**, a short distance from the village of Eynsford in Kent and not far from the M20/M25 junction. This remarkably compact house is only one of two in Britain to enjoy the luxury of a complete cover building and features an upper storey so that visitors can appreciate the mosaic pavement that dominates the middle of the building.

The other villa house to be so equipped is at **Brading** in the Isle of Wight. Remarkable for its array of sophisticated mosaic floors it is perhaps most easily compared with **Bignor**, not so very far away in West Sussex. Bignor's beautiful floors are now displayed under a series of early nineteenth-century huts which give little sense of the building's original appearance but which make for a charming visit. A trip to Bignor is best combined with the remarkable, and unique, site at **Fishbourne** not far away and close to Chichester. Fishbourne of course includes the unparalleled early series of mosaics laid in the palace that has been traditionally identified as the home of the client king Tiberius Claudius Togidubnus. Of other villas in Roman Britain the other most important sites that can be seen today are probably **Chedworth** and **Great Witcombe**, not far from one another in the Cotswolds. Chedworth is extremely popular but its visitor centre, museum and mosaics make for an extremely interesting place to visit. There is far less to see at Great Witcombe but the beauty of the setting makes for a reminder that villa owners chose the places for their houses carefully.

Villas and towns aside, Britain boasts a unique Roman site in the form of the spa baths and temple complex at **Bath**. The baths themselves form a magnificent centrepiece to the site but visitors today now also have an opportunity to walk through the dramatic subterranean remains of the temple precinct. The finds on display include the temple's pediment sculptures as well as curse tablets and other offerings from the sacred spring.

It is the **Roman army** in Britain though that has left the greatest quantity of physical remains, even in the south. The late shore 'forts' at **Richborough**, **Pevensey** and **Portchester** all survive to considerable heights, the latter two because they were used by the Normans as castle walls. **Dover** had a fort too, though now just a fragment is visible. Here the most astonishing survival is the lighthouse in the grounds of Dover Castle, once a member of a pair that guided ships into this key Roman port.

Further north and west, the **forts and fortresses** of Roman Britain remain the most potent reminders of this island's Roman past. In South Wales the II legion's fortress at **Caerleon** has not only barracks, defences and a fine museum, but also a complete amphitheatre. **Chester**, home to the XX legion, has half an amphitheatre, impressive defences and an equally remarkable museum as well as a shrine to Minerva still visible in its original location nearby across the river.

Of Roman **York** relatively little is visible apart from some of the defences, but the museum is one of the most important in the country. It is further to the north that the really exciting sites are now. On the west coast in Cumbria the museum at **Maryport** contains an important collection of Roman altars from the fort, and further south at **Ravenglass** is one of the most upstanding pieces of a Roman building in Britain – the fort bath-house. To the east in Hardknott Pass is **Hardknott fort**, still with defences and some of its buildings, erected to control the route across the hills.

To the east the alpha sites have to be **Wallsend** and **South Shields**. With pioneering zeal and foresight the archaeologists and local authority here have done extraordinary things and erected magnificent replicated buildings to add to the excellent museums. South Shields now has a wonderful replicated gate, commandant's house and barracks while Wallsend has a complete working Roman baths suite.

Nothing, however, can compare with the remains of the **Roman frontiers** themselves. In Scotland the weathered turf **Antonine Wall** is of comparatively limited appeal but the **Hunterian Museum** in Glasgow and the **Museum of Scotland** in Edinburgh, at either end of the Wall, more than make up for that. **Hadrian's Wall** is a different matter. Although much has been destroyed, and none stands to its original height, the forts of the central sector and some of the Wall that connected them at **Chesters**, **Carrawburgh**, **Housesteads** and **Birdoswald** can all be visited today and appreciated as magnificent testimony to the power of the Romans.

Not far to the rear is the extraordinary site of **Vindolanda**, with one of the richest collections of any in the country. So it is only appropriate here to mention the **British Museum** which houses Vindolanda's writing tablets. As the principal collection of finds it is without parallel. Here are the Thetford, Hoxne, Mildenhall and Water Newton treasures as well as Lullingstone's main finds: the Christian paintings and the marble busts, alongside a host of other material and set beside the remains of prehistoric Britain and post-Roman Britain – a reminder that the 360 years of Britain's time as a Roman province was just one episode in her rich and turbulent history.

NOTES

Abbreviations

Agr = Tacitus, *Agricola.*

Ann. = Tacitus, *Annales.*

BG = Caesar, *Bellum Gallicum* (The Gallic War).

CIL = *Corpus Inscriptionum Latinarum,* 16 vols. (Berlin, 1863–). Some of this material is now available on the Internet from the same source as *ILS* below: xiii (North Gaul and Rhineland), xvi (diplomas, regardless of findspot).

ILS = Dessau, H., *Inscriptionum latinae selectae,* 3 vols. (Berlin, 1892–1916).

Lactor 4 = Maxfield, V. and B. Dobson (eds.), *Inscriptions of Roman Britain,* London Association of Classical Teachers, 3rd ed. (London, 1995).

PNRB = Rivet and Smith (London, 1979).

RG = Augustus, *Res Gestae.*

RIB = Collingwood and Wright (1965; rev. ed., 1995).

RIC = *The Roman Imperial Coinage,* 10 vols. (London, 1923–).

Select Papyri = *Select Papyri: Public Documents,* vol. 2, Loeb Classical Library 282 (Cambridge, Massachussetts, 1934).

SHA = *Scriptores Historiae Augustae,* 3 vols., Loeb Classical Library 139 (Cambridge, Massachussetts, 1921). See also *The Lives of the Later Caesars,* trans. by A. Birley (London, 1976).

TV = *Tab. Vindol;* see Bowman (2003).

CHAPTER 1 (pp. 10–22)

1. *BG* iii.8
2. Pliny the Elder, *Natural History IV.*xvi.102
3. Rivet and Smith (1979), 39
4. Strabo, i.4.3, and iv.5.5
5. Diodorus, v.1–4
6. Strabo, iv.3.4
7. *BG* iii.8
8. *BG* iv.20
9. *BG* iii.13
10. Strabo, iv.5.2
11. Suetonius, *Caesar* xxv.2
12. *BG* iv.21
13. *Agr* 12.2
14. *Agr* 13.2
15. Niblett, in Todd (2003), 32
16. Frontinus, *Stratagems* ii.13.11

CHAPTER 2 (pp. 23–58)

1. '*feroci provincia*', *Agr* 8
2. Strabo, iv.5.3
3. *RG* 32. Tincomarus' name is incomplete on the monument that records the *Res Gestae.* It was originally restored as 'Tincommius' because coins naming 'TINC' also stated this person to be 'son of Commios'. A recent discovery of a coin with an expanded name has shown that 'Tincomarus' is correct.
4. *Agr* 13.2
5. The recent find of a Roman-type helmet in a massive hoard of late Iron Age coins in southeast Leicestershire points to such goods being gifts used as part of Roman patronage.
6. *Journal of Roman Studies* 24 (1934), 13–16
7. Suetonius, *Caligula* xliv.2
8. *Eclogues,* i.66
9. *BG* v.12, 14

10. Cicero, *Letters to his friends* ii.16.4
11. *Agr* 6.3
12. *Histories* iii.44
13. *ILS* 2701
14. Dio, lx.20
15. Ibid.
16. Black (1998)
17. Standing (2003)
18. *Agr* 14
19. Suetonius, *Vespasian* iv.1
20. *RIB* 91.
21. *Ann.* xii.31
22. *ILS* 216
23. See note 25.
24. *Ann.* xiv.38
25. See Braund (1984) for a discussion of Tacitus on this event, and the earlier Brigantian civil war under Didius Gallus. Tacitus may have confused different accounts of the same civil war.
26, *Natural History* iv.102
27. A *sestertius* struck in 85, depicting Domitian greeting an unnamed officer and three soldiers, is the only possible candidate (*RIC* 288B).
28. *Britannia* (1992), 147
29. *Britannia* (1998), 74
30. Suetonius, *Domitian* v, and xiii.2
31. *Agr* 21
32. Suetonius, *Domitian* x.3
33. *RIB* 2401.1; Pliny, iii.8.1; *TV* ii.225
34. *TV* ii.343
35. *TV* iii.643
36. *TV* ii.316
37. *TV* ii.343
38. *TV* ii.291
39. The evidence is itemized in de la Bédoyère (*Towns in Roman Britain*, 2003), 193–94.
40. *ILS* 2726, and most conveniently found in Lactor 4 (1995), no. 47.
41. *SHA* (Hadrian) v.2
42. *SHA* (Hadrian) xi.2
43. *SHA* (Antoninus Pius) v.4

CHAPTER 3 (pp. 59–78)

1. *SHA* (Marcus Aurelius) viii.7–8
2. Dio, lxxi.16.2, calling them the 'Iazyges'. Tacitus specifies them as the 'Sarmatian Iazyges' (*Ann.* xii.29), an emigrant people from southwest Russia then settled on the eastern border of Pannonia. Sarmatians cavalry are later testified at Ribchester (*RIB* 594, 595).
3. Dio, lxxiii.8
4. Dio, lxxv.5.4
5. *RIB* 730
6. *RIB* 791
7. *RIB* 1234
8. Herodian, iii.14.1
9. *SHA* (Severus) xxii.7
10. *RIB* 658
11. Herodian, iii.14.5–6
12. *RIB* 1956, at milecastle 52 a dedication to Cocidius.

13. See, for example, Casey (1994) and de la Bédoyère (in *Numismatic Chronicle*, 1998).

14. *RIB* 2291.

15. *RIB* 1912. This is the last datable military inscription from Britain.

16. Ammianus, xxvi.4.5

17. *De Excidio Britanniae* 14, 15

18. Zosimus, vi.5.2–3

CHAPTER 4 (pp. 79–100)

1. *Britannia* 27 (1996), 455–56

2. Creighton, in James and Millett (2001), 7–8

3. *Agr* 12

4. *Agr* 9.6

5. *TV* ii.154. The fort is now known to be only of second-century date and not to have had a timber predecessor, at least not on the same site. See Howe and Lakin (2004).

6. Herodian, iii.14.9

7. *Digest* xxxvi.1.48, and see E. Birley (1953), 51.

8. *Agr* 7.3

9. *RIB* 179

10. *RIB* 152

11. *TV* ii.250

12. Alston (1995), 95

13. Ibid., 79ff, and 97, where Alston itemizes activities that soldiers are testified on in Egypt. These included the construction of a harbour, and even the manufacture of paper.

14. *Agr* 21

15. On the forum-basilica inscription from St Albans (*Verulamium*), erected in 79 or 81.

16. *RIB* 88, 235

17. *TV* ii.225, Flavius Cerealis to Crispinus.

18. *RIB* 2504.29

19. Florus, i.47.4

20. Dio, lxii.3

21. *Agr* 13

22. *Histories* iv.74

23. *Agr* 19.4

24. *RIB* 725

25. Cicero, *Letters to Atticus* v.16.2, concerning Cilicia.

26. *CIL* viii.4508; see Lewis and Reinhold (1955), 146–47

27. *ILS* 2740, 1338, or see de la Bédoyère (1999), 132. For the date of *ILS* 1338, see also A. Birley (1979), 52.

CHAPTER 5 (pp. 101–129)

1. See, for example, Alston (1995), *passim*.

2. *Ann.* iv.5–6.

3. *ILS* 2288; the text, normally dated to the reign of Marcus Aurelius (161–80) seems to list 33 legions. Webster (1996), 114, states that it lists 'twenty-eight legions'. The text, however, seems plain enough.

4. Vegetius, ii

5. *Ann.* xii.38, and Vegetius, ii.10, 11

6. *Ann.* xiv.37

7. Hyginus, *de munitione castrorum*, 1

8. Polybius, vi.24

9. *ILS* 2446, *CIL* viii.18072

10. Vegetius, ii

11. Josephus, *Jewish War*, iii.7.2, 'each legion has its own 120-strong cavalry troop'.

12. At Carrawburgh under Hadrian, a century of an unspecified unit styled itself the 'Thruponian', instead of the 'century of Thrupo'. This probably means that Thrupo was dead, or retired, and that his post remained unfilled. *RIB* 1820

13. Vegetius, ii

14. For example, the First Cohort of Vardullians, part-mounted, which seem to have been in Britain since at least 98. They had the title by 124. *RIB* 2401.6 (diploma)

15. *Jewish War*, iii.4.2

16. *RIB* 1262, 'unit of scouts, based at *Bremenium* (High Rochester)'.

17. *Ann.* iv.6

18. *RIB* 1340. The text is incomplete and reads 'VEXILLATIO C[......] BRITAN(NICA)'. Strictly speaking, this could also refer to an infantry *cohors* of Britons, rather than the *classis*. However, use of indigenous auxiliaries in this way would have been most unusual. The fleet might seem an unlikely source of granary builders, but the fort at Dover was contemporary and they may already have gained appropriate experience.

19. *RIB* 823–26

20. '*quod multae, quod diversae stationes vos distinent*'. *ILS* 2487

21. *RIB* 814

22. Bowman (2003), 51

23. *RIB* 109 (Genialis at Cirencester), *Britannia* 17 (1986), 429, no. 3, and *RIB* 122 (centurial stone of XX at Gloucester, and a tombstone).

24. *RIB* 2415.39

25. *Ann.* xii.31

26. *Ann.* xiv.37–38

27. *Agr* 35

28. That dispersal of units was normal can be seen from evidence in Egypt. See Alston (1995), 157.

29. *RIB* 2401.1

30. A full list is provided in de la Bédoyère (*Companion to Roman Britain*, 1999), 65–83.

31. *Britannia* 29 (1998), 74, no. 44

32. *RIB* 605

33. *RIB* 1041, 2411.88, and 2411.89

34. *RIB* 1896

35. *RIB* 1365, near Benwell in the eastern sector.

36. However, in its first phase Birdoswald projected north of the Wall, which was at that stage made of turf, believed by some to indicate a cavalry garrison fort. When the Wall was consolidated in stone in the west by the mid-second century(?), the new Wall was built on a different alignment and brought the whole fort behind the Wall. Its garrison in the first phase might thus have been different.

37. *TV* ii.154

38. Hyginus, *de mun. cast.* 16

39. Arrian, *Tactica* 10

40. *Britannia* 17 (1986), 450–52, no. 84

41. See Frere and Wilkes (1989), 117ff.

42. Wilmott (2001), 68–69

43. *RIB* 1912

44. Polybius, *Histories* vi.27

45. One Roman foot (*pes*) is equivalent to 11.64 inches or 0.2957 m. 0.2957 x 2017 = 596.42 m. 596.42 x 596.42 = 355,717 sq m, which is 35.57 ha (88 acres).

46. Hyginus, *de mun. cast.* 2

47. Frere and St Joseph (1983), 20–21. In fact, they note that the unique conditions at Rey Cross (Cumbria) allow an internal grid to be reconstructed from the unusual number of entrances, showing that 15 plots resulted in the 8.15-ha plan. This would be enough for ten legionary cohorts and several

auxiliary units (in theory), which they suggest is a possible ballpark figure for a legion on campaign.

48. *RIB* 1024
49. *RIB* 2091, 2096
50. *RIB* 1542
51. In 128, Hadrian commended a cavalry cohort for building stone ramparts in little more time than it would have taken to make them from turf, which was 'cut to standard size and easy to carry and to handle'. The address was recorded on an inscription. *ILS* 2487
52. A. Johnson (1983), 62–63
53. *RIB* 1820, 1822. Another stone from the fort mentions a length of 112 ft (*RIB* 1818).
54. *RIB* 1556.
55. Vegetius, iii.8
56. 'By *[cohors IIII] Gallorum*, responsible for a *por[tam cum tu]rribus*'. *RIB* 1706
57. *RIB* 334, and *Journal of Roman Studies* 59 (1969), 246
58. *RIB* 978
59. Wilmott (2001), 70–71. The requirement for this sort of building is recorded in Vegetius; continual practice was essential, and a covered space was necessary during foul weather.
60. The text explicitly gives '*principia et armamentaria*'. *RIB* 1092
61. *RIB* 1280, 1281
62. *RIB* 1695
63. *RIB* 899
64. *RIB* 1843–84, 1672–73

CHAPTER 6 (pp. 130–159)

1. *Agr* 21.1
2. *Ann.* xii.32
3. *Ann.* xiv.31
4. *ILS* 2365
5. *Journal of Roman Studies* 11 (1921), 102
6. For example, the *conventus civium Romanorum*, 'Roman citizen corporation' at Lissus. Caesar, *Bellum Civile* iii.40.
7. *RIB* 92
8. A radical and interesting suggestion is that the early 'forum and basilica' at Silchester were in fact the headquarters of a short-lived timber Claudian legionary fortress, and that the mid-first century AD street grid at Silchester is in fact the fortress's layout (pers. comm. Mark Corney).
9. *RIB* 288
10. *Ann.* xiv.33
11. Pliny the Younger describes several instances during his tenure as governor of Bithynia and Pontus; for example, *Letters* x.39–40, concerning a theatre and gymnasium at Nicaea.
12. See *Select Papyri* nos. 356 and 357, concerning the lease of a tavern and the sale of a house.
13. *RIB* 674 (York), 250 (Lincoln), 161 (naming Gloucester, but found at Bath).
14. *RIB* 88. Antonius Lucretianus, on an altar to the Mother Goddesses.
15. *RIB* 311
16. *RIB* 933 (Old Penrith), 707 (Brough)
17. Boon (1974), 86–87
18. *RIB* 712
19. A *gynaecium*, in *Notitia Dignitatum*.
20. Ling (1997), 232, noting how sections of townhouses were converted into self-contained street frontage workshops.
21. *Insula* xxviii

CHAPTER 7 (pp. 160–181)

1. Strabo, iv.5.2–3
2. Diodorus Siculus, v.22
3. Ammianus, xviii.2.3
4. Hingley and Miles, in Salway (2002), 142ff
5. *RIB* 2409.26, but see also R. P. Wright, in *Britannia* 15 (1984), 257–58.
6. *Natural History* xxxiv.164
7. *RIB* 2404.3 (Bossington), 38 (Carmel)
8. *RIB* 2404.55
9. *RIB* 2404.32 (lead pig)
10. *Britannia* 27 (1996), 446–48
11. *RIB* 2404.24
12. *RIB* 2415.56
13. *RIB* 1092
14. *RIB* 156
15. Bayley, *et al.* (2001)
16. Baldock (Hertfordshire) has also produced remains of brooch manufacture. See Stead (1975).
17. *Britannia* 35 (2004)
18. *Journal of Roman Studies* 59 (1969), 235, no. 3
19. *TV* ii.154
20. *RIB* 2446.4. 16
21. *RIB* 2492.11
22. Wild (2002)
23. For example, *RIB* 17, a military tombstone found in London, is made of Lincolnshire limestone.
24. Pearson (2002), 82
25. Tyers (1996) provides the most comprehensive introduction, but de la Bédoyère (2000) summarizes the basics.
26. Kendal (1996)
27. *RIB* 151, 149
28. *RIB* 132
29. *Ann.* i.35
30. *Britannia* 27 (1996), 450–52
31. Shirley (1996)
32. Reece (1997)
33. 'The walls were most carefully constructed, with timber posts morticed and tenoned into sill beams joined by dovetail scarf joints.' McCarthy (2002), 75–76
34. *RIB* 2491.36 (Woodchester), 2491.43 and Rudling (1986) (Great Cansiron).
35. This is the same tribe that fled before Caesar in 57 BC.
36. Published in *Britannia* 8 (1977), 430, and Hassall (1978)
37. *ILS* 4751, and see *Lactor* 4, no. 215
38. *ILS* 7522, and see *Lactor* 4, no. 216
39. *RIB* 2456.8, found at Lancaster
40. *TV* ii.182, 207
41. See Robertson (2000), no. 134
42. Li (1963) provides a fascinating account of England's problems with gold and silver in the eighteenth century, which goes a long way to explaining the problems the Romans faced, but did not understand.
43. *Ann.* lxii.2
44. Fulford (2003), 323

CHAPTER 8 (pp. 182–205)

1. *Ann.* xiv.38
2. Lucius Julius Bellicus. *RIB* 2443.19, revised at 2504.29
3. Several are known, mostly of third- and early fourth-century date, for example one of Gordian III (238–44) from

Redruth, and one of Constantine I of 306–7 from St Hilary. *RIB* 2234, and 2233
4. Main (1998)
5. *RIB* 179
6. T. W. Potter, in Jackson and Potter (1996), especially 678, 685–86.
7. Lucas (1993)
8. Neal (1970), 158
9. Lucas (1993)
10. Meates (1979)
11. See *Current Archaeology* 193 (2004), 38
12. See *Britannia* (1998), 395
13. Perring (2003), 123, has even suggested that the *nymphaeum* is in fact a Christian baptistery, since the Chi-Rho has been found on a basin at the villa. This is, however, optimistic speculation based on very limited evidence.
14. Percival (1976), 118
15. Seneca, *Letters* 104.1
16. Pliny the Younger, *Letters* ii.17
17. Carter (1998)
18. Percival (1976), 124
19. Smith (1997)
20. Ausonius, xix.107–12

CHAPTER 9 (pp. 206–227)
1. Pliny the Younger, *Letters* x.106, concerning a petition by a soldier concerning his daughter.
2. See the *censitor*, pp. 95, 146
3. Millett (1990), 185
4. Roberts and Cox, in Todd (2003)
5. See de la Bédoyère (2004), 18
6. *RIB* 263, 363, 373. Census records from Egypt also indicate that some individuals were able to reach advanced ages.
7. *Journal of Roman Studies* 53 (1963), 160, no. 4
8. Roberts and Cox, in Todd (2003), 251
9. McWhirr, *et al* (1982), 181
10. *RIB* 109
11. de la Bédoyère (2001), 221
12. *ILS* 2926
13. *RIB* 261
14. *RIB* 109
15. Dio, lv.24.7
16. Swan (1992)
17. Cool (2004)
18. *RIB* 780 (Stratonician cavalry), 782 (cohort of Gauls), and 783 (VI legion)
19. A. Birley (1979), 113
20. For example, the so-called 'Golden Mummies' of Graeco-Roman date in the Bahariya Oasis.
21. Toynbee (1996), 41–42
22. *RIB* 685
23. *RIB* 3
24. *RIB* 9, 21
25. *RIB* 1065
26. *CIL* xvi.49, *AE* 1956.249
27. *RIB* 67, 87
28. See *Britannia* 31 (2000), 433–34
29. *RIB* 2448.9
30. For an alternative interpretation, see Henig and Soffe (1993), who regard the inscription as a collective dedication by a religious guild.
31. Wilson (2003)

32. *RIB* 2491.147
33. There are a few instances where attempts seem to have been made to use Latin letters to represent Celtic words, but that generally the phenomenon was that this simply did not occur. See Cunliffe and Davenport (1988), 128, no. 14, and the discussion on p. 129.
34. *RIB* 2503.167, 168
35. *RIB* 2502.32
36. Cunliffe and Davenport (1988), 118, no. 8
37. Rivet and Smith (1979), 498
38. The whole association with the 'Tigris' might be completely off-beam, since the 'Tigris' element of the name could equally well be an animal-based epithet for a military naval unit, e.g., the 'boatmen, styled the Tigers'. Roman naval units favoured such names.
39. Florus, i.47.4
40. *TV* ii.164
41. Ausonius, xix.107–12
42. Chadwick (1967), 229, and also de la Bédoyère (2003), 198–206
43. Claudian, xxii.247
44. Dio, lx.19; *Ann.* xiv.39
45. *Agr* 15
46. *Agr* 32.4
47. For example, the classic observation that adopting Roman customs was a mark of the Britons' enslavement. *Agr* 21
48. Tomlin (2003). The text includes an incomplete word beginning *leg....* Tomlin suggests a legionary connection. An alternative is *legitime*, meaning 'the due' or 'appropriate' sum of money, and known from other inscriptions to precede a sum of money.
49. *RIB* 2443.7
50. Varro, *De Re Rustica* i.17
51. Ibid. i.19
52. *RIB* 144, 147

CHAPTER 10 (pp. 228–253)
1. *Germania* 44
2. See, for example, Perring (2003) on the possibilities of 'gnosticism' being represented on Romano-British mosaics, and Ling (1997, p. 297) for a warning: 'it is safer ... to remain sceptical of hidden meanings unless there is good reason to believe that they exist'.
3. *BG* vi.13–19; *Natural History* xvi.249, xxx.13
4. *RIB* 89
5. See Tomlin (2003), 364, for a full discussion of the text.
6. *RIB* 274, and de la Bédoyère (*Companion to Roman Britain*, 1999), 172. The text states that three-*denarii*-worth of bronze was used to make the statue, at an overall cost of 100 *sestertii* (25 *denarii*).
7. *RIB* 218, 219
8. *Pharsalia* i.45
9. *RIB* 1578, 194
10. *RIB* 193
11. *Cuno–* = dog, *mag–* = high or great.
12. *RIB* 1534, 1527, 1527
13. *RIB* 1074
14. The temple is recorded on a first-century flagon (*RIB* 2503.127), and on an altar found reused in London's riverside wall; see *Britannia* 7 (1976), 378–79, no. 2, de la Bédoyère (*Companion to Roman Britain*, 1999), 167, or de la Bédoyère (*Towns of Roman Britain*, 2003), 204–5.

15. *RIB* 1792
16. *RIB* 658
17. White and Barker (1998), 81
18. *Britannia* 26 (1995), 373–76
19. *de Legibus* ii.8.20
20. Cunliffe and Davenport (1985), 130, 9A.1
21. *RIB* 155, 1314, 2065
22. *Journal of Roman Studies* 11 (1921), 102
23. *RIB* 678
24. *RIB* 627
25. *RIB* 2448.3
26. *RIB* 153
27. M. Pitts (2001)
28. Williams (2000)
29. By this date the civic basilica seems to have been given over to industry.
30. *Britannia* 8 (1977), 430, no. 18, and *Journal of Roman Studies* 52 (1962), 192, no. 7
31. *RIB* 316
32. *RIB* 1421, and de la Bédoyère (1999), 71
33. *RIB* 91
34. *Britannia* 7 (1976), 378, no. 1
35. *RIB* 1041
36. *RIB* 1042, 732 to 733
37. *Britannia* 32 (2001), 392, and *RIB* 2426.1
38. *Et nos servasti eternali sanguine fundo* ('and you have saved us with the shedding of blood of eternal life'). Line cited in Hammond and Scullard (1970), 695.

39. St Jerome, *Letters* cvii.2, calling them 'monstrous images'.
40. Tertullian, *de Corona* xv.3
41. *RIB* 4
42. *RIB* 2503.114
43. Cool (2000)
44. Johns (1997)
45. Varro, *De Re Rustica* i.1.6
46. Johns and Potter (1983)
47. *Natural History* xxxiii.139ff, 154
48. Webster (1983), and Perring (2003), 119

CHAPTER 11 (pp. 254–269)
1. de la Bédoyère (*Defying Rome*, 2003), 198–206
2. Constantius, *De Vita Germani*, 12–27
3. Gildas, *D.E.* 25ff. Bede (*H.E.* i.16) derived his version from Gildas.
4. Thomas (1998) illustrates a number of these. In this author's opinion, however, Thomas takes his interpretation of hidden 'messages and images' to an extreme and unsupportable level. See also McKee and McKee (2002).
5. See, for example, Henig (1995), 157.
6. Finberg (1955)
7. Barker, *et al* (1997), but summarized in White and Barker (1998).
8. Two good examples are Esmonde Cleary (1989) and M. E. Jones (1996).

BIBLIOGRAPHY

Abdy, R. A., *Romano-British Coin Hoards* (Princes Risborough, 2002).

Allason-Jones, L. and B. McKay, *Coventina's Well* (Chesters, 1985).

Alston, R., *Soldier and Society in Roman Egypt: A Social History* (Oxford, 1995).

Barker, P., R. White, K. Pretty, H. Bird and M. Corbishley, *The Baths Basilica, Wroxeter: Excavations 1966–90* (London, 1997).

Bayley, J., D. F. Mackreth and H. Wallis, 'Evidence for Romano-British brooch production at Old Buckenham, Norfolk', *Britannia* 32 (2001), pp. 93–118.

Bidwell, P. T., *Roman Exeter: Fortress and Town* (Exeter, 1980).

Birley, A., *The People of Roman Britain* (London, 1979).

————, *Garrison Life at Vindolanda: A Band of Brothers* (Stroud, 2002).

Birley, E., *Roman Britain and the Roman Army* (Kendal, 1953).

Black, E. W., 'How many rivers to cross', *Britannia* 29 (1998), pp. 306–7.

Boon, G. C., *Silchester: The Roman Town of Calleva* (Newton Abbot, 1974).

Bowman, A. K., *Life and Letters on the Roman Frontier: Vindolanda and its People* (London, 1994; rev. ed. 2003).

Braund, D., 'Observations on Cartimandua', *Britannia* 15 (1984), pp. 1–6.

Breeze, D. and B. Dobson, *Hadrian's Wall* (London, 1987).

Brown, P. D. C., 'The church at Richborough', *Britannia* 2 (1971), pp. 225–31.

Burnham, B. C. and J. Wacher, *The 'Small Towns' of Roman Britain* (London, 1990).

Carter, G. A., 'Excavations at the Orsett "cock" enclosure, Essex, 1976', *East Anglian Archaeology* 86 (1998).

Casey, P. J., *Carausius and Allectus: The British Usurpers* (London, 1994).

Chadwick, H., *The Early Church* (London, 1967).

Clarke, S., 'Abandonment, rubbish disposal and "special" deposits', in Meadows, K., C. Lemke and J. Heron (eds), *TRAC 96: Proceedings of the Sixth Annual Theoretical Roman Archaeology Conference* (Oxford, 1997), pp. 73–81.

Collingwood, R. G. and R. P. Wright (updated by R. S. O. Tomlin), *The Roman Inscriptions of Britain*, vol. 1. (1965; rev. ed. Stroud, 1995). For indexes to this work, see Goodburn and Waugh (1983).

Cool, H. E. M., 'The significance of snake jewellery hoards', *Britannia* 31 (2000), pp. 29–40.

—————, *The Roman Cemetery at Brougham, Cumbria: Excavations 1966–67*. Britannia Monograph Series 21 (London, 2004).

Coulston, J. C. and E. J. Phillips, *Corpus Signorum Imperii Romani. Great Britain: Hadrian's Wall West of the North Tyne, and Carlisle*, vol. 1, fasc. 6 (Oxford, 1988).

Crow, J., *Housesteads* (London, 1995).

Cunliffe, B., *Fifth Report on the Excavations of the Roman Fort at Richborough* (London, 1968).

—————, *Excavations at Portchester Castle I: Roman* (London, 1975).

—————, *Roman Bath Discovered* (London, 1984).

Cunliffe, B. and P. Davenport, *The Temple of Sulis Minerva at Bath: The Site*, vol. 1. Oxford University Committee for Archaeology Monograph 7 (Oxford, 1985).

—————, *The Temple of Sulis Minerva at Bath: Finds from the Sacred Spring*, vol. 2. Oxford University Committee for Archaeology Monograph 16 (Oxford, 1988).

Cunliffe B. W. and M. G. Fulford, *Corpus Signorum Imperii Romani. Great Britain: Bath and the Rest of Wessex*, vol. 1, fasc. 2 (Oxford, 1982).

Dannell, G. B. and J. P. Wild, *Longthorpe II. The Military Works-Depot: An Episode in Landscape History*. Britannia Monograph Series 8 (London, 1987).

Dark, P., 'Pollen evidence for the environment of Roman Britain', *Britannia* 30 (1999), pp. 247–72.

de la Bédoyère, G., *Finds of Roman Britain* (London, 1989).

—————, *Roman Villas and the Countryside* (London, 1993).

—————, *Hadrian's Wall: A History and Guide* (Stroud, 1998).

—————, 'Carausius and the marks RSR and INPCDA', *Numismatic Chronicle* 158 (1998), pp. 79–88.

—————, *Companion to Roman Britain* (Stroud, 1999).

—————, *The Golden Age of Roman Britain* (Stroud, 1999).

—————, *Pottery in Roman Britain* (Aylesbury, 2000).

—————, *The Buildings of Roman Britain* (Stroud, 2001).

—————, *Eagles over Britannia: The Roman Army in Britain* (Stroud, 2001).

—————, *Gods with Thunderbolts: Religion in Roman Britain* (Stroud, 2002).

—————, *Towns of Roman Britain* (Stroud, 2003).

—————, *Defying Rome: The Rebels of Roman Britain* (Stroud, 2003).

—————, *The Diary of John Evelyn* (Woodbridge, 2004).

de Jersey, P., *Celtic Coinage in Britain* (Princes Risborough, 2001).

Dobson, B. and J. C. Mann, 'The Roman army in Britain and Britons in the Roman army', *Britannia* 4 (1973), pp. 191–205.

Erim, K. T., 'A new relief showing Claudius and Britannia from Aphrodisias', *Britannia* 13 (1982), pp. 277–82.

Esmonde Cleary, A. S., *The Ending of Roman Britain* (London, 1989).

Faulkner, N., *The Decline and Fall of Roman Britain* (Stroud, 2000).

Finberg, H. P. R., *Roman and Saxon Withington*. Department of English Local History Occasional Papers 8 (Leicester, 1955).

Ford, S. D., 'The Silchester church: A dimensional analysis and a new reconstruction', *Britannia* 25 (1994), pp. 119–26.

France, N. E. and B. M. Gobel, *The Romano-British Temple at Harlow, Essex* (Gloucester, 1985).

Frere, S. S., *Britannia,* 3rd ed. (London, 1987).

Frere, S. S., M. Roxan and R. S. O. Tomlin (eds), *The Roman Inscriptions of Britain*, vol. 2, fasc. 1–8 (Stroud, 1990–95).

Frere, S. S. and J. K. S. St Joseph, *Roman Britain from the Air* (Cambridge, 1983).

Frere, S. S. and J. Wilkes, *Strageath: Excavations Within the Roman Fort 1973–86*. Britannia Monograph Series 9 (London, 1989).

Goldsworthy, A. and I. Haynes (eds), *The Roman Army as a Community. Journal of Roman Archaeology Supplementary Series* 34 (Portsmouth, Rhode Island, 1999).

Goldsworthy, A., *The Complete Roman Army* (London, 2003).

Goodburn, R. and H. Waugh, *The Roman Inscriptions of Britain: Inscriptions on Stone. Epigraphic Indexes*, vol. 1 (Gloucester, 1983).

Greene, K., *The Pre-Flavian Fine Wares: Report on the Excavations at Usk 1965–1976* (Cardiff, 1978).

Green, M. J., *The Gods of the Celts* (Stroud, 1997).

Grimes, W. F., 'Holt, Denbighshire: The works depot of the XXth legion at Castle Lyons', *Y Cymmrodor* 41 (London, 1930).

Hammond, N. G. L. and H. H. Scullard, *The Oxford Classical Dictionary* (Oxford, 1970).

Hanson, W. S., 'The organization of Roman military timber-supply', *Britannia* 9 (1978), pp. 293–305.

Hassall, M., 'Britain and the Rhine provinces: Epigraphic evidence for Roman trade', in J. du Plat Taylor and H. Cleere (eds), *Roman Shipping and Trade: Britain and the Rhine Provinces*. CBA Research Report 24 (London, 1978), pp. 41–48.

Hattatt, R., *Brooches of Antiquity: A Third Selection from the Author's Collection* (Oxford, 1987).

Henig, M., *Religion in Roman Britain* (London, 1984).

—————, *The Art of Roman Britain* (London, 1995).

Henig, M. and P. Booth, *Roman Oxfordshire* (Stroud, 2000).

Henig, M. and G. Soffe, 'The Thruxton Roman villa and its mosaic pavement'. *Journal of the British Archaeological Association* 146 (1993), pp. 1–28.

Howe, E. and D. Lakin, *Roman and Medieval Cripplegate. Archaeological Excavations 1992–98* (London, 2004).

Ireland, S., *Roman Britain: A Sourcebook* (London, 1995).

Jackson, R. P. J. and T. W. Potter, *Excavations at Stonea, Cambridgeshire 1980–85* (London, 1996).

James, S. and M. Millett, *Britons and Romans: Advancing an Archaeological Agenda*. CBA Research Report 125 (York, 2001).

Johns, C., *The Jewellery of Roman Britain* (London, 1996).

—————, *The Snettisham Roman Jeweller's Hoard* (London, 1997).

Johns, C. and T. W. Potter, *The Thetford Treasure* (London, 1983).

—————, *Roman Britain* (London, 2002).

Johnson, A., *Roman Forts* (London, 1983).

Johnson, S., *The Roman Forts of the Saxon Shore* (London, 1979).

Jones, B. and D. Mattingly, *An Atlas of Roman Britain* (Oxford, 1990).

Jones, M. E., *The End of Roman Britain* (Ithaca, 1996).

Jones, M. J., *Roman Lincoln* (Stroud, 2002).

Kendal, R., 'Transport logistics associated with the building of Hadrian's Wall', *Britannia* 27 (1996), pp. 129–52.

Leech, R., 'The excavation of a Romano-Celtic temple and a later cemetery on Lamyatt Beacon, Somerset', *Britannia* 17 (1986), pp. 259–328.

Lewis, M. J. T., *Temples in Roman Britain* (Cambridge, 1965).

Lewis, N. and M. Reinhold, *Roman Civilization* (New York, 1955).

Li, M.-H., *The Great Recoinage of 1696–99* (London, 1963).

Ling, R., *The Insula of the Menander at Pompeii: The Structures*, vol. 1 (Oxford, 1997).

————, 'Mosaics in Roman Britain: Discoveries and research since 1945', *Britannia* 28 (1997), pp. 259–96.

Lucas, R. N., *The Romano-British Villa at Halstock, Dorset: Excavations 1967–1985* (Dorchester, 1993).

Main, L., 'Excavations of a timber round house and broch at the Fairy Knowe, Buchlyvie, Stirlingshire, 1975–78'. *Proceedings of the Society of Antiquaries of Scotland* 128 (1998), pp. 293–418.

Mason, D. J. P., *Roman Chester: City of the Eagles* (Stroud, 2001).

Maxfield, V. and B. Dobson, *Inscriptions of Roman Britain*, 3rd ed. (London, 1995).

McCarthy, M., *Roman Carlisle and the Lands of the Solway* (Stroud, 2002).

McKee, H. and J. McKee, 'Counter arguments and numerical patterns in early Celtic inscriptions: A re-examination of Christian Celts; messages and images', *Medieval Archaeology* 46 (2002), pp. 29–40.

McWhirr, A., L. Viner and C. Wells, *Romano-British Cemeteries* (Cirencester, 1982).

Meates, G. W, *The Lullingstone Roman Villa, Kent: The Site*, vol. 1 (Maidstone, 1979).

————, *The Lullingstone Roman Villa, Kent: The Wall Paintings and Finds*, vol. 2 (Maidstone, 1987).

Millett, M., *The Romanization of Britain* (Cambridge, 1990).

Neal, D. S., 'The Roman villa at Boxmoor: Interim report', *Britannia* 1 (1970), pp. 156–62.

Niblett, R., *Verulamium: The Roman City of St Albans* (Stroud, 2001).

Painter, K. S., *The Water Newton Early Christian Silver* (London, 1977).

————, *The Mildenhall Treasure* (London, 1977).

Pearson, A., *The Roman Shore Forts* (Stroud, 2002).

Percival, J., *The Roman Villa* (London, 1976).

Perring, D., *The Roman House in Britain* (London, 2002).

————, '"Gnosticism" in fourth-century Britain: The Frampton mosaics reconsidered', *Britannia* 34 (2003), pp. 97–127.

Phillips, E. J., *Corpus Signorum Imperii Romani. Great Britain: Corbridge, Hadrian's Wall East of the North Tyne*, vol. 1, fasc. 1 (Oxford, 1977).

Pitts, L. F. and J. K. St Joseph, *Inchtuthil: The Roman Legionary Fortress* (London, 1985).

Pitts, M., 'Hayling Island', *Current Archaeology* 176 (2001), pp. 333–35.

Rainey, A., *Mosaics in Roman Britain* (Newton Abbot, 1973).

Reece, R., *The Future of Roman Military Archaeology*: Tenth Annual Caerleon Lecture (Cardiff, 1997).

————, *The Coinage of Roman Britain* (Stroud, 2002).

Richmond, I. A. and J. P. Gillam, 'The temple of Mithras at Carrawburgh', 4th series, *Archaeologia Aeliana* 29 (1951), pp. 1–92.

Rivet, A. L. F. and C. Smith, *The Place-Names of Roman Britain* (London, 1979).

Robertson, A., *An Inventory of Romano-British Coin Hoards* (London, 2000).

Rodwell, W. (ed), *Temples, Churches and Religion in Roman Britain*, BAR British Series 77 (Oxford, 1980).

Rudling, D., 'The Excavation of a Roman tilery on Great Cansiron farm, Hartfield, Sussex', *Britannia* 17 (1986), pp. 191–230.

Salway, P., *The Oxford Illustrated History of Roman Britain* (Oxford, 1993).

Sealey, P. R., *The Boudican Revolt Against Rome* (Princes Risborough, 1997).

Shepherd, J., *The Temple of Mithras: Excavations by W. F. Grimes and A. Williams at the Walbrook, London* (London, 1997).

Shirley, E. A. M., 'The building of the legionary fortress at Inchtuthil', *Britannia* 27 (1996), pp. 111–18.

Smith, J. T., *Roman Villas: A Study in Social Structure* (London, 1997).

Southern P. and K. R. Dixon, *The Late Roman Army* (London, 2000).

Standing, G., 'The Claudian invasion of Britain and the cult of *Victoria Britannica*', *Britannia* 34 (2003), pp. 281–87.

Stead, I. M., 'A Roman pottery theatrical face-mask and a bronze brooch blank from Baldock, Herts', *Antiquaries Journal* 55 (1975), pp. 397–98.

Swan, V. G., 'Legio VI and its men: African legionaries in Britain', *Journal of Roman Pottery Studies* 5 (1992), pp. 1–33.

Todd, M. (ed), *A Companion to Roman Britain* (Oxford, 2003).

Thomas, C., *Christian Celts* (Tempus, 1998).

Tomlin, R. S. O., '"The girl in question": A new text from Roman London', *Britannia* 34 (2003), pp. 41–52.

Toynbee, J. M. C., *Death and Burial in the Roman World* (Baltimore, 1996).

Tyers, P. A., *Roman Pottery in Britain* (London, 1996).

Wacher, J., *The Towns of Roman Britain* (London, 1995).

Webster, G., 'The function of Chedworth Roman "villa"', *Transactions of the Bristol and Gloucestershire Archaeological Society* 101 (1983), pp. 5–12.

Wedlake, W. J, *The Excavation of the Shrine of Apollo at Nettleton, Wiltshire, 1956–1971* (London, 1982).

Wheeler, R. E. M., *Maiden Castle, Dorset* (Oxford, 1943).

Wheeler, R. E. M. and T. V. Wheeler, *Report on the Excavation of the Prehistoric, Roman and Post-Roman Site in Lydney Park, Gloucestershire* (London, 1932).

White, R. and P. Barker, *Wroxeter: Life and Death of a Roman City* (Stroud, 1998).

Wild, J. P., 'The textile industries of Roman Britain', *Britannia* 33 (2002), pp. 1–32.

Williams, D., 'Wanborough Roman temple', *Current Archaeology* 167 (2000), pp. 434–37.

Wilmott, T., *Birdoswald: Excavations of a Roman Fort on Hadrian's Wall and its Successor Settlements 1987–92* (London, 1997).

————, *Birdoswald Roman Fort* (Stroud, 2001).

Wilson, R. J. A., *A Guide to the Roman Remains in Britain*, 4th ed. (London, 2002).

————, 'The Rudston Venus mosaic revisited: A spear-bearing lion?', *Britannia* 34 (2003), pp. 288–91.

Woodward, A. and Leach, P., *The Uley Shrines: Excavation of a Ritual Complex on West Hill, Uley, Gloucestershire, 1977–79* (London, 1990).

Zienkiewicz, D., *The Legionary Fortress Baths at Caerleon* (Cardiff, 1986).

ILLUSTRATION CREDITS

INDEX